GILES MILTON

SOLDIER, SAILOR, FROGMAN, SPY

Giles Milton is the internationally bestselling author of twelve works of narrative history. His most recent book is *Checkmate in Berlin: The Cold War Showdown That Shaped the Modern World*. His previous work, *Churchill's Ministry of Ungentlemanly Warfare*, is currently being developed into a major TV series. Milton's works—published in twenty-five languages—include *Nathaniel's Nutmeg*, serialized by the BBC. He lives in London and Burgundy.

Also by Giles Milton

SOLDIER, SAILOR, FROGMAN, SPY

GILES MILTON

HOW THE ALLIES WON ON D-DAY

SOLDIER, SAILOR, FROGMAN, SPY

PICADOR

Henry Holt and Company

New York

Picador
120 Broadway, New York 10271

Copyright © 2018 by Giles Milton
All rights reserved
Printed in the United States of America
Originally published in 2018 by Hodder & Stoughton,
Great Britain, as *D-Day: The Soldier's Story*
Published in the United States in 2018 by Henry Holt and Company, LLC
First Picador paperback edition, 2021

Maps drawn by Rodney Paull

Library of Congress Control Number: 2019286062
Picador Paperback ISBN: 978-1-250-13493-6

Typeset in Bembo MT Pro by Palimpsest Book Production Ltd,
Falkirk, Stirlingshire

Our books may be purchased in bulk for promotional, educational,
or business use. Please contact your local bookseller or the Macmillan
Corporate and Premium Sales Department at 1-800-221-7945, extension
5442, or by email at MacmillanSpecialMarkets@macmillan.com.

Picador® is a U.S. registered trademark and is used by Macmillan
Publishing Group, LLC, under license from Pan Books Limited.

For book club information, please visit facebook.com/picadorbookclub or
email marketing@picadorusa.com.

picadorusa.com · instagram.com/picador
twitter.com/picadorusa · facebook.com/picadorusa

1   3   5   7   9   10   8   6   4   2

To all who served

Contents

I want to tell you what the opening of the second front entailed, so that you can know and appreciate and forever be humbly grateful to those both dead and alive who did it for you.

Ernie Pyle, war correspondent

Preface

*T*HE LIBERATION OF *occupied Europe had been the Allied goal ever since the evacuation of Dunkirk in May 1940, when 330,000 beleaguered troops were rescued from the advancing Wehrmacht. But the early years of war had dealt the Allies such a string of crushing defeats that any talk of a cross-Channel offensive was wishful thinking. Although Hitler had cancelled his planned invasion of Britain in the autumn of 1940, his forces in North Africa and Russia had swept from victory to victory.*

By the winter of 1942 the tide had begun to turn. In Russia, German forces were trapped at Stalingrad and would soon surrender – a humiliating defeat for the Wehrmacht. In North Africa, the British Eighth Army had beaten the enemy at El Alamein. And in the Pacific theatre, the Americans – who had entered the war after the Japanese attack on Pearl Harbor in December 1941 – were making significant gains.

The tide was also turning in the North Atlantic, where German U-boats were being successfully targeted by heavily armed Atlantic convoys. By the late spring of 1943, Admiral Karl Dönitz would admit to having 'lost the Battle of the Atlantic'.[1] It was a costly loss, for it would enable large numbers of American troops and supplies to pour into Britain.

At the Casablanca Conference in January of that year, President Franklin Roosevelt had persuaded a reluctant Winston Churchill to establish a new Allied planning staff: its role was to prepare for an invasion of occupied France. The top job went to Lieutenant General Frederick Morgan, who was given a ten-word brief: 'to defeat the German fighting forces in North-West Europe'.[2]

The formal decision to press ahead with this cross-Channel invasion was taken by Churchill and Roosevelt at the Trident Conference in the spring of 1943, by which time Morgan's staff had increased dramatically. Yet it was not until December that General Dwight Eisenhower was appointed Supreme Allied Commander, with General Bernard Montgomery as commander of the 21st Army Group, comprising all land forces earmarked for the invasion. The organization hitherto led by Morgan was renamed: henceforth, it was to be known as Supreme Headquarters Allied Expeditionary Force (SHAEF), with its headquarters at Norfolk House in London. In March 1944 it moved to Bushy Park, west London, with an advance headquarters at Southwick House in Portsmouth. Eisenhower's staff numbered more than 900.

Morgan had envisaged an amphibious landing of three divisions. Allied troops would assault the gently shelving beaches of Normandy, where the coastal defences were weaker than at the Pas de Calais. But Eisenhower and Montgomery both felt that Morgan's troop numbers were too small; they added two more divisions to the planned invasion – now codenamed Operation Overlord – along with a major airborne component. They also expanded the landing zone to cover fully sixty miles of Normandy coastline, stretching from Sainte-Mère-Église to Lion-sur-Mer.

Some 156,000 soldiers were to assault five D-Day beaches: Utah, Omaha, Gold, Juno and Sword. The first two were assigned to the Americans, Juno to the Canadians and Gold and Sword to the British.

The goal for the invasion day was ambitious: a near contiguous beachhead stretching along much of Normandy's coast, with only a small gap between Utah and Omaha beaches. It was to extend fifteen miles inland and was to include the cities of Caen and Bayeux.

The imperative was to secure the coastal landing zone. First, there would be an intense pre-dawn bombardment from the air to obliterate the German coastal defences. This would be followed by a big-gun naval attack, with smaller rocket ships providing additional firepower. Next, an army of amphibious tanks would emerge from the sea and blast away any remaining guns. Specialist tanks would follow, along with armoured bulldozers. Then, once passages had been cleared through the beach debris in the opening hours of the first day, large numbers of infantry troops would be landed, followed by thousands of tons of supplies.

The logistical challenge was unprecedented. The number of American troops stationed in England had risen to 1.5 million by spring 1944, fully twenty divisions. There were also fourteen British divisions, three Canadian, one French and one Polish. These troops required thousands of jeeps and armoured vehicles, as well as artillery pieces, shells and ammunition. On D-Day itself, 73,000 American troops would be landed in Normandy, along with 62,000 British and 21,000 Canadian.

Secrecy and deception were to be of paramount importance to the operation's success: the Allies intended to dupe the Germans into thinking they would be landing at the Pas de Calais. To this end, they mounted Operation Fortitude, complete with phantom field armies, fake wireless traffic and the brilliant use of double agents working under the Double Cross System, whereby captured Nazi spies transmitted false intelligence back to Germany.

The commando raid on Dieppe (August 1942), the invasion of Sicily (July 1943) and the landings in Italy two months later gave a taste of the dangers to come. The amphibious landings at Salerno had faced stubborn resistance from German panzers, while those at Anzio came close to disaster. Yet Overlord was on a far more ambitious scale. Although the aerial bombardment of German coastal defences was a key ingredient, it was by no means certain that saturation bombing would destroy the coastal bunkers.

An additional concern was the lack of combat experience among Allied forces: many young conscripts had yet to be tested in battle and would require leadership from units that had already seen action. Yet even experienced troops often lacked the fighting spirit of the Germans. In virtually every previous engagement with the enemy – wherever the Allies had fought with equal numbers – the Wehrmacht had defeated them.

Allied forces would be doing battle against a formidable German military machine. Despite the hammering it was receiving on the Eastern Front, its soldiers displayed extraordinary bravado. Their fighting spirit was supported by superb weaponry. The Wehrmacht's Panther and Tiger tanks combined both power and strength: the thinly armoured British Cromwells and American Shermans were simply no match. Nor was Allied infantry weaponry as efficient as its German counterparts. The Wehrmacht's MG42 machine gun fired 1,200 rounds per minute; the Allies' Bren gun less than half that number.

Hitler's army in France and the Low Countries numbered fifty divisions – some 850,000 men – with the 15th Army defending the Pas de Calais and the 7th Army defending Normandy. Together they comprised Army Group B, commanded by Field Marshal Erwin Rommel.

Rommel disagreed with his superior, Field Marshal Gerd von Rundstedt (Commander-in-Chief West), about how best to defeat the anticipated Allied invasion. Von Rundstedt thought it impossible to prevent the coastal landings and argued that German panzer divisions should be held inland *in readiness for a counter-attack. His idea was to entrap the advancing Allied forces in an armoured pincer movement.*

But Rommel wanted Allied forces defeated immediately, while still on the beaches. To this end, in January 1944 he had embarked on a programme to strengthen the coastal defences, reinforcing concrete bunkers, planting anti-tank obstacles on the beaches and setting underwater minefields in the coastal shallows. By June of that year, some 6 million mines had been laid.

As an additional defence, potential landing fields had been studded with slanted poles to prevent the landing of gliders, while low-lying coastal meadows had been flooded so as to hinder the movement of Allied troops. This newly strengthened front line, the so-called Atlantic Wall, represented a significant obstacle to the Allied invasion.

Germany's defence of the skies above Normandy was entrusted to Luftflotte 3. This was a woefully ill-equipped force that had lost many of its planes to the Home Air Force, charged with defending northern Germany. Although there were some notable fighter aces in Luftflotte 3, they would find themselves facing an overwhelmingly superior Allied force that numbered more than 11,500 planes. These Allied aircraft faced far greater danger from ground-based anti-aircraft guns − a key part of the Atlantic Wall − than they did from Luftflotte 3.

Some of the coastal construction work had been undertaken by French conscripted labour, one of the many humiliations endured by Normandy's civilian population. Ever since the German occupation in 1940, the French had suffered a slew of indignities. A fledgling resistance soon sprang into being across France and by 1944 the Calvados branch of the Organisation civile et militaire, working along the Normandy coastline, was collecting intelligence about German defences and forwarding it to SHAEF.

The French resistance had also received air-drops of weaponry and explosives. The plan was for saboteurs to go into action in the hours before the invasion, destroying key bridges, railways and communication wires.

The Allied landings in Normandy were originally planned for 1 May 1944, but logistical difficulties caused them to be postponed for a month. By June, everything was in place. One thing alone had the ability to disrupt the invasion and that was the atrocious English weather.

SOLDIER, SAILOR, FROGMAN, SPY

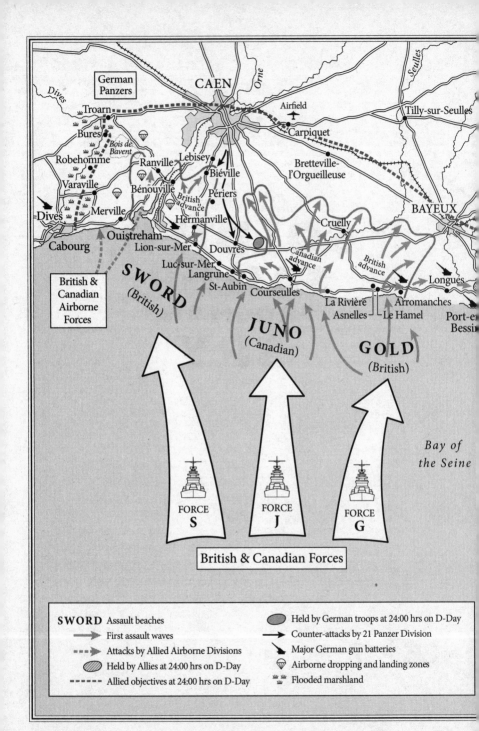

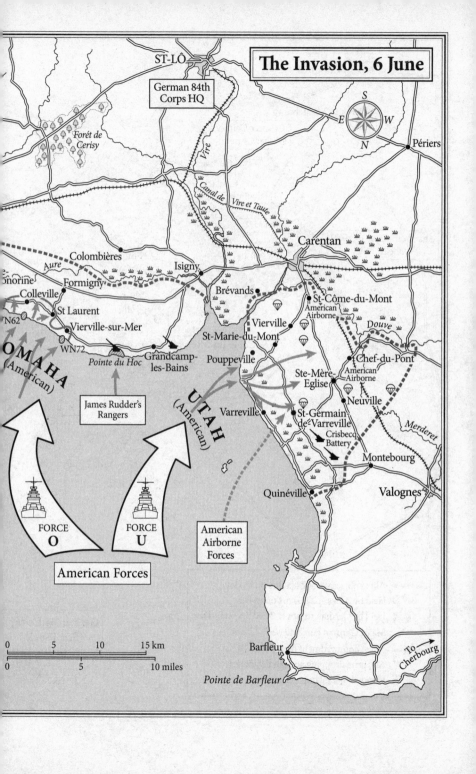

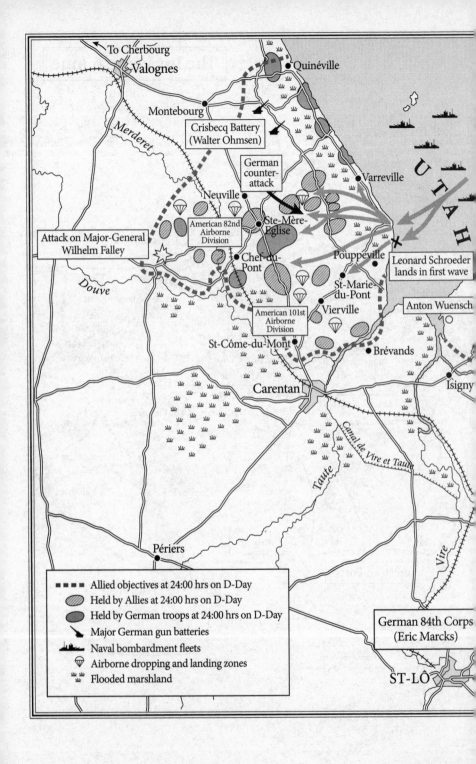

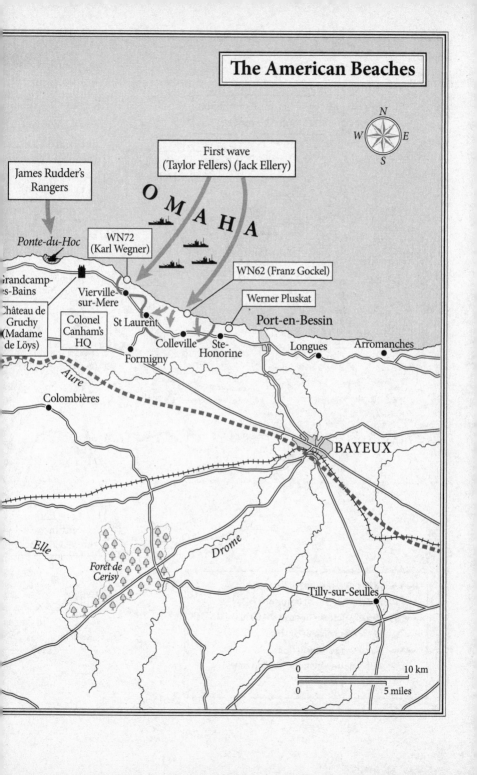

The American Beaches

James Rudder's Rangers

First wave
(Taylor Fellers) (Jack Ellery)

O M A H A

Ponte-du-Hoc

WN72
(Karl Wegner)

WN62 (Franz Gockel)

Grandcamp-
es-Bains

Vierville-
sur-Mere

Werner Pluskat

Port-en-Bessin

Château de
Gruchy
(Madame
de Löys)

Colonel
Canham's
HQ

St Laurent

Colleville

Ste-
Honorine

Longues

Arromanches

Aure

Formigny

Colombières

BAYEUX

Elle

Drome

*Forêt de
Cerisy*

Tilly-sur-Seulles

0   10 km

0   5 miles

N
W   E
S

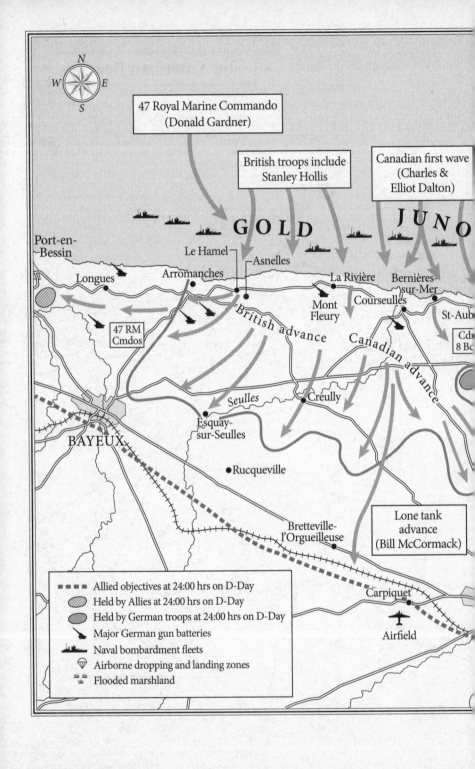

47 Royal Marine Commando
(Donald Gardner)

British troops include
Stanley Hollis

Canadian first wave
(Charles &
Elliot Dalton)

GOLD

JUNO

Port-en-
~Bessin

Longues

Le Hamel

Asnelles

Arromanches

La Rivière

Bernières-
sur-Mer

Courseulles

St-Aub

47 RM
Cmdos

British advance

Mont
Fleury

Canadian advance

Cd
8 Bd

Seulles

Créully

Esquay-
sur-Seulles

BAYEUX

Rucqueville

Bretteville-
l'Orgueilleuse

Lone tank
advance
(Bill McCormack)

Carpiquet

- - - - Allied objectives at 24:00 hrs on D-Day
Held by Allies at 24:00 hrs on D-Day
Held by German troops at 24:00 hrs on D-Day
Major German gun batteries
Naval bombardment fleets
Airborne dropping and landing zones
Flooded marshland

Airfield

The British and Canadian Beaches

East Yorks
in first wave

Lord Lovat's
commandos &
Philippe Kieffer's
French troops

Airborne bridge
destruction
(Tim Roseveare)

Airborne bridge
operation
(John Howard)

Airborne Merville
operation
(Terence Otway)

Langrune

Luc-sur-Mer

S W O R D

Douvres

Lion-sur-Mer

Ouistreham

Hermanville

Merville

Dives

Périers

British
advance

Bénouville

Varaville

Biéville

Robehomme

Ranville

Lebisey

Bois de
Bavent

German Panzer
counter-attack
(Hermann von
Oppeln-Bronikowski)

Bures

Troarn

Dives

German Panzers

CAEN

0   8 km

0   5 miles

Prologue

THE WIND HAD stiffened since lunchtime and now it was blowing a gale. It was sweeping in from the English Channel, a short sharp blast that was tugging at trees and snatching at the late spring blooms. In the formal gardens of the Abbaye aux Dames, the neatly clipped topiary had been whisked to a tangle.

For nine long centuries the abbey had loomed over the skyline of Caen, in northern France, a brooding monument to piety and power. Home to canonesses and nuns, saints and sinners, its God-fearing sisters had swished through the cloisters as they headed to the twilight service of evensong. They had prayed here until the revolution, when the candles were snuffed and the chanting faded.

But now, in the spring of 1944, the abbey had become home to a new type of novice. Eva Eifler was an unwilling German conscript who had spent that stormy June afternoon squinting at the clouds from one of the abbey's top-floor windows. With her prim dress and oval-rimmed spectacles, she might have been mistaken for a schoolmistress or governess, but she was too shy to be the former and too young to be the latter. Just eighteen years of age, and bashful to boot, there was still much of the child to be found in her awkward gait and gawkish smile.

Fräulein Eifler had been sent to Caen as a wireless operator with the Luftwaffe. Her job was to listen to messages, transcribe them on to paper and then forward them to be decoded. It was work that required intense concentration. 'Nothing was allowed to disturb me.' These words were drummed into her from the outset. 'Two seconds of inattention or disruption and I could miss the beginning of a message.' One mistake, one little slip, could send a Luftwaffe pilot to his death.

Now, as she stared at the sky on the afternoon of Monday, 5 June 1944, she was pleased to see yet more storm clouds banking up in the west. There would be little air activity that night, which meant a quiet time at work. It was a rare piece of good news. She had been working night shifts for the better part of a month and was suffering from extreme fatigue. She had no idea that events outside her control were about to turn the world on its head.

Fräulein Eifler's life had taken its first unwelcome twist in the previous year when she was drafted into the obligatory Reich Labour Service, bringing her schooling to an abrupt end. Shortly afterwards, while still just seventeen, she was sent to a training academy in the coastal port of Danzig where she learned to transmit military telegrams in Morse. Once proficient, she was ordered to pack her bags and prepare for a new life in France – one in which her loyalty was to the Luftwaffe and her duty was to the Nazi state.

She was distraught at the prospect of being wrenched from her siblings and confessed to being 'very nervous to be leaving my parents for the first time'. Life was so happy at home. But she had no choice in the matter. After the briefest of farewells she was transported into a world in which family and acquaintances no longer had any place. She had never felt so lonely in her life.

She was not entirely by herself. She shared her lodgings in the Abbaye aux Dames with four other young girls who also worked for the Luftwaffe. The five teenagers spent much of their time together, more out of solidarity than friendship, for it was dangerous to be alone in a city whose population was outwardly hostile. They tried to avoid 'even the smallest interaction with the civilians' lest any conversation be misconstrued. The only exception was their dealings with the local baker's daughter, a kindly girl who brought them 'chocolate biscuits in the shape of boats'.

If circumstances had been happier, the Abbaye aux Dames might have been a fine place to live: a palatial Benedictine convent founded by Matilda of Flanders. On the brighter days of spring, the sun tipped liquid light through the plate-glass windows and played a merry dance on the walls and floors. But the girls' working life was spent in an underground bunker known as R618: it was situated in the centre of town, deep below Place Gambetta. The R stood for

Regelbau – one of hundreds of 'standard design' bunkers constructed from heavily reinforced concrete. Secure and virtually indestructible, it was one of the Luftwaffe's principal telecommunications centres.

It was a grim place to work and Fräulein Eifler loathed every minute of her time there. 'The air was confined and humid, the light was artificial, and the accumulated weariness of the night made my eyes prick. I hated this room in which I was forced to spend most of my life. I had become some sort of robot.' She felt that her youth 'was being stolen' by the Nazis. The only bright point came during a 'severely chaperoned' trip to Paris in order to have her broken spectacles repaired. While she was there, she spent her hard-won savings on a pink negligée for her wedding night. It was an odd purchase given that she had neither fiancé nor suitor, and she surprised herself by making it. Hitherto, her only interaction with the opposite sex was with the coarse young lads who lurched around her desk in the bunker making jokes laden with innuendo.

The evening of Monday, 5 June had begun like any other. It was around 7 p.m. when Fräulein Eifler got changed into her grey-blue Luftwaffe uniform, with its lightning-flash symbol on the upper sleeve. Soon after, she set off for work in the company of the other girls, going on foot from the Abbaye aux Dames to Place Gambetta.

Their shift began punctually at 8 p.m. 'Each one of us had taken her seat at her work place,' she said, seated in front of a control panel linked to the port of Cherbourg. Fräulein Eifler sat perched on the edge of her chair with headphones clamped to her ears. She was soon transcribing the first of the incoming messages from field stations across Normandy. To her ears, they always sounded like gibberish. 'Endless lists of letters and numbers – A-C-X-L-5-O-W – that didn't mean anything to me.' As soon as each message had been transcribed, she would hand it to an officer who would take it to be decoded in the adjoining room.

This particular night was quieter than most. The weather had taken a turn for the worse and the girls were told that 'nothing abnormal was expected or signalled'. But as the clock slowly ticked its way towards midnight, Fräulein Eifler detected a change to the pace of the incoming messages. 'The movement suddenly accelerated.' There was a sense of urgency. They were coming faster. Every few seconds. And then, at exactly 01.00 hours, 'everything erupted'.

Messages began arriving at a stupefying rate from right across the coastal zone. Some came from the Cotentin peninsula. Others came from the countryside to the east of the city. They came from the Orne, the Dives and from Sainte-Mère-Église. Fräulein Eifler found herself 'working faster and faster, and as soon as I had finished, a hand behind me grabbed the paper straight away'. She didn't have time to turn around, nor even ask for a coffee. 'I was glued to my table, in front of jumbled-up alphabets.'

She lost all sense of time and had no clue as to how long she had been at her post. She knew that something momentous was happening – 'I could feel it' – but she had no idea of exactly what was taking place. 'Poised on my chair, headphones on, I wrote; I wrote like a maniac. I wrote until my wrists ached.'

In the small hours of the morning, when she was close to fainting from exhaustion, she felt a hand on her shoulder. It was an officer in the marines, coming to relieve her. Her night shift was finally at an end.

'What's happened?' she asked. 'Is it something serious?'

'Something serious.' He repeated the words in a grave tone of voice. Then he took his seat without adding anything more and began jotting down the latest message to be transmitted through the headphones.

Eva Eifler was drained by her work that night. She had a cramp in her hands and a crick in her neck. She noticed that her four girlfriends looked similarly exhausted. All had 'the same haggard, anxious look'.

The five of them followed each other into the control room that adjoined the one in which they worked. And it was only now – to their utter astonishment – that they realized what was taking place. 'The spectacle was incredible. On one wall, an enormous map of the French Channel coast was pinned with little markers and different coloured flags' – hundreds of them. Each flag denoted an Allied parachutist who had been dropped into the heart of Normandy. Those garbled messages that Fräulein Eifler had been transcribing were the very first reports of the Allied landings.

A soldier was standing in front of the map and adding or moving the flags, depending on the messages being received. New intelligence was arriving every second. Eva felt the atmosphere turn as chill as the grave. 'The look in everyone's eyes was tense. Their gestures were rapid and hasty. Yet no one was shouting.' Senior officers had been arriving all night and the room was now abuzz with commanders, many of them crisply dressed types in Nazi uniform. There was even a general or two. She had never seen that before.

As she stood there, staring at the map, she suddenly felt very frightened indeed. This, then, was it. This was the long-awaited *Invasiontag*. She had never imagined that she would be one of the very first people to know that D-Day had begun; that Allied paratroopers had started to land.

She stared at the map for a few more minutes, trying to take in the enormity of what was taking place. Then she rejoined her friends and they made their way back to their lodgings in the Abbaye aux Dames. 'We tried to reassure ourselves, but we had only questions without answers.' The sky was darkly menacing and the gutters were dripping with rain. Eva had a knot in her stomach and felt 'dumbfounded and anxious'.[1]

She was worried for herself and she was worried for her family. But most of all, she was worried about what the coming day would bring.

PART I
Know Thy Enemy

Operation Overlord had been planned in the greatest detail, with every minute of the day accounted for. However, the success of the landings would be contingent on accurate knowledge of the terrain, weather and German defences. RAF aerial reconnaissance had provided much information about coastal defences, but more detailed intelligence necessitated clandestine commando missions to the Normandy beaches.

The French resistance worked hard to collect up-to-the-minute intelligence about shore defences and troop movements. The Calvados branch of the Organisation civile et militaire used forbidden wireless transmitters to send information directly to SHAEF planners in England.

Resistance networks, known as 'circuits', were awaiting a coded radio broadcast to inform them that the landings were imminent and that sabotage operations should commence.

German forces in Normandy – the 7th Army – were part of Army Group B, commanded by Field Marshal Erwin Rommel. His newly strengthened Atlantic Wall was manned largely by conscripts and Osttruppen (men from occupied Soviet territories) of questionable loyalty. The 21st Panzer Division was also under his authority, but two additional panzer divisions could be released to Rommel only on Hitler's orders.

Field Marshal Erwin Rommel inspects the coastal defences of Normandy.
'It is this very area that the Allies will land,' he predicted.

I

Behind Enemy Lines

GEORGE LANE VIEWED his life in much the same way as a professional gambler might view a game of poker: something to be played with a steady nerve, a dash of courage and a willingness to win or lose everything in the process.

His addiction to risk had driven him to join the commandos; it had also led him to volunteer for a perilous undercover mission codenamed Operation Tarbrush X. In the second week of May 1944, Lane was to smuggle himself into Nazi-occupied France using the cover of darkness to paddle ashore in a black rubber dinghy. His task was to investigate a new type of mine that the Germans were believed to be installing on the Normandy beaches.

Lane had the air of a quintessentially British adventurer, one whose tweedy façade would not have looked out of place on the great Scottish hunting estates. His hair was waxed in the fashion of a young Cary Grant and divided into two by a carefully scoured parting. But there the similarity ended. His stare was colder than any actor could contrive and it was overlaid with a rigid sense of purpose. Lane would later recount his derring-do stories in an accent of such cut-glass clarity that it almost sounded fake. There was good reason for this. He was actually Hungarian – his real name was Dyuri Lanyi – and his formative years had been spent as a member of the Hungarian water polo team.

He had pitched up in Britain almost a decade earlier and had volunteered for the Grenadier Guards on the outbreak of war. But his foreign ways and Central European background had caused officials in the Home Office to serve him with a deportation order. Only swift action by his high-flying contacts ensured that the order was rescinded.

'Absolutely English in outlook and mentality.' So thundered his mentor, Albert Baillie, the Dean of St George's Chapel, Windsor Castle, who added that Lane had 'a genius for getting on with people'.[1] This was just as well, for he was to need every last drop of that genius in the weeks preceding D-Day.

The shoddy treatment he received from Whitehall bureaucrats might have put him off the Allied cause for good. Instead, it galvanized his stubborn spirit. In 1943 he signed up for the elite X-Troop, a British-led commando unit consisting of foreign nationals whose countries had been overrun by the Nazis.

Once accepted into this polyglot squadron he was given a fake identity and an invented backstory. He was also allowed to choose a pseudonym. He elected for Smith on the grounds that it was as English as a cup of tea. 'Don't be a bloody fool,' was the reaction of Bryan Hilton-Jones, the guts-of-granite commander of X-Troop. 'You can't even pronounce it properly.'[2] This was unfair – Lanyi's English was almost too perfect – but Hilton-Jones couldn't afford risks. He told him to settle for Lane (an Anglicization of Lanyi) and pretend to be Welsh, in order to explain away the occasional slips in his artificially clipped speech.

In the second week of May 1944, Lane was given a detailed briefing about his mission. Hilton-Jones told him that a new German mine had been discovered during an RAF bombing raid. A Spitfire had inadvertently dropped a bomb into the coastal shallows of northern France, triggering a series of spectacular detonations. It was fortuitous that these explosions had been caught on reconnaissance film, for it allowed scientists to assess them. They were concerned that the Nazis had developed 'some kind of new mine'[3] that could be detonated along an entire length of foreshore. The film was too grainy to reveal the working mechanism of the mine, but it was clear that such a weapon represented a potentially catastrophic threat to the planned Allied landings.

Hilton-Jones knew there was only one way to discover more and that was to send a man ashore. To this end, he began planning an audacious act of burglary, one that would require stealth, guts and an extra-large dose of bravado.

The plan was this: a high-speed motor torpedo boat would escort Lane and three comrades across the English Channel. They would then paddle ashore in a small black dinghy. Once there, two of the party would remain with the dinghy while the other two would slither up the beach, photograph the mine with an infrared camera and then beat a hasty retreat. If all went well, they would be back in England in time for breakfast.

But there was also the possibility that everything would go wrong. If so, the consequences would be grim indeed. Hitler's Commando Order dictated that all captured commandos were to be executed. That was terrifying enough, but before being shot, Lane and company were certain to be tortured by the Gestapo, whose agents were desperate for information about when and where the Allied landings might take place.

Most men would have weighed up the pros and cons when asked to take part in such a deadly mission, but Lane gave the same unflinching answer as he had when Hilton-Jones first asked if he would like to join the commandos. 'You bet I would!'[4]

Operation Tarbrush X was scheduled for 17 May, when a new moon promised near-total darkness. Lane selected a sapper named Roy Wooldridge to help him photograph the mines, while two officers, Sergeant Bluff and Corporal King, would remain at the shoreline with the dinghy. All four were fearless and highly trained. All four were confident of success.

The mission got off to a flying start. The men were ferried across the Channel in the motor torpedo boat and then transferred to the black rubber dinghy. They paddled themselves ashore and landed undetected at exactly 1.40 a.m. The elements were on their side. The rain was lashing down in liquid sheets and a stiff onshore squall was flinging freezing spray across the beach. For the German sentries patrolling the coast, visibility was little better than zero.

The four commandos now separated, as planned. Bluff and King remained with the dinghy, while Lane and Wooldridge crawled up the wet sand. They found the newly installed mines just a few hundred yards along the beach and Lane pulled out his infrared camera. But as he snapped his first photograph, the camera emitted a sharp flash. The reaction was immediate. 'A challenging shout in German rang out and within about ten seconds it was followed by a scream which sounded as if somebody had been knifed.'[5] Soon after, three gunshots ricocheted across the beach.

It was the signal for a firework display unlike any other. The Germans triggered starshells and Very lights (two different types of flare) to illuminate the entire stretch of beach and then began firing wildly into the driving rain, unable to determine where the intruders were hiding.

Lane and Wooldridge scraped themselves deeper into the sand as they tried to avoid the bullets, but they remained desperately exposed and found themselves caught in a ferocious gun battle. Two enemy patrols had opened fire and it soon became apparent that they were shooting at each other. 'We might have laughed,' noted Lane after the incident, 'if we had felt a bit safer.'[6]

It was almost 3 a.m. by the time the gunfight ended and the German flashlights were finally snapped off. Sergeant Bluff and Corporal King were convinced that Lane and Wooldridge were dead, but they left the dinghy for their erstwhile comrades and prepared themselves for a long and exhausting swim back to the motor torpedo launch. They eventually clambered aboard, bedraggled and freezing, and were taken back to England. They would get their cooked breakfast after all.

George Lane and Roy Wooldridge faced a rather less appetizing breakfast. They flashed signals out to sea, hoping to attract the motor torpedo boat and then flashed a continuous red light in the hope of attracting attention. But there was never any response. As they belly-crawled along the shoreline, wondering what to do, they stumbled across the little dinghy. Lane checked his watch. It was an hour before dawn, precious little time to get away, and the Atlantic gale was whipping the sea into a frenzy of crests and troughs. It was not the best weather to be crossing the English Channel in a dinghy the size of a bathtub.

'Shivering in our wet clothes, we tried to keep our spirits up by talking about the possibility of a Catalina flying boat being sent out to find us and take us home.' Wooldridge glanced at his watch and wryly remarked that it was the date on which he was meant to have been going off on his honeymoon. Lane laughed at the absurdity of it all. 'There he was, poor bugger, with me in a dinghy.'

Any hopes of being rescued by a flying boat were dealt a heavy blow in the hour before dawn. As the coastal town of Cayeux-sur-Mer slowly receded into the distance, Lane suddenly noticed a dot in the sea that was growing larger by the second. It was a German motor launch and it was approaching at high speed. He and Wooldridge immediately ditched their most incriminating equipment, including the camera, but kept their pistols and ammunition. Lane was considering a bold plan of action: 'shooting our way out, overpowering the crew and pinching their boat'.[7] But as their German pursuers began circling the dinghy, Lane was left in no doubt that the game was up. 'We found four or five Schmeisser machine guns pointed at us menacingly.' The two of them threw their pistols into the sea and 'with a rather theatrical gesture, put up our hands'.[8]

They were immediately arrested and taken back to Cayeux-sur-Mer, zigzagging a careful passage through the tidal waters. Lane swallowed hard. Only now did it dawn on him that he had paddled the dinghy through the middle of a huge minefield without even realizing it was there. 'It was an incredible bit of luck that we weren't blown to bits.'

The two men feared for their lives. They were separated on landing and Lane was manhandled into a windowless cellar, 'very damp and cold'. His clothes were drenched and his teeth were chattering because of the chill. He was also in need of sustenance, for he had not eaten since leaving England.

It was not long before an officer from the Gestapo paid him a visit. 'Of course you know we'll have to shoot you,' he was told, 'because you are obviously a saboteur and we have very strict orders to shoot all saboteurs and commandos.' Lane feigned defiance, telling his interrogators that killing him would be a very bad idea. The officer merely scowled. 'What were you doing?'

Lane and Wooldridge had cut the commando and parachute badges from their battledress while still at sea, aware that such badges would condemn them to a swift execution. They had also agreed on a story to explain their predicament. But such precautions proved in vain. The German interrogator examined Lane's battledress and told him that he 'could see where the badges had been'. Lane felt his first frisson of fear. 'They knew we were commandos.'

His interrogation took a turn for the worse when the Gestapo demanded information about the Allied landings, which they knew were imminent. 'They kept threatening me and I kept saying, "I'm sorry, I can't tell you anything important because I don't know anything important."'[9] He was refused food and water – the price to be paid for keeping silent – and faced increasingly aggressive questioning. Not until dusk did the interrogation come to an end. The two of them were locked into separate cellars and prepared themselves for a sleepless night.

Lane had been trained in psychological warfare and retained a clarity of purpose. With D-Day imminent, it was imperative for him and Wooldridge to make their escape. In pitch darkness, he groped his way around the cellar and discovered that the chimney pipe was tied to the wall with a piece of wire. He unhooked the wire, shaped it and then inserted it into the lock of his cell. After a moment of fumbling there was a click and the door sprang open. Not for nothing were the commandos known as the elite.

The corridor was completely dark. Lane groped his way forward using the walls as his guide, but as he did so he tripped over a German sentry lying on the floor. 'I'd go back if I were you,' barked the guard. 'There's another sentry around the corner.'[10] His escape attempt was over before it began.

Lane was always cool under pressure but even he got the fright of his life when his cell door was opened at dawn by a doctor dressed in a white gown. 'I thought, My God, what's going to happen now?' He was blindfolded, as was Wooldridge, and the two of them had their hands roped behind their backs. They were then bundled into a car and driven off at high speed. Lane asked where they were going. He got no answer.

'As I lay back in the seat, I realized they had tied the blindfold so tightly that I could see underneath it, through the gaps on either side of the bridge of my nose.'[11] Unlike in England, the Germans had not removed the road signs so Lane was able to snatch glimpses of the passing villages. 'Shortly before we stopped, I had been able to see a signpost that said: La Petite Roche Guyon.'[12]

He assumed that this was his journey's end; that he would be dragged from the car and shot.

★

As the German military car came to a halt in a private drive, the doors were opened and Lane's blindfold was removed by one of the sentries. When he looked up, he blinked in disbelief. 'My God!' he whispered under his breath. 'What a strange place! Just look at it!'[13] A fortified château stood bolted to the rock, a one-time feudal redoubt whose Enlightenment overlords had converted it into an eighteenth-century pleasure palace. The vertical outcrop behind was crowned by a medieval donjon, the original tower, while the castle itself still bristled with battlements and buttresses. Château de La Roche-Guyon was the hereditary fiefdom of the La Rochefoucauld dynasty, which had been ensconced here in pomp and splendour since the reign of the illustrious Sun King, Louis XIV. The addition of a sandstone façade had done much to tame the martial exterior, but the barbed-wire fences and concrete bunkers were testimony to the fact that this was once again a military edifice.

Lane had little time to admire the view. He and Wooldridge were shunted inside the entrance hall and led into two separate rooms. Just when Lane thought that his morning could not get any more bizarre, a guard appeared with a piping hot cup of tea.

The room in which he was being held had been left unlocked, so he unlatched the handle and peeked out. 'There was the fiercest looking dog' – an Alsatian – 'that I've ever seen in my life.' It growled and was heaved back by a guard. 'And I thought, I better stay put.'[14]

Lane still had no idea why he had been brought here, but that was soon about to change. 'After a little while, a very elegant officer came in and, to my amazement, we shook hands.' The officer spoke English with an accent as sharp as a blade. 'How are things in England?' he asked. 'It's always very beautiful at this time of year, isn't it?'[15] Lane pinched himself as this Alice in Wonderland world grew ever more strange. A sharp pang of hunger brought him to his senses: he told the officer that he hadn't eaten anything for almost forty-eight hours. The German apologized profusely and immediately ordered some food: fresh chicken sandwiches and coffee. 'Simply marvellous', thought Lane. His spirits were rising by the minute.

As he was eating, the officer turned to him and said, 'Do you realize you are about to meet someone very important?'

Lane shrugged. Nothing could surprise him any more.

'I must have your assurance,' said the German, 'that you're going to behave with the utmost dignity.'

Lane gave the officer an audacious dressing down, telling him 'that I happen to be an officer and a gentleman and I cannot behave in any other way'. But then he paused, for his curiosity was piqued, and he asked, 'But who am I going to meet?'

The officer stiffened slightly as he snapped out his reply. 'You are going to meet His Excellency Field Marshal Rommel.'

Lane was knocked sideways. Rommel, the Wüstenfuchs or Desert Fox, was one of the titans of the Third Reich, the seemingly invincible general who had won a string of victories in North Africa before meeting his nemesis in General Montgomery. Vanquished in the hot desert sands, yet still worshipped by his troops, he had been decorated by the Führer with the highest honour of all, the Knight's Cross with Oak Leaves, Swords and Diamonds. There were some who murmured that his finest days were behind him, but he had nevertheless been given command of Army Group B, defenders of the northern French coastline. Château de La Roche-Guyon was his operational headquarters.

'I'm delighted,' said Lane to his officer, 'because in the British army we have great admiration for him.'[16] This was true enough: his conduct during the North Africa campaign had earned him a reputation for fair play and chivalry.

Lane was so enthused by the prospect of meeting Rommel that he forgot all fears of his probable execution. He was intrigued to come face to face with the man whose mission was to ensure that the Allied invasion of France would fail.

The officer suggested that he clean himself up as soon as he had finished the last of his sandwiches. Lane was the first to admit he was 'pretty grubby', but even he was taken aback when he was handed a nail file and asked to remove the dirt from his fingernails. Once the manicure was complete, he was led through the castle's corridors towards the library. It was here that his meeting with Field Marshal Rommel was to take place.

The castle's sumptuous interior left Lane breathless. The Rochefoucauld dynasty lived in a bauble of opulence, with a war-chest of treasures that had been acquired (or pillaged) over the centuries by a succession of gaunt-faced counts and dukes. Gobelin tapestries jostled with hunting trophies, and portraits of illustrious seigneurs crowded the walls of the Hall of Ancestors. Here, too, the plump-cheeked Duke François de La Rochefoucauld – celebrated author of maxims – peered at guests through layer upon layer of smoke-blackened varnish.

Lane was led towards the galleried library, where his gaze was immediately drawn to the figure seated behind a writing desk at the far end of the room. It was Field Marshal Rommel, with his glacial eyes and sharply cleft chin. He wore his hallmark expression of impatience.

Lane had heard stories of how Rommel liked to unnerve his visitors by making them 'walk the whole length of a room', a form of mild psychological torture that enhanced his own stature while diminishing that of his guest. But on this occasion, he 'immediately got up, walked towards me, motioned to a round table on one side of the room and said, *Setzen Sie sich*' – 'sit yourself down'. Lane, who spoke perfect German, pretended not to understand: it would give him more time to field answers to the questions he was sure to be asked.

Several other high-ranking officials joined them at the table, including General Hans-Georg von Tempelhoff (Army Group B's chief of staff) and Captain Helmut Lang (Rommel's aide-de-camp). Once all were seated, Rommel turned to address Lane. 'So you are one of these gangster commandos, are you?'

Lane waited for this to be translated into English before feigning indignation. 'Please tell His Excellency that I do not understand what he means by gangster commandos. Gangsters are gangsters, but the commandos are the best soldiers in the world.'[17]

Rommel seemed to appreciate the answer for a brief smile swept his face. 'Perhaps you are not a gangster,' he said, 'but we've had some very bad experiences concerning commandos.'

This much was true. Over the previous months, Lane's fellow commandos in X-Troop had staged a series of hit-and-run raids on the coastline of France. But Lane was hardly going to admit such activities. He said that he had trouble believing what he was hearing from the field marshal.

'Do you realize that you have been taken prisoner under very strange circumstances?' continued Rommel.

Lane took issue with his choice of words. 'I hardly think they were *strange*,' he said. 'More unfortunate and unhappy.'[18]

'You know you are in a very serious situation.' This bald statement of fact was followed by a piercing stare: Rommel accused him of being a saboteur. Lane considered this for a moment before launching himself on to a high-wire of bravado. 'If the Field Marshal took me for a saboteur,' he said, 'he would not have invited me here.'

Even Rommel was taken aback by the boldness of Lane's response. 'So you think this was an invitation?'

'Naturally, yes, and I take it as a great honour. I'm delighted to be here.'

Lane was playing his cards with abandon, aware (as the Dean of Windsor had remarked) of his genius for getting on with people. He knew he was halfway to winning the game when Rommel's vulpine face broke into a broad smile. The ice was broken and the conversation now developed into something more akin to banter than interrogation.

'How's my friend Montgomery?'

'Unfortunately I don't know him,' said Lane, 'but he's preparing the invasion so you'll see him fairly soon.' He added that he knew little more about Montgomery than what appeared in *The Times*. As an afterthought, he told Rommel that it was an excellent newspaper. 'I think you ought to read it.'

Rommel was warming to the game. 'I do,' he said. 'I get it from Lisbon.'

'Well then, you'll see that he's preparing the invasion and they'll be here shortly, fighting you.'

Rommel scoffed. 'Well that'll be the first time that the English do any fighting.'

'I beg your pardon!' Lane spluttered offence. 'What happened at El Alamein?'

'That was not the English,' said Rommel. 'The English always get other people to do their fighting for them. The Canadians, the Australians, the New Zealanders, the South Africans.'[19] Lane – a Hungarian Jew fighting for the British – found it hard to keep a straight face.

Rommel soon returned to the subject of the Allied landings, asking Lane where he thought the soldiers would land. Lane retorted that he was only a junior officer: he was not privy to the invasion plans. 'If it was up to me,' he said, 'I would probably go for the shortest crossing.'[20]

Rommel nodded and then offered an opinion that took Lane by surprise. 'The great tragedy is that the British and Germans are fighting against each other, instead of combining our strength and fighting against the real enemy, which is the Russians.'

Lane responded by criticizing Nazi Germany's treatment of the Jews. 'We abhor the way you treat them.'

'Ah well,' said Rommel. 'People have different ideas about it all. It's impossible to talk about it.'

There was a lengthy pause and Lane surmised that the interrogation was coming to an end. He was determined to prolong it, for he found it fascinating. 'I was enjoying myself tremendously, so I asked the interpreter if, as the field marshal had asked me so many questions, I would be permitted to ask a few of my own.'

Rommel scoffed at his impertinence but nodded nonetheless.

'What I'd like to know is this,' said Lane. 'France is being occupied by you. How do the French people react to being occupied?'[21]

His question provided the cue for what Lane would later describe as 'the most wonderful dissertation' about the occupying army, with Rommel explaining in concise terms how Germany had brought leadership and order to France. 'The French people,' he declared, 'had never been so happy and so well organised.'[22]

'My goodness!' exclaimed Lane. 'I'd love to see that!'

'You can see it for yourself,' said Rommel, 'as you travel through France.'

Lane laughed in scorn. 'Every time I travel with your boys, they blindfold me and tie my hands behind my back.' At this, Rommel turned to Lang, his aide-de-camp, and asked if this was strictly necessary.

Lang nodded. 'Oh yes,' he said. 'These are very dangerous people.'[23]

These ominous words signalled the end of the interview. The meeting was over. Lane was faultlessly courteous to the end, thanking the field marshal for his time. He was hoping for a stay of execution, but as soon as he was outside he was blindfolded once again. He and Wooldridge were then driven off at high speed to Gestapo headquarters in Paris, arriving early that evening. 'It frightened the life out of me when I realized where I was,' admitted Lane, who was even more terrified when he heard the screams of prisoners being tortured.

Yet his own Gestapo interrogation was conducted in such dilatory fashion that he couldn't help wondering if Rommel had 'interceded on our behalf and prevented both Roy and I from being executed'.[24] In the event, he was neither shot nor tortured. Instead, he was sent to Oflag 9/AH, a prisoner-of-war camp in central Germany.

At the same time as Lane and Wooldridge were being transported to Paris, Rommel returned to his inlaid Renaissance desk – the one on which the 1685 Revocation of the Edict of Nantes had been signed – and wrote a letter to his beloved wife, Lucie-Maria. He told her of his extraordinary interview with a 'sensible British officer'[25] whose charm and bravado had spared him his life.

Those close to Rommel were not surprised by the field marshal's generosity to his prisoners. 'He upheld a code of chivalry that had become strange to our times.' So thought Hans Speidel, his chief of staff, who added that Rommel's behaviour was 'regarded by many as a sign of weakness'.[26] But it was also a private display of strength. In saving George Lane from execution, Rommel was directly contravening Hitler's Commando Order.

In his daily letters to Lucie-Maria, Rommel confided all the tittle-tattle about life at La Roche-Guyon. '*Meine liebste Lu*', he would begin, before recounting stories about his beloved dogs, Treff and Ebbo, his wild boar hunts with the Nazi-sympathizing duke and the fact that spring had yet to arrive in the valley of the River Oise.

'The weather is still cold,' he wrote on that same May evening, 'and finally rain. The British will have to be patient a little longer.'[27] He had no inkling as to when the Allies might come and his interrogation of Lane had left him none the wiser. Yet he had a hunch as to *where* they might come. He disagreed with Lane's contention that they would land at the Pas de Calais. The gun batteries and beach defences at Cap Gris Nez were so formidable that any assault would end in slaughter. 'They won't come there, for sure,'[28] he told the journalist Lutz Koch.

He was increasingly certain they would land in Normandy, on the shores of Calvados, where the sweeping sands made a perfect landing zone for infantry and artillery alike. During an inspection of the long beach at Saint-Laurent-sur-Mer, he had turned to the officer in charge, Major Werner Pluskat, and said, 'Pluskat, in my opinion, it is this very area that the Allies will land. This is exactly the type of place that the Allies will choose. They did so in Italy.'[29]

In this, as in so many of his military hunches, Rommel was to be proved correct. The Allies had indeed chosen it as one of their five landing beaches. They had given it the codename Omaha.

*Beach obstacles on the Normandy coast were a key part of the Atlantic Wall.
German soldiers are seen here diving for cover as the Allied reconnaissance
plane sweeps overhead.*

2

Atlantic Wall

THIRTY MILES TO the south-west of Rommel's headquarters, in the hamlet of Le Rousset d'Acon, Irmgard Meyer had spent that late May morning relaxing in the dining room of her new home. She was looking forward to the steamed asparagus that her French maid was preparing for lunch.

Frau Meyer was young, vibrant and in the early stages of pregnancy; her move to France had come as a bolt from the blue. She had been staring blankly out of the window of her parents' house in Stuttgart when she noticed an open-top saloon sweeping up the drive. Out stepped her husband's chauffeur who was bearing an important message from Normandy. All leave for officers had been cancelled, a sure sign of increasing tensions. Irmgard's husband, Hubert, was an officer in the 12th SS Panzer Division. In the light of the new restrictions, he wanted his wife to come to Normandy. 'Totally illegal,' he later admitted, 'but I hadn't had any leave for ages.'[1] He told her to travel back with his driver that very morning, 'before things begin to happen'.

Irmgard Meyer knew that the Allies would land at some point soon. 'People were always talking about the possibility of an invasion. It was an open secret that the English and the Americans were both expected somewhere up there.' Now, on receipt of her husband's message, she telephoned her cousin and asked her to take temporary care of her two young children. She then hurriedly packed her bags. 'I just wanted to see my husband one more time, because neither of us knew whether we would meet each other again.'

It was a seven-hour drive to Normandy and it was evening by the time she arrived. She was enchanted when she first glimpsed the hamlet in which her husband had his lodgings. Le Rousset d'Acon was a place of bucolic charm and the house itself was uncommonly picturesque, with an artist's studio and a patchwork garden studded with blooms. It was going to be 'a beautiful spring'. After the bombing raids on Stuttgart, Le Rousset d'Acon was 'just like peacetime'.

But the Meyers' private idyll was not to last. The commander of the 12th SS Panzer Division, Fritz Witt, had also brought his wife to France, as had a number of other senior staff. Now, General Witt decided they should all live together in a requisitioned mansion, Château de la Guillerie.

There was a touch of architectural fantasy to this communal home. With its leaded windows and monstrous brick chimneys it could almost have been conjured up by mad King Ludwig of Bavaria. In different circumstances it might have been a droll place to stay, but Frau Meyer was upset by the enforced move because she no longer had her husband to herself. 'There were too many people and we were never alone, we had constantly to make conversation with other people in the evenings.'

There were but two consolations. One was the large lake in the park, a delightful place to swim. The other was getting to know the dashing young officers of the 12th SS Panzer Division. The men of Hubert Meyer's panzer regiment certainly looked the part. Frau Meyer was particularly taken with the hawkish Max Wuensche, always decked in 'his splendid black tank uniform'. He would strut around the drawing room of Château de la Guillerie with an air of imperious disdain, his blond hair oiled, his eyes piercingly cold. Hero of the Third Battle of Kharkov, in which he led a crushing assault on the Soviet front line, he had been decorated with the Knight's Cross, the most prestigious military award in Nazi Germany.

Another master of armoured warfare was Kurt 'Panzer' Meyer, also a veteran of the Eastern Front, who was said to have ordered the massacre of the village of Yefremovka. His dutiful Nazi wife (also at the château) was pregnant with her fifth child. 'Little Meyer,' he would jest to Irmgard, who shared the same surname, 'I'm going to have my son before you do!'[2] It would be a moment of double celebration, for his wife would be rewarded for her fertility with the *Mutterkreuz* or Mother's Cross.

Presiding over this group of elite officers was General Fritz Witt, their hollow-eyed commander. He had won his spurs in

France, Greece and on the Eastern Front, where he was said to have ordered the massacre of 4,000 civilians in cold blood. Atrocities like this were never mentioned in front of the ladies at Château de la Guillerie. Instead, the men regaled their wives with tales of Arctic-style blizzards and the blood-bond camaraderie of life in the SS. Their lofty arrogance was epitomized by one of their lieutenants, Walter Kruger, who expressed his 'absolute confidence in victory from first to last'. This confidence was predicated on the fact that his men had received 'a proper training in the Hitler Youth'. They also had a 'sense of order [and] discipline',[3] except when they swigged too many pitchers of sharp Normandy cider. Then, they would erupt into rowdy choruses of the Horst Wessel song, the Nazi anthem.

These Eastern Front veterans were the men on whom Rommel was pinning his hopes. He wanted them to swing into action as soon as the Allies landed on the beaches, engaging the invaders when they were still seasick and vulnerable. He warned Hans Speidel, his chief of staff, that if the panzers were not able to 'throw them off the mainland in the first forty-eight hours, then the invasion will have succeeded and the war is lost'.[4] It was a policy that put him in direct confrontation with Germany's Commander-in-Chief in the West, Field Marshal Gerd von Rundstedt, and also with Hitler himself. They wanted these elite forces held in reserve.

One day, Irmgard's husband, Hubert, paid a visit to the nearby Luftwaffe post responsible for conducting reconnaissance flights over England. The commodore told him that his pilots had 'been unable to penetrate airborne defences in England for weeks, because of the fighters and flak, and that he simply could not say how advanced the invasion plans were'.

This ought to have caused deep alarm, for it suggested both the readiness of the Allies and the inadequacy of the Luftwaffe. Yet it did nothing to shake the confidence of Hubert Meyer and his officers. They were convinced they would be able to crush the Allied invaders within hours of the landings. They were also convinced that the showdown was in the offing. 'It was going to be soon,'[5] said Meyer with a hint of relish.

He just didn't know when. And he didn't know where.

★

The lack of news about Allied intentions was a source of particular anguish to Franz Gockel, a wide-eyed teenage soldier from north-west Germany. Young Gockel inhabited a different world from those battle-hardened SS officers. An unwilling conscript, he had been drafted into the army on his seventeenth birthday, in December 1942, and posted to Normandy in the following autumn. And it was here that his troubles really began, for he spent his days in a concrete bunker just above the beach at Saint-Laurent-sur-Mer. It was the very spot where Rommel had made his prediction of an Allied landing.

Gockel's unwilling move to Normandy marked the abrupt end to a childhood already scarred by the Nazi school curriculum. He still had the smooth-faced chubbiness of a schoolboy, albeit one decked in oversized army fatigues. His jacket hung loose on his shoulders and his cap was too large for his head. The flattened hair underneath might have been licked and patted by an over-anxious mother. Shy and endearingly innocent, he was quick to blush when girls were mentioned. In letters to his parents, he told them about picking wild cowslips and drinking milk fresh from the cow. He was particularly sad at missing another Mother's Day, 'the second that I can't spend with you'.[6]

His twenty-eight comrades were mostly teenagers like him. They were stationed a few hundred metres inland, where they manned the main compound of WN62, a *Widerstandsnest* or fortified strong-point. It was one of fourteen on this five-mile stretch of coast. Each strongpoint was an interlocking chain of bunkers and dug-outs armed with a veritable arsenal of machine guns, field guns and mortars. The size of ninety tennis courts, or thereabouts, WN62 was self-contained and almost self-sufficient – equipped in the fashion of a medieval fort, complete with its own enceinte or enclosure, a ditch-like counterscarp and fortified redoubts that lay some distance from the principal bunker.

Gockel had pulled the short straw in its defence, for he was stationed just metres from the beach, crouched in a machine-gun pit scraped into a shoulder of cliff. It was so close to the sea that the stiff spring gale flung salt-spray through the narrow embrasure. If and when the Allies attacked, he would be the very first German soldier they encountered. He knew this and it filled him with dread.

His task was to squat behind his MG 42 and spray the advancing troops with a hail of bullets.

For hour upon endless hour Gockel studied the soup-coloured swirl of the English Channel through his field glasses, searching for any hint of enemy vessels. But those long hours were always empty ones, for there was 'nothing but the coming and going of the waves'.[7] The only change to this forlorn vista came with each receding tide, when the submerged coastal defences were gradually exposed to reveal skeletal structures that resembled the carcass of some washed-up galleon. They included Czech hedgehogs, designed to thwart the movement of armoured vehicles, and 'Rommel's asparagus', stout poles stuck upright in the sand and topped with Teller mines. Any flat-bottomed landing craft brushing against them would be blown sky-high. These were the outermost defences of the Atlantic Wall, that chain of fortified obstacles that stretched from the Arctic fjords to the beaches of southern France. By the first week of June 1944, they had been in situ for long enough to become slung with dense mantles of kelp.

The 1,000 or so young conscripts defending this lonely stretch of foreshore held an ace card up their sleeve. While the shoreline itself was ideal for an Allied landing, the land behind the beach presented a world of difficulties for any would-be invader. A stack of cliffs and bluffs sheared upwards from the shingle, extending fully five miles along the shoreline. The lower slopes were a tangle of briars as impenetrable as any barbed wire, while the upper reaches presented an even greater challenge. The contours stiffened into a chaotic redoubt of crumbling turrets and crenellated gullies. Here, amid the thick clumps of wild gorse, vast sandstone corbels projected outwards at dizzying heights.

Such a dramatic backdrop brought small comfort to these teenage defenders, who complained of hunger, homesickness and lack of sleep. Gockel had the additional anguish of a troubled conscience. 'As a good Catholic boy, I know what to do and what not to do,'[8] he wrote in a letter to his parents. Yet life in the Wehrmacht was giving him a catechism of such vulgarity that it could scarcely be repeated in the confessional. It reached its nadir in the sharp evenings of late spring, when he and his comrades would gather at their regiment's orderly room, housed in a requisitioned manor in the hamlet of L'Épinette. Here, over pitchers of local cider, they would listen spellbound as rough-edged veterans of the Eastern Front bragged about fucking their way through the army whores. Gockel had not even kissed a girl: he had arrived in Normandy with romantic dreams of capering in the haystacks with local farm girls. He was not, as he put it, 'envisaging encounters like these'.[9]

He was particularly mortified when he found himself caught up in a bar with a bunch of foul-mouthed veterans. The bar girl was dressed in a décolleté bodice that provoked a string of obscenities from his well-sluiced comrades.

'Dammit,' roared one in guttural German, 'I'd like to see this one naked.'

'Don't get excited,' interjected another. 'She's probably got the *Property of the Wehrmacht* stamped on her round arse.'

Gockel turned 'red with embarrassment' and was led away by his friend, Heinrich, who saw his discomfort and told him not to 'pay attention to these show-offs'.[10] Gockel never repeated such stories to his parents. Instead, he sought solace in the burgeoning landscape. In one letter home, he wrote that 'everything feels like spring; nature is displaying itself at its most peaceful.'[11] As the sun grew in warmth, the apple trees of Calvados gave a coquettish display of brilliant pink and white buds. But paradise is rarely free from menace and the orchards of Normandy were no exception. 'Above us, at about 8000 or 9000 metres, observation planes were circling, leaving a white trail of condensation behind them.'[12]

At the end of May, an officer named Lieutenant Hans Heinze came to inspect Gockel's bunker. As he did so, a German plane crash-landed into the foreshore, having been hit and damaged during a rare reconnaissance mission over southern England. Lieutenant Heinze ran over to the concussed pilot, only to find him muttering incoherently. 'My God,' he kept repeating, 'England is completely awash with ships.' Heinze told Gockel and his friends not to worry, saying that it was the deluded ramblings of someone in severe shock. 'If there really were a lot of ships, then our Luftwaffe would bomb them.'[13] Yet he was clearly rattled, for he repeatedly reminded the young soldiers of the importance of keeping a close watch on the sea.

Gockel despaired of those endless hours spent staring at the horizon. There was nothing to break the slate-grey monotony of it all, not even ships, for the fishing skiffs of Grandcamp were no longer allowed out of port. What he never realized was that while German pilots were spying from the air, the Allies were spying from the ground. And they were doing so in most unusual fashion.

Guillaume Mercader was one of those rare individuals who seemed to have it all, a dashing Gallic pin-up with a beaky nose and a slick of jet-black hair. His powerful physique was matched by an enviable winning streak. Mercader was a champion cyclist whose stash of mantelpiece trophies bore testimony to his competitive spirit. In 1936 he had received the sponsorship of La Perle, the racing-bike manufacturers. He had soon proved his worth, winning the prestigious Caen to Rouen road-race just a few months after being signed up. He had subsequently become something of a legend in his native Bayeux.

Over the previous three years, he had used his local stardom to good effect. He ingratiated himself with the local Gestapo and then requested permission to continue his training along the coastal road that led from Courseulles-sur-Mer to Grandcamp, a distance of forty miles. The road had been declared a forbidden zone by the German military authorities for obvious reasons: it was the main point of access for all the defences of the Atlantic Wall.

Mercader's charm was such that he was granted permission to use that off-limits road. The soldiers who saw him on his bike had no inkling that he was diligently noting every pillbox, bunker and machine-gun nest. It was an *espionage de folie*: Mercader was the only spy in history to gather intelligence from the saddle of a La Perle racing bicycle, dressed in lightweight shorts and a skintight jersey.

He always carried the requisite papers, signed and stamped by the Gestapo. But his work was nonetheless dangerous, as he knew only too well. 'I was very often stopped close to Pointe du Hoc, an area under intense surveillance, and also a long way from my home.'[14] Tucked into his vest and pants was a stash of plans and diagrams that would have got him executed if discovered.

By the spring of 1944, Mercader had been gathering intelligence for more than three years and his 'circuit' of resisters, the Calvados

Organisation civile et militaire, was working with the smooth efficiency of a derailleur gear. Mercader was in contact with almost
ninety agents, including three gendarmes and a handful of railway
workers. The former supplied him with identity cards 'for agents
in difficulty',[15] while the latter kept a close eye on troop movements.
Farmers also proved their worth. Mercader had won the confidence
of local men like Jean Coulibeuf and Jean Picot who 'could move
about the countryside without being suspected'. They were invaluable in supplying 'important information about the minefields, the
defences deeper inside the land, and the type and importance of
the units and the ammunition dumps'.[16]

Once in possession of all the latest information, Mercader would
cycle over to 1 Rue Saint-Malo in Bayeux (headquarters of the
local resistance) where the intelligence reports were collated and
handed to a local engineer named Eugène Melun. He transmitted
them by wireless to England where they were processed by staff of
the Special Operations Executive and forwarded to the Supreme
Headquarters Allied Expeditionary Force. Within a day or two of
Guillaume Mercader cycling along the coastal road of Normandy,
the architects of Operation Overlord were in possession of the very
latest news of the German beach defences.

This was invaluable, for the success or failure of D-Day would be
dependent on the seaborne assault on the coastline. Mercader knew
that a great number of men – more than 2 million troops in fact –
were stationed across England, all of them awaiting shipment to France.
The lives of many of those soldiers, and certainly those in the first
wave, would be dependent on the accuracy of the French intelligence.

On Friday, 2 June, Guillaume Mercader caught a train to Paris
in order to meet with a solicitor by the name of Robert Delente,
a fellow native of Normandy. Delente's skills went far beyond
resolving legal disputes. For more than three years he had been
orchestrating the Calvados circuit of resisters, in which Mercader
was the star turn. He now had some sensational news for his young
protégé, informing him that there was to be 'an imminent landing'[17]
of Allied forces. Furthermore, he said that the exact date of the
landing would be broadcast on the BBC as one of the hundreds of
coded *messages personnels* that filled the airwaves every evening. Each
of these messages transmitted information to the resistance.

Delente was very specific in his instructions to Mercader. 'For what concerned specifically our region, we had to listen at 6.30 p.m. for the phrase, *Il fait chaud à Suez* [*It is hot in Suez*]. This would be repeated in quick succession. It would then be followed by a second message, *Les dés sont jetés* [*The dice are thrown*]: also broadcast twice.'[18]

As soon as he heard these two duplicated messages, Mercader was to inform his fellow resisters that the Allied landings were imminent. It would be the signal for them to start their acts of sabotage, blowing bridges and cutting communication wires. It would also be the signal that D-Day had finally arrived.

Women played a key role in transmitting messages in the hours before D-Day. It was exhausting work for those on nightshift in Underground Headquarters, Portsmouth.

3

The Weather Report

NINETEEN-YEAR-OLD ELSIE CAMPBELL had been at work for an hour or so on the evening of Saturday, 3 June when she was struck by the feeling that life was about to take a turn for the better. This was partly because it was almost her birthday. At midnight she would be twenty – no longer a teenager – and she was intending to celebrate. Her friend Brenda had promised a birthday luncheon at the Red Lion in Fareham. But the pub lunch was not the principal cause of her excitement. She had just made a momentous discovery – an exhilarating one.

Miss Campbell worked in one of the most secure strongholds in the country: a sprawling underground bunker buried 100 feet beneath the Hampshire coastline. Fort Southwick was the nerve centre for Operation Overlord, a hub from which radar reports were cross-referenced with messages from ships at sea in order to provide an accurate picture of what was taking place in the English Channel. As such, it was a key part of the D-Day chain of command.

Miss Campbell and her girlfriends referred to the fort as a 'rabbit warren'.[1] It was indeed – a labyrinth of tunnels that had been hacked through the Portsmouth bedrock by army sappers two years earlier. It was deep enough to withstand the heaviest Luftwaffe bombing raid.

The tunnels had been lined with fluorescent tubes and the light in this subterranean world was bright and shrill. Time held little meaning for the 700 staff who worked here, as the lighting was constant, whether it was midday or midnight. The electric glare was certainly no substitute for daylight. Several of Miss Campbell's fellow workers had been obliged to undergo sessions of sun-ray treatment in order to return colour to their pallid skin.

This grid-like warren of tunnels was packed with state-of-the-art wireless equipment. The first time Miss Campbell descended the 168 stairs that led into UGHQ – the acronym for Underground Headquarters – she found herself glimpsing an alternative world that was driven by the latest technology. At its heart was the Operations Plotting Room, an excavated chamber that stood higher than a double-decker bus. It contained a gigantic table-top map of the English Channel, studded with scores of miniature ships. Each time a ship moved, the corresponding miniature was likewise shifted.

In close proximity to the Operations Plotting Room was the Q Message Room (Q was the code for deception) as well as the naval cipher officers. There was also a wireless telegraphy office and a 'crypto' office that always seemed to be locked. Miss Campbell never discovered what took place behind its doors.

Her shift that day had begun like any other. As she made her way on foot to Fort Southwick, she paused for a moment at the top of Portsdown Hill in order to admire the panorama spread out below. The sky was lead-grey and the dirt-coloured sea was in full churn as it surged in from the Atlantic. This blustery backdrop did nothing to distract from the 'wonderful view of Portsmouth Harbour'. As far as she could see, there was 'a solid mass of ships and landing craft of every description'.[2] There were hundreds of them, thousands even: battleships, destroyers, corvettes, mine-sweepers, tugs and landing craft – ships of every possible shape and size. Above them hung huge white barrage balloons, bloated like the famous Michelin man. Attached to the vessels by invisible wires, these puffed-up bladders offered a protection of sorts against the Luftwaffe. Miss Campbell's workmate, Doris Buttle, was quick to notice that they were much lower in the sky than usual on that particular evening. It gave her a moment's pause for thought. She couldn't help wondering if 'something momentous was about to happen'.[3]

Miss Campbell took her seat beside a team of like-minded young women: Molly Carter, Sarah 'Skippy' Wilson and Mary Deacon-Pickles, some working in signals, some working on the switchboards. They were a close-knit band with a shared outlook. One of their colleagues, Alison Edye, felt as if she were living 'in a honeycomb with all the other busy bees'.[4] All were dressed in bell-bottom trousers rather than skirts, 'in view of the damp in the tunnels',[5] and each of them sat in front of an RCA AR88 receiver, tuning the dials in order to keep it at a frequency of 535 kHz.

After an hour or so of work, they looked forward to the 'corned beef sarnie'[6] that was delivered to their desks by the canteen staff. On occasions, they were also given cups of cocoa enriched with fat from the corned beef cans. It sounded disgusting and tasted little better, but it provided them with energy to push through the night.

Nothing of significance happened during the early part of Miss Campbell's shift, just the usual 'ships passing to and fro'. But a little after 10 p.m., she detected an unexpected change in tone in the messages. 'A signal' – far more powerful than usual – 'gave news of a convoy sailing from the West Country.'

This was most irregular and what made it even stranger was the fact that its destination flashed up as 'the Far Shore'. Miss Campbell knew that this was one of the codenames for Normandy. With growing excitement, she began to track other signals before whispering to her friends. 'It was obvious that the second front, so long awaited, was at last taking place.'

Elsie Campbell was extremely sharp; she now started to note down the positions of the ships in order to calculate the most likely time when the men would be landing. 'By studying all the signals, it was possible to work out that D-Day was planned for Monday, 5 June.'[7] If all went to schedule, the men would be starting their historic landing in France within the next thirty hours.

Miss Campbell would be proven correct in her calculation but wrong in her assumptions – for that tempestuous June night was to be full of surprises.

Lashed by rain and shivering into his bones, Howard Vander Beek spat a curse at the waters of the English Channel. This was the sort of night to be spent on land, in the cosy warmth of the Minerva Inn. It was the sort of night to draw the curtains and batten down the hatches. But it was certainly not the sort of night to be out at sea.

Vander Beek and his American crew were braving a sharp spring storm that was pitching six-foot waves against the hull of their diminutive vessel, LCC 60. Vander Beek had sea legs of steel and a stomach of concrete, yet even he was finding the sea 'abusively choppy and disagreeable'. He had been warned that 'the Channel weather was the worst in twenty years', but he hadn't expected it to be quite so relentless. He and his crew had been at sea for eight hours and they were feeling 'weary and cold from the bitter winds'.[8] Vander Beek wiped the spray from his Westclox watch. Almost midnight. Another six hours to go.

Vander Beek was the senior officer aboard LCC 60 – a strong-jawed, white-toothed twenty-seven-year-old from Oskaloosa, Iowa. His wave of blond hair and sharply knotted tie lent an Ivy League preppiness to his nautical dress – at least it did when he was on dry land. But now, after so many hours at sea, his hair was sluiced with salt and his necktie sodden and listing.

Vander Beek was known as 'Boss' and he was a natural leader. This was just as well, for his job was to sail in the vanguard of Force U, the huge fleet of ships destined for Utah Beach. It consisted of twelve separate convoys that had sailed from their anchorages at Belfast, Plymouth, Torbay, Weymouth and Dartmouth before grouping together in the English Channel. It was one of the greatest flotillas in history, consisting of 865 vessels that included battleships, destroyers and frigates. Yet Force U was just one of five fleets that were destined to sail to Normandy on D-Day, one for each beach. Since Utah was the furthest of the five landing beaches, its fleet had been the first to set sail. The other four were not due to leave their ports for some hours.

In the stormy blackness of the English Channel, only a handful of the leading vessels were visible through the spindrift. When Vander Beek glanced back into the night, they appeared to him as 'silent dark hulks crashing through the ever-mounting waves'.

His responsibility was an onerous one for someone so young, yet his position at the front of Force U was just one of his duties. Once the fleet had arrived at its anchorage off Utah Beach, he had an even more exacting task to perform. He was to guide the scores of landing craft to the shore, leading them to the exact spot where the men would begin their invasion. One slip, one mistake, and disaster could ensue. For if the men were landed at the wrong place, the long months of training would all have been in vain.

Such an important mission required a special ship and LCC 60 was exactly that. She was a control vessel powered by two

255-horsepower engines that enabled her to cruise at close to four-teen knots. The men had nicknamed her Lily Cup Cruiser, but the quaintness of the name did not equate to comfort. Just fifty-six feet long and little wider than a London bus, her below-decks space was minuscule and crammed with weaponry and nautical equipment that included smoke-pots for signalling, an odograph for measuring distance and two fathometers or depth finders. These last two items would be needed to help guide the landing craft to the shore.

The role entrusted to Vander Beek and his men was so important that it had been kept under wraps. The vessel, too, had been kept concealed until a few days before their departure from Plymouth. This secrecy had engendered a close camaraderie among the crew. 'Solid kinship', was how Vander Beek saw it. He had trained for more than a year with three of the men and fought with three others in Sicily. They shared opinions in the same way as they shared their food. And now, as the Channel gale flung 'raw salt spray' into their eyes, they were all sharing the same thought: that this was the worst possible night for launching the largest seaborne invasion in history.

The weather was not the only reason for their anxiety. Something unsettling had happened a week earlier, something so alarming that it was still preying on their minds. It had taken place one evening when they tuned into Axis Sally, an American broadcaster producing propaganda for the Nazis. She was popular with the crew, even though a traitor to her country, because she played the latest American hits. But on this particular evening the music was to strike a discordant note. She had just played 'As Time Goes By' when, to Vander Beek's astonishment, she addressed him and his men directly. 'Tonight I want to talk seriously with Sims [Gauthier] and Howard [Vander Beek] and their crew over in Plymouth.'

The men could scarcely believe their ears. 'You are sitting there thinking that you will soon be in on an invasion of this mighty continent,' she said. 'Your stupid leaders are making plans to force you to sacrifice your lives to do it. This is a huge fortress, and if you come near it, all of you will die violent deaths.' She suggested it would be better for them to go back to their loved ones in the United States 'while you still can'.

Axis Sally's comments left the men with a deep sense of disquiet.

Not only did she know their names, but she also knew all about their secret vessel, LCC 60. She described the boat, outlined her function and even discussed the men's recent activities, down to 'the scraping and painting the crewmen had done that very Saturday afternoon'. They listened 'in frozen silence', mystified as to how she could know such things.

They got their answer soon afterwards. Two of the crew recalled chatting to 'a friendly old British couple' while they had been scraping down the hull. The couple had heaped praise on the Americans and then asked a number of detailed questions. Seduced by the couple's smiles, the men had been happy to provide answers.

It was clear that Axis Sally could only have received her information from this seemingly benign pair of pensioners. Vander Beek realized that they had been 'able to garner all they wanted to know about us in order to transmit it by wireless for Sally's use that evening. Well trained and cleverly disguised, they had been Nazi spies.'[9] He never discovered whether or not the authorities arrested the couple. Even if they had, the damage had been done. The element of surprise, so crucial to the invasion, seemed to have been lost.

Howard Vander Beek's sense of unease was shared by the men on board one of the Force U destroyers following in their wake. USS *Corry* was a bolts and steel leviathan in comparison to Vander Beek's tiny craft — a big-gunned destroyer with a top speed of almost forty knots. She was well equipped to deal with anything that the German shore batteries might hurl at her. Yet an atmosphere of collective doubt had pervaded the vessel ever since she left harbour. To those on board, it felt as if there were a dark spell hanging over the ship. When the vessel's radio operator, Bennie Glisson, had descended into the mess hall for his dinner that evening, he found it 'as silent as a tomb'. He turned to his shipmates and attempted to lighten the atmosphere. 'You guys act like you're eating your last meal.' No one laughed, nor even looked up, so he ate his turkey dinner in silence. The usual banter had been replaced by an all-pervading gloom that was 'comparative to a funeral crossing'.[10]

The loss of morale had taken hold on the previous evening, when the ship's captain, Lieutenant Commander George Hoffman, gathered the crew on deck for a pre-sailing pep talk. Instead of lifting their spirits with a rousing call to arms, he warned them of the dangers that lay ahead and concluded by saying that each and every one of them was 'expendable'.[11] It was an unfortunate choice of vocabulary. One of Benny Glisson's fellow radio operators, Lloyd 'Red' Brantley, felt the optimism vanish in a flash. 'People were kind of in shock.'[12]

Captain Hoffman was unaware of the damage he had done. He had spent the last four hours on the bridge, staring into the rain-slashed darkness as he tried to keep his eye fixed on the LCC 60. Also on the bridge was Robert Beeman, a smart young graduate from Yale who had worked in naval intelligence before being assigned to USS *Corry*. His job was to transmit information to and from the ship's operation centre below decks.

The relationship between Beeman and Hoffman was one of cool politeness, but there were unspoken tensions that had hitherto been kept bottled up. Beeman harboured private doubts about Commander Hoffman and felt he attached too much importance to outmoded naval traditions and too little to the technicalities of modern warfare. Hoffman was godson of Admiral George Dewey, the walrus-moustached hero of the Battle of Manila Bay, and he 'liked us to know that his middle name' – Dewey – 'linked him to the famous admiral'.

There was certainly a touch of the martinet about Hoffman. A stickler for convention, he 'firmly believed in the privileges and responsibilities of a commanding officer' and was happy to let it be known that he had been awarded the Legion of Merit for sinking an enemy U-boat. He was rather less quick to acknowledge that he had been 'royally chewed out' by his naval superiors for ramming a crippled surfaced submarine, an action that could have seriously damaged his own ship. His naval bosses were so infuriated that they published their rebuke in the Anti-Submarine Warfare bulletin.

Hoffman seemed to have learned little from his mistakes. For now, as he steered USS *Corry* across the English Channel, he made another serious misjudgement. While still in shallow water, the ship's sonar equipment detected something untoward on the seabed. This news was relayed to the bridge, where it prompted very different reactions from the two men at the controls. Beeman knew from experience that sonar readings were to be treated with caution, as they were often distorted by fish, kelp or even thermal gradients. 'As we all knew, most of our contacts were *not* submarines.'[13]

But Hoffman took the decision to attack, displaying the same rashness as he had when he rammed the submarine. He ordered a 600-pound Mark VII depth charge to be dropped on to a target that might have been no more malign than a clump of seaweed. It was a dangerous gamble. The sea was just twenty-five fathoms deep and the depth charge was huge. When it exploded, it did so with such violence that USS *Corry* took much of the impact. The engine's drainpipe was shattered, the radar knocked out and the main control system for the ship's big guns was crippled. Although the engine and radar were patched up after a tense four hours, the control system was damaged beyond repair. USS *Corry* would be going into battle without being able to fire her five-inch guns automatically. They could still be used under manual control, 'but with considerable loss of accuracy and rate of fire'.[14]

The ship ploughed on through the night, one of many hundreds in that vast fleet. It was stifling down in the bowels of the ship and the only noise was the throaty hum of the engines. There had been radio silence for hours, as all the ships of Force U were maintaining a blackout. But shortly before dawn, 'all of a sudden', three digits flashed over the system. Lloyd Brantley, the radio operator, looked at his code sheet and blinked in astonishment. 'Oh my God!'[15]

He immediately showed the message to his fellow radioman, Mort Rubin. 'Jesus Christ!' said Rubin. The message informed them that D-Day had been postponed. The entire fleet of 865 vessels was told to turn in its tracks and head back to England.

Rubin was sceptical. 'Could this be a fake message sent by the Germans?' he wondered. 'If so, it was certainly a beauty.' Even if it was genuine, it was every captain's nightmare. There was also the real possibility that some of the ships wouldn't receive it and Rubin had visions of 'a lone destroyer or minesweeper going in on its own private war and tipping our hand to the Germans'.[16] It was imperative to inform the rest of the fleet.

Still in the vanguard was Howard Vander Beek's LCC 60, which had been quick to pick up the coded *Post Mike One* postponement message. Within seconds of confirming its veracity, the craft swung back towards England in the hope that the hundreds of other vessels would follow suit.

In such choppy seas, this was a procedure fraught with complications. Many vessels were towing tugs, entailing 'seamanship of a high order'. One false manoeuvre could easily result in tow-lines getting fouled around the screws. But as the weakest of dawns began to lick away the darkness, the mighty Force U performed perhaps the greatest U-turn in history, wheeling through a gigantic semicircle and heading slowly back to England.

There was bitter disappointment aboard the LCC 60. Howard Vander Beek's men were 'exhausted, saltwater-soaked and hungry'. For more than eighteen hours they had been pitched up crests and lurched into troughs, as if they were riding some sort of liquid bucking-bronco. Now, they were told to head for Weymouth and await further orders.

The only consolation came when Vander Beek was invited to spend the rest of that day in a 'cosy old dwelling' that belonged to a kindly English family. He ate 'a wholesome meal' and was then led to a 'warm soft feather bed'.[17] Yet he still felt a deep sense of disappointment. The first attempt at landing in occupied France had been thwarted not by Rommel, nor even by the German coastal guns, but by an enemy far closer to home: the atrocious English weather.

It was an enemy that had one last trick to play.

The wind was still gusting strongly on Sunday morning when Professor Walter Stübe arrived for work in his gilded office on the second floor of the Luxembourg Palace in Paris. The giant swastika at the front of the building was snapping angrily at the flagpole and the low cloud was whipping through the eaves and gables of the French capital.

Stübe was chief meteorologist to the Luftwaffe and he knew more than most about frontal systems and Atlantic depressions. He also knew that his world had been contracting with alarming speed. Just three years previously, he had access to advance weather information from as far afield as Jan Mayen Land, Greenland and Spitsbergen. But the German weather station on Jan Mayen Land had been abandoned and the one on desolate Sabine Island, in northern

Greenland, had been destroyed by American bombers. Although meteorologists were still collecting weather data in Spitsbergen, little useful information ever reached Professor Stübe. This left him at a serious handicap. Unlike his Allied counterparts, who received data from across the North Atlantic, Stübe was reliant on information from Luftwaffe pilots returning from missions at sea.

His only other source was a naval officer in Le Havre, who telephoned him each evening with barometer readings and precipitation statistics. One who observed Stübe at work said he was engaged in 'the most incredible crystal-ball gazing' and Stübe himself was acutely aware of the impossibility of forecasting with any accuracy. 'This,' he remarked to one visitor, 'is why I have white hair.'

Stübe met with senior staff officers at that Sunday's 10.30 a.m. conference. He assured them there was no possibility of any Allied invasion for the next few days because 'the weather situation was becoming worse.' Information from Le Havre revealed that 'the barometer was definitely going down and the cloud cover was eight-tenths below six hundred metres and ten-tenths above that.'[18] In such conditions, Allied planes could not operate.

Stübe had studied previous Allied attacks (in Italy and elsewhere) and noted that they only invaded when there was a cast-iron guarantee of fine weather. Another sure sign that the invasion was not imminent was the fact that the northern coast of France would be under a full moon for the next three days. In Sicily, the Allies had attacked when the moon was in its first quarter. And in the deserts of North Africa, the British had never attacked during a full moon.

Once the morning conference was over, Professor Stübe telephoned his projections to Major Hermann Mueller, the chief meteorologist at Field Marshal von Rundstedt's underground headquarters in Saint-Germain-en-Laye. Stübe knew that von Rundstedt was 'very conscious of the weather and took it quite seriously':[19] he wanted to give him the latest update. Major Mueller had also received some new data and it differed slightly from that of Stübe. It suggested that an airborne operation would be 'broadly possible'[20] and a seaborne landing conceivable, although the stormy conditions in the Channel made it far from ideal. Mueller agreed with the professor's assessment that an imminent landing was most unlikely.

He nevertheless asked for a review of the situation later that day, when the latest data had been received from Le Havre.

The updated information, when it arrived, only confirmed the two men's earlier assessment. There was 'no promise of good weather in the future' and the stormy conditions were likely to intensify. The Luftwaffe considered the outlook so unfavourable that the anti-aircraft units were allowed to stand down.

Field Marshal Rommel shared his weathermen's belief that there would be no Allied invasion for the foreseeable future. He noted that 'the enemy has not made use of three periods of fine weather in May for his invasion' and was convinced that 'further periods of fine weather in the coming weeks cannot be reckoned on.'[21] The gunmetal sky only served to confirm this opinion. When Rommel had awoken on that Sunday morning, the wind was moaning through the turrets of La Roche-Guyon and tugging at the heads of the giant rhododendrons, tearing at petals and strewing them into the gullies where they collected like patches of damp snow. The morning sky was so half-hearted that Rommel had been obliged to switch on his desk lamp.

His mind was now made up. He would leave for Germany that very morning in order to be with his wife, Lucie-Maria, for her birthday on 6 June. He had bought her a pair of hand-made grey suede shoes that were costly, chic and very Parisian. He was determined to give them to her in person.

Rommel had another reason for heading to Germany, one of even greater importance than his wife's suede shoes. He was hoping to meet with Hitler in order to implore him to place the two panzer divisions stationed outside Paris – the 12th SS and Panzer Lehr – under his sole command. Rommel feared that without these panzers, he could not defeat the expected Allied invasion.

After a snatched breakfast of toast and honey, he bade a hasty farewell to his staff and climbed into his black convertible Horch. He placed the shoebox beside him and then turned to his chauffeur. 'We can go now, Daniel.'[22] He was anxious to get under way, for it was a twelve-hour drive to the family home in Herrlingen, southern Germany.

As the Horch swept down the drive, the sentries snapped a salute before closing the wrought-iron gates to Château de La Roche-Guyon.

★

Military planning officer Goronwy Rees shared one thing in common with Field Marshal Rommel: he knew that the Allied invasion was predicated upon fine weather. He was also one of only a handful of people to know exactly how Operation Overlord would unfold. He had served on General Montgomery's staff for many months and helped to plan every aspect of the invasion. Now, as the big day approached, he had to get the finalized Operation Orders signed off by the various commanders-in-chief.

This was more time-consuming than he was expecting. When he took the document to Air Marshal Trafford Leigh-Mallory, 'he insisted on reading the whole bloody thing from start to finish, trying to correct commas.' Rees did his best to hurry him along. 'It's impossible to alter anything,' he said. 'It's all been agreed.'[23] But Leigh-Mallory was unmoved. He felt sure that in detail lay victory.

The success of Operation Overlord was contingent on there being a full moon and a flooding dawn tide. This greatly constricted the options for the date of the landings. Success was also contingent on the weather. Smooth seas, clear skies and nothing more than a light wind were all deemed essential. And this is where the problems began.

When General Eisenhower summoned his chief weatherman, James Stagg, to a meeting at 4.15 a.m. that Sunday, he was unaware that his three teams of meteorologists were at war with themselves. The American forecasters thought their British counterparts too cautious. The British thought the Americans too confident. And the naval forecasters were infuriated by James Stagg's self-importance. 'A glory hound',[24] was the opinion of Laurence Hogben, a young New Zealander on the last team.

The Americans were led by two 'loud-mouthed' Californians, Ben Holzman and Irving Krick, who had spent their pre-war years forecasting for Hollywood movie-makers. The bull-headed Krick was particularly irksome. Dismissed by his rivals as 'a salesman to his fingertips',[25] his brash overconfidence led him to claim he could produce reliable forecasts for up to five days. This infuriated the British, who slapped him down with the retort that the English Channel was rather less predictable than the west coast of America.

It was a put-down that carried some weight. The British meteorological team was led by the veteran Charles 'C.K.M.' Douglas, a gaunt and austere individual whose 'distant manner'[26] masked an anabatic brain and a photographic memory of weather patterns stretching back to Edwardian times. He contended that Channel forecasts could not be predicted beyond forty-eight hours.

James Stagg's task was to collate the three individual forecasts and knock them into a coherent report. But this was far from easy. Although he liked to present himself to General Eisenhower as a weatherman extraordinaire with his pulse on every frontal trough, he was not a trained meteorologist and his views were, as one of his forecasters put it, 'not worth a damn'.[27]

He was increasingly drained by having to walk 'on a not-very-tight tightrope',[28] especially as Eisenhower treated him as if he were in possession of a magic weather-wand. 'Just name us five, fine calm days and we'll go for it.'[29] It sounded so easy, yet proved so difficult. That Sunday's pre-dawn conference had been particularly tense, for Stagg had been forced to admit to Eisenhower that he saw no change to the atrocious spring weather. Indeed, he said that the cloud cover would be so thick in the coming days that air support would be impossible. Eisenhower gave a grim response. 'If the air cannot operate, we must postpone.'[30]

In the hours since that pre-dawn meeting, Stagg's day had taken a turn for the worse. His mid-morning conference call with the meteorologists 'was the most heatedly argumentative'[31] of them all, with no one agreeing on anything.

But every cloud has a silver lining and Stagg's came in the form of a large cold front sweeping eastwards across the Atlantic. If the charts were correct, this would bring clear skies and calmer seas for much of Tuesday, 6 June. Not only was there a clear window of opportunity for the landings, but the air force would also be able to operate.

That Sunday evening, 4 June, as the clocks in Southwick House chimed 9.30 p.m., Stagg addressed General Eisenhower and his staff in the old library. The double blackout curtains had been tightly drawn, but the rain could be heard drilling hard against the panes of glass. Eisenhower's three commanders-in-chief were present – Admiral Sir Bertram Ramsay, General Bernard Montgomery and Air Marshal Sir Trafford Leigh-Mallory – along with their chiefs of staff.

Stagg delivered his upbeat forecast for 6 June and then answered questions from the assembled company. Once this was done, he left the room while Eisenhower made his final decision as to whether or not to launch the invasion. He was still chatting in the corridor when the Supreme Commander strode out of the library with a detectable spring in his step. 'Well Stagg,' he said with a broad smile, 'we're putting it on again. For heaven's sake, hold the weather to what you told us.'[32] A final and irrevocable decision would be taken at 4.15 a.m. the next day, but Eisenhower had fired the starting gun and it would soon be too late to halt the invasion.

As Stagg scuttled back to his tented billet in the woods that surrounded Southwick House, he hoiked his collar against the driving rain. The wind was still whipping a gale and the night sky was 'heavily overcast with low cloud'.[33] It was typically English weather.

By June 1944, southern England was a vast marshalling yard for military supplies. Here, women of the Auxiliary Territorial Service check that tyres are fully inflated.

4

Codebreaking

THE RAIN WAS still tipping down on the following morning, 5 June, with a sky so filled with menace that it felt as if summer had packed its bags and left for good. In a thousand army encampments and in 279,000 khaki tents, men slouched under flapping canvas and waited in vain for the skies to clear. They drank tea by the urn and chain-smoked their Player's Navy Cut until their lungs ached.

The previous months had seen southern England transformed into a vast marshalling yard that stretched from Dover to Devon. Eleven thousand planes and a third of a million vehicles had been parked and concealed to hide them from the Luftwaffe's prying eyes. But as the great day approached they were moved to the coast, and by the first week of June the backwater lanes of six counties had been churned to sludge by monstrous mechanized vehicles, the like of which had never been seen before: armoured bulldozers, amphibious half-tracks and Dodge four-by-fours. Bumper to bumper they travelled, with the open-backed Chevrolet trucks carrying sharply dressed GIs with pressed kit and parted hair.

That summer, fields sprouted munitions instead of wheat – thousands of acres of mortars, howitzers and anti-aircraft guns. A staggering 23 million tons of matériel had been shuttled across the Atlantic from North America; so much, indeed, that it required 170 miles of new railway lines to shift it across the British countryside. And in the skies above, British Spitfires and Lancasters were now flanked by American Liberators, Dakotas and twin-boomed P38 Lightnings.

O America! To one little boy evacuated from Clapham to the West Country, the arrival of the spick-and-span GIs was more entrancing than any travelling circus. The Americans gleamed. They had white teeth. And (better still) their low-slung pockets were stashed with endless packs of Spearmint chewing gum. By contrast, their British counterparts looked dour and downtrodden, like 'jumble-sale champions' with ill-fitting fatigues and outsized boots.

That boggle-eyed little boy* watched mesmerized as the Americans swept by 'in magnificent, gleaming, olive-green, pressed-steel, four-wheel-drive juggernauts, decked with what car salesmen would call optional extras of a sort never seen on their domestic equivalents'. These included 'deep-treaded spare tyres, winches, towing cables, fire-extinguishers'. In their wake came the motorized jeeps, 'caparisoned with whiplash aerials and sketchy canvas hoods which drummed with the rhythm of a cowboy's saddlebags rising and falling to the canter of his horse across the prairie'.[1]

By the end of May, all these vehicles – American, British, Canadian – had been travelling on a one-way road to the coast. The countdown to Operation Overlord had begun in earnest and all the soldiers heading to Normandy were 'enclosed' in marshalling camps that were sealed off from the outside world. 'All of a sudden, barbed wire appeared all the way around.' So noted one sergeant in the artillery. 'Red caps, blue caps with dogs, patrolling outside. Nobody was allowed to leave, nobody could come in.'[2]

There were 1,200 such camps, along with a dozen marshalling zones near the coast and 133 airfields spread right across the British Isles. And it was at one of these airfields, tucked neatly into a fold of rural Dorset, that an operation of the greatest secrecy was about to be launched. This anonymous base was to be the starting point for the opening act of D-Day, a curtain-raiser of such bravado that none of those taking part expected to come through it alive.

The men had been transported to the airfield in sealed wagons. It was crucial – lest there be any traitor in their midst – that the camp's location remain unknown. En route from their previous billet on Salisbury Plain they saw nothing of Blackmore Vale and the Stour valley, they glimpsed none of the surrounding villages with names so redolent of Olde England: Lytchett Matravers, Winterborne Stickland, Gussage St Michael. They knew only that

---

* That little boy, John Keegan, was to become one of the most celebrated military historians of the twentieth century and author of *Six Armies in Normandy*.

they were being locked into 'one of the many high-security tented camps behind guarded barbed-wire fences'. There was a sign on the main gate: 'SECRET – KEEP OUT UNLESS ON DUTY'.[3] Armed guards patrolled the perimeter. Dogs were on standby. If any of the troops were to break out, they risked being shot.

The camp to which they had been transported was Tarrant Rushton in Dorset, an RAF airfield, and Denis Edwards and his pals from the Oxfordshire and Buckinghamshire Light Infantry had been brought here amid rumours that 'something was definitely about to happen'.[4] But as hours drifted into days and the rain continued to sluice down, they wondered if they would ever get airborne.

These men's D-Day mission was crucial: they were to spearhead the initial assault on occupied France with an audacious *coup-de-main* – a swift and surprise attack that would require them to be dropped deep behind enemy lines. Long before the seaborne forces landed, they would be fighting their way through the French countryside with the goal of seizing two vitally important bridges, one at the village of Ranville and one at Bénouville.

The capture of these bridges was vital to the success of D-Day. They were the principal crossing points for two waterways, the River Orne and the Caen Canal, which ran northwards to the coast. If they remained in German hands, the Allied troops landing on Sword Beach risked being trapped inside their beachhead. If that happened, the SS panzer divisions would be able to sweep across the bridges and drive the newly landed men back into the sea.

Nineteen-year-old Denis Edwards looked too young to be entrusted with such a hazardous mission. With his scrubbed cheeks and boyish grin, he might have been mistaken for a member of the Boy Scouts or Sea Cadets. Yet he was far from naïve and harboured no illusions as to the perils that lay ahead. 'Terrifyingly dangerous', is how he described it. 'There were so many possibilities for things to go badly wrong.' His young comrades in D Company were equally twitchy. 'What if the Germans counter-attacked?' they asked. 'What if the seaborne forces didn't break through the German defences in time?'[5] The architects of the operation could provide few answers. Like everything else on D-Day, the outcome would rest with those on the ground.

The unpredictability of their mission made them jumpy, and none more so than Edwards himself. He was praying that he would be able to display the same bravery as his father during the Great War. Old Man Edwards had earned himself the nickname of Rubber-Guts because of his willingness to report on enemy artillery positions from the precarious vantage point of a hot air balloon. The balloon had become a favourite target for German pilots, who would strafe it with bullet holes and then watch it sink to the ground at ever increasing speed. But they never managed to puncture it completely and Rubber-Guts had the last laugh when he got to bury the fabled German fighter ace, the Red Baron, Manfred von Richthofen, after he was shot down over his sector of battle.

The lads in Denis Edwards's team had one critical advantage over the thousands of other men about to be deployed. Their commander, John Howard, had proved himself a veritable alchemist when it came to training them, knocking base metal into something approaching gold. A thirty-two-year-old Oxfordshire policeman with a deep sense of purpose, Howard had the rugged features of an outdoorsman – one whose tough working-class childhood had left him with deep resources and a powerful sense of self-belief.

Over the course of several months, he had pushed his men through a training programme unlike any other, with a relentless focus on physical fitness. He forced them to swim glacial rivers (naked, and in midwinter), trudge thirty miles through bog land and slither across firing ranges on which live-bullet exercises were under way.

His programme might have dropped straight from the sports curriculum of one of Britain's more draconian boarding schools. Edwards and his friends had grown used to being 'roughly roused'[6] from their beds in the shivering chill of midwinter and transported to the ice-bound wilderness of Salisbury Plain. They would then have to find their way back to camp without being captured by the patrols sent to hunt them down.

It was a gruelling regime. For the first few months, the men were half broken by hardship. One of Denis Edwards's comrades, Wally Parr, had almost collapsed from exhaustion and there were times when he 'wanted to chuck it in', especially in midwinter. 'Your feet are raw and you've got blisters and blood everywhere and your back's aching and you're spending night after night on Salisbury Plain, sleeping on the frozen ground in the freezing fog.'[7]

One thing alone kept them going and that was their absolute devotion to their commander. They cursed him for being 'the hardest of task-masters'[8] and they hated him when he wrenched them from their early morning slumbers. But they knew he was a consummate professional, one whose mantra was blunt and uncompromising: 'Win at everything.'[9]

Only when they were near broken would he allow them a night out in Salisbury, where they played as roughly as they trained. They 'would drink the pubs dry and engage in pitched battles with the Americans', challenging them to violent fist-fights. Even in this, they strove to win. The Salisbury locals grew to dread the days on which Howard's men were unleashed. 'We were seen as a bunch of hooligans as we fell upon the city.'[10]

Trained, briefed and furnished with weapons, they now waited for the big day to arrive. But the skies turned grey and the rain tipped down and there was no hope of an airborne operation for the foreseeable future. And then the news got worse. They were told that the 12th SS Panzer Division and the 21st Panzer Division had both been moved closer to the two bridges they were charged with capturing. 'Just our bloody luck,' they said to each other when they were warned that these 'were the elite of the zealous Hitler Youth movement and Nazi fanatics every one'.[11]

By Monday morning, 5 June, the men were tetchy and anxious to get under way. It was still blowing a gale and rain was whipping through the canvas encampment, but there was a whisper afoot that they would soon be given the green light. Edwards was told that although conditions 'were far from ideal for an airborne operation',[12] the seaborne troops could not be held aboard their ships for much longer. It was possible, indeed probable, that they would be heading to France within the next twelve hours.

Guillaume Mercader awoke early on that grey Monday morning and slipped into his La Perle cycling gear: he was to spend much of the day in the saddle, fighting the stiff westerly as he pedalled through the Forêt de Cerisy towards Lamberville. It was no weather to be on a bike: the gusts were so strong that he had to pump hard to make any headway.

Mercader was due to meet several members of his resistance circuit, including Père Martin, the local Catholic priest, and a chatelaine named Mademoiselle de Siresme. The latter was not only the proprietor of the village château, but she also owned a significant tract of land. As such, she was able to provide information on where the latest German anti-glider posts had been positioned.

Mercader covered a great deal of ground that day and it was mid-afternoon by the time he headed back to his home in Bayeux. As he cycled northwards, he was surprised to see what he later described as 'very important and unusual activity of the Allied air force'. There were many more planes in the sky than was normal and they seemed to be heading for targets deep inland. Puzzled as to why they had chosen such an overcast day for a large-scale raid, he wondered if it heralded anything of significance. He was none the wiser when he unlatched the front door, stowed his bike and made his way down to the cellar in order to listen to the BBC's *messages personnels* on his clandestine wireless.

There were hundreds of these messages each evening and they were gibberish to everyone except the intended recipient. *Napoleon has lost his hat* might be the signal for sabotage. *John has a long moustache* might refer to a bridge in need of destruction.

It was now more than seventy-two hours since Mercader had been forewarned of the message that would alert him to the Allied landings. Two phrases were to be broadcast at around 6.30 p.m., the signal for his saboteurs to go into action. They would also signify that the Allied landings would be happening within hours.

On this particular evening, he tuned into the BBC at 6 p.m. as usual, paying only cursory attention to what was being said. Listening to such gibberish was both monotonous and tiresome. But on the dot of 6.30 p.m., he got the surprise of his life.

Il fait chaud à Suez. It was the first part of the phrase for him.

There was a short pause in the broadcast. And then came the second message. *Les dés sont jetés.*

He was 'stunned by listening to these coded messages' and found it hard to take in the enormity of it all. This, then, was it. The Allied invasion was about to begin.

He suddenly stood up, thinking on his feet. 'Quickly enough, I came to myself.' He snapped off the wireless and dashed back upstairs, 'climbing the steps from the cellar four at a time'. Breathless with excitement, he told his wife, Madeleine, what he had just heard. 'The night,' he said, 'was going to be long.'

Still weary after an exhausting day, he climbed back on his bicycle and set off to inform his agents 'of an immediate landing'.[13] It was essential that everyone in the circuit should get the news.

Guillaume Mercader was not alone in hearing the message that evening. Fellow resister Robert le Nevez had been listening to the same BBC broadcast when he heard the call to arms for his Saint-Clair circuit of saboteurs. *Le champ du laboureur dans le matin brumeux.* (The field of the ploughman in the morning mist.) It was the signal for them to swing into action. He immediately cycled over to the house of his friend, André Héricy, and broke the extraordinary news. 'It's this evening! D'you understand!'[14]

Héricy was an impulsive twenty-three-year-old carpenter who had joined the Saint-Clair resistance circuit two years earlier, one of a generation of youngsters who felt that their youth had been stolen by the Germans. He had been waiting for this moment since 1940. Now, he blew a hasty kiss to his wife and ten-week-old son and followed his friend out into the wind and drizzle. 'I took my bike and, hop, nothing was going to stop me that night!'[15] The two young men sped across the moonlit countryside to a dank coppice behind the farm at Saint-Clair, the agreed rendezvous for their fellow saboteurs.

Twelve others had already gathered by the time they arrived, along with their bandit leader, Captain Jean. His real name was Jean Renaud-Dandicolle and he was revered by the younger lads. The captain's first display of Gallic brio had come a few weeks earlier when he parachuted into Saint-Clair like an avenging angel, a transmission set tucked neatly into his backpack. He told the would-be saboteurs how he had spent the previous months serving with General de Gaulle in London.

He was well briefed on what needed to be done. Their primary mission was a most important one: to blow up the main railway line between Caen and Laval. This railway was 'essential for the conveyance of German weapons towards the beaches'.[16] It was also essential for the movement of troops. Unless it was destroyed, the

Germans would be able to move thousands of soldiers northwards to the coast.

Captain Jean asked for five volunteers from that band of twelve. Héricy was quick to raise his hand, as were Nevez and three others. The captain gave each of them a gift from his box of tricks: a pistol, some detonators and a large bag of explosives. He then offered them a choice of Sten gun or automatic rifle – weapons that had been dropped into the area just a few nights earlier. The men changed into American jackets, a disguise of sorts that was intended to confuse any German sentry they might encounter. 'We had to make the Germans believe that it was the work of an American commando [group], rather than the French resistance.'[17] This would minimize the risk of reprisals against the civilian population.

Lightly disguised but heavily armed, they now made their way to the village of Grimbosq, pedalling at speed through the darkness and 'using back roads and making detours'. They concealed their bikes in the undergrowth and crept through the tangle of dripping briars that fringed the railway line. Up ahead was a high stone embankment that loomed into the night. Beyond it was a fork in the tracks. This was their goal, a crucial junction in the Caen to Laval line. It was a tense moment, for there were German sentries within spitting distance, but the saboteurs used the curve in the tracks to remain out of sight.

They now worked as fast as they could. 'We collected the lumps of plastic explosive before kneading them and fixing them along each rail at a junction, so as to blow up eight rails at a time.' They had been given three types of detonators: thirty seconds, three minutes and five minutes. Héricy conferred with the others as to which one to use. 'Seeing as nobody had disturbed us, we opted for the green, five-minute detonator.'

His heart was thumping hard. All five had been dreaming of this moment for years. 'Only one thing mattered to us,' said Héricy, 'to kick the Germans out of France.'[18]

They triggered the detonators and then 'jumped like madmen towards the rampart'. Here, a damp woodpile offered protection from the blast. If all went to plan, they had just five minutes before this entire stretch of railway would be blown to the heavens.

★

Those long hours since dusk had proved no less eventful for Colonel Helmuth Meyer, a 'thin-faced, exuberant and sly' Nazi intelligence officer whose pinched features hinted at the devious brain within.

Colonel Meyer was in charge of counter-intelligence for the 15th Army and he also ran the only unit engaged in radio monitoring. He believed his work to be of paramount importance to the war effort and was bitter to discover that it was not taken seriously by his superiors.

Meyer insisted on his team adopting a methodical approach to their work. 'He even went so far as to have his intercepting radio crew listen to the broadcasts made from the jeeps of the military police in England as they directed troops along the roads.'

But one thing took priority over all others. He was 'ardently interested' in learning more about the Allied invasion plans and felt sure that the clue lay in the infernal BBC *messages personnels*. 'He had worked out all sorts of devices to ferret out the meaning of messages.' These 'devices' included interrogation and torture: 'Gestapo and SS methods to extract information from French resistance men who were caught'. Such methods, coupled with radio eavesdropping, had enabled him to gather a vast dossier of information as to the Allied intentions. But there was one vexing problem that seemed to have no obvious solution: 'to decide what was true and what was false'.[19]

Meyer was based at Tourcoing, a provincial city some twenty minutes' drive to the north of Lille. This was the headquarters of the 15th Army and its offices straddled a large tract of land between Rue de Melbourne and the Canal de Tourcoing. At its heart was a concrete bunker known as Maikäfer R608 (a *Maikäfer* is a large beetle) – the most secretive building on the site. Here, in a secure underground office divided by a glass partition, Helmuth Meyer's team eavesdropped on the thousands of Allied messages transmitted each day.

By the late spring of 1944, he was directing a team of thirty counter-intelligence specialists whose skill at identifying individual Allied wireless operators was outstanding. Heinz Herbst claimed he could recognize operators by the manner in which they transmitted their Morse. 'One might linger on a dash or falter with a dot.' By such signs, 'we would be able to recognize the individual operator, and we referred to them by nicknames we had given them.'[20]

Colonel Meyer had received a most tantalizing tip-off from the Berlin Abwehr, or military intelligence service, just a few months earlier. It was a tip-off that had the potential to change the course of the war. He had been informed that the Allies were intending to use their *messages personnels* to broadcast a general announcement to the French resistance, informing it of the forthcoming invasion. This message was to be the opening lines of a poem by Paul Verlaine. The first line would be transmitted exactly a week before the invasion. The second would signal that the Allied landings were imminent.

Listening to these messages was now moved to the top of the agenda – a painstakingly dull business for those working in Meyer's intelligence team. Their principal goal, drummed into them time and again, was 'to find out where the invasion would begin'.

The long hours of eavesdropping eventually yielded a choice nugget of gold. The first excerpt of the Verlaine poem was picked up at 9.20 p.m. on Thursday, 1 June. *Les sanglots longs, des violons de l'automne.* (*The long sighs of the violins of autumn.*) Sergeant Hans Reichling heard the phrase in his headphones and instantly switched on the wire-recorder in order to catch the repeat. He then rushed into the adjacent office where Meyer was seated at his desk. 'Sir, the first part of the message is here.'

Meyer listened to the recording and gave a brisk nod. 'Now something's going to happen.' It was vital not to miss the second excerpt of the poem, which would alert him to the fact that the invasion was imminent.

It duly came at 9.33 p.m. on Monday, 5 June. Reichling was once again listening to the BBC messages when he heard the second line of verse: *Blessent mon coeur d'une langueur monotone.* (*Wound my heart with a monotonous languor.*) It was the breakthrough he needed. Unless it was an elaborate hoax on the part of the Allies, the troops would be landing within hours.

This was such priceless intelligence that Meyer dashed through to the officers' mess and thrust the message into the hands of Major-General Rudolf Hofman, the 15th Army's chief of staff. He immediately realized its importance and flashed a general alert to the 15th Army headquarters. From here, it was transmitted to Army Group B, where it was received by Colonel Staubwasser. He forwarded it to von Rundstedt's headquarters, from whence it was sent directly to the German Supreme Command (OKW) in Berchtesgaden. Within a very short space of time, it was in the hands of General Alfred Jodl, the all-important Chief of Operations Staff. But there it stopped. 'The message remained on his desk.'

General Jodl was in a position to order a general alert. He could have sent a warning to every command post in northern France, as well as to the Kriegsmarine and Luftwaffe. But he hesitated. He simply did not trust Meyer's intelligence. Over the past weeks there had been too many false alarms. He therefore declined to forward the warning to the very army charged with defending the Normandy coastline.

Colonel Meyer knew nothing of this at the time. Indeed he only learned of Jodl's decision when it was too late. Not only was he furious, but he also declared himself 'the most frustrated man'[21] in the Wehrmacht. Not for the first time, his hard-won intelligence had been ignored. His exceptional team had discovered that the Allies were coming. They knew the landings were imminent. But on that critical evening, when so much was at stake, the commanders on the beaches had been left completely in the dark.

The Supreme Commander of Allied forces, General Dwight Eisenhower, had confirmed the launch of the invasion in the hours before dawn, having been reassured that the weather was set to improve. 'Okay,' he said briskly, 'we'll go!'[22] It was a laconic send-off for the greatest seaborne fleet in history.

He would later return to his mobile headquarters, a large trailer parked in a gloomy nook of woodland just a mile or so from Southwick House. If circumstances had been different, it might have been a bucolic spot to camp. Wild clematis trailed through the lower branches and dog rose rampaged through the damp shadows. But the surrounding encampment was dismal, a place 'where sunshine was exiled, where rain soaked our entire canvas headquarters days on end, giving everything a damp, musty odour'.[23]

If the setting was downcast, the trailer itself was positively regal, a three-carriage unit that Eisenhower jokingly referred to as his circus wagon. It had been specially designed by Mr G.V. Russell, whose pre-war years had been spent creating 'lavish night clubs'[24] for the starlets and roués of Hollywood. The advent of war had seen him turn his talents to mobile homes, transforming Eisenhower's Lockheed trailer into a self-contained battle headquarters complete with kitchenette, shower and chemical lavatory, as well as air conditioning, portable power and state-of-the-art radio equipment. The floors were of polished black linoleum, the walls were tinted pearl-grey and the upholstered furniture was made of green leather. You could cook, watch films and plan an invasion – or you could do all three at once. In comparison to Rommel's sumptuous headquarters at Château de La Roche-Guyon, it lacked the hunting trophies, duodecimo volumes and sculpted marble busts. But it was a uniquely self-contained unit. The invasion could falter or the world could come to an end, yet Eisenhower could continue to direct its aftermath from his high-tech wagon.

He was not alone that Monday evening. He was in the company of Harry Butcher, his personal aide, in whom he had placed his trust. Butcher was an unlikely candidate for such a demanding job. A handsome young journalist, he was a gregarious raconteur who served up his gossip with twin dollops of wit and charm. He had been first introduced to Eisenhower by the general's younger brother, Milton, and the two of them immediately became friends. Eisenhower admired Butcher's laissez-faire approach to life (he detested rules) while Butcher appreciated Eisenhower's quiet intensity. When playing bridge, he was amazed to discover that Ike 'could determine after the first round of bidding with astounding accuracy the number of cards of each suit held by the other three players'.[25] When Eisenhower gambled, he did so to win.

Two years after their first meeting, Eisenhower was in need of a naval aide and asked Butcher if he wanted the job, even though he knew little of naval affairs. He had previously been editor of *Fertilizer Review* and his professional expertise was in chemicals and muck. Some would later claim that muck-raking was the only métier in which Butcher really excelled. Yet even muck can contain nuggets of gold and the memoirs that Butcher kept while working for Eisenhower were to provide an insight into the insecurities of a man about to send two and a half million men into battle.

He soon made himself indispensable, becoming – in the words of one admirer – Eisenhower's 'front office boy, full time aide, personal friend, eager publicist and chief diarist'.[26] Butcher himself referred to his role as 'kibitzer, water boy, cigarette girl and flunky'.[27] He was certainly a jack-of-all-trades but he was also a master of one, as Eisenhower was quick to acknowledge. 'Butcher's job is simple,' he confessed. 'It is to keep me sane.'[28] But keeping Eisenhower sane on the eve of D-Day was not easy. The Supreme Commander chain-smoked his Chesterfields as he pondered over the fate of the men he was sending into battle. 'How many youngsters are gone forever,'[29] he had written eight weeks earlier. Now, there were certain to be many more deaths and each one would weigh heavy on his soul.

Harry Butcher was not the only one with him on that tense Monday evening. Also present was Kay Summersby, his Irish chauffeur-cum-secretary who had been first introduced to him two years earlier. She had the wistful beauty of a 1940s movie star: high cheekbones, a retroussé nose and dark eyebrows that had been plucked and sketched into perfect arcs. Miss Summersby was living in the shadow of tragedy, for her fiancé had been killed by a landmine just eight months earlier. 'She's not a very well person,'[30] confessed Eisenhower, who perhaps sensed a fellow traveller in her highly strung nature. As he took to her, so she also took to him. Indeed, she had a general preference for 'the breezy easy-going Yanks to the stiff-upper-lip swagger stick-carrying British officers'.

There were abundant rumours (never proven) that she was Eisenhower's mistress. 'She was perky and she was cute,' thought Ike's son, John. 'Whether she had any designs on the Old Man, and the extent to which he succumbed, I just don't know.' Eisenhower's wife, Mamie, suspected something was afoot and was furious when, during a brief home leave in West Virginia, he kept calling her Kay by mistake.

Miss Summersby was certainly one of the few who seemed able to soothe his anxieties. She was also unique among army chauffeurs: 'better than any man at driving that big Packard in a total blackout and through London's pea-soupers with those pinpoint headlights'.[31] On arriving back at Southwick House, she would knead and buffet Eisenhower's shoulders in an effort to reduce his stress. 'Um, that's good,' he would say to her in that slight, mid-Atlantic accent of his. But he never really relaxed, and certainly not in the hours when the great fleet was sailing for France. 'In those tense pre-dawn hours, no matter how much strength I used, I could not undo the knots at the base of his neck.' Eisenhower was indeed in an alarming state of nervous exhaustion. 'His eyes were bloodshot and he was so tired that his hands shook when he lit a cigarette.'[32]

Summersby feared that the responsibilities were too much for one person. She noticed that he had tears in his eyes when she drove him back from meeting the American paratroopers about to depart for Normandy. He was, she said, 'the loneliest man in the world'.[33]

The tensions of that Monday evening grew almost too much to bear. The three of them sat in virtual silence in Ike's nickel-plated trailer, 'each with his own thoughts and trying to borrow by psychological osmosis those of the Supreme Commander'.[34] This little trio, with their hang-ups, insecurities and feigned bravado was like a microcosm of every platoon heading for Normandy.

By 1.15 a.m., Butcher had had enough. 'To hell with it,' he said, and took himself off to bed. Summersby stayed for longer, trying to persuade Eisenhower to rest. 'I think you ought to go and lie down for a little while.' Finally, hours later, he agreed. 'You should do the same.'[35]

As she made her way back to her quarters through the tented encampment, she had the dreamy impression that she was wandering through a Native American village. She felt rootless, displaced and sad. War had changed them all.

André Héricy and his band of saboteurs had been hiding behind their damp woodpile for what seemed like an eternity. 'We waited. Waited. And then, one by one, we lifted our heads and looked at each other anxiously.' There was no explosion. Just silence. 'Those five minutes seemed to last an hour.'

When it finally happened, it did so quite without warning. There was an eruption of such magnitude that the very core of the earth seemed to shudder. 'We dived down again, covering our heads with our hands.' They were fortunate to have the protection of the woodpile, for the explosion was one of unbelievable violence and was followed by a downpour unlike any other as 'debris and gravel rained down from the sky.' Ballast, track and even the sleepers were hurled into the surrounding woods.

When the deluge finally came to an end, the five saboteurs rushed forward to inspect the damage. They could scarcely believe the destructive force of the explosion. For more than fifty metres, the railway had simply disappeared. The ballast had been stripped away. Even the tracks were missing. In the few places where they were still in situ, they were sticking into the air like giant metal fingers. Héricy was exhilarated. 'We felt like kings.'[36] They were so fired with adrenalin that they reached for their guns and opened fire on the surrounding apple trees, shooting up that year's crop.

Then, realizing the foolishness of what they were doing, they darted back into the forest before the German sentries could get on their trail. After retrieving their bikes, they set off into the night, cycling as fast as possible back to Saint-Clair. As they did so, they could hear the low growl of planes in the midnight sky.

It was D-Day.

PART II
Midnight

The Allied planners of Operation Overlord feared their seaborne troops would get trapped on the beaches. At the western end of the landing zone, the Germans had flooded the coastal meadows: the only route inland was via four raised causeways. At the eastern end, troops could advance only if they controlled two key bridges over the River Orne and Caen Canal.

The Allied plan was to capture these bridges, at Bénouville and Ranville, and destroy five others. Shortly after midnight, 181 British troops from the 6th Airborne Division were to land by glider and seize the bridges: a further 7,000 troops would land by parachute and destroy the remainder.

Simultaneously with the British operation, 13,000 American paratroopers were to be dropped at the landing zone's western end. Their task was to capture the raised causeways and the town of Sainte-Mère-Église.

The role of the French resistance was to blow bridges, viaducts and railway junctions – anything that would prevent the Germans from moving reinforcements towards the coast.

Field Marshal Rommel's strategy was the exact reverse of the Allied one: he intended to trap the Allied forces inside their beachhead by thrusting his armoured panzers northwards to the coast. But the German advance was contingent on controlling bridges, causeways and Sainte-Mère-Église. If Rommel lost the latter, he would also have lost the main highway to Cherbourg.

John Howard's Horsa glider crash-landed thirty yards from Bénouville Bridge. 'We're here,' shouted one of the mission's pilots. 'Piss off and do what you're paid to do.'

5

The Midnight Hour

Denis Edwards and his comrades received the order to emplane at around 10 p.m. 'Okay, chaps,' barked John Howard, 'get in the gliders.'[1] All were relieved to be getting under way. They'd spent the preceding hours checking and re-checking their kit, drinking yet more tea (this time laced with rum) and making endless trips to the lavatory. Wally Parr noticed that 'everyone was pissing like hell'. They'd smeared grease on to their faces and used a burned cork to make themselves even darker. Parr displayed a characteristic lack of tact by handing the cork to one of the two black men in the company, Private 'Darkie' Baines. 'I don't think I'll bother,'[2] said Baines.

In a chill twilight still awash with rain, Parr chalked 'Lady Irene' on to the side of the plane, an affectionate reference to his young wife. Then he joined Edwards and the others inside the fragile plywood and canvas glider that would, in theory, deliver them to France. They shared the dubious distinction of being in the lead glider and it would fall to their platoon of thirty men (plus John Howard) to storm Bénouville Bridge and seize it from the Germans. They would have the support of a further sixty men who were to land just a minute or so later in the other two gliders. Three more platoons had been assigned to seize Ranville Bridge.

John Howard visited each plane in turn and gave the men a last-minute pep talk. 'Speed is essential,' he reminded them. 'We've got to take these bridges and we've got to hold them.'[3] He gave a fleeting smile. 'See you there, lads. Don't be late.'[4] The men greeted his words with much back-slapping and jesting. 'Good luck,' they shouted to each other. 'See you over the other side.'[5]

They all knew the risks and there was plenty of gallows humour as they strapped themselves into the gliders. 'If they'd lined them with silk,' said one, 'the thing would be ideal to bury the lot of us in.'[6] Only the two pilots, Jim Wallwork and John Ainsworth, remained upbeat, telling the men that 'although we may lose a wing or two', they felt sure 'they would be able to put us down close to our targets.' They added that they 'fully expected to finish the trip the right way up',[7] expressing themselves with a breezy confidence that did little to reassure anyone.

It was close to 10.35 p.m. by the time everyone was inside their Horsa glider, or 'hearse-glider', as they called it. Edwards sensed 'a strong undercurrent of tension' and admitted he was 'becoming increasingly scared'.[8] Wally Parr was also on edge. The plane was pulsing with stress, the men on board 'like two boxers in a room, hitting and dancing on their toes, waiting to have a go at it'. No one wanted to betray any sign of fear, but even Howard would later confess to having 'a terrible lump'[9] in his throat.

At 10.56 p.m. the engine of the Halifax tow-plane increased in volume from a hum to a deafening roar. Edwards felt sick to his stomach. 'My muscles tightened, a cold shiver ran up my spine, I went hot and cold.'[10] This was it. They were off. There was no turning back.

The Halifax was gathering speed and the men braced themselves for the violent jerk that always occurred when the tow-rope reached full tension.

'*Twang!*' The glider gave a sickening lurch forward as it was dragged down the Tarrant Rushton airstrip. It was lifted from the ground for a moment, seemingly weightless, before thumping back on to its wheels and jolting the men's stomachs into their mouths. Then it got airborne once again and this time it remained in the air. Edwards closed his eyes and managed to lose himself in 'a fantasy dream world' in which he was back at the comfortable barrack room at Bulford Camp. But when he opened his eyes again he was thrust into the present, 'scared half to death' and feeling deep anxiety about the battle ahead, 'much as a condemned man must feel on his last morning when he is being led from the condemned cell to the gallows'. He was resigned to his own death. 'The hand of destiny had guided me to this point in my life,' and it was time to face the inevitable. 'You've had it, chum,' he told himself. 'It's no good worrying any more.'[11]

The men started to sing, lustily and with growing confidence. They belted out 'Roll Out the Barrel' and 'Abey, Abey Abey, My Boy' and 'I'm Forever Blowing Bubbles'. One of their number, William Gray, squeezed himself around in order to look out of the little portholes. Far below, he could just make out the seaside town of Worthing. It was glinting in the moonlight and beyond it lay the waters of the English Channel, lit to a glancing sheen. The cloud cover was breaking, yet there was no sign of the massive armada that he knew must already be under way.

They had been in the clouds for little more than an hour when 'all hell started up'.[12] Anti-aircraft ack-ack fire exploded upwards into the night sky, a clear sign they had crossed the French coastline. Soon afterwards, there was another loud twang as the glider detached itself from the Halifax. There had been 'a continuous high-pitched scream of wind forcing its way through the cracks and crevices in the thin fabric covering of the wooden fuselage',[13] but now they had cut their link to the mother plane there was nothing but an eerie swishing noise so unsettling that they all began singing again.

'For God's sake, shut up.' Lieutenant David Wood, the platoon commander in the second glider, was urging his men to keep silent. 'We've cast off. You can't be singing.' He pointed to the ground below. 'They'll hear us.'[14]

In the lead glider, the two pilots were preparing for a dangerous and most unpleasant manoeuvre. In order to avoid a slow descent that involved endless circling, they would tip the Horsa's nose into a sickening dive. Once done, there was no turning back. The glider would hurtle to earth at a speed in excess of 100 mph and only their skill would prevent it from smashing into the ground. The men clutched their bellies as they were pitched forward, with only their harnesses keeping them strapped to their seats. 'We plummeted earthwards at what felt to us like breakneck speed until we were within 1,000 feet of the ground.'[15] There was a horrendous judder as Wallwork and Ainsworth fought hard to lift the nose back into a sweeping glide, instead of a dive. In the mottled moonlight, Wallwork could see the bridge, the village and the landing zone.

There was a quiet intensity in the glider. They were close to the land. This was the moment they were dreading. A few days earlier, an RAF reconnaissance plane had revealed freshly dug holes in the fields and anti-glider poles stacked up nearby. If the poles had been installed, the gliders would be in big trouble.

'*Link arms!*' Wallwark yelled to the men from the front of the glider. Each man clutched his neighbour and braced himself for the impact to come. Wally Parr pulled his legs sharply towards him. He'd been warned they could be ripped off. He also knew that the undercarriage might be shredded as they hit the ground. He glanced through the porthole. Trees were rushing past as blurred silhouettes and fields were 'racing underneath us'.[16] There was a bump, a jerk and a heavier bump: the glider was grazing the ground at alarming speed.

Edwards gripped his neighbour as the glider 'lurched forwards like a bucking bronco'. For a moment, he thought they were all right. But 'the darkness was suddenly filled with a stream of brilliant sparks as the skids hit some stony ground.'[17] A sickening tearing sound shook the glider from end to end, 'like a giant canvas sheet being viciously ripped apart'. It was followed by a deep roar that pitched the men from their seats. Parr's torso was jackknifed towards the porthole; he noticed 'the wheels go skidding past'.[18] Edwards felt as if he were being wrenched to pieces. Even the unflappable John Howard thought that this was it. 'The most hellish din imaginable.'[19] And then, in a terrifying shower of sparks and debris, the crippled remnant of the glider slammed itself to a violent halt. The two pilots were pitched forward with such force that their seats were sheared off the floor bolts. They shot through the cockpit screen and into the field, thereby earning themselves the distinction of being the first Allied troops to land in France on D-Day. It was unfortunate that they were scarcely conscious.

Less than five miles away as the crow flies, a young German adjutant named Helmut Liebeskind had spent the previous ten minutes pacing the orderly room of his regimental command post in the village of Vimont. He was feeling anxious. Something was not right.

Over the previous fortnight, he had become increasingly convinced that the Allies would soon be landing. 'We read in the German papers and Swiss papers that Stalin was urgently in need of another front.' He also felt sure they would land on the very stretch of coast where he had been stationed, although he admitted he had no evidence for this. 'I calculated that it would be in Normandy for the simple reason that we had been posted there.' He was 'in a state of tension' that preyed on his nerves, especially as he was given 'constant orders to stand-to and then stand-down'.[20]

Earlier that afternoon, Liebeskind had attended his daily meeting with his regimental commander, Hans von Luck. The two men enjoyed a solid working relationship of the sort that might be found between an office junior and his boss. Von Luck was impressed with the efficiency of his twenty-two-year-old adjutant, while Liebeskind was more than a little star-struck by the much decorated major. Von Luck was ten years his senior and had fought with distinction in Poland and France before winning himself a golden German Cross for punching his tanks deep into Soviet Lithuania.

There was a great deal that was impressive about von Luck. His features were perfectly aquiline – 'a hawk-like nose, deep-set penetrating blue eyes, a jutting chin, a large broad forehead' – and he was punctilious about etiquette. 'His manners and his manner-isms were those of an Old World aristocrat.'[21] He was a habitual winner when in combat and had every intention of playing a winning game when the enemy Allies finally landed in France.

At that afternoon's meeting, Hans von Luck had confided to Liebeskind that he did not believe they would be coming any time soon. He had just received the latest meteorological reports and contended that no commander would dare to invade in such inclement weather. 'Heavy seas, storms and low lying clouds would make large-scale operations at sea and in the air impossible.'[22]

Von Luck's assurances helped calm Liebeskind's fragile nerves. As darkness fell, he took a drive through the local countryside, where two of von Luck's panzer battalions were conducting field exercises. Seeing that everything was going to plan, he returned to his quar-ters in order to wash, shave and dress for dinner, slipping into the starched tunic he liked to wear beneath his uniform. He had then headed to the nearby Château de Vimont that had been requisi-tioned by the regiment and transformed into an officers' club. Here, one could dine on the sort of fresh produce that had been unavail-able in Germany for years – 'butter, cheese, crème fraiche and meat'[23] – along with unlimited quantities of wine, cider and Calvados.

But Liebeskind's dinner had not proved as enjoyable as he had hoped, for it was interrupted by 'disturbing reports' of heavy bombing raids taking place just a few miles to the west. One officer warned him that the number of planes seemed to be multiplying by the minute.

Aerial raids were nothing new and scarcely a night passed when planes could not be heard overhead. But Liebeskind was unsettled enough to leave the club earlier than intended and return to the regimental orderly room in Vimont.

At exactly 0.10 a.m., he once again slipped on his over-jacket and stepped outside into the damp night air. He wanted to see for himself what was taking place. When he glanced at the sky, he could hear 'the sound of engines in the air' but was unable to see anything, for 'there was a low but thin cloud base that concealed everything'. As he stood there, 'wondering what on earth was going on', he suddenly got the shock of his life. Through a break in the cloud, he glimpsed 'the shadowy forms of multi-engine bombers with freighter gliders attached'.[24] He was one of the very first German soldiers to witness the opening act of D-Day.

He dashed back inside to phone this news through to Hans von Luck, who had spent the evening in his sparsely furnished lodgings in the nearby village of Bellengreville.

'*Major* – ' exclaimed the breathless Liebeskind. 'Gliders are landing in our section. I'm trying to make contact with No II Battalion. I'll come along to you at once.'[25]

Hans von Luck felt a terrible sinking feeling in his stomach. The men whom Liebeskind was attempting to contact – No II Battalion – were still out in the field, conducting exercises in the very area where the Allied gliders were landing. This would have been ideal, had it not been for the fact that they had been issued with blank cartridges. Now, as he paced up and down the room, he found himself muttering into the gloom. 'A dangerous situation,' he said. 'A dangerous situation.'[26]

Silence. Absolute silence. Denis Edwards was lost in a dream world all of his own. 'From somewhere out in endless space there zoomed towards me a long tracer-like stream of multi-coloured lights, like a host of shooting stars that moved towards me at high speed.'[27]

72

The Germans were shooting at him, or so it seemed, until he had a vague realization that he was seriously concussed and that the millions of little stars were inside his head.

The silence inside the wrecked glider was intense. 'No one stirred, nothing moved.'[28] John Howard was only dimly aware of being alive. His head was smashed and he couldn't see a thing. 'God,' he thought in terror. 'I'm blind.'[29] But as he stirred from his wooziness, he realized his helmet had been rammed hard over his eyes. He could discern other crashing noises, distant but distinct. It was the other gliders coming in to land. Harry Clark, on the second glider, had just been catapulted through the side of his wrecked plane. Richard Smith, on the third glider, was 'shot like a bullet'[30] through the cockpit screen. He landed in a thick puddle of mud.

The noise of the gliders might have caused alarm in the village adjacent to where they had crashed. Yet nothing stirred. The inhabitants of Bénouville had been in their beds for several hours and were only dimly aware of what was taking place outside. To the few still awake, the sound of aircraft in distress was just another inconvenience of war. Georges Gondrée, owner of the nearby café, stirred in his sleep and 'assumed it was the noise of an English bomber crashing'. If so, 'it was likely that the crew would have bailed out and been captured by the Germans'.[31] His wife, Thérèse, was more curious. 'Get up!' she whispered to her husband. 'Don't you hear what's happening? Open the window.'[32] When he still didn't stir, she nudged him hard. 'Get up. Listen. It sounds like wood breaking.' As Monsieur Gondrée sat up in bed, he could hear 'snapping and crunching sounds'.[33]

One of the German soldiers patrolling Bénouville Bridge that night was eighteen-year-old Private Helmut Roemer. He had heard 'a swishing noise followed by a bang'[34] but thought nothing of it. Stricken planes had crashed into the countryside on countless occasions and he saw no reason to sound the alarm. It would make him deeply unpopular with his comrades, who would be pitched from their beds and ordered to search for surviving airmen.

Denis Edwards was fast recovering consciousness, along with those around him. 'The realisation that we were not all dead came quickly as bodies began unstrapping themselves.'[35] There was a sudden stirring. Men who had been unconscious a few minutes earlier now began to push themselves out of the shattered fuselage.

'We're here,' yelled Oliver Boland, pilot of the second glider. 'Piss off and do what you're paid to do.'[36]

'Charlie, get out!'[37] shouted Wally Parr to his buddy, Charles Gardner. He and Charlie were trained to operate as a two-man team and Parr, who had been knocked out in the landing, was suddenly pumped with adrenalin. They both jumped out of the stricken glider and landed in knee-deep marshy water. Moonlight was shining through the fractured cloud and they could see the steel girder bridge looming into the night. It was just thirty yards away. The pilots had done a magnificent job.

'Come on, lads!'[38] The urgency was apparent in Den Brotheridge's voice.

'Charge!'[39] roared Howard.

Parr and Gardner were first to the bridge. 'Lit by moonlight, I see this damn thing towering above me.' Parr's mouth went dry. 'I couldn't spit sixpence, my tongue was stuck to the top of my mouth.'[40]

Denis Edwards was just a few paces behind: he heard Howard shout once again: 'Come on boys. This is it!'[41]

Thérèse Gondrée was still leaning out of the window, trying to figure out what was happening. Since she spoke German, she called out to the sentry on the bridge, just a few metres away. She saw his face suddenly change: 'his eyes were wide with fear'. He was unable to speak and 'was literally struck dumb by terror'.[42]

Private Roemer was indeed petrified by what he saw. 'Soldiers, their faces smeared all in black, started coming towards us and in the half-moonlight, we saw they were British.' He fired his Very light and screamed the alarm.

'*Achtung!*'

Howard's men were by now on the bridge and 'shooting around themselves wildly'. Roemer had no intention of resisting. Together with two others, Erwin Sauer and a Polish conscript, they decided 'to leg it'.[43] They leaped from the bridge and hid in an overgrown elderberry bush.

William Gray spotted a German to his right 'and let rip at him'. As the man slumped to the ground, the others also began 'letting fly with rifles and automatics'[44] and hurling grenades on to the bridge. They had no hesitation about killing any German who stood in their way, working rapidly and methodically, attacking the defenders' roadside pillbox with grenades by dropping them through the slits.

'Come out and fight, you square-headed bastards.' Wally Parr was bawling at no one in particular. He and Charlie Gardner found themselves working as a highly dangerous double-act, pitching explosives into the German dug-outs that surrounded the bridge. They'd practised it so many times that it seemed almost routine. 'I dashed to the first one, put my rifle to the side of it, whipped out a 36 grenade.' Gardner was right behind him with the Bren gun. 'I slung open the door, pulled the pin, slung it in, shut the door and waited.' There was a booming explosion from beneath their feet. Then Parr kicked open the door again and Gardner sprayed the dug-out with his machine gun. They repeated this at each dug-out.

After one such attack, Parr heard a voice 'groaning and moaning': someone inside was still alive. It was no time for squeamishness. He held Gardner back, pulled a 77 phosphorus grenade from his belt and lobbed it inside. 'If the shrapnel didn't get them,' he said, 'the phosphorus would.' There was another massive explosion and Parr gave a little smile. 'It went off a treat.'[45]

The men worked with clinical efficiency, aware that it was kill or be killed. They had been trained not to feel any emotion: this was a fight to the death. 'We were not taking any prisoners,' said one. 'Anything that moved, we shot.'[46]

The teams from the other two gliders had by now reached the bridge and joined the fray. Grenades, phosphorus bombs and tracer bullets were creating a spectacular display in the night sky. 'A tremendous sight', thought John Howard as he looked around him. There were three different colours, red, yellow and white, 'with the enemy firing at us, and my men firing at them'.[47] The Germans had by now managed to get their machine guns and Spandau into action, causing the air to be 'rent with gunfire'.[48] The battle was starting to intensify. Parr and Gardner had completed their first task, 'and so we tore across the bridge'[49] and reached the Café Gondrée, where a dead German was lying in the road. They were supposed to rendezvous with Den 'Danny' Brotheridge at an agreed point, some thirty yards from the café.

'Where's Brotheridge? Where's Danny Brotheridge?'

Parr ran back to the bridge and saw a second body sprawled lengthways on the road. 'I ran past him thinking it was another German.' But the uniform gave him a jolt. 'I stopped, turned around, went back to look at him.' It was Den Brotheridge. He was lying on his back with his hand towards the bridge and his feet towards the T-junction. Parr knelt down and lifted his head slightly. 'He was conscious and he said something. I couldn't hear what he said.' Parr begged him to speak louder. 'I'm sorry, sir, but I can't hear.'

Brotheridge tried to speak, but then 'he just closed his eyes and gave a big sigh and lay back.' He was mortally wounded, with a bullet through his neck. Parr pulled his hand from under his head. 'It was covered in blood.'[50]

Another of the men, Jack Bailey, came running over. 'What the hell's going on?'

'It's Danny,' muttered Parr. 'He's had it.'

'Christ almighty,'[51] said Bailey. He knew, as did all the others, that Den Brotheridge's wife, Margaret, was about to give birth to their first child.

Den Brotheridge's death caused a pause in momentum. Even John Howard confessed to having a lump in his throat as his body was dragged off the bridge. Brotheridge was one of the few men in his platoon who was more than just a comrade. But there was no time for sentimentality: a burst of German bullets sent the men diving for cover. News of other injuries reached Howard. Sandy Smith, platoon leader from the third glider, had a broken wrist. And Corporal Webb had got caught in friendly fire from a Sten gun and been shot through the leg and shoulder.

But there was good news to accompany the bad. Howard's sappers had successfully cut all the fuses and wires planted by the Germans, who had been intending to blow the bridge rather than let it fall into Allied hands.

Howard had still heard nothing from the men storming Ranville Bridge, half a mile down the road. Corporal Tappenden was continually trying to raise them on the wireless, but the line was always dead.

He was still fiddling with the dials when an open-topped German staff car was seen speeding towards the T-junction at the western end of the bridge. Inside was a German paratrooper, Heinrich Hickman, and four young soldiers. Hickman knew nothing of the glider landings, but as he approached the bridge he instantly recognized the sound of the Sten gun. It had to be the enemy.

He slammed on the brakes and climbed out of the car with great caution, creeping to within fifty metres of the bridge. When he looked up, he saw Wally Parr and his men running full-tilt across the structure. He was terrified. 'The way they charged, the way they fired, the way they ran across the bridge . . . I'm not a coward, but at that moment I got frightened.'[52]

He reached for his Schmeisser submachine gun and fired it from the hip at one of the shadowy figures on the bridge. The bullets just missed William Gray, who fired back. He also missed, but the shots came close enough to convince Hickman to flee. He crawled back to his staff car, cursing the bridge sentries for the 'cushy life'[53] that had softened them. He then slammed the car into gear and sped off towards Caen, a journey that should have taken no more than fifteen minutes. But the Allied aerial bombing was so intense that he would not arrive until after dawn.

As Denis Edwards dashed across the bridge, he sensed that the defence was starting to crumble. 'As we neared the far side of the bridge, still shouting, firing our weapons and lobbing hand grenades, the Germans jumped to their feet and ran for their lives, scattering in all directions.' It marked the end of their short fire-fight. The battle was over as dramatically as it had begun. 'Relief, exhilaration, incredulity – I experienced all these feelings upon realizing that we had taken the bridge.'[54]

There was more good news to come. Corporal Tappenden was still fiddling with his wireless set when he received news that Ranville Bridge had also been captured. Denis Fox and his men had taken it without a shot being fired.

Howard now needed to transmit this news to headquarters in England so that the follow-up forces would know that both bridges were in Allied hands. The pre-agreed signal was 'Ham and Jam' – Ham for Bénouville Bridge and Jam for Ranville. Tappenden went back to his wireless and endlessly repeated the victory message: *Ham and Jam, Ham and Jam.* But there was never any response.

When Howard overheard him some minutes later, he was still shouting into his wireless, only the message had changed somewhat. 'Ham and Bloody Jam,' he bawled. 'Ham and Bloody Jam.'

'What's all this Ham and Jam about?' asked a dreamily voiced John Vaughan, who was wandering aimlessly in the darkness, suffering from severe concussion. He knew the coded message, of course, but he was in a world of his own. Howard handed him a hip flask of whisky, 'which seemed to help him collect his senses'.[55] Yet he was still badly dazed, so he was led away to the newly installed medical post.

Wally Parr and Charlie Gardner were by now standing guard over the Café Gondrée. Nearby there was a large iron grille in the ground, used for lowering beer barrels into the cellar. When Parr peered through the grille, he found himself looking down on Madame Gondrée and her two little daughters, who had moved to the cellar for safety. 'She was nestling the one in her left arm, into her bosom. The one on the right was staring up at me.'

The two young girls got the fright of their lives when they saw this 'black-faced monstrous soldier', but Parr was also shaken by seeing them. Only now did it strike him that they were fighting in a country filled with civilians.

'Madame, go in,' he shouted. 'Liberators – invasion – go in.'

When Madame Gondrée still didn't move, he handed down a chocolate bar to the elder girl, Georgia. He was touched when she nervously took it from his hand. 'They were the first two children to be liberated in the invasion of Europe – liberated by a Cockney soldier with a bar of chocolate.'[56]

Parr was unaware that Georges and Thérèse Gondrée had been working for the British for some years. Thérèse spoke fluent German (she was from Alsace) and had been eavesdropping on the local sentries when they came to her bar each evening. Her husband spoke English (he had worked for Lloyds Bank) and passed on this information to the resistance. It was their intelligence that had enabled Howard's men to be so well briefed about the German guns, bunkers and machine-gun nests.

John Howard's team had scored a magnificent victory in capturing the two bridges, but they were now in a precarious position – undermanned, under-armed and surrounded by hostile forces. Denis

Edwards was acutely aware of their predicament. 'With the bridges now in our hands, we had to defend them against whatever counter-attack might be made.'[57]

Not for the first time during his posting to Normandy, Major Hans Schmidt found himself torn between his love for the Führer and his desire for the local ladies. As commander of Bénouville Bridge, he ought to have kept the garrison on full alert each night. He also ought to have remained at his post. But given a choice between duty and pleasure, it was invariably the latter that took precedence. On this particular night, he had spent much of the evening with his French lover, an 'obliging local lady'[58] whom he hoped to make even more obliging by showering her with an array of gifts that included good food and fine wine. If this didn't work, he had supplies in reserve that he hoped would do the trick.

But his intimate soirée was to be rudely curtailed by the noise of gunfire coming from the direction of the bridge. He immediately summoned his driver and escort, persuaded the young lady to accompany him to the bridge and clambered into his open-top Mercedes, still clutching the bottle of unfinished wine and a plate of half-eaten food. There was to be one unscheduled stop en route to the bridge. The lady in question decided she'd had enough excitement for one night and demanded to be dropped at her house, leaving the food and wine for Schmidt to finish on his own. As for the little parcel, it could be collected at a more suitable time.

Once she was gone, the Mercedes roared down towards the bridge in tandem with the motorcycle escort. Schmidt was unaware that he was driving headlong into a trap. The escort was the first to be targeted: it was hit with a broadside of gunfire from the men of D Company, who were lying in wait. John Howard watched as the motorcycle crashed off the road and 'slewed right into the river, killing the rider instantly'.

Schmidt's Mercedes was hit just seconds later. Tod Sweeney had been hiding on the left bank, awaiting anything that might approach the bridge. In the years before the war, he had taken the vows of a novice monk and spent his nights in solemn prayer. Now, the only prayer on his lips was that he might disable the Mercedes. As he let rip with his Sten gun, the car's tyres burst and the vehicle careered to a standstill. Sweeney ran towards the car, only to be confronted by an enraged Major Schmidt, whose evening had taken a decided turn for the worse. He had been deprived of his wine, his woman and his car, along with his dignity. He started shouting in perfect English 'that he had lost his honour and demanded to be shot'. This wish was politely declined. Instead, he was dragged over to John Howard's command post where he harangued the medic, John Vaughan, telling him 'about the futility of the Allies believing for one moment that they could win the war against the master race'. He once again demanded to be shot and this time his wish was granted, although not in the manner he had intended. Vaughan shot him with morphine, using the largest syringe he could find, and thereby 'induced him to take a more reasonable view of things'. The drug worked wonders. 'Within ten minutes, he was thanking me profusely for my medical attention.'[59]

When Howard's men went to search the Mercedes, they found it was a staff officer's car unlike any other, filled with wine glasses, dinner plates and cosmetics, as well as a neatly wrapped parcel of French lingerie.

As Major Schmidt sank into a morphine-induced slumber, Hans von Luck was growing increasingly frustrated. He had been joined at his billet by Helmut Liebeskind, who had raced over to Bellengreville within minutes of first telephoning news of the enemy parachutists. Now, the two men tried to organize the first tentative counter-attack against the Allies.

Von Luck grabbed the telephone and shouted orders to anyone he could reach. 'All units are to be put on alert immediately.' He wanted the panzers to attack 'immediately and independently', even though he knew this ran counter to official orders. They were forbidden from fighting without first getting clearance from the highest authorities.

Von Luck also managed to track down one of his company commanders, Lieutenant Brandenburg, who had been taking part in that night's field exercise equipped with nothing more than blank cartridges. Now, he was hiding out in a cellar in the village of Troarn. 'Brandenburg, hold on,' ordered von Luck. 'The battalion is already attacking and is bound to reach you in a few minutes.'[60] Lieutenant Brandenburg replied with a weary 'Okay.'

The first counter-attack came as no surprise to John Howard: he knew the Germans would try to retake the bridge. His men had scarcely dug themselves in when they heard 'the sound of powerful engines from the west'. It was obvious what they were. 'The clanking, rattling and squeaking noises heralded the movement of tanks' and they were getting louder with every passing second. Denis Edwards immediately realized that 'they were coming our way'.[61]

Wally Parr was by now stationed close to the T-junction at the far end of the road that led to Bénouville Bridge. He was hiding on the right bank while others took up positions on the left. As the noise of the tanks grew louder, Parr received an urgent message.

'Go back to the glider, for Chrissakes, go and get the PIAT.'

The PIAT was an anti-tank weapon and the only one powerful enough to knock out a German armoured vehicle.

Parr swung into action. 'I said to Charlie, "Hold my rifle" and I ran. I ran down as fast as I could, across the bridge.' On the way, he bounded past Howard.

'Where the hell are you going?'

'We've got tanks.'

'I can damn well hear them.'

'The PIAT's still in the glider.'

'Jesus – go. Get it, man. Run!'

Parr dashed over to the glider, dragged out the PIAT and then struggled back across the bridge. It was exhausting work. 'The sweat was lashing off.' When he finally paused to catch his breath, he looked down at the PIAT. To his dismay, he noticed that the firing mechanism had been twisted in the crash-landing. The gun was useless.

'Charlie, Charlie, for Chrissakes, the PIAT's smashed.'

The two of them decided to improvise by priming the PIAT's mortars. Parr's idea was 'to stand behind the hedge and throw 'em over the top and hope for the best'. They had almost finished preparing them when the ground beneath them trembled violently. It was as if a giant fist were wrenching the riverbank. 'There was a God-almighty smash and the biggest explosion and firework display I'd seen for a long time.'[62] It took some seconds for Parr to realize what had happened. His comrades on the other side of the road had managed to assemble the second PIAT and this had been placed in the hands of Charles 'Wagger' Thornton, a young sergeant with unflinchingly cool nerves. He knew that to be effective, the PIAT needed to be fired at very close range, no more than thirty yards. In a notable display of self-control, he waited until the lead tank was almost upon him before opening fire.

He scored a direct hit, sending the mortar deep into its belly, where it exploded with unbelievable violence. This, in turn, triggered all the ammunition inside the tank, a chain reaction that created 'an amazing firework display accompanied by deafening cracks and thuds that could be seen and heard over a large area'.[63] The noise was just as well, for it covered the 'cries and screams of the trapped tank commander'[64] who was burned alive. The sight of the explosion proved a powerful deterrent for the other German tanks. They turned in their tracks and beat a hasty retreat.

The high point of that exhilarating night was neither the battle for the bridge nor the success against the tanks. It came when Howard heard 'the increasing drone of many engines and, looking up, saw the skies full of countless aeroplanes coming from the direction of the sea'.

And then, like a miracle unfolding before their eyes, the sky was filled with billowing parachutes. The men could hardly believe it. 'A sight,' said Howard, 'none of us could ever forget, as they drifted to earth illuminated by the ground flares.' It was the first of the 7,000 troops of the 6th Airborne Division due to land in Normandy over the coming hours. Even the most hardened members of D Company found themselves choking back the emotion. For Howard, it was 'one of the most awe-inspiring sights of my life'.[65]

It was also the best possible news. They were no longer alone.

German coastal defences presented a formidable obstacle to the Allied landings. Heavy artillery targeted the landing craft while machine guns aimed at newly landed troops.

6

At German Headquarters

Fifty miles to the west of the parachute landings, at the 84th Army Corps headquarters in Saint-Lô, General Erich Marcks was enjoying a glass of chilled Chablis, one of the many deliciously ill-gotten perks of life in France. Marcks was in unusually good humour. The clock had just struck midnight (occupied France was an hour behind British Double Summer Time*) and it was his birthday. He was turning fifty-three, although he looked somewhat older, and had the air of an old warhorse, with a vulpine face 'expressing self-discipline' and a strong will 'that might have been that of a scholar'. But his most striking feature was his artificial leg, a souvenir of the Eastern Front, that 'creaked as he rose to greet his visitors'.[1] He sounded like an antiquarian relic from the reign of old King Friedrich, all stiff back and aching bones.

On this particular night, his visitors included Major Wilhelm Viebig, Major Friedrich Hayn and Lieutenant Colonel Friedrich von Criegern, all senior staff of the 7th Army. They had arrived at the general's operations room with a birthday cake, the bottle of chilled Chablis and the intention of introducing a touch of levity into General Marcks's life. But they knew the celebration would be perfunctory, just like the general himself. He was a no-nonsense puritan with a frosty disdain for frivolity: 'ascetic, with a thin face, strong, earnest and absolutely correct in his manner'.[2] Commander of the 84th Corps, Marcks was in charge of the divisions manning the Normandy beaches.

The cork was popped, a toast was raised and the Chablis briefly savoured. 'In a few minutes the ceremony was over.'[3] And then the

---

* Double Summer Time – two hours ahead of Greenwich Mean Time – provided an extra hour of evening daylight for British workers to get home before the blackout.

general turned back to the huge situation map of the south coast of England, which showed the disposition of the thirty Allied divisions preparing for the invasion – Canadians in the east, British in the middle and Americans in the west. Marcks was studying intently 'the little flags, the red or blue lines and curves, the shaded ovals and overlapping curves'.[4] He was paying particular attention to the five airborne divisions set out neatly on the maps.

There was good reason for his attentiveness. On the very next morning, at dawn on 6 June, all the divisional commanders of the 7th Army were due to meet in Rennes in order to discuss how best to deal with an Allied landing on the Cotentin peninsula. General Marcks himself was to play the role of an Allied paratrooper commander, deploying his forces from the air. The others were to demonstrate 'how they would wipe these paratroopers out'.[5]

Marcks was taking the exercise extremely seriously. After examining the map of the Allied forces, he turned to a second map – this time of Normandy – that marked the various developments over the previous two months. It made for uncomfortable viewing. Allied bombing targets had been highlighted in red pen and they revealed an alarming pattern to the destruction.

Marcks's bony finger slid across the map from east to west as he joined up the red dots: Hamm, Maastricht, Amiens, Rouen, Caen, Cherbourg – all the major railway junctions had come under heavy aerial bombardment. So had the subsidiary lines, such as the one connecting Metz with Bar-le-Duc. And it was not just railways that had been targeted. The road bridges over the Seine between Paris and Rouen had been knocked out, along with those over the Loire at Orléans and Nantes. As Marcks studied the map, he got a chilling insight into the Allies' strategic planning. He felt sure that their aim was to trap the 7th Army on a small island of land. It was every general's nightmare.

One of the trio of officers with General Marcks that night was Friedrich Hayn, his intelligence expert. Along with the Chablis, Hayn had brought a birthday message that was rather less welcome. He warned Marcks that 'methodically and with ever-growing accuracy, the Allies were aiming at inshore targets.'[6] These included the Ginsterhöhe radar station, the V1 site south of Cherbourg and several synthetic fuel plants. The German 7th Army was in a precarious situation.

General Marcks was studying a plan of German artillery positions when the field telephone rang loud and shrill in the operations room. It was precisely 1.11 a.m. – an unforgettable moment, according to Hayn. 'The general's body stiffened, his right hand clutched the edge of the table and with a jerk of his head, he beckoned to his chief of staff to listen in.' The message was as stark as it was sensational: enemy parachutists were landing in huge numbers along the banks of the River Orne. The report, said Hayn, 'struck us like lightning'.[7]

There followed a heated discussion in the operations room. Some felt the paratroopers were merely liaison parties sent to help the French resistance. Hayn disagreed. 'Too close to our front line,' he said. 'The resistance people would never risk that.' He was adamant that they had come to capture positions of tactical importance. If so, 'the situation had become serious indeed'.

The men were still discussing the landings when the phone rang again. It was 1.45 a.m. 'Enemy parachutists south of St Germain de Varreville and at Sainte Marie du Mont.'[8] Colonel Hamann, acting commander of the 709th Division, had just received the reports from Valognes. There were also rumours of parachutists landing at Sainte-Mère-Église and on both banks of the Merderet River.

Hayn was by now seriously alarmed. 'Three jumping areas near our front line. Two of them, moreover, near important passages across our flooded districts.'[9] He turned to General Marcks and gravely informed him that the invasion was imminent. Marcks was not so sure. 'Let's wait and see.'[10] But he was sufficiently worried to cancel the wargame planned for the following morning: he ordered the various divisional commanders to remain at their posts.

'The *kriegsspiel* [wargame] is countermanded: the gentlemen are requested to return at once to their units.'[11] Some of the generals were successfully contacted, but others could not be reached. General Hellmich, General von Schlieben and Lieutenant General Falley were already en route to Rennes.

News of the landings was swiftly phoned through to Rommel's headquarters at La Roche-Guyon. The duty officer, Lieutenant Borzikowski, immediately raised the alarm, waking everyone by sounding the sirens. Among those roused from his sleep was

Rommel's personnel officer, Colonel Leodegard Freyberg. He sat bolt upright in bed, listened to the sirens for a moment and decided 'it was just another false alarm'. He was about to go back to sleep when there was a heavy pounding on his door. He switched on the light and found himself staring at his chief clerk, Sergeant Heine, in full combat dress.

'Are you crazy, Heine? What's happening to you?'

'Sir, the invasion has begun. All personnel must immediately proceed to their respective bunkers.'

Freyberg threw off his bed covers and immediately got dressed. 'Well this is it,' he thought. 'At last it's started.'[12]

But not everyone was convinced. Rommel's chief of staff, Hans Speidel, glanced at the overcast night sky and felt sure that it was a false alarm. 'Darn it, that's odd! That's no way to start an invasion, and in weather such as this, of all things!'[13] He decided not to trouble Rommel until he was sure that this was indeed the start of the landings.

'This *is* the invasion.' From his base in Cherbourg, General Max Pemsel, the 7th Army's chief of staff, put in a frantic call to General Hans von Salmuth, commander of the 15th Army. But the general was sceptical, for he refused to believe the Allies would land in such bad weather.

'Have any sea landings taken place?' he asked.

'No,' said Pemsel. 'Not one man has landed. Nothing so far.'

General von Salmuth thought it was a fuss about nothing. He hung up the phone and said to one of his staff, 'Now I'm going to sleep.'[14]

By now, reports were being received from across Normandy. Many were wired through to Caen, where Eva Eifler was struggling to keep up with the transmissions coming through her headphones. It was impossibly exhausting. No sooner were they deciphered and transcribed than they were forwarded to General Marcks, as well as to all the commanders in the coastal area.

Hayn felt as if everyone had been given a shot of adrenalin. 'Our Army Corps Command Post was humming like a beehive.'[15] But he also felt a profound sense of disquiet. The old general had been wrong-footed by the paratrooper landings and it was some time before he was prepared to accept that this might indeed be the invasion.

'Alarm coast!' He suddenly snapped these two words to Wilhelm Viebig, his chief of operations. It was a codeword that everyone knew: it signified that the Allied invasion was under way.

'*Alert!*' A call also flashed out from the 15th Army's wireless operators. It was the invasion. This was it. The 7th Army's operators responded in kind.

'Alert! Alert!'[16]

While General Erich Marcks and his staff tried to make sense of what was going on, others were getting more direct experience of the Allied paratrooper landings. Walter Ohmsen, the senior commander of the huge gun battery at Crisbecq, was studying the night sky with his field glasses when he heard a thunderous roar sweeping in from the sea. Ohmsen harboured no illusions as to what would happen next. For the last six weeks, his battery had been relentlessly pounded by enemy bombers.

There was good reason why it was being targeted. Crisbecq was situated on the eastern coast of the Cotentin peninsula, less than five miles to the north of Utah Beach, and Allied reconnaissance planes had spotted a serious danger lurking inside this concrete and steel redoubt. It was armed with three long-barrelled 210mm Czech Kanone that had a range of twenty-one miles and were powerful enough to punch a hole in the largest battleship. They also presented a formidable threat to the planned beach landings, for they were within range of every beach from Morsalines to Pointe du Hoc.

Sub Lieutenant Ohmsen was almost thirty-three years of age (it was his birthday on 7 June) and one of a breed of professionals who had joined the navy during the Weimar Republic. After fifteen years at sea, he was more used to life on the waves than on dry land. But Crisbecq's proximity to the coast had led to it being placed under the direction of the Kriegsmarine, the German navy, with Ohmsen as its commander, so he spent his days staring at the sea rather than sailing on it.

There was a touch of the hangdog about Ohmsen, a look that was accentuated by his jug ears and tired eyes. He was suffering from severe sleep deprivation after weeks of aerial raids that had caused extensive damage to his armour-plated home. Forty of his men had been injured and their living quarters reduced to ruins.

The trenches and foxholes that surrounded the battery had also been destroyed. After such intensive carpet-bombing, Crisbecq looked like the surface of the moon.

'Let's hope the enemy waits till we are ready.'[17] These words were the constant refrain of Ohmsen's colleague, Corporal Hermann Nissen. But Ohmsen knew that his men would never be ready unless the bombing raids came to a halt.

He made his final inspection of the day's work at 11 p.m. on 5 June: his men had spent much of the afternoon repairing the communications wires damaged after the previous night's raid. Now they had changed back into their naval dress uniforms with their characteristic gold buttons and epaulettes.

Once the inspection was complete, Ohmsen ordered two gun crews to man each battery, some fifty men in total. The rest were sent to relax in the nearby Château de Fontenay, a fine country manor requisitioned as their billet. Ohmsen himself joined Lieutenant Krieg in the small command bunker, an underground concrete room that housed the radios, telephones and technical equipment for the big guns. He was expecting another long night.

'*Enemy aircraft!*'[18] The familiar cry went up shortly after midnight. It heralded a sprint to the underground bunkers, whose ten-foot reinforced ceilings could withstand almost anything. Moments later, hundreds of Allied planes swept in from the sea. As they passed over the battery, a stream of high explosive fell through the air.

'There wasn't a man who wasn't scared to death,'[19] admitted Ohmsen after the raid. The explosions packed such a punch that the concrete shuddered violently in its earthen tomb. He feared the entire structure would collapse on top of him.

'It looks to me like it's going to start tonight,'[20] shouted Lieutenant Krieg over the din of the explosions. His reasoning was that the raid was far heavier and longer than usual. By the time it ended, the battery had been hit by some 600 tons of high explosive.

No sooner was it finished than there was a loud hammering on the door of the command bunker. 'Herr Oberleutnant – a direct hit on the chateau. The quarters are wrecked. Lots of men are buried. The ruins are burning. There are many dead and wounded.'

Ohmsen remained cool under pressure, ordering Lieutenant Krieg to head to the château with all the available men. 'Get them to draw spades and shovels. And hurry up. We can't afford any losses now.'[21]

The men bounded through the darkness towards the dull orange glow of the burning château. But they soon found themselves running into trouble. A burst of machine-gun fire erupted from nowhere and hit two of the men, killing them instantly. The rest beat a hasty retreat to the battery.

'Herr Oberleutnant, we came under fire! I presume from enemy paratroops.'

Ohmsen was shocked by this piece of intelligence: a difficult night was turning into a desperate one. 'Get a fighting patrol ready!' he snapped. 'Oberleutnant Krieg will lead the patrol.'[22]

The men were issued with machine guns and grenades and ordered to find out what was taking place. They returned soon enough, bringing with them twenty prisoners of war that included 'an American captain dressed in camouflaged uniform'.[23]

A search of their kitbags left Ohmsen stunned. They contained the most sophisticated equipment, including miniature compasses, radio sets and highly detailed maps of the area around Crisbecq. What impressed him most was the fact that they had the exact map coordinates of his machine-gun posts. This was something that he had tried to calculate himself, but had never succeeded in doing.

Ohmsen did his best to interrogate the men, but they refused to answer his questions so he locked them into an underground room. He then reached for his field telephone and called Commander Hennecke at Cherbourg in order to warn him that Allied paratroopers were landing in the area around Crisbecq.

'Are you quite sure, Ohmsen?'

'I have twenty prisoners of war to prove it.'

This was evidence enough for Hennecke: he hung up the phone and sounded the general alarm.

Ohmsen now sent a second group of men over to the burning château with orders to dig out the survivors of the bombing raid. The group would eventually return with a large number of wounded comrades, many of whom had suffered terrible injuries to their 'stomach, legs and so on'.[24] It made for a sickening sight. Twenty of the most severely wounded were given morphine and assured that they would be evacuated at first light.

Ohmsen's most pressing concern was his three naval guns. He needed to know if they had been damaged in the raid. He now went to check on them and was pleased to note that all three were still in perfect working order. It was a welcome early birthday present.

By 1 a.m., the parachute landings in and around Bénouville were causing total confusion to German commanders on the ground, not least because the British had dropped dummy soldiers alongside real ones. There was a corresponding confusion among those doing the jumping. Major Tim Roseveare had been parachuted into the countryside close to Bénouville Bridge, one of some 7,000 airborne troops. Shortly before his jump, RAF pathfinder planes had dropped beacons to mark the various landing zones. Now, as Roseveare neared the ground, he found himself landing within a stone's throw of the beacon. He thanked his lucky stars and gave silent thanks to the plane's pilot. 'By a splendid piece of navigation, Squadron Leader Miller had put me down 50 yards from the Rebecca-Eureka homing beacon.'[25] This beacon – a specialist piece of kit – enabled an airborne paratrooper equipped with a Rebecca transceiver to locate a ground-based Eureka transponder.

But as he peered into the gloom, Roseveare recognized none of the features he had been expecting. No clock tower. No villages. No river. Even the fields looked different. It suddenly dawned on him that he had landed at the wrong beacon. He and his men, who were scattered across the surrounding meadows, had been dropped in entirely the wrong place.

This realization might have triggered panic, but this was no time to lose one's head. Roseveare prided himself on his crisp efficiency and was delighted when his squadron's sergeant, Bob Barr, picked himself out of the dirt, brushed down his fatigues and 'gave me a smart salute'. The world suddenly felt better again. 'It did my morale a lot of good,'[26] he later admitted.

This was just as well, for Major Roseveare was in charge of an operation of equal importance to the one undertaken by John Howard and his men. His squadron (the 3rd Parachute) was to penetrate deep into enemy territory and destroy five bridges over the River Dives, a crucial act of demolition that would prevent the Germans from bringing heavy armoury to the coastal area.

Of the five, the bridge that crossed the River Dives at Troarn presented the greatest difficulties. Not only was it deep behind enemy lines (it was almost ten miles from the coast) but it had been built to endure, a squat fortress of solid masonry with buttressed pillars and five low arches. If the bridge-busters were to be successful in its demolition, they would need speed, daring and luck. Necessity outweighed the risk: the bridge carried the main road from Caen to Le Havre and was therefore a strategic imperative.

Tim Roseveare was the perfect leader for such a mission, a splendid-looking young adventurer with a twinkle in his eye and an impeccable moustache. When he posed for the camera, he did so in style, astride an Ariel motorcycle and sporting an Airborne beret and a pair of metal-framed tinted glasses. In the years before the war, he had worked for M.G. and R.W. Weeks, a firm specializing in sewerage and water supply. Now, he was entrusted with supplying water to the very place where the Germans least wanted it – on the principal highway through Normandy.

Roseveare had landed more than three miles from his intended drop zone, as he discovered when he saw a road sign at a nearby crossroads. Undaunted, he began gathering men and locating the parachute-containers filled with explosives and equipment. Not all of his men had experienced such soft landings as his own. One chirpy young sapper named Bill Irving had landed virtually on top of a German soldier, or so he thought. He grappled for his knife and was about to slit the man's throat when he realized it was Sapper O'Leary, one of his comrades. O'Leary was not best pleased – 'he nearly bottomed me for it'[27] – but Irving managed to talk him around.

After half an hour spent gathering men and supplies, Roseveare took stock of his situation. He had thirty sappers, a small troop of soldiers and a large quantity of armaments – including the 500 pounds of plastic explosive needed to blow the bridge at Troarn. These were all loaded into a collapsible trolley and then the party set off across country, looking for all the world as if they were heading home from the local store with the week's groceries.

Not for the first time, Roseveare had luck on his side. 'Out of the murk, a jeep and trailer appeared.' It had been landed by glider and designated as a field ambulance. Roseveare peered inside its canvas hood and saw it was 'packed to the gunwales with bottles of blood and bandages and splints and all the sort of field dressing equipment and instruments and this and that'.[28] Medicine was important but so were jeeps. Pulling rank, he commandeered the vehicle, reasoning that it 'might make all the difference between success and failure'.[29] Ever gracious, he told the medics they could come with him. Then he jumped into the driving seat and prepared for the joy-ride of his life, pumping his foot hard on to the accelerator of his newly acquired set of wheels.

The jeep was comically overladen, with more than a dozen men squeezed inside, more on the trailer and two extras clinging on to the bonnet. 'A bit dodgy,'[30] thought Bill Irving as he clung on for dear life and tried to anticipate the twists and turns of Roseveare's erratic dash through the pitch-black country lanes. Nerves, excitement and the sheer thrill of being set loose behind enemy lines engendered a spirit of recklessness among the men. They skirted Ranville at high speed then burned a passage through Hérouvillette and Escoville, whose windows were shuttered to the world.

Roseveare drove with such cavalier abandon that they were soon approaching Troarn. But as the inclines stiffened, the weight of the jeep and trailer began to act like giant brakes. Roseveare took the decision to shed the medics and their supplies. 'We unloaded the old bottles of blood and splints and bandages'[31] and transferred most of the explosives from the trailer into the jeep. He also divided his men into two groups. Eight of them, including himself, would head towards Troarn in the jeep. Another party, led by Tim Juckes, would set out on foot to destroy the two bridges at Bures-sur-Dives. A third group, Canadians, had already been entrusted with blowing the other bridges.

He revved the engine and headed for Troarn, but soon found himself driving into trouble. As he steered through 'a murky gloom', he drove 'crash-bang'[32] into a barbed-wire barricade (thankfully unmanned) that was blocking the road into Troarn.

Bill Irving jumped down from the bonnet to take a closer look. It was not good news. 'The jeep was well and truly enmeshed in the barbed wire' and could move neither backward nor forward. The men, their car and their explosives were sitting ducks. Someone located the wire-cutters and Irving was tasked with crawling under the vehicle and snipping the jeep free, while Roseveare directed his torchlight on to the tangled mess. Irving wryly noted that this would have been 'very helpful', were it not for the fact that it made him a perfectly illuminated target for any passing German patrol. 'I felt,' he said, 'like a pea waiting to be plucked out of a pod.'

But on this occasion both pea and pod were safe. Irving freed the jeep and cut through the barricade: Roseveare meanwhile sparked the engine and inched the vehicle rather more cautiously towards the crossroads that led into Troarn. Irving had run ahead of the jeep and was about to wave the all-clear when he got an unexpected surprise. 'Whistling past me was a German on a bicycle, obviously returning from a night out.'[33] He was cycling fast, but not fast enough, for he was dragged off his bicycle, thrown to the ground and shot with a Sten gun.

'That's done it,'[34] hissed Roseveare, furious that his men had not knifed the cyclist to death. 'Very foolish.'[35]

It was indeed foolish, for the burst of Sten fire woke all the Germans in Troarn. In a flash, Roseveare's troop found themselves in a hostile town whose every window seemed to conceal an enemy soldier.

There comes a moment in each operation when the momentum falters and stalls. Roseveare knew this from his long months of training. At such a critical juncture, leadership is crucial. He might easily have slammed his jeep into reverse and made his escape, but a surge of adrenalin overrode all thoughts of retreat. He shoved his foot hard on to the accelerator and rounded the corner that led into the main street. And it was then, as he put it, that 'the fun started'.[36]

It was crucial to pass through the town at high speed, but the jeep and trailer weighed the same as a small lorry and responded to the accelerator with sluggish indifference. Try as he might, Roseveare could not get it above 35 mph. As they bowled down the main street, they came under a hail of gunfire. Roseveare was in his element. This was far more exciting than his desk job at M.G. and R.W. Weeks. 'There seemed to be a Boche [German] in every doorway, shooting like mad.'[37] One of the sappers, Sam Peachey, was clinging to the rear of the jeep and blasting away with his Bren gun. Bill Irving was doing the same at the front bonnet, 'blazing away with my Sten gun at anything that moved'. Roseveare was meanwhile slamming the wheel from left to right, zigzagging down the street. 'Some crazy mad driving,'[38] thought Irving as he was lurched sideways. It felt even crazier to Joe Henderson, who had started the ride on the bonnet and ended it on the trailer. He could never quite work out how.

Others were less fortunate. At some point during their dash through town, Sam Peachey was flung from the jeep and jettisoned on to the pavement. (He was later captured and made a prisoner of war.) Another of Roseveare's joy-riders, David Breeze, found himself musing on 'the cost of replacing all the plate-glass shop windows, so rudely shattered'.[39]

They were halfway through town when they saw an alarming sight. A German soldier had set up a machine gun in the middle of the road and was about to open fire. Undaunted, Roseveare squeezed every last drop from the jeep's overheated engine. 'As the speed rose rapidly, we careered from side to side of the road.'[40] He bore down on the machine gunner, who chose prudence over bravery and dashed into a nearby doorway. He 'got the hell out', noted Bill Irving from his precarious vantage point on the front bonnet. Just seconds after they passed his gun, the soldier was back behind the trigger 'and in a moment a stream of tracer went out over our heads'.[41]

The men were now on a downhill slope and fast approaching the river. Roseveare mumbled a brief prayer of thanks. 'By the grace of God, those steep hills were the only thing that saved us.'[42] He knew, as did the German machine gunner, that the MG-34 couldn't fire effectively down such a gradient.

The men leaped out as soon as they reached the riverbank and prepared to blow the bridge as fast as possible. They had trained for this moment for months and knew exactly what to do. Joe Henderson and David Breeze covered the road behind them while Bill Irving clambered on to the bridge with another of the sappers, Corporal Tellers. Their task was to lay the demolition charges intended to destroy the middle of the structure.

They strung a line of charges right across the roadway and connected all the wires and fuses to the detonator – 'a very simple process'. As additional fireworks, the men wired the trailer, laden with explosives, and left it on the central arch of the bridge. Once done, Roseveare yelled to everyone to get back aboard the jeep.

Irving asked him if he wanted to light the fuse.

'No, you light it.'

Irving wondered if Roseveare declined out of courtesy or prudence. He decided it was the latter. 'If the damn thing didn't go off, it was nothing to do with him.'

He was still lighting the fuses when Roseveare started to drive away. Irving made a final check and then legged it after the vehicle. 'It was rather like trying to catch the bus that you've just missed.' He was hauled on board just as the night sky was lit by a brilliant flash and a 'great bang'.[43] The fuses had worked.

'Down, down, down she goes!'[44] hooted Roseveare. He was jubilant with success. Tons of shattered masonry were rent apart and lifted far into the night sky, before crashing back down into the River Dives. The entire central span – some twenty feet in length – was no more. For Roseveare, an expert in water management, it was his Moses moment, only one that came with an exquisite twist. Instead of parting the waters, he had parted the bridge that spanned those waters. In doing so, he had cut the principal road that led towards the planned Allied beachhead.

This news was good enough, but Roseveare would soon learn that there was further cause for celebration. Tim Juckes's party had managed to destroy both bridges at Bures-sur-Dives while the Canadian group had blown their two targets at Robehomme and Varaville. Five key bridges had ceased to exist. It was a job well done.

As Roseveare and his men made their escape through the night, avoiding Troarn, they came across an elderly Frenchman milking his cow. Roseveare paused for a chat.

'When I informed him that he was being liberated, he was not impressed.' Roseveare thought that 'perhaps he did not understand my accent'.[45] This may have been so. But that elderly farmer may also have been nervous as to what additional terrors that troubled night might bring.

Allied parachute drops were launched in the early hours of 6 June. Soldiers were weighed down with weapons, food and supplies. Those landing in Sainte-Mère-Église found it hard to dodge the intense German gunfire.

7

Landing by Moonlight

ONE OF THE key Allied objectives that night was the capture of Sainte-Mère-Église, a two-horse town that had shuffled through the centuries with only a nod and a wink to the outside world. Here, the unhurried traditions of rural France could be found in abundance: an early rise, a generous *déjeuner* and a long evening in which to catch up on the gossip.

Sainte-Mère-Église only awoke from its slumbers on market day, when local spinsters would peddle their home-churned butter and cream. Few paused to consider that their little town might be a place of vital strategic significance; that Sainte-Mère-Église was the glittering goal for American paratroopers in the early hours of Tuesday, 6 June.

Yet even a cursory glance at the map would have revealed why it was so important. Not only was it situated just five miles from Utah Beach, but it straddled the main road that ran through the Cotentin peninsula: as such, it was a crucial artery for the German army. At the peninsula's northern end stood the coastal port of Cherbourg, with its vast docks and deep harbour – deep enough for the *Titanic* to have called here on her fateful maiden voyage. An hour's drive to the south stood the town of Carentan, with its canal and its interchange of roads. Between the two stood Sainte-Mère-Église. Control the town and you controlled everything.

The curtain-raiser to that night's events had occurred at around 10 p.m., when Raymond Paris, a young assistant to the local notary, had been roused by a violent banging on the front door. He opened the upstairs window and saw two of his friends standing in the street below.

'Come quickly!' they shouted. 'There's a fire at Julia's place.'[1]

He glanced towards the elderly lady's house on the far side of the town square and could see a dull glow coming from inside. It was the home of Juliette Pommier, who took care of children in the village.

Paris woke his father, a local fireman, and the two of them rushed into the square to get a water-pump from the storehouse. In doing so, they risked serious punishment. The German curfew had begun an hour earlier and no one was allowed outside without a *laissez-passer* – something that the fireman did not have. But Paris and his father took the risk. They went to knock on the door of another fireman, who sounded the general alarm, and within seconds windows and doors were opening as everyone sought to find out what was happening.

Paris junior grabbed a pump, along with buckets, hoses and nozzles, and then he and his father quickly made their way to the house. 'It was hard work for us, because the hoses were very heavy and we were soon out of breath.'[2]

The alarm bell was clanging loudly and it brought dozens of people rushing into the square. Everyone was urged to form a human chain in order to fight the fire, which was fast spreading out of control.

The mayor of Sainte-Mère-Église, Alexandre Renaud, arrived a few moments later, by which time much of the house was engulfed in flames. 'The men were running with their canvas buckets. They threw their contents into a huge tub.' But no matter how much water they put on the fire, it continued to spread.

The strong wind was scarcely helping matters. It was fanning the flames horizontally and Monsieur Renaud was alarmed to see that 'pieces of burning paper and straw were being blown towards the barn, which was twenty metres away and full of straw and wood.'[3]

The crowd in the square had been joined by a group of young German soldiers, who had come to watch the local inhabitants trying to extinguish the fire. Among them was Rudi Escher, a twenty-year-old conscript from Coburg in Bavaria. He and his army comrades had spent the hour before dark larking around in the church square. Now, they kept themselves amused by watching the locals trying to douse the flames.

Eventually even this got boring and they were about to go to their barracks when they heard a sharp cry from one of their fellow soldiers at the top of the church tower. An aeroplane had just passed over very low and he could see 'eight or ten parachutists starting to descend'. For Escher and his friends, this was the worst possible news. 'We thought it was the crew ejecting from a crippled plane,' and this meant only one thing. 'Our orders were to track down and capture any enemy parachutists.' They abandoned all thoughts of going to bed. 'We grabbed our weapons and went off in the direction where we thought they had landed, leaving two sentries in the church tower.'4

It was dark in the fields and the men could scarcely see their own boots, let alone the enemy parachutists. After an hour or so, they gave up their search and returned to Sainte-Mère-Église, where Raymond Paris was still directing efforts to douse the flames. As he picked up yet another bucket, he became aware of a loud roar and glanced at the sky. He saw 'an enormous wave of aeroplanes coming from the west to the east'5 and had a brief thought that this could be the start of the Allied invasion. But the planes swung north and headed in the direction of Crisbecq battery.

Monsieur Renaud had also been watching the aircraft and was still looking at the sky when he got the shock of his life. 'Just at that moment, a big transport plane, all lights ablaze, flew right over the tree-tops.' It was flying so low that everyone instinctively ducked as its vast shadow swept across the square. It was immediately followed by a second plane, and then a third. Within seconds, they were coming 'in great waves, almost silent, their great shadows covering the earth'.6

Raymond Paris could scarcely contain his excitement: this, surely, was the start of the invasion. It was still not completely dark, for there was a full moon. He could quite clearly see 'that the side doors of the aeroplane were open'.7

Everyone was now looking at the sky, staring at the planes, waiting for something to happen. And then, quite without warning, 'what looked like huge confetti dropped out of their fuselages and fell quickly to earth'.8

'Paratroopers!' cried the mayor.

'That's it!' said Paris sharply. 'It's the invasion!'9

★

Inside one of those planes, American pilot Julian 'Bud' Rice was wiping a stream of sweat from his forehead as he gazed at the fire below. He had just emerged from a dense bank of coastal fog: now, he could clearly see the T-light on the ground. It marked the drop zone for the paratroopers aboard his plane. He cut the throttle in a desperate attempt to slow the engines of his lumbering Douglas C-47 Skytrain. As he did so, all hell broke loose from the ground. Anti-aircraft bullets burst upwards, tearing through the plane's metal shell and piercing holes in the tail. Rice knew that if a single bullet pierced the gas tank in the wing, the entire plane would explode. '*Scary?*' he said to himself. 'You bet!'[10] Yet it was also exhilarating. He had spent more than eighteen months training for precisely this sort of mid-air drama and felt ready for anything.

Just twenty-two years of age – and decked in leather cap and flying goggles – Rice looked every inch the professional pilot. Indeed there was a sense in which he'd been awaiting this moment all his life. At the age of seven, he had watched Charles Lindbergh take off from a Panama airfield in his famous monoplane, *Spirit of St Louis*. The young Rice had vowed that one day he, too, would become a pilot. Now, his moment had come.

The drama unfolding in the night sky above Sainte-Mère-Église had begun earlier that evening when he and his fellow pilot, Larue Wells, had been summoned to a packed operations room at Cottesmore airfield in Rutland. Addressing the crowd was their jaunty lieutenant colonel, Walter Washburn, who brought news that was extremely exciting. 'Gentlemen,' he said, 'you will be taking part in the largest airborne armada ever created.' His rhetorical flourish was packed with a punch. They were to drop 13,000 paratroopers behind enemy lines on the Cotentin peninsula.

More than 800 aircraft were to take part in Missions Albany and Boston, crossing the English Channel in an aerial convoy so vast it would stretch back fully 300 miles. It was an operation that carried huge risks. The planes were to fly in a succession of V formations, like migrating birds, and would be so close to each other that their wingtips would be almost touching. There was to be no radar or radio communication and they would have to fly across the Channel at just 500 feet in order to escape detection by German radar stations.

Lieutenant Colonel Washburn did not mince his words when

detailing the dangers. The pilots would face German flak, anti-aircraft fire and possibly dense sea fog. 'Watch your airspeed,' he told them, a warning that carried a nasty sting in its tail. The planes were to be so heavily laden that their engines would fatally stall if they fell below 100 mph. Once stalled, they could not be restarted.

Washburn also warned that there were only enough navigators for one in ten of the planes taking part in the operation. The other nine would be flying blind. Julian Rice knew exactly what this meant: 'Dead reckoning navigation and straining eyesight by lead pilots and navigators looking for the dim amber wing lights of the other groups.'

Yet even these wing lights were to be switched off soon after leaving the English coastline. As the giant formation swept out across the Channel, the only guide for Rice, Wells and all the other pilots would be the small-cupped blue lights on the plane in front of them, lights that ran along the upper fuselage. 'Hang in close and tight,' advised Washburn in a spirit of breezy confidence, 'so you don't lose your way.' He made it sound as if they were off for a stroll in the park.

Many of the pilots gathered in the operations room had questions, but Washburn's briefing was at an end. 'Keep the formation tight,' was his last injunction. 'Give your troops a good trip. Good luck. Let's go!'

As he strode out of the room, he paused, turned and offered one final warning. 'No paratrooper is to be returned to England,' he said. 'Any paratrooper refusing to jump will be court-martialled.'[11] It was a parting shot that left a chill in the air.

Julian Rice's squadron was to play a particularly crucial role on that night's mission. The planes were carrying the American paratroopers[12] whose specific task was to capture Sainte-Mère-Église. A mission of such importance required a commander fit for the task. Edward 'Cannonball' Krause was just such a man. A veteran survivor of Biazza Ridge in Sicily, where his men had fought off a ferocious German panzer attack, Krause had a fearsome reputation among all who served under him. With his cropped hair and crumpled fatigues he looked every inch the professional soldier, yet there was something unsettling about the blank expression and detached gaze. Few liked him and most feared him. One labelled him 'a psycho' who would kill anything that stood in his way. Another criticized his 'very abrasive personality' and added, 'I doubt if many people would have nice things to say about him.'[13] Few did, yet Krause had trained his men to within a whisker of their lives, turning them into a hardened force of elite fighters. If anyone could be entrusted to capture the most important goal in the Allies' western landing zone, it was Cannonball Krause and his men of the 3rd Battalion.

On the previous evening, he had gathered them together at the Cottesmore airbase and delivered an electrifying call to arms. Bill Tucker was one of those assembled on the tarmac and was particularly impressed when 'Blood and Guts' Krause whipped a tattered American flag from his pocket, as if he were a magician with a box of tricks. 'This was the first American flag to fly over Gela, Sicily,' he said, 'and the first American flag to be raised over Naples. And tomorrow morning, I will be sitting in the Mayor's office in Sainte-Mère-Église and this flag will be flying over that office.'

Tucker had long felt ambivalence towards his commander. 'I continued to both like and dislike Krause.'[14] Yet he had little doubt that he meant what he said about capturing the town and even less doubt that he would achieve it.

There was good reason why Krause was so confident. Experience had taught him that a highly trained group of assault troops could wreak havoc on enemy defences if they had the twin advantages of darkness and surprise. Under the cover of night, sentries could be stalked, positions ambushed and gun emplacements wrested from sleeping guards. For the attack on Sainte-Mère-Église he favoured the knife over the gun. It was silent, terrifying and deadly effective.

It was gone 9 p.m. on 5 June when the paratroopers marched out to their respective planes. The C-47s stretched as far as the eye could see. Bill Tucker tried to count them all, for it was a means of keeping his nerves at bay, but he quickly gave up. He felt both anxious and excited, with 'a sense of tremendous anticipation' about everything that was to come.

The deepening twilight had long since swallowed the planes at the far end of the airfield and time seemed to have been placed on pause. Tucker felt there was 'a quiet feeling in the air, something like when the birds and monkeys in the jungle all stop making noises'.[15] He knew that the entire jungle would soon be asleep: the perfect time to strike at the German defences in Normandy.

Pilot Julian Rice was already at the controls of his plane when the twenty-one paratroopers in his 'stick' arrived. He watched as they hauled themselves aboard, got strapped into their canvas seats and prepared for take-off. He could sense the tension: only the powerfully built jumpmaster seemed to have total confidence in what lay ahead. Rice studied him as he boarded the plane, his face darkened with black smudges. 'He looked to me like he could win the war single-handed.'

Rice went through the pre-flight check and then 'threw in a prayer or two'[16] for good luck. He knew they would need both prayers and luck if they were to make it safely to France. He fired the engines of his C-47 at the same time as all the other pilots. The noise was so deafening that it shook the earth beneath them. Bill Tucker's nerves were lost to 'the beat and roar of hundreds of aircraft engines'.

At exactly 11 p.m., a green flare signal could be seen coming from the control tower. Everyone knew what it meant: 'The invasion was on!'[17] No more postponements; no more last-minute glitches. Within seconds, the first of the C-47s was preparing for take-off. At the allotted moment, Rice taxied to the end of the runway and locked the tail wheel in position. Then, with a confident thrust of his fist, he 'shoved the twin throttles to the firewall'.[18] The engines roared as the plane gathered speed down the runway, giving a shudder and groan before lumbering into the night air above Cottesmore.

Bill Tucker twisted his head slightly to get a final view of the ground. 'Along each side of the runway there were literally hundreds of people lined up two and three deep: US and RAF ground personnel, ATS (Auxiliary Territorial Service) English girls, cooks and bakers.' He was struck by the fact that everyone was as still as statues. 'They just stared at our plane and without moving there seemed to be a tremendous gesture of a salute and perhaps a blessing.'[19]

Julian Rice had flown any number of missions, yet he still experienced a moment of panic as the plane left the ground. It hit a twisting vortex of prop-wash – disturbed air – caused by the C-47 just ahead of him. The turbulence was so powerful that it threatened to hurl the plane back to the ground. But Rice fought the controls and managed to keep it airborne. Soon after, they were joined in the moonlit sky by the seventy-one other planes of their group. Once all were airborne, they assembled into their pre-arranged V formations.

So long as the amber wing lights were illuminated, it was relatively easy to keep together. But these were switched off as they passed over the Isle of Portland and out into the English Channel. Thereafter, their only guide was the small blue fuselage light on the plane in front.

On several occasions this light faded into the darkness, leaving nothing but the moonlit silhouette of the adjacent plane. Rice and his comrades called this their 'sweat time'. They knew they were never more than 100 feet from a catastrophic mid-air collision. A fortnight earlier they had come close to experiencing just such a collision while participating in a practice exercise. From nowhere, Rice had seen flashing navigation lights coming towards him at high speed. He managed to dodge them but the plane behind was not so fortunate. The two aircraft rammed into each other at high speed – 'the sky lit up'[20] – as they both exploded in mid-air. Twelve men were killed in the crash.

Now, as they passed to the east of Guernsey, Rice glimpsed a magnificent sight being played out below them. 'The English Channel was striped with the wake of thousands of ships heading for the landing beaches of Omaha and Utah.' This was Force O and Force U – a naval armada on such a scale that it outclassed even the aerial convoy in which he was taking part. The ships were ferrying to Normandy the American troops that would be landing on Omaha and Utah beaches in just seven hours.

'*Lord keep us safe . . . Lord keep us safe.*' Above the roar of the engines, Rice could hear these distant words replaying themselves over and over in his headphones. It was some time before he realized that it was the sound of his own prayers.

The skies over the Channel were clear and the coastline of Normandy was visible as a finely etched line against the dark sea. But now, as the planes approached land, a most alarming sight could be seen looming in the night sky. Rice knew in an instant that they were heading into disaster.

'Suddenly, without warning, the shit hit the fan.' As he piloted his plane over the French coastline, the entire formation flew into a dense wall of fog. It swallowed everything. Not only did the blue lights disappear, but the entire formation vanished. Rice couldn't even see the wings of his own plane, let alone any others. Such a perilous situation demanded an immediate action known as emergency dispersal manoeuvre, whereby the pilots broke formation and spread out in the fog-bound sky. It was not for the faint-hearted. 'I shoved the fuel mixture to rich, boosted the throttle setting and revs-per-minute to climb mode, synchronized prop pitch, kicked the hard left rudder and pulled back the yoke.'[21]

In the rear of the plane, the paratroopers wondered what the hell was going on. They gripped their safety harnesses and clutched their stomachs as the plane screamed its way out of the fog-bank, climbing at a near impossible angle. Many regretted the steak and ice cream they had eaten before take-off. Bill Tucker managed to hold his somewhere between his stomach and his throat, but his friend Harry Baffone lost the battle 'and had to use his helmet to throw up'.[22]

To Rice and Wells, 'those few minutes in the soup felt like an eternity.' When they broke out of the fog, planes were scattered everywhere. The night sky was filled with C-47s, each following its own erratic trajectory. The danger was far from over. Indeed, it was only now about to start. 'A heavy barrage of enemy anti-aircraft shells burst right, then left. Black-gray flak clouds were everywhere.'

On the ground, the German anti-aircraft batteries had an unrivalled view of the moonlit planes as they weaved across the sky. 'Machine-gun tracer streams were searching us out. Staccato rat-a-tat of bullets pierced the tail assembly.' This gave a severe jolt to the elevator controls and the plane lurched downwards as it headed for the ground. Rice and Wells fought to keep control of the craft, wrenching the nose heavenwards again. 'The sky was now a smoky yellow haze. Exploding shells filled the air with turbulence, which jerked our plane up and down like a yo-yo.' They were not the only ones in danger. Scores of other planes were weaving a random passage across the sky as they took evasive action.

As the C-47s passed over the town of Sainte-Mère-Église, Rice got his first clear view of the fire below. The men needed to jump

– and soon – for they were exactly on target. Pathfinder parachutists had landed just a few minutes earlier in order to set up their T-lights on the designated dropping zones: Rice could clearly see the T-light intended for the men on board his plane, but they were travelling so fast that to let them out now would condemn them to a speedy death. Their parachutes would be shredded by the air speed.

Rice had clocked up more than 800 hours of flying time and knew there was only one way to slow a C-47 in mid-air – a two-man manoeuvre that would be both rough and brutal. 'Co-pilot Wells extended the flaps and lowered the landing gear in order to produce instant drag, while I kicked the rudder and yanked the elevator and aileron controls.'

It was like slamming on the brakes. There was a violent shudder as the plane seemed to hit a solid wall of air. 'Sorry, guys,'[23] mouthed Rice to the paratroopers behind. Seconds later, he flicked on the green jump light. They were travelling at 118 mph – terrifyingly close to the speed at which the engines would fatally stall – and flying at a height of 750 feet. For the twenty-one paratroopers on board, it would be like jumping off the eightieth floor of the Empire State Building, a perilous but mercifully short jump, albeit under heavy German gunfire.

'Stand up and hook up.'[24] The red light flashed and the men got in line. 'Jesus Christ, we don't get paid enough for this,'[25] shouted Bill Tucker's friend Larry over the roar of the engines. 'Check equipment.' But there was barely time. The red light flashed to green and the jumpmaster pushed them out. 'Twenty-one. Okay. Twenty. Okay. Nineteen. Okay.'[26] As Tucker leaped into the void, he heard Krupinski yell, 'Son of a bitch. I'm hit again.'[27]

Paratrooper Ken Russell knew he was in trouble before he even left the plane. The fire in Sainte-Mère-Église was lighting the night sky and picking out the men as sharply defined silhouettes. In those long seconds in the air, Russell had a bird's-eye view of those who had jumped before him. 'Lieutenant Cadish, H.T. Bryant and Laddie Tlapa landed on telephone poles down the street.' They were impaled. 'It was like they were crucified there.'

He saw another of his comrades hit by machine-gun fire while still in the air. Unfortunately, the lad was armed with powerful gammon grenades and the resulting explosion was as harrowing as it was catastrophic. 'He was blown away. Instantaneously. I looked around and there was just an empty parachute coming down.'

Russell himself felt shells and bullets jerking at his chute as he drifted towards the ground. He once again looked down and got another shock. The heat of the fire was sucking the parachutists downwards and pulling them into the burning building. One of his friends – he thought it was Vanholzbech – was dragged into the heart of the inferno. 'I heard him scream. I saw him come down into the fire and the chute come down. He didn't scream any more.'

Russell was caught in his own nightmare. He was heading straight for the church tower of Sainte-Mère-Église, along with one of his comrades. 'I hit first, and a couple of my suspension lines, or maybe more, went around the church steeple.' He slid down the slate roof, which shredded both his clothing and skin until he came to a sudden halt, hanging by the fragile suspension lines, suspended and helpless like a fly in a web. As he looked up, he saw John Steele also land on the church. His chute had wrapped itself over the steeple.

From his precarious vantage point, Russell witnessed his friend John Ray land just in front of the church. As he did so, a red-haired German soldier ran out from behind the building, glanced upwards and noticed both himself and Steele dangling there like trapped insects. The German was about to take aim at them both when distracted by John Ray. In a flash he swung his gun towards Ray and shot him in the stomach.

Russell knew that he would be next. He didn't stand a chance. But Ray, 'while he was dying in agony, got his .45 out'. He took aim and shot the German soldier in the back of the head, killing him. Seconds later, he also died of his wound.

Russell's platoon of some thirty-six men was one of many that had suffered a catastrophic landing. If all had gone to plan, they would have come down just outside the town, regrouped and then launched a concerted attack on the German garrison. Instead, they had been impaled, shot and landed in impossible positions in the heart of town. Worse still – although Russell did not know this at the time – only four of them were still alive.

He knew he had to get down from the church roof as a matter of urgency. He reached for his trench knife, cut the parachute risers and tumbled headlong into the street below. He was fortunate not to break a bone.

'After jumping to the ground, I dashed across the street and the machine-gun fire was knocking up pieces of earth all around me.' He dived for cover into a grove of trees close to the edge of town, feeling like 'the loneliest man in the world'. He had never wanted to be a soldier: he was a young student from Maryville, Tennessee, who should have been graduating that very evening.

As he crawled out of the coppice, he spied a German soldier shooting at paratroopers still coming down from the sky. The only weapon he had was a gammon bomb and he now prepared to throw it at the German. 'Scared to death' was how he felt. It was 'the first time I'd ever used them'. He lobbed it through the air and it blew up right on target. 'The gun stopped.' Russell had killed his first German.

As he stumbled across a field, he spied another paratrooper who had landed far from his drop zone and was hopelessly lost.

'Do you know where you're at?'

'No'.

'I don't either.'[28]

The two of them teamed up and decided to go in search of others. Russell was unaware that his commander, Edward Krause, was crouched in a field just a few hundred yards away.

Krause himself was lucky to be alive. As his plane had emerged from the coastal fog-bank, it had come within thirty feet of colliding with another three aircraft. Even the cool-headed Krause had been ruffled. 'As close to being crashed in the air as I ever hope to.' But his troubles were far from over. The plane was still taking evasive action when he jumped, plunging to earth from an altitude of more than 2,000 feet – 'the longest ride I had in over fifty jumps'. Worse still, four planes passed beneath him as he descended to the ground. 'I really sweated that out.'[29]

Ever the professional, he landed on target and set up a command post before starting to gather his troops. He decided not to assault Sainte-Mère-Église until he had several hundred men, enough to give him a reasonable chance of capturing the town. He still had high hopes of being in the mayor's office before dawn.

Sixteen-year-old Jeanne Pentecôte, the butcher's daughter, had been hiding in the family cellar when the first wave of planes flew overhead. As she listened to the low roar from outside, she heard her uncle calling to her.

'Oh my God!' he cried. 'Come, look at this. We'll never see this again!'[30] She rushed to the front door just in time to see the first of the parachutists arrive.

Young Henri-Jean Renaud, the mayor's son, was also at home when he heard the thrum of plane engines. He leaned out of the window and saw 'successive waves of planes which passed over at very low altitude'. When his mother, Simone, saw him and his brother hanging out of the window, she pulled them back inside. 'No, no!'[31] she shouted, and told them to get down on their knees and pray.

A few minutes later Henri-Jean heard the front door opening. It was his father bringing the news. 'It's really the landing,' he cried. 'It's not a commando raid. It's just too big. It's the liberation!'[32]

Raymond Paris was still in the market square. 'Some of the parachutists landed as close as four or five metres from where I stood. I could see them pulling on the strings of their parachutes to cushion their landing.'[33] One fell into the lime trees next to the town pump and Paris and his friends went to help.

The sight of the parachutists momentarily stunned the Germans, among them Rudi Escher. He saw 'a lot of airplanes about us and the dark sky full of bright parachutes'.[34] When he looked more closely at the church, he noticed that 'one was hanging from the spire'.[35] This was John Steele.

Escher and his comrades swung into action as soon as they recovered from the shock. Raymond Paris was standing about fifteen metres from the town pump when 'a nearby German soldier suddenly lifted his machine gun to fire on a parachutist.' Paris was appalled. 'I tapped him on the shoulder saying, "Don't shoot – civilian,"'[36] to distract him. The parachutist was very lucky, for the German soldier held his fire.

Others were not so fortunate. Mayor Renaud watched in dismay as another paratrooper tumbled into the still-burning house. 'Sparks flew and the fire burned brighter.' He saw another man shot in the legs as he was about to land. A third crashed into a tree and desperately sought to get down before being spotted. But the German flak was already trained on him. 'The machine guns fired their sinister patter. The poor man's hands fell and the body swung to and fro from the cables.'[37]

The situation spun even faster out of control when a huge transport plane crashed to the ground close to the town's sawmill. It erupted into a sheet of flame.

Paris was by now seriously alarmed. 'There was the sound of the bell, the noise of the airplanes, the bursts of automatic gunfire, the shouts and cries of the German soldiers, the cries of the French and the screams of the women, who obviously were terrified.'[38]

Rudi Escher and his German comrades were also alarmed. 'With Americans landing everywhere, we were afraid for our lives.' They had no desire to fight. Some discussed what to do while others went to gather equipment and canisters discarded by the newly landed paratroopers. 'We got some cigarettes and chocolate and thought we were doing pretty well out of it.'

The telephone line to their command post, a mile out of town, was still working. One of Escher's men called and asked what they should do. 'We were told, initially, to stay put.' This was the worst possible news, for 'there was by now quite a bit of shooting' and the situation was becoming increasingly dangerous.

'While we were standing by the church wondering what to do, one of our men' – Alfons Jakl – 'fell down dead, shot through the heart.' This persuaded the men to flee the town while they still could. 'Leaving our dead comrade behind, we retrieved our bicycles, which were stored in a barn, and cycled back to our unit.' They rode in single file, 'one behind the other, each of us frightened of being shot by the Americans'.[39] Their flight from Sainte-Mère-Église left a window of opportunity for the Americans, for there were now fewer than two dozen German troops still inside the town. A key section of the German front line was extremely vulnerable.

PART III
The Night

The precisely planned American airborne operation was designed to support the troops landing on Utah Beach. The 101st Airborne Division was to seize the raised causeways leading inland from the coast, while the experienced 505th Parachute Infantry Regiment – part of the 82nd Airborne Division – was to spearhead the attack on Sainte-Mère-Église.

However, Allied strategists knew it would not take much for their exact plans to go seriously awry. If so, improvisation alone would save the day.

A key operation for British airborne forces was to silence the guns of Merville Battery, a huge gun emplacement situated close to Sword Beach. This formidable undertaking – assigned to the 9th Parachute Battalion – depended on a precision drop of men and weaponry.

German commanders were confused by the seemingly random nature of the airborne landings, a situation compounded by the cutting of communication wires. News of the aerial assault reached Hitler's OKW (Supreme High Command) at 4 a.m.: it came with a request to release the two SS panzer divisions – which the sleeping Führer alone could grant.

French civilians were also taken by surprise by the nocturnal airborne landings. Many feared it was another hit-and-run raid, like the disastrous commando assault on Dieppe, but they nevertheless risked their lives by providing shelter and first aid to wounded paratroopers.

The fight for Sainte-Mère-Église was bloody and violent.
The town was in American hands by dawn, when paratroopers felt
safe enough to pause for a cigarette.

8

Sainte-Mère-Église

M ARCELLE HAMEL WAS having a troubled night. The moon was gleaming through the window of her schoolhouse lodgings, bathing the room in pale light. Outside, the sky had been washed to silver. Her thoughts were with her close friend Jean, who had left for North Africa on just such a June evening four years earlier. Since then, she had received very little news. She didn't even know if he was still alive.

She tried to make herself comfortable on the sofa bed she shared with her mother. Their living arrangements were far from satisfactory, but they had no choice. They had been evicted from their home in Octeville, near Cherbourg, exactly a year earlier, when it was requisitioned by the Germans. Ever since, twenty-eight-year-old Marcelle and her family (her mother, aunt and grandparents) had been living in rented lodgings in the village of Neuville.

The nocturnal stillness was broken by the faint hum of planes. The Hamels had grown used to such a noise, for bombing raids had been a regular occurrence for weeks. Nor was Mademoiselle Hamel particularly afraid. The Neuville schoolhouse was a solid stone building that lay some distance from any obvious military targets. The small German garrison at Sainte-Mère-Église was almost two miles away and the railway station even further.

But on this occasion the noise was more persistent than usual and she noticed that the sky to the north was glowing a reddish-brown colour. She was sufficiently disturbed to wake her mother: the two of them went down into the yard to see if they could work out what was being bombed. But by the time they were outside there was only 'the faint rumble of a bombardment near Quinéville'. Even that soon faded to nothing and an all-pervading silence once again took hold.

'It's just like last time,' said Madame Hamel. 'They must have bombed the blockhouses [strongpoints] on the coast.'

They returned to the darkened house and climbed back into bed. But Marcelle Hamel still couldn't sleep and stared blankly at the dim rectangle of window-light. In this 'sort of semi-consciousness' she had the impression of seeing 'fantastic shadows appearing from nowhere, dark against the chiaroscuro of the sky, like huge black parasols'. They seemed 'to rain softly down on to the fields opposite and disappear behind the black line of the hedgerow'. She pinched herself to check she was not dreaming.

She threw on some clothes, went downstairs again and stepped outside. The sky was filled with the drone of engines and the hedges seemed to be alive with curious snapping sounds.

She noticed that Monsieur Dumont, a local widower, was also outside. He shuffled over and pointed 'to the material of a parachute hanging from the roof of the covered playground'.[1]

Others in Neuville had also been woken by the noise. Denise Lecourtois, daughter of the café owner, had been jolted from sleep by the 'loud bellowing of the aircraft that passed overhead'. She peered anxiously out of the first-floor window and was astonished to see paratroopers descending in the nearby fields. From behind the curtains, she watched them 'slowly enter the village, hugging the walls of the houses'.[2] She was terrified and clambered back into bed, pulling the eiderdown over her head in the hope that all would be well in the morning.

Intrigued by the parachute, Mademoiselle Hamel decided to investigate, stepping out from the schoolyard and walking a short distance along the lane. Here, she was met by an unexpected sight. Seated on her neighbour's front wall was a young man, heavily armed with rifle, gun and knife. As she stared at him, the silhouetted figure beckoned her over.

Her curiosity got the better of her. She asked him in her near-fluent English if his plane had been shot down. Answering in excellent French, but speaking in a whisper, he broke the news she had been awaiting for four long years. 'It is the great invasion. Thousands and thousands of parachutists are descending here tonight. I am an American soldier, but I speak your language well, for my mother is French. She's from the Basse-Pyrenees.'

Mademoiselle Hamel found it hard to take in everything she was being told. Excited, frightened and confused, she stuttered a series of questions. 'What's happening on the shore? Is there a landing? What about the Germans?'

The soldier declined to answer. Instead, and with urgency in his voice, he asked her for information about the Germans in the area.

'There are no Germans here. The nearest ones are stationed in Sainte-Mère-Église, about two kilometres away.'

The soldier nodded and asked if there was somewhere safe for him to look at his map. He was lost and wanted to find out precisely where he had landed. When Mademoiselle Hamel suggested the schoolhouse, he said he didn't want to place her at risk.

'Monsieur Dumont and my old aunt will keep watch over the school,' she said. 'One in front, the other at the back.'

This seemed to reassure the soldier, for he now followed her into the house. She noticed he was limping and asked if he was hurt. He said he had sprained his ankle, but declined to have it bandaged. He pulled out a highly detailed Ordnance Survey map, along with a torch, and flashed his light on to the coastal area, asking her to show him where he had landed. When Marcelle pointed her finger to Neuville, the soldier expressed surprise at being so far from where he was supposed to be.

Once she had shown him how to reach his landing zone, a few kilometres to the west, the soldier refolded the map, packed it into his rucksack and then delved into his pocket for some bars of chocolate. He gave them to Monsieur Dumont's children, who had just entered the schoolhouse. They were 'so astonished' they neglected to eat them.

Mademoiselle Hamel was surprised that the man appeared so calm. He seemed in complete control of everything. But when he shook her hand to thank her, she noticed that his palm was sweaty, even though the night was cool. Now, without further ado, he turned to leave.

'Goodnight to you all!' he said in French. And then he turned to Mademoiselle Hamel and added in whispered English, 'The coming days will be terrible. Good luck to you, miss. Thank you. I will think of you all my life.'

She couldn't quite believe what was happening and had to pinch herself for the second time that night. The man abruptly vanished into the night 'as if he were but a vision in a dream'.[3]

Marcelle Hamel was not alone in receiving an unexpected visitor in those early morning hours. In the nearby village of Videcosville, the farmstead of Saint-Laurent was also playing host to a guest from the sky, albeit in more grisly fashion. Charles Levaillant and his eighteen-year-old brother, Hubert, were both sleeping deeply that night, having spent the previous evening carousing with friends. They first knew something was awry when they were woken by a sharp cry from one of the domestic staff.

'Hurry up! There's an American!'

The two brothers sat up in their beds for a moment, still groggy-headed, then threw on some clothes and rushed downstairs. A horrific sight greeted them. An American paratrooper stood by the front door, pale, exhausted and bearing terrible wounds. As twenty-year-old Charles stared at him in the moonlight, he noticed that 'his two hands had been torn off by a grenade and were transformed into bloody pieces of flesh.'[4] He pulled the man inside, sat him down and gave him a large shot of Calvados.

The commotion had by now wakened their mother, Madame Levaillant, who came downstairs and looked over the injured youth before ordering a bed to be brought into the living room. She was seemingly unfazed by the sight of the terrible wounds and gave him a dose of morphine from the phial she found in his kitbag. But she could also see that the poor lad needed more than morphine if his life was to be saved. His wounds required professional medical attention – and fast.

Charles offered to go for help, lacing his shoes and fetching his bicycle from the barn. He then made a spirited dash along the country lanes towards the nearby village of Quettehou, where he banged on the door of Monsieur Cardet, the trustworthy assistant pharmacist. Cardet got dressed and hurried back to the farm with Charles, but he shook his head when he saw the extent of the man's wounds. There was no option but to inform the Germans and get the soldier transported to hospital.

With great reluctance, Charles got back on his bike and cycled over to the German command post, where the local *kommandantur* was stationed. He felt bitterly sorry for the paratrooper. He was so young, perhaps the same age as him.

In the chaos of landing, and with radios broken or malfunctioning, Lieutenant Colonel Edward Krause was unaware that a small group of fellow Americans had seized the initiative and were engaged in hand-to-hand fighting in the streets of Sainte-Mère-Église. Among them was Ronald Snyder, a plucky twenty-year-old sergeant whose unit had spearheaded the invasions of both Sicily and Salerno. This, his third combat jump, had been the worst. He had fallen out of the plane head first and the jolt of the opening chute had sent a violent jerk through his body. 'Vast tracers lit the sky like silver confetti,' an exploding firework display that might have been exhilarating had it not been so uncomfortably close. To his alarm, Snyder realized that the tracer fire was 'ripping through my canopy'. He was still gaining speed when he hit the ground 'and slammed into a cow pasture like a sack of cement'.

His intense training now reaped dividends. He picked himself up, brushed off the wet mud and began looking around for anyone he could find. 'It was very dark, bewildered cows were everywhere and confusion reigned.' But he soon located his comrade, Lieutenant Orman, and the two of them lit their Very lights as a signal for fellow paratroopers. After assembling a small group, Snyder led them through the shadows towards the outskirts of town. As they reached the first buildings, another wave of C-47s passed overhead. The men watched, 'sickened and enraged, as volumes of silver tracer ripped through the fuselages'. Snyder whispered to his ten men: they would have their revenge by creeping into town and killing the Germans still manning the guns.

Krause had prepared them for exactly this sort of guerrilla attack. 'We moved quickly, filing past the darkened houses that lined the street named Chef-du-Pont. Enemy vehicles were roaring by on the main road ahead and suddenly one truck braked to a stop and troops from the back began firing wildly down the street.' Snyder split his men into two, ordering one group to cover the truck while he led the others down a connecting street so as to attack from a more secure position. 'This was always the main principle of our tactics. Never attack the strongpoint head on, but circle around and hit it from the flank.'

The first truck had left by the time they re-entered the main street, but other vehicles were coming and going as the Germans tried to make sense of the confusion. Snyder shouted the order to shoot, and 'we directed all of our fire and drove them out of town in a hail of bullets.'⁵

He and his band felt as if they were engaged in a lonely battle for Sainte-Mère-Église, but other parachutists were also converging on the town. Not for nothing were these men known as the elite. Among the more audacious of this advance guard was James Eads, a twenty-one-year-old engineering student from Illinois, whose original mission had been to capture one of the four raised causeways connecting Utah Beach and Sainte-Mère-Église. But like so many parachutists that night, Eads had been dropped in the wrong place at the wrong time.

Scarcely had he landed (in a heap of cow manure) when he glimpsed three soldiers running towards him. 'I could see the coal-bucket-style helmet and thought, Oh hell.' But his intensive training kicked in. He reached for his pistol, which was already loaded with a round in the chamber and seven in the clip. 'I thumbed back the hammer and started firing.' He was a good shot and the Germans were easy targets. 'The third man fell with my eighth round, right at my feet.'

Eads's ordeal was far from over. A German machine-gun nest opened up at him from a position seventy-five yards away. It was so accurate that the rounds were snapping through the leaves just above his head. 'Dammit,' he swore, 'is the whole Kraut army after me?' A bullet tore through his musette bag and another ripped through his map case. And then came an unexpected boom as the German position erupted into a sheet of flame.

'I got those over-anxious Kraut machine gunners with a grenade,' said a paratrooper who had appeared from nowhere. He looked down at Eads, still sprawled in the manure. 'Holy cow! You stink!'

In common with Snyder and his men, Eads and his companion now headed into Sainte-Mère-Église, vowing that nothing would stop them from accomplishing their mission. At one point they heard the stomp of hobnailed boots rounding a curve in the road.

Eads reached for his gun and 'started firing short bursts at the last man, then the second. All three fell.' Shortly afterwards, he spied a further ten Germans approaching. 'They were almost on top of us when we opened fire. All fell. Our surprise was complete.'

Surprise had always been the key element in the Americans' favour and Eads and his comrade used it to deadly effect in those early morning hours, playing a vicious game of guerrilla warfare. Although the situation on the ground was chaotic, they had but one goal – to wrest the little French town from its German occupiers. Adrenalin provided added impetus to their turbo-charged sense of purpose; it also overrode any feelings of fear. As the two of them darted through the outskirts of town, they were horrified to see 'troopers lying everywhere, almost all of them still in their chutes'. On approaching the main square, Eads even noticed one 'hanging from the spire of the church'. This was John Steele, who was wondering if he would ever make it down alive.

As the two men crouched in the shadows, a German troop-carrier roared into sight and advanced towards them at speed. Both began firing, aware that it was kill or be killed. 'One of us got the driver of the truck and it stopped and out of it the Krauts came.' Eads reloaded and was about to start firing again 'when I heard my buddy grunt and saw him fall'. He had been hit – fatally so – bringing their two-man spectacular to a deadly close.

Eads was now alone, with 600 rounds of ammunition and a keen will to survive. He had landed just ninety minutes earlier, yet those minutes had already carried him to hell and back. As he sidled across the square looking for comrades, he spied the hiding place of four German soldiers. He crept up and double-checked that his tommy gun was fully loaded before shooting them all down. He had rapidly learned to appreciate that gun. 'It's just like a garden hose. You aim it in the general direction of your target, hold on the trigger and wave it back and forth.' Some ammunition was invariably wasted, 'but you can't hardly miss hitting with some of them'.

Soon after, Eads noticed a group of fellow paratroopers hiding behind a low wall. There were eight of them, two of whom had been hit. Eads looked at their wounds and found that one was already dead 'and the other was past help'.[6]

This beleaguered group of men now tried to take stock of their situation, but with no working radio it was impossible to get any clarity. Sainte-Mère-Église was in a state of utter confusion, with no one in control and no one knowing what to do next.

The plan for capturing the town was more complex than simply driving out the Germans. It was imperative that the inevitable counter-attack be halted before it reached the outskirts, and this meant seizing the main road that led both north and south.

The northern approach had been assigned to Benjamin 'Vandy' Vandervoort, 3rd battalion commander of the 505th Parachute Infantry Regiment. He ticked the checklist of every attribute required by an officer of the Airborne: steel nerves, a sharp brain and a total insensibility to pain. He had imposed such a punishing training regime on his men that they cursed and damned him behind his back. But he would also earn their grudging respect. In the words of one stalwart who accompanied him to Normandy, 'if he had told us to follow him to hell, we would have gone with him.'[7] Such loyalty was fortunate, for he was indeed leading them into hell.

Vandervoort had suffered a disastrous landing. His plane had been flying too high and too fast when the moment came to jump. His chute opened so violently that it tore his neck and 'snapped blinding flashes in front of my eyes'. He landed heavily on a steep slope and felt a sharp pain in his ankle. He 'knew at once it was broken'. Frustrated but undeterred, he crawled into a hedgerow and 'shot myself in the leg with a morphine syrette [syringe with flexible tube] carried in our paratrooper's first aid kit'.

His injury would have put many men out of action, but Vandervoort was determined to see the night through. He reached for his Very pistol, loaded it and 'began to shoot up the green flares that were the visual assembly signal for my battalion'.[8]

One of those who saw the flare was Lyle Putnam, the battalion's medic. He made his way towards it and found his commander 'seated with a rain cape over him, reading a map by flashlight'. Vandervoort described his injuries and asked Putnam to examine his ankle 'with as little demonstration as possible'. It didn't take long to determine that the bone had 'a simple rather than a compound fracture'. When Vandervoort heard this, 'he insisted on replacing his jump-boot, laced it tightly, formed a makeshift crutch from a stick and moved with the outfit as an equal and a leader, without complaint.' Putnam had never warmed to Vandervoort, finding him 'a very proud individual'.[9] But even he was impressed at the manner in which he shook off the pain of the fracture.

By 2.30 a.m., Vandervoort had gathered together some fifty men. These now headed north, with orders to dig entrenched positions along the main road to Cherbourg. Vandervoort was unable to make the hike with a broken ankle, but he spotted two young parachutists with an ammunition cart and ordered them to wheel him there. They were indignant, telling him that they hadn't 'come all the way to Normandy to pull any damn colonel around'. They soon regretted their outburst. 'I persuaded them otherwise,'[10] said Vandervoort in typically laconic fashion. His men soon established an effective roadblock on the route out of town. Long before Sainte-Mère-Église itself was in Allied hands, the road to the north was secure.

Soon afterwards, the southern approaches were also sealed off with roadblocks, as was the country lane leading west to the little village of Chef-du-Pont. Leslie Palmer Cruise helped his twenty comrades place three rows of landmines in the road; they then dug themselves into foxholes. Sainte-Mère-Église was being squeezed from all sides.

They had not been there long when they heard the welcome thrum of an American jeep, one of many hundreds landed by glider that night. But their spirits were soon to take a knock. The jeep's driver had spied the roadblock and assumed it to be German. Only when it was too late did Cruise realize he was going to try to force his way through. 'Down the road they rode on full throttle.' He waved frantically into the darkness, but the vehicle was approaching at a terrific speed.

'*Hit the ground!*'

Cruise shoved his head into his foxhole as the jeep bowled towards him. It all happened in seconds. The engine roared like a beast and then the earth was rocked by a thunderous explosion.

'*Kapow! Boom!*' Cruise's eardrums almost burst. There was 'a deafening crescendo of explosive sounds as a number of our mines blew the jeep and its troopers into the air'. He lifted his head just in time to catch a glimpse of the unfolding catastrophe. 'Hell broke loose' as the jeep's trajectory changed from horizontal to vertical. Its chassis was blown to the heavens and fragmented into chunks of twisted steel. Then, 'in an arching skyward path, they landed in the hedgerow beyond.' Seconds later, the smaller lumps fell to earth and Cruise once again buried his head to avoid 'pieces of jeep and mine fragments raining down around us'. When all the mangled wreckage had landed, he and his comrades emerged to examine the damage. 'The smoking remains of the jeep were lying in the ditch of the roadside'[11] and all its occupants had been blown to shreds.

The Airborne Division's drop from the sky had gone spectacularly awry for many of the 13,000 paratroopers that night. Some had landed in the sea and been dragged to a watery grave. Others had drowned in the inundated meadows around Sainte-Mère-Église. Men had also been scattered many miles from their drop zones and found themselves with neither weapons nor equipment. They felt helpless and useless – the jokers in the pack – and yet these fright-ened stragglers were destined to play a vital role that night.

Tom Porcella was one of many whose first hour in France was particularly woeful. Even before he jumped, he was torn with anguish about what lay ahead. A devout Christian, he found the same ques-tion repeating itself in his head. 'Will I be able to kill a man?'

As it transpired, killing was the very last thing on his mind when he splashed down into one of the flooded meadows. His feet squelched deep into the mud and he was sucked beneath the surface of the water: he 'thought he was going to drown'. But if he lifted himself on to tiptoe, he could just about clutch at short gasps of air through his nostrils. 'My heart was beating so rapidly that I thought it would burst. I pleaded, "Oh God, please don't let me drown in this damn water in the middle of nowhere."'

His boots slurped even deeper into the mud as he attempted to cut the leg straps of the chute that was pulling him down. 'I came up for another breath of air . . . I wanted to scream for help . . . As I was gasping for air, I kept on saying Hail Marys.' His prayers were eventually answered, for he managed to extract his boots from the glue-like mud and heave himself into shallower water. But now he faced a new danger: a crippled plane was hurtling towards him at high speed and it 'sounded like the scream of a human being about to die'.

He lurched forward, desperate to escape its trajectory. The water held him back. 'Oh my God! It's coming towards me!' But it bucked as it passed overhead and crashed into an adjacent field, exploding into a sheet of flame.

Porcella was still in shoulder-high water when he heard a voice. '*Flash . . .?*'

It was his battalion's password, for which the answer ought to have been 'Thunder'. But he neglected to answer, for he recognized the voice as belonging to his buddy, Dale Cable. It was a near-fatal mistake. 'Pushing the weeds from side to side, my right hand hit against an object and I heard the click of a trigger.' Cable repeated the password and this time Porcella gave the requisite reply. He was met with a torrent of abuse. Cable was furious 'and proceeded to give me hell for not answering the first time'.

Other comrades had also landed in that flooded meadow. Tommy Horne had come down close by, along with Tommy Lott and Kenneth High. As the four of them emerged from the water, they were hit by a blast of German machine-gun fire. They all scattered in the darkness. When the fire-fight was over, Porcella was once again alone.

But not for long. By now it seemed as if there were an American paratrooper in every field and Porcella found himself teaming up with a young soldier named Cantenberry. They were making their way along a country lane when they heard the unmistakable sound of an approaching German motorcycle. Porcella's instinct was to hide but Cantenberry took a rather different approach. 'I'll shoot the son of a bitch.' He meant it. Porcella watched in appalled fascination as Cantenberry raised his rifle and waited until the motorcyclist was about fifty feet from where he was standing. 'Gee,' he thought. 'The Ten Commandments say "Thou shalt not kill." There is either something wrong with the Ten Commandments or there is something wrong with the rules of the world today.'

Cantenberry fired a single shot and scored a direct hit. 'The German was suspended in mid-air, while the motorcycle continued to go on and crashed into the side of the road.' It was like the scene from a cartoon, only far more deadly. Out of morbid curiosity, Porcella went to take a look. The blond-haired German soldier 'just laid there in the middle of the road, laying on his back, his arms were outstretched'. He guessed the youth was about twenty years old, almost the same as him. It was a terrible shock. 'The first dead German I had seen.'[12]

Like so many paratroopers, Porcella was lost, bedraggled and unable to undertake the mission assigned to him. He felt like an irrelevant wanderer in the unfolding drama. Yet he was unwittingly playing an important role in the events of that night, for the wide scattering of airborne troops was causing considerable confusion among German generals. They could not work out the Allied game plan. Until they knew the answer, they were unable to deploy their troops effectively.

Edward 'Cannonball' Krause had spent the previous hour and a half assembling enough men for his assault on Sainte-Mère-Église. In that time, he had gathered a force of almost 200 paratroopers, some from his own battalion and some from units landed far from their intended drop zones. This impromptu band of soldiers now set off along a secluded path that wound its way into town. Leading from the front was 'a slightly inebriated Frenchman' who had been seized by one of Krause's men and forced to show them the way. 'We made him go first,' said Krause, 'so that he would not lead us into any gun position.'[13]

Krause was unaware that other members of his battalion had already converged on Sainte-Mère-Église. Robert Snyder and James Eads were not alone in penetrating the town's defences: young Chris Christensen had also led a group through the mud-churned fields. It had been tough going, 'much like running an obstacle course with all those damn hedgerows'. It had also been scary, and Christensen 'had this eerie feeling of being watched'. As they entered the deserted streets on the outskirts of town, there was the acrid smell of cordite in the air. Christensen noticed strange objects hanging in the trees and went to investigate. The sight was too ghoulish for comfort: dead paratroopers swinging head down from the branches.

He was still reeling from this macabre spectacle when Lieutenant Colonel Krause appeared from nowhere. Krause might have congratulated Christensen for his initiative in leading a frontal advance; instead, he criticized him for getting distracted by corpses. Christensen had never liked Krause and this reprimand was the final straw. He privately hoped there would be 'an enemy sniper in the vicinity who would see and realize he was an officer and plug him between the eyes'.[14]

Krause was unpopular but efficient. He sent a company of men into the heart of town with orders to flush out any remaining Germans. Among those involved in this dangerous operation was Bill Tucker, who now encountered his first French civilians. 'These were the people that were being liberated,' he said, 'but they didn't look all that joyful at the time.'

Tucker was accompanied by his friend, Larry Leonard, who set up their machine gun under a tree. Tucker felt a shiver of nerves. 'It was suddenly very quiet and I felt very strange. It seemed as if something was moving very close to me and I swung the gun around, but didn't see anything until I looked above me.' Another dead parachutist was hanging from the branches. He had been shot and was 'swaying back and forth' like a heavy human pendulum. Tucker was mesmerized. All he could think was that the man 'had very big hands'.

The two of them now ran across the square in front of the church, looking for a new place to set up their machine gun. As they passed the church door, Tucker stumbled over a dead German. 'His skin was sort of blue and there was blood on the corner of his mouth running out.'[15] This was probably the soldier killed by John Ray as he lay dying in agony.

The men sent by Edward Krause to sweep through Sainte-Mère-Église achieved their goal in less than one hour. They took some thirty prisoners and killed a handful more. But most of the Germans, like Rudi Escher and his friends, had already fled.

Krause himself headed straight to the town hall, whipped out the American flag from his haversack and hoisted it on to the flagpole. He then radioed a message through to Colonel William Ekman, commander of the 505th Parachute Infantry Regiment. There was more than a touch of self-aggrandisement in his choice of words.

'I have secured Sainte-Mère-Église.'[16] This was true enough, but he made it sound as if he had achieved it single-handed.

Lieutenant Colonel Krause knew that the Germans were certain to launch a counter-attack within hours. He also knew that he must hold the town until reinforcements arrived from Utah Beach. Winning Sainte-Mère-Église was only half the battle. Holding it looked set to prove rather more difficult.

A staggering 6,939 vessels headed to Normandy on D-Day. Many were moored at Southampton harbour. 'A mass of shipping stretching right out of sight.'

9

Night Assault

IT WAS A pig of a night, with rain lashing down and a brisk sea
gale that was strengthening with every hour that passed. Forty
miles from the French coast and wishing he was dead, Cliff Morris
was clutching his stomach as he fought to hold down his supper.

The journey had been bad enough at the beginning, when they
were still sheltered by the land. Even then, the shallow-draught
landing craft had been pitched half-sideways by the swell, causing
Morris and his pals to reach for their pink seasickness pills. But
now it was like riding a liquid seesaw. 'Instead of just tossing and
rolling about', their vessel was 'being lifted clean out of the water
and landing back with a dull thud that shook every beam and threw
all its occupants from one side to the other'.[1]

Morris had a thumping headache caused by the tablets and was
regretting the tinned soup, cocoa and biscuits that were swilling in
his stomach like lukewarm bilge water. The hearty camaraderie that
had marked the beginning of the voyage seemed to belong to
another era. Now, the back-slapping and singing had been replaced
by the deep vroom of the engines and the terrifying creak of the
landing craft's wooden frame.

Morris feared that the craft would either capsize or split apart.
If so, there was no hope of rescue, for the man in charge of the
fleet, Rear Admiral Arthur Talbot, had told the captain of each
ship that 'under no circumstances' were they 'to stop to pick up
survivors'. In case his injunction left any room for doubt, he had
reiterated that any capsized vessel was to be abandoned to its fate.
'Drive on!' he had told the assembled captains in a tone of gung-ho
abandon. 'Drive on!'[2]

By the time Morris and company were mid-Channel, they were
beyond caring. The thick stench of diesel that hung heavy in the

stagnant compartments below decks was only adding to their misery. 'We felt so bad that we began to wish we were dead.'³

Morris was by no means alone in his predicament. There were twenty-two landing craft in his little flotilla, as well as an American cutter and a hospital ship. All these storm-tossed vessels were under the overall command of Rupert Curtis, a briskly spoken captain with a keen eye and genial smile. But this mini-fleet, codename S9, was only one tiny part of Force S, a massive armada of more than 1,000 ships and landing craft tasked with storming Sword Beach, the most easterly of the five landing beaches.

To Cliff Morris and his comrades, the sight of Force S filling the massive harbour at Portsmouth had been little short of breath-taking. 'The whole of Cowes Roads and Southampton Water, as far as the eye could reach, was packed with shipping. Thousands of ships and landing craft of all kinds filled the sea; in the sky were serried ranks of balloons, hundreds and hundreds of them, the farthest mere pinpricks in the sky.'⁴

It became even more impressive once they were out at sea, 'a mass of shipping stretching right out of sight'.⁵ It was as if the whole world had taken to the water. Morris and friends had learned in their schooldays of the mighty Spanish Armada, the greatest invading force in history, yet King Philip's flotilla was a mere speck in the ocean compared to the fleet now under sail. Morris himself was on LCI 503, a medium-sized landing craft, yet even this was far larger than the galleons in King Philip's fleet. And LCI 503 was just one wheel in the cog. On that blustery June night in 1944, no fewer than 6,939 vessels were heading towards Normandy, including more than 4,000 landing craft. The service personnel numbered almost 200,000, larger than the population of most English provincial towns.

Each of the landing craft in Rupert Curtis's S9 flotilla had some 200 men aboard, all commandos, who had spent weeks studying the shoreline on which they would be landing. But only now – once they were at sea – did they learn that their destination was Normandy. They were told they would be landing at Ouistreham, a coastal village that none of them had heard of and few of them could pronounce. The only thing they knew for sure was that '144 big guns would be firing on us.'⁶

They were to land under the leadership of Simon Fraser, the 15th Lord Lovat, a flamboyant Highland chief with a patrician charm and an indomitable spirit. His friend, Iain Moncreiffe, described him as a *grand seigneur* with an 'indefinable star quality'.[7] Indefinable, perhaps, but also carefully nurtured by his lordship. Only Lovat would have the swagger to go into battle with a Highland piper at his side. And only he would have the panache to wear a mono-grammed shirt under his battledress. Known to his friends as Shimi Lovat – an anglicized version of his Gaelic name – he spoke the English of the ruling elite, all drawled inflexions and liquid vowels. Although his ancestral estates were deep in the Scottish Highlands, there was not a dram of Gaelic brogue.

Just thirty-three years of age, Lord Lovat had the wind-blown air of an Elizabethan pirate-adventurer. But his ancestral pedigree was a great deal more distinguished than that of a mere buccaneer. One of his medieval forebears was reputed to have slain a nine-foot dragon, while another, his fourteenth-century Scottish namesake, had defeated the English three times in a single day at the Battle of Roslin.

Lesser men might have been cowed by such a heritage. Not so Lovat. Appointed commander of the 1st Special Service Brigade, he had vowed to create the finest unit ever to go into battle.*

In common with other front-line leaders, Lovat knew that only the best prepared men would pull through D-Day. To this end, he trained them halfway to death, with enforced marches and full-scale practice assaults on the Sussex coast between Angmering and Littlehampton. By the beginning of June, he believed his commandos were 'a military machine as perfect as any which history can show'.[8]

Lovat had learned from experience that men could achieve great things if properly led. To this end, he hand-picked a choice selec-tion of unit leaders. Cliff Morris and his comrades in 6 Commando had Derek Mills-Roberts as their standard-bearer, an ex-solicitor who found life on the front line decidedly more stimulating than resolving divorces and house purchases.

A close chum of Lovat since their days together at Oxford

---

* In 1941 Lord Lovat's first cousin, David Stirling, had founded the elite 'L' Detachment Special Air Service Brigade, which became the SAS.

University, Mills-Roberts had fought guerrilla skirmishes in Arctic Norway, escaped with his life from the disastrous 1942 Dieppe raid and whirled his way through the North African desert storms. 'Jet-propelled with consuming energy' was how Lord Lovat described him. He was a pit-bull of a man who spoke in 'blistering language' and was 'not to be trifled with, drunk or sober'.[9] Both friends and foes alike were terrified of him 'as he strutted around waving his big stick'[10] – it was a shillelagh or Irish blackthorn cudgel – looking for all the world like a brute with a grudge. Commando Donald Gilchrist said that 'when he exploded, everyone felt the blast.' Yet the men in his troop soon came to realize that 'Mills-Bomb-Roberts' represented their best hope of surviving D-Day in one piece. 'For all his bark, he was a born leader and the lads would have followed him everywhere.'[11]

This devotion on the part of his soldiers was extended to Lovat himself, whose 'ice-cold brain'[12] had understood something of paramount importance in everything that was to come. To win a war, you needed to understand the psychology of those who were fighting it. You needed to fire them up and make them believe in themselves. At times, that meant putting on a darn fine show, one so loud and exuberant that it would be remembered for years to come. And that is why, when the commandos had embarked at Portsmouth on the previous evening, Lovat had planned it to unfold like some martial version of a Mardi Gras carnival, with colour, festivity and most of all noise.

Rarely had men gone to war with such panache as Lovat's commandos. It began with his personal bagpiper, Bill Millin, blasting out old favourites from the helm of Rupert Curtis's landing craft. Curtis himself was almost overcome with emotion. 'The skirl of the pipes worked some strange magic that evening, for it set the troops in the waiting transports cheering from ship to ship, so that the Solent rang and echoed with the sound.'[13]

Next, Lovat got the various captains to play their gramophones through the ships' loudspeakers, sending a cacophony of joyous tunes over the Solent. There was a moment's pause in the music, in which Curtis heard guffaws of laughter coming from the wardroom below. It was Lord Lovat, entertaining two of his colonels. But the laughter was soon drowned out by the craft anchored behind his own. Denis Glover, the ebullient captain of Derek Mills-Roberts's landing craft, started blasting 'Hearts of Oak' over the water. Even the leonine Mills-Roberts seemed tamed. 'Stirring chords,'[14] he admitted as he bawled the rousing words of the chorus: *We'll fight and we'll conquer again and again.*

Cliff Morris and friends were determined to enjoy every second of their departure from England. It was a wilder send-off than they had ever imagined. 'Everyone was now on deck laughing and shouting and the radio playing away with swing music. What a feeling! I do not think anyone had a care in the world.'[15] Others felt a burst of patriotism. 'I never loved England so truly as at that moment,'[16] confessed commando Reginald Barnes. One man alone was alarmed by everything that was to come. The medic of 4 Commando, Dr Joe Patterson, had been casting nervous glances at the sea beyond the harbour. 'It was blowing half a gale from the south-west and banking up black and beastly for what promised to be a dirty night.'[17]

Eight hours later, in the rain-swept period before dawn, the party was well and truly over. Derek Mills-Roberts cast his eye over the men on board and was appalled by what he saw. Most were 'abominably sick'[18] and some were so ill they were unable to move. Only Lord Lovat seemed immune. He had borrowed Curtis's bunk and was sleeping soundly. 'I can snore through any form of disturbance,' he would later say, 'provided I go to bed with a clear mind.' On this particular night, his mind had been titillated by the discovery of a copy of Dr Marie Stopes's bedroom guide for young couples. 'Remarkable,' thought his lordship as he flicked through the pages. 'Full of surprises.' He summoned over a young bachelor named Peter Young in order to give him a brief education in matters of the flesh. 'Soft beds and hard battles had something in common after all!'[19] he quipped.

Up on deck, Commander Curtis was fighting hard with the wheel as he steered his landing craft through a sheet of driving spray. This was far from easy, for 'the seas were heavy and hitting our small, shallow-draught craft hard, causing them to roll and plunge sickeningly.'[20] Curtis had a bosun's legs and anchors for feet, yet even he was finding it hard to stay upright. Worse than this, he had to keep his vessel within the narrow channel swept by minesweepers earlier that evening, one of ten channels cleared through to the Normandy coast. He knew that Rommel's offshore minefields, packed with more than 6 million mines, represented a deadly threat to the Allied fleet.

All vessels had been forbidden the use of navigation lights and their only guidance was the blue stern light of the ship in front. Curtis kept his eye on this 'very dim' light, but it kept vanishing into the sea spray. His only consolation was being in occasional radio contact with HMS *Starling*, one of the escort ships, commanded by the legendary Frederic Walker. He was a U-boat hunter extraordinaire who had sunk more German submarines than any other Royal Navy captain. Curtis hoped that he would display similar mettle when he came to land his commandos on the beaches.

The night crossing was bad enough for the commandos of Flotilla S9, but it was even worse for Lionel Roebuck and his comrades in the East Yorkshire Regiment. They were in the vanguard of Force S and were due to land on Sword Beach in the first wave at 7.25 a.m., more than an hour before the commandos. They felt like lambs to the slaughter. They had undergone little intense training and done no simulated landings. Although they had been pushed through a fitness regime, it was never so arduous that it prevented them from catching the evening train to Guildford and getting royally drunk. Once back at camp, they would lark around in their tents and piss in each other's boots.

If their training was rudimentary, then so was their embarkation. There was none of the pageantry laid on by Lord Lovat. Instead local ladies served them tea and home-baked cakes on the quayside (at threepence a serving, paid for out of their own wages) before they boarded their landing craft.

Roebuck's bunk area was in a watertight compartment. If the compartment were to be holed by an enemy torpedo, it would be immediately sealed, along with all the men inside. Roebuck mulled over the prospect of drowning in an enclosed metal box before deciding it was 'not a pleasant thought with which to start off the long sea voyage'.

The East Yorks may not have had such a colourful send-off as the commandos, but the atrocious weather soon placed everyone on an even keel. Roebuck had made the mistake of wolfing a glutinous meat stew and a large brick of chocolate, all washed down with a pitcher of strong tea. As the gathering storm caused his landing craft to reel and lurch, he felt his supper swilling into his throat. He swallowed hard, and swallowed again, but it was no use. He was violently sick, first on deck and then over the side. His head was spinning and his legs had turned to jelly. His only consolation came when he looked at his mates. Many were 'in a far worse condition' than him and 'lay green and immobile on their bunks'.[21]

Their sorry predicament was not helped by the ship's cooks, who lit their petrol stoves mid-Channel and began frying up a night-time breakfast that few could stomach: greasy bacon, tinned sausages and fried bread slopping around in pools of liquid suet.

Roebuck noticed that his friend Micky Riley was studying a map of the French coastline. For the first time it had the real names of the coastal villages and ports. It was from Riley that Roebuck learned that they would be landing at a place called Lion-sur-Mer.

They were given some last-minute additions to their vast rucksack of equipment: 200 French francs (in 5 franc notes), a box of water sterilizing tablets and 'dire warnings against drinking milk'. One of the last pieces of advice – off the record, of course – concerned 'the problems of taking too many prisoners'.[22] Dead Germans, they were told, were a lot less trouble than captured ones.

The men pondered this for a moment. If they were being advised to shoot captured Germans, then the Germans were undoubtedly being told to shoot them. It was an uncomfortable thought, but one that belonged to the future. First, they had to survive the terrors of the landing. There was not long to go. Within a few hours, the entire stretch of coastline from Lion-sur-Mer to Franceville-Plage would be visible through the early morning drizzle.

The wind was still snapping angrily at the foreshore when Lieutenant Raimund Steiner took a final look outside his coastal observation post at Franceville-Plage. Almost midnight. He stood on the wind-swept beach for a moment and watched the low cloud scudding across the moon. There was drizzle in the air and a white crest on the waves. 'Bad weather,'[23] he muttered to himself. 'Not the kind of weather for an invasion.'[24] He stepped back inside his bunker, slipped into pyjamas (contrary to army regulations) and prepared for an early night.

Steiner was in desperate need of sleep. Over the previous two weeks, his nights had been shattered by the relentless aerial bombardment of the gun battery at Merville, a massive fortified redoubt whose 160 gunners and sentries were under his command. It was a formidable defensive position whose four gun emplacements were buried in eighteen feet of concrete and earth. Its guns had a sweeping field of fire, positioned to dominate the sandy foreshore between Ouistreham and Langrune.

Steiner was young to be in charge of such an important battery – a youthful twenty-four-year-old with a boyish face and melancholic eyes. There was good reason for the haunted expression: he had lived through a nightmare ever since the Nazis marched into his native Austria in 1938. First, Hitler's henchmen had come for his father, a distinguished Innsbruck councillor, and tortured him in Dachau for his outspoken liberal opinions. When the old man was released after eleven months of hell, Steiner found himself confronting someone he barely recognized. 'An emaciated man stood there in our doorway. He was shaking and in tears and all the hair had been burned from his head.' He died of his injuries just months later.

Once the Nazis had dealt with the elder Steiner, they came for Raimund himself, putting him through a political re-education process before conscripting him into the Mountain Artillery Regiment. Injured in Norway, half-starved at Stalingrad and grievously wounded in Yugoslavia, he was sent to Normandy to convalesce. When he reported for duty at Merville, still wearing his mountain breeches, he was greeted with sarcasm by Major-General Wilhelm Richter, commander of the 716 Infantry Division. 'Ha! A gentleman in baby's nappies, I see,'[25] sneered Richter. 'Get yourself a correct officer's uniform.'

Steiner was never going to become a Nazi, but he was nevertheless appalled by the debauchery of the local battery officers, especially Lieutenant Siegfried Ebenfeld. When they first met, Ebenfeld drunkenly introduced him to his French mistress. 'Her thick makeup was smeared and a false eyelash had stuck to one cheek.' Steiner snapped a military salute. 'That can wait until morning,' slurred Ebenfeld. 'Where's supper?'[26]

It was little wonder that Steiner's men spent half their time drunk, for the nightly bombardment of their bunker had brought them close to breaking point. Among those who lived in this underground world was the battery's twenty-eight-year-old sergeant major, Hans Buskotte. Only a week earlier, he had emerged from his casement with shredded nerves and a pounding in his skull. A bomb had exploded on the concrete roof above him and scoured a crater the depth of a jackboot. Buskotte told Steiner that he felt 'as if someone had hit his helmet with a hammer'.[27]

Steiner was more fortunate than his men, for his living quarters were a few hundred metres to the north of Merville Battery, amid the sand dunes of Franceville-Plage. From here, he was in regular telephone contact with Hans Buskotte.

Steiner had fallen into a deep sleep on the night of 5 June and had no idea that thousands of paratroopers had already landed in Normandy. The first he knew something was wrong was when he was abruptly woken by the ring of his telephone. He glanced at his watch: it was 0.25 a.m. local time (1.25 a.m. in Britain). He lifted the receiver and heard a frantic voice at the other end.

'Herr Leutnant,' said a breathless Hans Buskotte, 'a cargo glider has come down at our battery and we are in close quarters fighting.'[28] He said that the glider had crash-landed into the bunker's minefield and was now a burning wreck.

Buskotte's news shocked Steiner: this must surely be the start of the Allied invasion. He immediately phoned his commander, Major-General Richter, who was furious at having been woken from his sleep. 'When an aircraft crashes, don't imagine it is an invasion,' he snapped. Steiner insisted it was serious, speaking in his strong Austrian accent. This merely provoked a torrent of anti-Austrian invective from the general. Steiner was shaken and angry. 'He did not take me seriously. He was not interested.'[29] Indeed, Richter hung up the phone without another word, logging the call at an incorrect time in the regimental diary.

Steiner was so alarmed by Buskotte's phone call that he got dressed and stepped outside. He heard a distant thundering that soon grew into a roar. And then he saw a sight he would never forget, 'an endless stream of bomber formations' flying so low in the sky that he 'could see the engine exhausts glowing and flaming'. Steiner followed their trajectory as they bombed Merville and the west bank of the River Orne.

When he glanced back towards the bunker, he saw dozens of massive gliders swooping in from the sea. He was amazed. 'I could not understand how such things could fly.'

The gliders were still passing overhead when Hans Buskotte called for a second time. On this occasion, the panic could be heard in his voice. He was deep inside the bunker's underground command post, with his eye clamped to the rubber eye-piece of the periscope. Through this coin-sized disc of glass he could see the moonlit silhouettes of figures crawling through the thick mud and cutting their way through the coils of barbed wire. When he swung the periscope through 180 degrees, he got a wider view. Shadowy forms were also advancing through the minefield.

And then, lit by the ghastly glow of a burning glider, he saw an even more alarming sight. The attackers were dragging behind them weapons of destruction, including 'flamethrowers, compressed air-drills and explosives'. It was made all the more unreal by the fact of watching it through the periscope. 'The enemy gets closer, in a large semi-circle. Here, a shadow jumps up and sinks into a crater. Over there crouches a dark shape as the earth swallows it.'[30]

This was no small-scale raid. And these were no amateurs. Buskotte watched them drag a machine gun into position and felt a tight lump in his throat. He had but one thought in his head. 'We are outnumbered.'[31]

Less than twenty yards away, Alan Mower was having exactly the same thought as he slithered through the quagmire. One of a small group of parachutists charged with assaulting the Merville Battery, this was his first time in action. It was not going well. He had landed heavily on the roof of a farm building and badly injured his leg when he tumbled to the ground. Worse still, his knee had somehow rammed itself into his stomach 'and knocked the wind out of him'. He was in such pain that he almost lost consciousness. As he lay there collecting his breath, he peered into the darkness in the hope of seeing his comrades. But there was no one.

'*Boiled beef. Boiled beef.*' He called out the password as loud as he dared. He was hoping to hear the pre-agreed reply, *Carrots*, but no one answered. He crept over to a nearby orchard, tripping over a dead comrade as he did so. 'Sorry, mate,' he said as he helped himself to the man's ammunition.

When he reached the orchard he bumped into Private 'Towny' Townsend, one of the soldiers from his platoon. 'This is a right fuck-up,'[32] said Townsend. He told Mower that he had stumbled across two more of their platoon – Bobby Clarke and 'Arsie-Tarsie' Hughes – who had been killed in the jump.

In a field just a few hundred feet away, Sid Capon was feeling equally despondent. He was fortunate to have landed without hurting himself and had immediately looked around, expecting 'to see hundreds of us'.[33] Instead, all he could make out was a few dead cows and the unmistakable silhouette of Bert Hill.

'*Punch,*' shouted Hill. It was the code word for their platoon.

The pre-agreed answer was *Judy*, predictably enough, but Capon was still dazed from the jump and merely muttered his own name. 'Thank Christ for that,' answered Hill, before giving him the bad news. 'We've lost everything bar a few grenades.'[34]

As the other men from the Merville assault team landed and collected their scattered equipment, they made their way to the agreed rendezvous. When Alan Jefferson pitched up, he found his commanding officer, Terence Otway, 'looking very peculiar indeed'.[35] The reason for this soon became apparent. 'The drop's a bloody chaos,' he said. 'There's hardly anybody here.'[36] Jefferson looked round and saw just a handful of men. 'It dawned on us that something had gone frantically wrong.'[37]

The men had been alerted to the possibility of disaster shortly before leaving England. Brigadier James Hill had warned the airborne forces of the extreme danger of their mission. 'Gentlemen,' he had said, 'in spite of your excellent orders and training, do not be daunted if chaos reigns. It undoubtedly will.'[38] Hill was rarely wrong and this occasion was no exception. The landing had been a total disaster. Otway had trained no fewer than 750 men for the assault on Merville. Of these, fewer than 100 had made it to the rendezvous. The rest had been shot, captured or sucked into the flooded meadows. Otway himself had tried to pull several of them from the viscous mud, but their sixty-pound kitbags made it impossible. 'The suction was unbelievable. We just couldn't get them out.'[39] They all drowned.

Otway explained to Jefferson that he had none of the special explosives needed to destroy the Merville guns, nor mortars, nor anti-tank guns, nor even any wireless sets. The gliders had failed to land inside the battery perimeter fence, as intended, and the medical teams had yet to be located. Equally distressing was the fact that every single Lancaster bomber supporting the operation had missed its target, a testimony to the difficulties of bombing at night. Instead of hitting the battery, they had dropped their 1,000-pound bombs on the men's intended route into the Merville compound.

Otway waited for fifteen minutes, agonizing over what to do. In that time, another fifty stragglers arrived at the rendezvous. But he still had only a fifth of his men and many of his platoon leaders had failed to materialize. He turned to Jefferson, a junior subaltern, and promptly promoted him to commander of C Company. 'Well, don't just stand there. Get on, go and see your company.' Jefferson did just that and discovered that it consisted of five men, two of whom were seriously injured. 'It was really lamentable.'[40]

Otway was caught in a terrible dilemma. 'Do I go with 150?' he asked himself. 'Or do I pack it in?' He turned to Joe Wilson, his batman, and betrayed a rare moment of weakness. 'I don't know what I'm going to do, Wilson.'

Wilson stiffened and replied, 'There's only one thing, sir.' He then handed Otway a hip flask 'as if it were a decanter on a silver tray'[41] and added, with the calm deference that only a former valet could truly muster, 'Shall we have our brandy now, sir?'[42]

In the space of a few minutes, Otway dramatically modified the plan of attack. He divided the men into four assault groups, each composed of twelve men, and also formed two diversion parties. A small reserve group was to be held back, along with the few medical officers who had by now arrived. The assault was to be led by Allen Parry, who had spent the last twenty minutes up a tree, trying to attract stray parachutists with his lamp and whistle.

There was one glimmer of good news. Two of Otway's men, Dusty Miller and Paul Greenway, had proved that their commander's exhaustive training programme had not been in vain. Despite losing their mine-detectors and their marking tape, they had nevertheless 'crawled through the minefield, neutralising the mines with their fingers'. Once this was done, they had 'sat on their backsides and dragged their heels on the ground, making a path through the minefield'. Even Otway felt this beyond the call of duty. 'Quite extraordinary,'[43] he said.

When it was clear that no one else was going to arrive, Otway ordered the men to move up to the barbed-wire perimeter fence, a 2,400-yard crawl through waterlogged craters and shell-holes filled with mud that was 'greyish and wet and nasty and sticky'.[44] Some of the craters were huge. To Alan Mower's eyes, they looked 'big enough to drop houses in'.

He was momentarily distracted by a voice in the darkness. 'Look over there!' He glanced up and saw 'a ball of fire in the sky' and heard the deep roar of engines. 'Hope the poor bastards get out of that,' said the lad who was sharing his muddy crater. But the plane was doomed. 'The bomber literally broke in half and two tiny dots of men on parachutes fell out – but only two.' Seconds later, an out-of-control glider skimmed over their heads, 'so close that it almost seemed possible to touch it'. It was hit with a burst of anti-aircraft fire and seemed to pause in mid-air, as if trying to remain airborne. Seconds later, it burst into flame and crash-landed into an orchard some fifty yards away. Mower knew that twenty-two of his comrades and friends had been on board.

'*Move up!*'[45]

The men resumed their crawl through the mud and puddles and only stopped when they reached the outer ring of wire that surrounded the Merville Battery. A burst of German machine-gun fire caused them to push themselves deep into the wet mud.

'Give us covering fire,'[46] yelled Mike Dowling.

Jefferson raised his head to take a peek at the battery. 'The moon was coming and going behind clouds and we had our first sight of the casements, looking like toads squatting there, somehow nasty.' He couldn't see how they could capture the battery's four casements with so few men, yet he was willing to have a go. He slithered over to his little group and gave them an impromptu pep talk. 'We're here, we're trained for it, we're ready for it,' he said.

'If we don't do it, imagine what will happen to your wives and daughters.'[47]

It was already 4.45 a.m., far later than intended, and Otway knew that it was now or never. But the assault could not begin until gaps had been blown through the perimeter fence. Mike Dowling crawled forward with two Bangalore torpedoes – a tube-shaped explosive used to clear low-lying obstacles – and slipped them under the barbed wire. Even though the moon was partially obscured by cloud, Alan Jefferson could see Dowling 'grinning hugely and thoroughly enjoying himself'.[48]

The blast of the torpedoes was the prelude to the assault. Two violent explosions blew wire and clods of earth into the night sky. 'Get ready, men.' Allen Parry gave a shrill blast on his whistle. Jefferson blew his hunting horn.

'Get in! Get in!'[49] yelled Otway.

'Bastards! Bastards! Bastards!'

Sid Capon was bawling at the top of his voice as he charged towards the open gap in the wire. He was heading for the first casemate, one of the four semi-underground gun emplacements, along with Alan Mower and Alan Jefferson. Its flat domed top looked like a mini-volcano in the half-light of the cloud-covered moon.

'Mines!'[50] yelled a voice. Bullets were zipping through the air and smacking into the wet earth.

Jefferson was hurtling forward when something slapped hard on his leg. 'I went down like a sheep on its back.' Sprawled in the mud and sprayed with shrapnel, he watched the others continue their charge. He felt inexplicably calm. 'My goodness,' he thought, 'the training has worked.'[51]

Allen Parry had also been brought down by gunfire. 'I was conscious of something striking my left thigh, my leg collapsed under me and I fell into a huge bomb crater.' He saw one of his men run past, 'looking at me as if to say: "Bad luck mate"'.[52]

Parry was in a bad way. 'My left leg was numb and my trouser leg was soaked in blood.'[53] He removed his whistle lanyard and tied it to his leg as a tourniquet, but he did it in the wrong place and lost all feeling. After reapplying it, he was able to drag himself out of the crater and continue the fight.

Private Smith hit a mine that exploded in front of him, gouging out an eye. Hal Hudson received multiple wounds to his stomach and clutched at his open belly with his hand. He could feel sticky blood pumping out and tried desperately to staunch the flow.

'Are you all right?' asked Otway as he ran past.

'I think so.'

'He's been hit in the stomach,' said a voice from the gloom.

'Oh, bad luck.'[54]

Mower and Capon were now so close to casemate one that they could see the camouflage netting. Mower saw 'dead Germans all around',[55] most of them sprawled in a churn of mud. Capon noticed that the rear steel doors were ajar and seized the moment, hurling two fragmentation grenades inside. The effect of the explosion in a confined space was devastating.

'*Kamarad! Kamarad! Russki! Russki!*' Those who survived the initial blast came running out with their hands up. They wore greatcoats and soft hats and looked totally unprepared for what had just hit them.

'What the hell are they on about?' thought Capon.[56] Only later did he realize that they were Russians fighting for the Germans.

Parry was watching everything unfold from the distance of a few feet. 'The chaps fired like hell into them and shrieks came from them.'[57] Many were nursing gaping wounds. 'The last chappy was a big chap, he wore glasses and was in a terrible state.'[58]

Alan Mower peered through the blackness of the casemate, then cautiously moved inside. He could see a field gun on a platform with a stack of shells all around it. He was about to lob a grenade on to the pile when he was struck by 'a terrific belt in the back' that felt 'like thousands of red-hot needles'. He collapsed on to the wooden floorboards of the casemate, 'unable to control his legs, which were kicking involuntarily'. He wondered if he was dead. His comrade, George Hawkins, had also been hit. A third comrade was killed by shrapnel to his head.

'For God's sake, take my things off,' Mower was shouting into the gloom. When no one responded he turned to the injured Hawkins. 'Let's crawl in here.' The two of them pushed deeper into the casemate, both in great pain.

'Don't leave us, don't leave us!' they pleaded with Paddy Jenkins when they saw him entering the casemate. Mower was by now in such pain that he begged Jenkins to shoot him. 'For Christ sake, finish me off, please.'

Jenkins stayed cool. 'Don't be silly, you'll be all right.'[59]

He stepped back outside, only to stumble over a German soldier feigning death. 'I've just seen this bastard move.'[60] He shouted it to no one in particular before shooting the man with his Lee Enfield rifle and giving him the *coup de grâce* with his bayonet.

'Don't leave me, don't, please.'[61] Hawkins was crying for help as he watched Mower being lifted on to a cart. Scores of injured men lay sprawled in the mud and bullets were still zinging through the darkness. Yet the attack was nowhere near as disastrous as it appeared. Harold Long and a clutch of his fifteen men had reached the fourth casemate and almost overwhelmed it, while Barney Ross and his team had made it to the third. It was so dark that his men could scarcely see a thing, but they managed to locate the air vents and used them to hurl their grenades into the chamber below. 'By the time we got round to the front of the gun,' said Ross, 'the guys had had enough.'

'*Kamerad! Kamerad! Kamerad!*' Yet more Russians emerged from the darkness. Ross had lost so many men that he felt no sympathy. 'We'd have liked to have shot the bloody lot.'[62]

Hans Buskotte had been monitoring the unfolding assault through the lens of his underground periscope. He had always thought that the casemates were impregnable, but he now saw they had their vulnerable points. When the air in the bunkers became 'so thin that the lungs protest',[63] it was necessary to open the vents. Otway's men had been quick to spot this vulnerability and exploited it by tossing their grenades inside.

Still at his observation post at Franceville-Plage, Raimund Steiner was trying to make sense of what was taking place. He had put a call through to the battery just a few minutes earlier and was distressed to hear the suffering of his men. 'Down the line I could hear my men were suffocating. Some were praying, some were swearing and all were fighting against suffocation.'[64] It sounded as if the bunkers were being attacked with flame-throwers. He hung up the phone and decided to see for himself what was happening, setting off with a radio operator and a couple of others. But by the time they reached the crossroads at Franceville, they could go no further. 'The situation was chaotic. Nobody knew who was friend or foe. Houses and trees were on fire and the sky was red.'[65] Steiner had fought in Norway, Russia and Yugoslavia, but he had never seen anything like this. 'We were crawling through the middle of an inferno.' He panicked. 'I didn't know what I should do. I was still a young bloke. It was hopeless.'[66]

In desperation he radioed divisional headquarters and called for the German artillery to fire on the bunker. It was a last throw of the dice in the attempt to halt the attack. His message reached headquarters but got corrupted in the process. Instead of one gun firing on the battery an entire barrage opened up, targeting such a wide area that Franceville itself was hit. 'Everything was reduced to nothing. It was terrible.' When the bombardment finally ended, Steiner was surrounded by carnage. His radio operator had taken the full blast of a nearby explosion. 'Only the top of his body was left, shredded to pieces.' His under-officer was moaning wildly. 'One of his feet had been severed.'[67]

Terence Otway was one of the first to realize that the battery had been captured. All four casemates had been abandoned by the defenders. This should have been a moment of celebration, but the assault was not yet over. It was imperative for his men to destroy the battery's big guns.

It was now, at this moment of victory, that the battle took a most unwelcome twist. When Allen Parry entered casemate one, he saw to his 'intense dismay' that the gun was 'a tiny old fashioned piece, mounted on a carriage with wooden wheels'.[68] It was not the huge cannon he had been led to expect. There was worse news to come. The rest of Merville's guns were not heavy-duty 150mm artillery pieces, as had been believed. 'They were only very, very ancient 75 millimetre guns of Czech manufacture.'[69] As such, they represented very little threat to the troops soon to land on Sword Beach. Allen Parry was devastated. 'This was an awful anti-climax and made me wonder if our journey had really been necessary.'[70]

Even worse was the fact that the guns could not be destroyed, for all the explosives had been lost during the landing. The men stuffed grenades down the barrels, but these didn't have 'any effect on very shiny, polished hard metal'.[71] The men destroyed the breech-blocks and wrecked whatever they could, but it was hardly the devastation they had been intending.

The realization that Merville was by no means as deadly as supposed left the men with a terrible sense of deflation. Worse by far, their victory had come with a very high price tag attached. When Otway did a head count, he discovered that only 75 of the 150 men involved in the assault were still standing. All the rest had been killed or wounded.

Barney Ross had been instrumental in capturing casemate three and had initially felt his team had 'done a great job'. But he was now having second thoughts. As he looked at the small number of survivors, he thought, 'My God, what's happened to all the guys?' Many of the men had become friends after two years of training together. Now, most of his closest pals were missing. 'My God, where's he gone?' he asked himself of one of them. He realized that he was 'bloody lucky to get out of this'.[72]

The capture of Merville was not the triumph it was supposed to be, yet there was one aspect to the attack that would have been welcomed by all at Supreme Headquarters. Terence Otway had been warned that his Merville assault would require 750 men and an entire arsenal of sophisticated weaponry. In the event, he had attacked the battery with only a fifth of his troop, a mixed group of men equipped with very little weaponry. This depleted force had nevertheless managed to seize Merville after a surprisingly short fight.

Even more heartening was the fact that the battery's defenders had thrown in the towel as soon as the going got tough. This boded well for the beach landings soon to begin. For if such a small group could capture a mighty battery, then it stood to reason that larger groups would be able to knock out the coastal casemates and bunkers with relative ease.

Such logic was lost on men still nursing their wounds. Most felt profoundly dejected and there was a real danger that despondency would drain their remaining morale. Allen Parry was quick to see the need to give his men a lift. Injured in the leg and transported into field headquarters in a wheelbarrow, he summoned all the swagger he could muster when greeting Major George Smith, commander of the 9th Battalion headquarters. 'He took a brandy flask from his pocket, gulped a mouthful and beamed. "A jolly good battle, what?"'

Smith gave a vigorous nod. Black humour was not always appropriate but on this occasion it seemed to work, for 'the grim faces of the men burst into smiles'.[73]

The first sight of the Allied fleet terrified the German lookouts. 'There must be ten thousand ships out there!' said one. 'This must be the invasion.'

10

First Light

D AWN ARRIVED EARLY in the Bavarian Alps. Long before the bells of St Paul and St Johannes clanged their morning sentinel, the sky above Berchtesgaden was washed with the first light of day. Within an hour, the high-altitude ridge of the Watzmann would be traced with a fine ribbon of silver. But night still clung to the northern flank of this alpine wilderness and Hitler's mountain refuge, the Berghof, was steeped in darkness. Shielded by the steep contours of the Obersalzberg and flanked by a deep phalanx of mountain spruces, it stood isolated from the outside world. Here, in a modest bedroom on the first floor, the Führer slept undisturbed.

Hitler had only retired to bed a couple of hours earlier, after spending a convivial evening with his guests, Albert and Margarete Speer, Martin Bormann and his wife, and Karl von Puttkamer, his loyal naval aide, whose comb-scraped hair and piercing eyes made him an instantly recognizable figure at the Berghof. Also present were Hitler's two secretaries and his lover, Eva Braun.

Hitler had been animated for much of the evening and Puttkamer noticed that he was taking great pains 'to act as an accomplished host'.[1] Once dinner was over, the Führer suggested that his female companions join him in the great hall so that he could play them his favourite composers on the gramophone: Wagner, Lehar and Strauss, interspersed with some lighter music specially chosen to amuse the ladies. It was the early hours before Hitler decided it was time for everyone to retire to bed. None of the Berghof staff expected him to wake before mid-morning.

In the valley below, a five-minute drive down the mountain road, stood the Reichskanzlei or Chancellery, where Alfred Jodl, Wilhelm Keitel and other senior generals in the OKW (Oberkommando der Wehrmacht or Supreme High Command of the German Armed Forces) had their lodgings. Here, too, was Martin Bormann's vast mountain chalet where he lived with Frau Bormann and eight of their ten children. Karl von Puttkamer also lived in the house, a pleasant enough arrangement as he got along well with the Bormanns.

Puttkamer, the acting duty officer that night, had been dozing for several hours when the telephone next to his bed rang at exactly 4 a.m., abruptly awakening him. He immediately recognized the voice at the other end as belonging to General Jodl's personal assistant, but the subject of his call took him completely by surprise. There had been parachute landings in Normandy, large ones, but 'nothing precise was known and first messages were extremely vague'. He wanted to know whether or not Hitler should be informed.

Puttkamer counselled against such a move. Hitler had been given a sedative by his physician, which meant it would be extremely difficult to rouse him. Puttkamer also feared that 'he might start one of his endless nervous scenes' that had been known to continue for hours. He suggested that they hold off until morning, when they would have more information. Then, the call over, he 'switched off his light and went back to sleep'.[2]

Puttkamer was not alone in getting a call that night. General Walter Warlimont, deputy to Jodl and Keitel, was also woken with news of the landings. He immediately called his boss.

'Colonel General, sir, this is Warlimont. Blumentritt has just called and told me that in the judgement of OB West, the real invasion has begun.'

There was a moment's silence as Jodl digested this news. 'Are you sure of all this?' he said. 'I am not so sure that this is the invasion.'

He declined to authorize the release of the two panzer divisions stationed outside Paris, as was being requested by Rommel's army commanders in Normandy. Indeed he reminded Warlimont there were already enough regular troops 'to cope with the situation'. He added that any decisions about the panzer divisions could wait until morning, when Hitler could review the situation.

'I will call Blumentritt and tell him immediately, sir,' said Warlimont. Yet he remained surprised by the decision, for it had long been agreed that the divisions, the 12th SS and Panzer Lehr, should be immediately deployed in the event of an invasion.

He hung up the phone 'slowly and thoughtfully'.³ He feared that Jodl had just made a terrible blunder.

The first rays of daylight had arrived a little earlier in Normandy, yet darkness still lingered in the sunken country lanes that wound through the Cotentin peninsula. Most of the roads were deserted, for it was still too early for farm traffic and the German patrols were few and far between. But on the little lane that linked Périers and Étienville, a Mercedes Phaeton was travelling at high speed through the gloom. In the back seat sat Lieutenant General Wilhelm Falley, commander of the 91st Airlanding Division, crisply dressed in military uniform and with the Iron Cross dangling from his neck. Beside him sat Major Joachim Bartuzat, his supply officer, a sharp-eyed, sharp-nosed Nazi with more than a hint of menace in his thin upper lip.

Their destination was the Château de Bernaville, an ornate eighteenth-century pile that had been requisitioned as the head-quarters of Falley's division. It was an elegant residence with high-ceilinged salons and parquet floors that harked back to a more enlightened age.

'Come on, step on it,' barked Falley to his driver, Corporal Baumann. 'It's nearly daylight.'

'We're practically there, Herr General.'

Falley had left his château headquarters six hours earlier in order to attend the war games session that General Marcks had convened in Rennes. Marcks's cancellation message had never reached Falley, yet he had decided to abandon the trip after becoming alarmed by the number of Allied aircraft passing over the Cotentin peninsula.

'Turn back,' he said to his driver. 'We're going back to head-quarters.'⁴

Now, after speeding northwards through the flat pastureland around Saint-Lô, they were almost back at the château. As Corporal Baumann swept along the narrow D-15, the familiar sight of the Ferme de la Minoterie was lit by the carbide lamps of Falley's Mercedes. This was home to the Lagouge family, who had been brusquely roused from their slumber by an unexpected visitor just a few minutes earlier.

That visitor was Malcolm Brannen, an American paratrooper who had landed from the sky in a 'thicket of briars and nettles'. He had soon stumbled across other men, all 'whispering the password and receiving the countersign'. Among them were a couple of paratrooper engineers, whom he had found cutting the roadside communication wires 'in many pieces'.

Like so many lost paratroopers, Brannen was determined to prove his worth during the remaining hours of darkness. When his men stumbled across a stray canister filled with supplies, they broke it open and helped themselves to a bazooka and twelve rockets. Newly armed, they headed in a northerly direction with the intention of waking the occupants of the first house they came across. They needed to find out exactly where they had landed.

As they headed over the fields, they came across two tents and two motorcycles. It was clearly a German field command post that had been left unguarded. Brannen promptly disabled the motorcycles 'by slashing all the tyres' while the others upended the contents of the command post. They then continued across the moonlit field, where Brannen ran into two more comrades, Harold Richard and Sergeant Hill. He now had a party of fourteen.

Just fifty yards from where they were standing was the Ferme de la Minoterie. Twelve of the men split up and surrounded the house, while Brannen and Richard pounded on the front door. 'In a few seconds, a very excited Frenchman came rushing – or gushing, is more like it – out of the door.' Several other members of the family could be seen peering out of the windows and wondering what on earth was happening. Brannen spied a number 'of little kiddos, wide-eyed at seeing the American uniforms instead of the usual German ones'. From the farmer, he learned that they were between Picauville and Étienville.

'Good,' he thought. 'We now had a definite location from which we could plan on future moves.'

As he was standing by the door he heard the distant roar of a car. He looked at Harold Richard and both had the same thought: to stop it in its tracks. Their warlike expressions were enough to strike fear into the Lagouge family. They knew that the car almost certainly belonged to one of the German officers based at the nearby Château de Bernaville and beat a hasty retreat.

As the car sped towards the farm, Lieutenant Richard ran to one side of the house while the others crossed to the far end. Brannen himself stood in the road and held up his hand at the oncoming vehicle, signalling it to stop. To his alarm, 'the car came on faster', for Corporal Baumann had sensed danger and slammed his foot hard on the accelerator. But speed could do little to save him.

'All of us fired at the same time, as a dozen or more shots rang out.' They came so thick and fast that Brannen feared he would be hit. 'I fell to the road and watched the car as it was hit.' It crashed into the stone wall next to the house and the driver 'was thrown from the front seat of the car'. Bannen saw him run towards the farmhouse, desperately seeking cover. He took a pot-shot with his Colt automatic, 'grazing his shoulder'. The injured corporal was captured soon afterwards and taken prisoner.

Major Bartuzat was in more serious trouble. He had just time to shout a single word to Falley – 'Careful!' – before he was gunned down inside the car. Brannen later found him 'slumped onto the floor with his head and shoulders hanging out of the open front door, dead'.

As for Falley himself, he had been thrown from the vehicle, injured but alive. From his vantage point in the hedge, Brannen could see him crawling across the road in a desperate attempt to reach his Luger, which had been flung from its holster. The lieutenant general looked up and saw Brannen. 'As he inched closer and closer to his weapon, he pleaded to me in German, and also in English: "Don't kill, don't kill!"' Brannen had a moment's reflection. 'I'm not a cold-hearted killer, I'm human,' he said to himself, 'but if he gets that Luger, it's either him or me.'

He pulled the trigger and hit Falley directly in the forehead, killing him instantly. 'The blood spurted from his forehead about six feet high and, like water in a fountain when it is shut off, it gradually subsided.'

As the men prepared to leave, Brannen 'tore the general's hat apart, looking for further identification of name or unit'. He found 'only a name printed on it – the name was Falley'.[5] He had just claimed the scalp of the first German general to be killed on D-Day.

It was not yet 5 a.m.

★

Within minutes of the attack on Lieutenant General Falley, Helmut Eberspächer was scrambled to his Focke-Wulf 190 fighter with orders to get airborne with immediate effect. Lancaster bombers had been striking the coastline with impunity for some hours and it was essential that the Luftwaffe hit back. But this was no easy matter, for the skies belonged to the Allies in that pre-dawn period, just as they would for much of the day. The Allies would fly 14,075 sorties on D-Day, the Luftwaffe just 139. Of the hundred or so Allied planes shot down, most were hit by ground-based anti-aircraft batteries.[6]

But not all. Twenty-eight-year-old Eberspächer was a professional fighter ace; a clean-shaven *wunderkind* who had learned to perform acrobatic miracles in his Focke-Wulf, jumping out of the clouds on to his unsuspecting quarry and then machine-gunning it to the ground. Such tactics were only possible because his plane was a nimble little masterpiece of aerial menace, equipped with two machine guns, four auto-cannon and a BMW radial engine that enabled it to climb to 3,000 feet in under a minute.

Against such a versatile enemy, the Allies' Lancaster bomber was a lumbering giant with a cruise speed of just 200 mph, less than half that of a Focke-Wulf. Nor did it have the thrust of its Luftwaffe enemy: as the German fighter soared upwards into the clouds, the Lancaster would still be hundreds of feet below, chugging along like a dependable workhorse. Combat between a Focke-Wulf and a Lancaster was like pitting a cheetah against a sloth.

Eberspächer got rapidly airborne and circled the dawn sky, where the moon still shone brighter than the nascent sun. As he headed towards the Normandy coast, his keen eyes detected an enticing prey. 'I noticed a row of bombers flying below the moon-lighted cloud cover.' These four bombers were from RAF 97 Squadron and they had already dropped their payload of bombs close to Pointe du Hoc. Now they were heading for home.

On board one of those planes, and crouched into the wireless seat, was a boyish-looking twenty-three-year-old named Albert Chambers. Chambers had married his sweetheart, Vera Grubb, just eight months earlier, one of the many British servicemen who had chosen to tie the knot before heading into the fray. On his ring finger he wore a gold band bearing his initials, AC, and the words 'Love Vera' on the inside.

Helmut Eberspächer felt a sudden thrill when he spotted the four-strong squadron of Lancasters. He thrust his plane upwards and ascended rapidly into the heavens, managing to remain unseen by the British planes. 'Similar to a shadow theatre, the bombers stood out against the clouds. However, they could not see me against the dark earth.' He would later write in his logbook that it was 'a favourable flying position'.[7] He knew that he stood a high chance of crippling the Allied planes. After selecting his first victim, he swooped downwards out of the sky, slicing through the air with all the grace and elegance of a bird of prey. As he did so, he unleashed a deadly spray of 13mm bullets.

At least one of the bullets ripped straight through the side of Albert Chambers's plane. Many more pierced the engines, crippling the plane's power supply. The motors spluttered, coughed and died, and Wing Commander Jimmy Carter found himself in a frantic struggle to keep the craft airborne. Carter was an experienced pilot, having undertaken raids on Berlin, Frankfurt, Brunswick and Leipzig, among many other cities. But he now found himself in a hopeless battle against gravity, trying to control eighteen tons of aircraft that had lost all power. In truth, only a magician could have kept the plane aloft, especially once its engines burst into flames. French farm workers watched aghast as the stricken aircraft tumbled nose over tail from the sky. It hurtled to the ground at a dizzying speed, somersaulting wildly before it eventually plunged into a field near Carentan. It hit the ground with such force that the wreckage was buried deep in the mud. As it did so, the crew were instantly killed and the gold ring on Albert Chambers's finger was flung into a nearby marsh.[*]

Once Eberspächer had destroyed Chambers's plane, Lancaster ND739, he latched on to the other Lancasters and managed to cripple two more in that fleet of four. 'Within a few minutes, three British Lancaster bombers went down in flames.'

---

[*] Albert Chambers's gold ring would remain in the earth until January 2012, when its chance discovery led to the unearthing of Lancaster ND739. Inside the crumpled fuselage were three RAF jumpers, a Waterman pen and a silver-plated cigarette case mangled by the force of the impact. There were also bloodstained RAF maps, four unused parachutes and a cockpit dial. Strangely, there was no trace of any bodies.

Helmut Eberspächer's morning work was done. He had just added three more kills to a record that would eventually earn him the Knight's Cross. He wheeled his Focke-Wulf through a giant arc and then headed back to the aerodrome where he was based, so as 'not to become another casualty of the morning's invasion'.[8]

That pre-dawn hour had been one of equal turmoil in Château de la Guillerie, home to the senior officers of the elite 12th SS Panzer Division. Hubert Meyer and his pregnant wife, Irmgard, first learned something was wrong when they were woken in the middle of the night. 'Wake up, the invasion's started.'[9] It was Major-General Fritz Witt, commander of the division. 'On your feet, Meyer, the invasion has begun.'[10] Meyer rose sharply from his bed, threw on his uniform and raced down the château's grand staircase in order to telephone the 711 Infantry Division headquarters for more information. He couldn't quite believe what he was being told, not least because the wind was ripping through the shrubs in the garden.

'No, it's *not* the invasion,' said a weary voice at divisional head-quarters. 'They aren't paratroopers, they're just straw dummies.'

A relieved Meyer transmitted the message to everyone in the château and then returned to his room. But he had scarcely fallen back to sleep when he was woken again by another shout.

'Wake up! The invasion's begun and this time it's the real thing!' He turned to his wife and told her not to worry. 'You stay here and sleep and wait and see what happens.'[11] Frau Meyer was happy to oblige. Her pregnancy had left her exhausted and she wanted nothing more than to remain under the blankets.

Meyer once again phoned divisional headquarters and this time received confirmation that paratroopers had indeed been dropped. This in itself was alarming, but Meyer was especially concerned on account of his wife's pregnancy. He rushed back upstairs to warn her as to what was happening. 'They have landed, but I don't know where and you have got to get out of here as soon as possible.' Frau Meyer was still sleepy and it was some moments before his words made any impression. 'Get up immediately and pack! You can't take anything [large] with you because you are going in a car with two other women, Frau Wuensche and Frau Witt.' The fact that Major-General Witt was sending his own wife home reinforced the sense of urgency.

Irmgard asked if she could take their dog, but her husband refused. She then asked if she could take the camera. 'No, I need that. I want to take pictures of the invasion.'[12]

With that he turned to leave the room, leaving his wife to pack a few essentials. Frau Meyer felt suddenly deflated. Her enchanting spring in northern France had been rudely interrupted.

While Major-General Fritz Witt awaited orders to move the 12th SS Panzer Division towards the coastline, Werner Pluskat was crouching in his coastal bunker near Sainte-Honorine-des-Pertes, his powerful artillery binoculars glued tightly to his eyes. He had headed to the bunker some three hours earlier, when he first heard rumours of the parachute landings. Since then, he had sat there with two of his ordnance officers, Fritz Theen and Ludz Wilkening. It was still quite dark, though the moon was full, and the air was full of mist. No one spoke. All three felt as if they were waiting for something to happen.

Pluskat picked up his binoculars every few minutes and stared out to sea, but 'there was absolutely nothing to be seen.' Even the heavy swell seemed to have calmed since the previous evening.

'Just another false alarm,' he said to Theen.

The tension increased when another wave of bombers passed overhead. Pluskat instinctively picked up his binoculars and once again looked towards the horizon, but still he could see nothing, 'partly because of the mist on the sea and partly because there were extremely heavy clouds that night passing across the face of the moon'.

As the first light of dawn began spreading across the sky, Pluskat detected a blur on the horizon. He stepped back in puzzlement. And then he looked once again through the binoculars. Something was wrong.

'Take a look.'

He handed the binoculars to Theen, who raised them to the horizon and gasped.

'My God!' he said. 'It's the invasion!'

Both men were astonished. The entire horizon from east to west 'was filled with shipping of all kinds'. Pluskat could scarcely believe that such a fleet could have gathered 'without anybody being the wiser, without anybody giving a warning'. It was barely credible.

He would have been yet more alarmed had he known that he was observing but a single invasion fleet, Force O, destined for Omaha Beach. There were another four flotillas advancing on the coastline of Normandy and each presented an equally formidable threat.

Pluskat wondered if he was witnessing some sort of mirage. But no, the blur on the horizon was moving. As he watched, 'he was absolutely petrified by the sight of this steady armada approaching the Normandy coast.' It was advancing 'relentlessly' towards him.

Frantically, he snatched at the telephone and put in an urgent call to Major Block at divisional headquarters.

'There must be ten thousand ships out there!' he said. 'It's un-believable . . . This must be the invasion.'

Major Block gave a loud snort. 'Now look, Pluskat, are you really sure there are that many ships? The Americans and British together don't have that many ships.'

'For Christ's sake, come and see for yourself.'

Block's voice betrayed his cynicism. He still didn't believe what he was being told.

'Oh, to hell with you,' shouted Pluskat as he threw down the receiver. But he soon thought better of it and rang Block again. 'Can I open fire?'

In the intervening time, Block had received other calls confirming a huge fleet sailing towards the shore. But he refused to give the fire command. 'No, no,' he said. 'We're too short on ammunition. No gun must fire until the troops are nearing the beaches.'

Pluskat put down the phone and turned to Theen, repeating what he had been told in a tone of weary resignation. And then, for good measure, he added, 'That's the way it is. I've known it all along. We're a suicide squad.'[13]

Admiral Theodor Krancke, the commander-in-chief of Navy Group Command West, was in charge of all German naval vessels operating in northern France, including the coastline of Normandy. A dapper officer of the old school, he had stood down the high-speed coastal patrol boats on the previous evening on account of the foul weather in the English Channel. In doing so, he had committed a rare blunder, leaving himself blind to the tumultuous events taking place out at sea. Many coastal radar stations had been destroyed by Allied bombing, while those still operable were sending out gibberish due to the success of Operation Taxable, an ingenious Allied operation in which masses of tinfoil strips, known as 'chaff', had been scattered from planes. These rendered German radar signals unintelligible.

Not until 3.09 a.m. did an uncorrupted radar report reach Krancke's office in Paris. *Several units with course south.* 'Several units' meant several ships. 'Course south' meant they were heading to Normandy. The report suggested that something untoward was taking place in the English Channel, although it was not immediately clear what it might be. Krancke was sufficiently alarmed by this news to inform the coastal shore batteries to prepare for action. He also telephoned the E-boat flotilla in Le Havre, where Lieutenant Commander Heinrich Hoffmann was on night duty. 'Stand by,' he said, 'ready to sail immediately.'

Just a few hours earlier, Hoffmann had spoken to his anxious wife on the telephone. She had given him the latest news about their young son and then confessed her fears that the invasion was imminent. 'Heinrich, I'm restless tonight. Is there anything afoot?'

Hoffmann had done his best to reassure her. 'Things are very quiet, darling. Nothing is going to happen tonight.'

But now he was not so sure. After learning of the strange signals coming from the Channel, he couldn't help thinking of what his wife had said. And the more he thought about it, the more he began to wonder if this was indeed the invasion.

Hoffmann had been patrolling the English Channel for two years and knew its waters almost as well as his native Marburg. He also knew that he had a reputation for being a man of action and that his men had coined a little phrase they liked to repeat. 'When Hoffmann gets to a place, things start happening.' Now, he decided to investigate the strange signal coming from the Channel, ordering the crew of his patrol boat, T-28, to make themselves ready, along with two accompanying vessels.

The three-strong flotilla had slipped out of Le Havre at 3.30 a.m. and headed south-west, pushing through the sea at a steady twenty-three knots and following a course roughly parallel to the coastline.

Hoffmann stood on his command platform, his white sailor's cap pushed backward, peering into the darkness. The others stayed below decks, protected from the spray.

When they were some twenty-five miles from Le Havre, Hoffmann sighted a huge fleet of planes heading inland. It was clear that they 'were after targets other than his small naval force'. The sky was starting to clear and the first streak of dawn was breaking through the cloud.

As he stared at the murky horizon, he noticed that everything had turned hazy. It was as if a milky-white mist had settled over the water. And then, to his astonishment, he spotted a single plane 'crawling out, under the white blanket'. This was the very moment, as he followed the plane's trajectory, that the terrible truth dawned. It was laying a smokescreen over the sea. Someone had something to hide.

Hoffmann glanced at his watch. It was now 5 a.m. Soon it would be daylight. He knew it was now or never. In the last remaining minutes of semi-darkness, he rammed his throttle to maximum and steeled himself for piercing the smokescreen in order to discover what lay on the other side.

When he finally burst through the screen, he blinked in disbelief. He found himself face to face with the most astonishing sight in the world: fifteen destroyers, half a dozen battleships and hundreds of other vessels. This was Force S, destined for Sword Beach.

Hoffmann's own little flotilla was minuscule in comparison. Indeed he would liken it to 'sitting in a rowing boat', exposed and vulnerable. *When Hoffmann gets to a place, things start happening.* Not for the first time, the phrase repeated itself in his head. And now he decided to attack.

'To all, Z forward.' He relayed the pre-agreed message to the other vessels. He then raised the red flag over his bridge and cranked his engine to maximum. 'To all, Toni Dora Six.'[14] It was the signal to fire. Seconds later, eighteen torpedoes were knifing through the dark waters of the Channel.

Force S was under attack.

PART IV
Dawn

The Allied planners of Operation Neptune (the invasion's seaborne element) decided that troops should land at low tide and at dawn: this was in the hope of achieving tactical surprise.

A short aerial bombardment of the coast was to be followed by a concentrated naval bombardment. As landing craft neared the shore, rocket ships would unleash further salvoes. A final element of surprise was the use of specially invented armoured vehicles: Britain's 79th Armoured Division of amphibious tanks were to emerge from the sea at the same time as the infantry hit the beaches.

Greatly strengthened over preceding months, the German Atlantic Wall presented a forbidding challenge to infantry landing from the sea. At high water, beach obstacles and mines were concealed; at low water, the beaches were dangerously exposed.

Many German troops were stationed in coastal Widerstandsnest, *or strongpoints. These semi-underground concrete bunkers enabled them to fire their MG 42 machine guns through small embrasures. The guns had been carefully positioned so that they could hit every inch of beach.*

The French coast was dotted with villages whose populations had remained in situ. The Allied beach plan paid scant heed to the fact that families risked being caught in one of the heaviest bombardments in history.

American soldiers prepare for the four-hour run-in to Utah Beach.
Many were violently seasick. In the far distance are the US destroyers, with
attached barrage balloons to hinder German bombers.

II

On Utah Beach

THE SKY WAS still dark when Al Corry, a young American bombardier, was shaken from his sleep and summoned to a pre-dawn briefing with his commanding officer.

'Come on, get up, time to get up!'

Still groggy with sleep, he and his comrades threw on their flying gear and made their way to the briefing room. Corry noticed a marked difference to previous pre-dawn briefings. 'Normally there was a lot of mumbling going on, guys talking on the way to the briefing room, just discussing various little things.' Not on this particular morning. 'It was real quiet still,' he said. 'Everybody sensed something.'

Corry had scarcely taken his seat when his commanding officer, Colonel Story, burst into the room. He was a pugnacious warlord, 'a real hot jockey' who looked as if he were ready to take on the entire German army. 'He had his hat cocked back on his head and a short stubby cigar in his mouth.' He greeted the assembled airmen with a smile. 'Hey guys, good morning, good morning, good morning. Well, here we are. This is it.'

His words were met with silence and blank faces, a cue for him to continue. 'This is the big day we've been waiting for. That's what we all came here for.'

Still there was silence.

'We're going to France at six in the morning,' he said, spelling it out in blunt language. 'As air support for the Allied forces invading the Normandy coast of Europe. This is to be the invasion.'

His words were met with a roar of approval from the assembled company. Corry joined in. 'Oh boy,' he yelled. 'Yea botz! Yea botz all right!' He'd been looking forward to bombing the enemy's shore defences ever since arriving in England. For pulse-inducing thrills, it was a lot more gratifying than attending lectures at Syracuse University.

A note of caution was sounded by one of the training officers. He produced a map of the Normandy coast, handed the men sheets of transparent paper and instructed them to draw a thin red line on their maps. 'This side of the line would be all Allied troops,' he told them, pointing to the shore, 'and beyond that line would be enemy territory.' It was essential that Allied soldiers were not accidentally hit as they made their way on to the beaches.

Corry and company got airborne well before dawn and headed southwards across the English Channel, one small component in the largest aerial armada in history. More than 1,000 RAF bombers were taking part in the raid, accompanied by 1,635 American planes – a mixed fleet of bombers that included twin-engined B-26 Marauders, B-17 Flying Fortresses and B-24 Liberators.

As Corry's Marauder approached the coast, the low-lying cloud gave him his first twinge of disquiet. 'We're going to have to go down lower,' he told the pilot. 'I can't see the target! I can't bomb. I can't identify that bomb line on the ground. The cloud's too low.'

He was acutely aware of the dangers of descending beneath the cloud: their plane would be exposed to the highly accurate German flak batteries. But there was no alternative if they were to unleash their heavy bombs on the right side of the red line, so the pilot plunged to 3,000 feet.

'Not low enough,' said Corry. 'We've got to break through this darn layer.'

The pilot continued his descent until they reached 1,250 feet, whereupon they emerged from the lowest layer of cloud. As Corry peered out of the gunner's window he caught a brief glimpse of the shoreline below. He could see they were approaching their target – the bunkers and defences set just behind the beach.

He felt sorry for the infantry soon to land. 'I could see what they were heading into and I prayed for all those brave young men about to come face to face with death.' Given the choice of being in a plane or a landing craft, he would always choose the former. 'I thought, Man, I'm up here looking down at this stuff and they're out there waiting to get on that beach.'

There was no time for further reflection: they were right on target and it was time to bomb the coast. 'I set my inter-valometer [time device] so that every two seconds a bomb would release.' He also used a manual trip switch to pick off gun nests he could identify on the ground. Seconds later, he watched the bombs explode on the beach below. 'I could see Germans on the far side, running, running away from the front, and a couple of trucks.' As soon as the bomb bay was empty, Corry gave a shout to the pilot. 'Break off and head west,' he said. 'Take a right-hand turn.'

As they veered over the Cotentin peninsula, he got a panorama of the landscape below. 'It looked like a real old castle with a moat around it.' It was made even more picturesque by the flashes of light bursting upwards from the ground. It took just a few seconds for him to realize that the flashes were actually 88mm flak guns aiming at their aircraft.

'Here they come! Let's get out of here!' He was shouting to the pilot. 'Bank off to the left. Keep going down.'

The panic could be heard in his voice.

'Give it some speed and let's get the hell out of here.'

The pilot tried to dodge the flak but it was no use.

'They're bracketing us,' yelled Corry. The German gunners had them in their sights.

As the pilot took evasive measures, something smacked into the plane with such force that it was as if a heavy boot had kicked it sideways. There was a sickening rat-tat-tat as the fuselage was riddled with gunfire and then came a shriek of twisted metal as something slammed through the cone of the plane. For Corry, seated up front, it happened in a flash. 'I felt that someone had slapped me in the chest with a sledgehammer.' Was this the end? 'My chest did not exactly hurt but it was sore. Putting my hand inside my jacket, it felt kind of wet. I pulled it out – my fingers and hand were covered with blood.'

He felt inside for a second time and was relieved to discover that it wasn't coming from his chest. 'It was coming from my little finger, which had a big slice cut off the end.' A piece of shrapnel had severed it in two. He reached for the memo book he kept in the jacket pocket next to his heart. 'I found a small jagged flak fragment stuck in the cover.'[1] That memo book had saved his life.

Corry's Marauder had a lucky escape. Within minutes the plane was limping back across the English Channel, surviving the voyage and landing without incident, despite its dents and bruises. Corry was served tea and fresh doughnuts by the Red Cross girls who worked at the airfield.

Their pre-dawn mission had been a success, or so it seemed. In common with most of the Marauder pilots targeting Utah Beach, they had flown parallel to the shoreline – and at very low altitude – enabling them to hit their targets with commendable accuracy. Corry had seen with his own eyes the bombs exploding on the correct side of the red line. But the attack on Utah was the exception rather than the rule – the result of good judgement rather than good orders. Shortly before the bomber fleet got airborne, Eisenhower had agreed to a request from the Eighth Air Force that pilots be allowed to delay their bombardment for up to thirty seconds as they passed over the coast. This was to avoid hitting the shore-bound infantry below, but it had unfortunate consequences. The 329 B-24 bombers targeting Omaha Beach dropped 13,000 bombs in that pre-dawn period. Virtually all of them exploded in the cliff-top pastureland, killing cows and damaging farms but leaving the German coastal defences completely untouched. They didn't scour a single crater into the beaches, as was intended, in order to provide cover for the infantry soon to land.

'The Air Corps might just as well have stayed in bed,'[2] commented one American officer watching the bombing raid from a few hundred yards offshore. An English captain was equally damning. 'That's a fat lot of use,' he said. 'All it's done is wake them up.'[3]

This was not entirely correct. On Utah Beach, the Germans were already awake.

The great Allied fleet assembling ten miles offshore from Utah had pulled off the most spectacular conjuring trick in history. Force U's 865 vessels had got within striking distance of Rommel's Atlantic Wall seemingly without raising any suspicions.

More astonishing to those on board was the fact that the Germans had aided their navigation by neglecting to extinguish the blinking beam of the lighthouse at Cape Barfleur. It was as if they never really believed the Allies would land from the sea.

The Force U flagship, USS *Bayfield*, had been first to arrive at the pre-agreed rendezvous, at 2.29 a.m. 'Anchor holding, sir, in 17 fathoms.'[4] Those were the words shouted up to Captain Lyndon Spencer on the bridge. The USS *Nevada* followed in her wake, another lumbering ghost of a ship that was visible as a pewter-grey silhouette washed with moonlight. To Ross Olsen, one of *Nevada's* impressionable young lieutenants, it felt as if they 'were sneaking up on the enemy' as part of some high-stakes game of cat and mouse. He noted that everyone was talking 'in whispers, thinking that we might be heard by the Germans on the beach'. This, of course, was ridiculous: they were still a long way from shore. But it was a sign of everyone's edginess and even Olsen couldn't help wincing when the captain cut loose the anchor, for 'it made a tremendous noise as the anchor chain went through the hawsepipe.'[5]

USS *Nevada* was one of the eighteen ships that made up the bombardment group – battleships, cruisers and destroyers whose task was to unleash a storm of high-explosive shells on to Utah Beach in the hour before the landings. These ships had manoeuvred far closer to the shore than the USS *Bayfield* and were relying on smokescreens to remain hidden from the Germans.

Also hiding behind smokescreens were hundreds of other ships, all jockeying for space in the crowded seas. These were the mine-sweepers, support craft and Rhino ferries – huge barges lashed together and laden with jeeps, trucks and armoured bulldozers that would be needed to shunt debris from the beaches. The Rhinos had been towed from England by the larger landing ships, many of which were carrying smaller landing craft.

'*Now hear this! Stand by all troops!*'

The cry could be heard through the darkness as amplified voices played through the loudspeakers of USS *Bayfield*. Within seconds, there was frenetic activity as hundreds of boat-hands sprang into action. Landing craft dangled on their crane-like davits, whistles screeched, boatswains blasted orders and the smaller landing craft began firing their engines in preparation for the long run-in to the coast.

'*Stand by all troops!*'[6]

For one twenty-five-year-old American captain, this was the moment he had been awaiting for almost three years. Leonard Schroeder was in command of F Company of the 8th Infantry, with five landing craft that each contained thirty-two men. The boats were to land on the beach in a V formation, with Schroeder's boat in the middle of the V. His men were in the vanguard of the invasion of occupied Europe: if all went to plan, they would be the first to splash through the surf and storm the vaunted Atlantic Wall.

Schroeder was a bulldozer of a man, with a thickset face and a pronounced nose. He was known as Moose, an appropriate moniker for someone as stock-solid as the giant animal of his native North America. He was also likeable – a no-nonsense team player with big hands and a big heart. He had pushed his men hard, leading them through mock landings and using live ammunition. In doing so, he had transformed them from teenage volunteers into a highly competent force. He compared them to a team of football players who would shout down their rivals in order 'to pump themselves up before a match'. But in private, he saw them as blood brothers who had developed a 'sincere and honest'[7] bond. Each man had become dependent on the other, which was exactly what he intended.

Some had a feeling of dread as the fateful hour drew near, but they disguised it with fake camaraderie. Among those picked for the initial assault was twenty-five-year-old Malvin Pike, who felt the tensions increase as the hour for landing approached. Even on the eve of their departure from England, he had observed a strange hush in the mess canteen. 'Nobody was talking. About all you could hear was the knives and forks hitting the side of the plate.'[8] It was unsettling, as if they were condemned men eating their last supper.

Once aboard the *Bayfield*, they had listened attentively to the speech by Brigadier General Theodore 'Teddy' Roosevelt, the only high-ranking general scheduled to land in the first wave on D-Day. He spoke touchingly, powerfully, before ending with a vow. 'I'll see you tomorrow morning, six-thirty, on the beach.'[9] He meant it and his men were visibly moved.

Leonard Schroeder received a more succinct message from his battalion commander, Carlton McNeely. 'Well, Moose, this is it. Give 'em hell.'[10] But for all the fighting talk, the two men 'choked up' as emotion got the better of them. They each knew they might well be killed. Schroeder wrote a long letter to his wife, telling her how much he loved her.

He and his men were among the first to board their landing craft, at around 2.30 a.m. They had spent a relatively tranquil night aboard USS *Bayfield*, but now they faced a rough ride through choppy seas during the four-hour run-in to the beach.

Boarding was difficult. In near-darkness, the men had a dizzying clamber down rope netting that was strung like a web over the sides of their transport ships. They were burdened with everything they would need for the next few days – backpack, rations, grenades, Bangalore torpedoes and mortars, as well as trenching tools, portable stoves and radio transmitters. The boats bucked and pitched in the rolling swell and Schroeder was aghast to learn that several soldiers had plunged from the netting and been crushed to death.

As the first landing craft picked their passage through the fleet and moved into formation, they were greeted by a sharp blast from a ship's loudspeaker. 'Good luck, fourth division.'

'Jesus Christ,' hissed one of Malvin Pike's comrades. 'I don't know why in the hell they want to make that darn racket.'

'Well, I can't believe the Germans don't know we're here,'[11] said another. It was a sobering thought. It was possible that even now, the enemy were spying upon them.

It was crucially important that the men landed at the correct point on Utah Beach. The task of guiding them to shore fell to Howard Vander Beek, whose little craft, LCC 60, had been tossed violently across the Channel for the second time in forty-eight hours. His fourteen-strong crew wore the haggard expressions of men at the limits of their endurance. They had snatched just four hours' sleep since their first abortive crossing and Vander Beek 'had a feeling of being led to oblivion', even though it was him doing the leading. His job was to ensure that the troops, tanks and armoured vehicles landed at the correct place. If he got it wrong, the entire assault would be in jeopardy.

Vander Beek had been warned of his responsibilities by Roosevelt himself. 'Well, my boy,' he said, 'my life is now in your hands.' So were the lives of the 620 men scheduled to land in the opening minutes of the invasion.

LCC 60 pushed off into the damp night in the company of a little patrol craft. When Vander Beek looked to his rear, he could just about make out the grey shadows of the ten landing craft packed with the men of E Company and F Company. Further away were another ten craft with the men of B Company and C Company. Even more distant, and lost to the darkness, were the larger landing craft carrying the amphibious tanks. These were to be released into the sea at 5,000 yards from shore and would travel to the beach under their own steam.

Vander Beek's flotilla was just the first wave. It would be followed by hundreds of other vessels laden with jeeps, tanks and armoured vehicles, as well as 21,000 troops of the 4th Infantry Division.

The control craft's wireless suddenly crackled into life and brought the first unpleasant surprise of the morning. 'A Germanized-English voice from the beach came in on our radio frequency.' The speaker was posing as a British Red Cross worker asking to be rescued from the beach, but it was obviously a bluff. Vander Beek felt 'the first icy chill of confrontation with the enemy'.

For what seemed like an eternity, the flotilla pushed through the night until the first glimmer of day streaked the sky. By 4.30 a.m., Vander Beek could see 'a faint silhouette of the Nazi-held territory before us'.[12] It was a pale, low-lying and wind-blown coastline almost entirely devoid of features. Finding the designated landing zone would not be easy.

The LCC 60's navigator, Sims Gauthier, had spent much of his time below deck, relaying messages to the *Bayfield* as he sought to keep track of their exact position. Shortly before 5.30 a.m., he clambered up the metal ladder in order to confer with Vander Beek. Both men were admiring the flotilla fanned out behind them when their accompanying patrol boat flipped on to her side – quite without warning – and began to sink. She had almost certainly struck an underwater mine.

Vander Beek watched in shock as the crew scrambled out of the upturned vessel, only to lose their grip on the hull of the boat and slip into the freezing water. Gauthier felt sickened by the sight of the men 'screaming, hollering and asking for help'. But there was nothing they could do: they were under strict orders not to stop.

Just twelve minutes after the patrol craft was lost, disaster struck one of the tank-carrying landing craft, LCT 597. Gauthier had returned to his navigation table below deck when he felt the force of a tremendous explosion. 'Our little craft was lifted up out of the water and we came down again and there was a shock wave that came through that vessel.' He rushed back on deck in time to see what had happened. The tank craft 'had just been blown sky-high and everything just disappeared in a matter of seconds'.[13]

It was terrible to observe. Sam Grundfast, the ship's commanding officer, was one of only three dazed survivors: the detonation had flung him through the air with the force of a giant catapult, so fast and violently that he had no idea what had happened. One moment he was on deck, the next he was underwater. He opened his eyes 'and saw the surface of water somewhere above my head'.[14]

'*Skipper! Skipper!*' He could half hear the watery voice of his comrade, Richard Abernathy, who had managed to haul himself on to a chunk of floating wreckage, along with one other crew member. Everything else – ship, tanks and men – had plunged to the bottom. Like so many others that morning, these three marooned survivors would have to endure a long time in the frigid water before anyone came to their rescue.

Vander Beek was still trying to make sense of the unfolding disaster when there was a 'deafening, thunderous roar'[15] as wave after wave of bombers cut through the sky. As they crossed the coastline, they dumped their high explosives on to the German bunkers and machine-gun nests.

Shortly afterwards, USS *Nevada* led the long-range saturation bombardment of the shoreline, pitching thousands of tons of sand and debris into the dawn sky. The fireworks display was so spectacular that the crew on the *Bayfield*, anchored ten miles offshore, were left speechless. The ship's stores officer, Cyrus Aydlett, had never seen anything quite like it. 'The heavens seemed to open, spilling a million stars on the coastline before us, each one spattering luminous tentacle-like branches of flame in every direction.'

But this was just the opening act. Next came 'mammoth streaks of fire, expelled by rocket launchers'[16] designed to cause maximum damage to the shore defences. They skimmed the water at such a low level that the men instinctively ducked. At close range, it was terrifying to observe the destructive power of these rockets. Vander Beek watched in awe as 'violent explosions and spectacular blazes transformed the scene'.

The sun had just risen, at 5.58 a.m., but it was a gloomy, half-hearted sort of dawn that was struggling to shrug off the night.

'Low-lying clouds and billowing smoke and dust blocked out the colours [the dawn] might have painted the dull French coast.'[17] Visibility was so reduced that it was hard to make out the shoreline. Sims Gauthier was trying to work out exactly where the men should land, but 'the airborne debris, spreading smoke, dust and fog, curtained much from view.' Worse still, he and his men were soaked to the skin, for 'the raw Channel wind wafted salt spray upon our faces [and] waves often doused us with sea water.'[18]

The original battle plan had called for the amphibious tanks to be launched at 5,000 yards from the coast. They would then chug their way to the beach, half submerged and invisible to the soldiers manning the German shore defences. But Vander Beek was alarmed by the heavy swell: the wind was blasting off the land at twenty knots and the waves were more than five feet high. He took the decision to launch the tanks much closer to the shore, at 3,000 yards, where the land offered some protection.

To his eyes, these amphibious vehicles looked like 'odd-shaped sea monsters, depending upon huge, doughnut-like balloons for flotation, wallowing through the heavy waves and struggling to keep in formation'. These sea monsters were in fact thirty-three-ton Sherman tanks that would go into action as soon as they hit the beach.

Vander Beek guided the giant flotilla to within 500 yards of the coast. Even here, so close to shore, the low sea wall and tufted sand dunes were scarcely visible through the salt-haze and spray. As they came within spitting distance of the beach, the LCC 60's crew bade a noisy farewell to the troops about to land, with 'shouted cheers, gestured support and encouragement, but only a few on each boat returned acknowledgement'. They felt desperately sorry for the men. 'Some were too busy using helmets to bail out seawater seeping over their low-set craft.' Others, suffering from acute seasickness, were vomiting over the sides. 'Most, however, stood pressed together, motionless, salt-water soaked and chilled by fear and cold.'[19]

This sickly band of men was in the vanguard of the Allied army. In less than three minutes, it would find itself pitched against the Nazi war machine.

★

Robert Beeman had a grandstand view of the unfolding events, for he was standing on the windswept bridge of USS *Corry*. He was less interested in the landing craft than in the German coastal batteries, whose guns were pointed towards the *Corry*. He had been observing the batteries through his naval binoculars and had counted no fewer than seventy-five big guns within range. USS *Corry's* position just 3,500 yards offshore made her a sitting duck.

Beeman was also troubled by the damage done to the ship's mechanical system two days earlier, on their initial crossing of the English Channel. Captain George Hoffman's attack on a non-existent submarine had left the vessel with guns that could only be fired manually. This would put them at a serious disadvantage if it came to a duel with the huge guns on the foreshore.

As Beeman fretted over their predicament, it seemed as if a miracle might be on its way. Two Allied planes could be seen approaching from the north and as they passed over USS *Corry's* accompanying vessels, USS *Fitch* and USS *Hobson*, they laid a thick smokescreen by spraying a chemical mixture into the air. This made them invisible to the German gunners.

Beeman was expecting them to do the same for his own vessel, but to his dismay the planes headed back out towards the Channel. USS *Corry* was left 'in plain view of the Germans'. When this news reached the men below decks, a terrible doom fell over the ship. The chief radio technician, Francis McKernon, turned to the radar man, Pete McHugh. 'Without smoke cover, we can't last much longer.' Just three days earlier, in a moment of black humour, McKernon had played devil's advocate by betting ten dollars that the *Corry* would get hit. Now, he regretted such flippancy, especially when he learned that the sea temperature was just 13 degrees centigrade. 'Man alive,' he said, 'someone's gonna have a cold swim.'[20]

The big German guns opened fire a few minutes later. Beeman was still on the bridge and he studied their trajectory with mounting alarm. 'Suddenly, several large splashes appeared in the water off the port beam, about 250 yards distant.' He counted four separate explosions, five or ten yards apart, in a perfectly straight line. He could scarcely believe the 'ability of the gunners to place their shells in so tight and precise a pattern'.

The men running the ship's systems equipment were below decks and dependent on receiving regular updates from the bridge.

'They're firing at us!' shouted Beeman down the wire. As he said this, he saw 'a row of flashes on the high ground behind the beach'.[21] Exactly fifteen seconds later, a row of waterspouts erupted in the sea just 150 yards from USS *Corry*. The aim of the Germans was getting increasingly accurate and it was clear they would hit the ship unless she shifted position.

'Right full rudder,' commanded Captain Hoffman. 'Twenty-five knots.'[22] It was a manoeuvre fraught with danger, for the vessel was operating in a mine-swept channel just 750 yards wide. Her turning circle was only a fraction less than the channel.

Deep below in the engine room, Grant Gullickson and his team were awash with sweat as they toiled to keep the boilers pumping at full blast. Over the noise of belching pipes and gurgling pumps, Gullickson could hear the big guns roaring into action.

The ship was still in a sharp turn when a German mortar slammed into her with full force. She gave a deep shudder as 1,500 tons of steel were lifted from the water. It was as if she had been shoved sideways by a giant fist, causing chaos in the quarters below deck, as well as on the bridge above. Robert Beeman was flung ten feet through the air. As he crashed to the deck, he was showered with debris and shrapnel.

Francis McKernon was also hurled from his seat. He was winded and only semi-conscious. There were lifeless bodies all around him. 'They're all dead,' he thought. 'I'm the only one alive.' He turned his gaze to the young lad seated behind the 20mm anti-aircraft gun. He was still strapped into his seat, but 'slumped backwards with his eyes closed and his arms hanging limp'.[23]

The situation was worse below decks. Benny Glisson, the radio-man, was shunted violently from his chair and tossed upside down. 'Everything seemed to explode at once and I felt like I'd fallen into a concrete mixer.'[24] Grant Gullickson was in the forward engine room when the turbines were split open by the explosion. Steam erupted from the cracks and the pipes burst in two, with devastating effect. One of the boiler-men, 'Big Ski' Ravinski, took the full force of the blast and was left horrifically scalded.

Three direct hits had punctured a hole in the ship's boiler room and seawater was now gushing in. Benny Glisson had smashed his leg in the explosion and had a deep gash on his head. 'Everything was literally a mass of wreckage, debris and twisted steel.' He looked round to see 'a hole there big enough to drive a truck through'.

One of his comrades had 95 per cent burns – so bad, indeed, that when medics later gave him a transfusion, 'the only place to stick a needle was the inner side of his big toe'. Another lad had 'a gaping wound about eight inches long just above his knee' while three more 'were covered with oil and so badly burned that they were unrecognizable'. One young crew member had been trapped against a bulkhead and 'live steam was spewing at him from a broken pipe'.[25] He was only saved when the cold-water tank above him burst.

A torrent of seawater ripped through the partition and Grant Gullickson found himself up to his waist. He 'grappled to open the hatch'[26] in order to make his escape. His friend Ernie McKay was also trying to get out. The floor plates beneath him were torn apart and he saw water surging towards him. He was 'completely disorientated, having been spun round'[27] and tipped into the bilge.

Emil Vestuti heard a voice crying for help.

'Vestuti, Vestuti, help. I can't see.'

Vestuti reached out to help, but it was no use. 'When I went to grab his arm, the skin came off.'[28]

McKernon was still semi-conscious when Captain Hoffman seized him by the shoulders and shook him hard. Hoffman knew that his ship was seriously damaged, but had no idea of the catastrophic situation below the waterline.

'We've lost control of the steering,' he said. 'But we're still moving! If you're okay, I want you to go aft, steer north and get us out of here.'

McKernon rushed back to the bridge, still dazed, only to discover that steam was belching from a massive crack that ran across the main deck. It spanned more than a foot and was widening fast. The ship had broken her back.

'Steer north!' McKernon yelled to the men in the steering hatch. He still hoped they might sail out of danger. 'Get us out of here.' But when Big Joyich tried to move the rudder, it was completely jammed.

McKernon glanced amidships and saw a flood of water rushing towards him.

'Everybody out!'[29] he shouted down the steering hatch into the blackness below.

Mort Rubin was still below decks when the ship lost all power. There was a sudden 'black silence' that felt like the end of everything. 'In the quietest times, noises permeated the ship – fans, motors and assorted equipment.' But now there was nothing. 'This was death.'[30] Terrified of getting trapped, Rubin hoisted himself up to the deck.

He found a hellish sight. Men were panicking, screaming for help, begging for morphine. Those not wounded were trying to unlash the boats and life-rafts. Others were searching for the life jackets that would keep them afloat. McKernon helped the chief gunner's mate hurl five-inch gunpowder canisters into the sea. Three feet long and unsinkable, they would be invaluable floats.

It was clear to everyone that the ship was doomed. Water was sluicing over the ruptured deck and in places it was already two feet deep. Lieutenant Commander Hoffman gave the order that every captain dreads. 'Abandon ship! Abandon ship!'[31]

The water was up to the rail by the time Mort Rubin ditched his boots, belt and pistol and slipped into the water. It was shock-ingly cold. As he inflated his lifebelt, a splash of shrapnel broke the water around him.

Some of the wounded had been helped into the boats and rafts; they now tried to put some distance between them and the stricken vessel to avoid being dragged under when she sank. There was not enough room for everyone and many, like Mort Rubin, found themselves in the freezing water.

McKernon jumped in and plunged deep below the surface. He had to claw his way back up, spluttering and coughing as he clutched at the air. He found himself close to Hoffman and several others. 'Looking back at the jack-knifed *Corry*, we saw the stern and bow slanted upward at right angles above the water.'[32] The upper bridge and smokestacks were still visible. The rest was already submerged.

The German shellfire now began targeting the men in the water. Robert Beeman was struggling through icy three-foot waves when a shell exploded near one of the life-rafts, causing shocking injuries. One of his comrades, Norman Bensman, was hit 'and the upper half of his head was sliced off by shrapnel.' Another comrade 'was blown to bits'.[33]

Beeman clutched at a gunpowder canister and fought his way through a thick slick of engine oil. Some men inadvertently swallowed it, causing them to vomit. Several were half smothered by it.

There was worse to come. Francis McKernon and others were trapped in a corrosive cloud of chemical vapour released when the generators blew up. Those closest to the cloud began to gag in the water. A few were blinded and thrashed around helpless in the oily waves.

With the invasion now in full swing, the men knew they faced hours in the water before being rescued. The survivors would eventually be picked up by USS *Corry*'s companion destroyers, *Fitch* and *Hobson*. By that time, Gullickson was so cold that he was unable to grasp the line dropped down into the water.

'Buddy, it's great to see you,' said the voice of the man who pulled him out. 'Everything's going to be all right.'[34] Gullickson nodded weakly, aware that he was one of the lucky ones. When he went to see his friend Charlie Brewer, lying on a bunk below decks, he saw that he had been killed by shrapnel in his brain.

In the bleak haze of dawn, the first wave of landing craft approached the shore in V-formation, exactly as planned. As the beach became visible through the dampness, the two men standing at the rear of each craft let rip with their 30-calibre machine guns, flinging a hail of bullets on to the beach. Malvin Pike was crouched in the water-logged bottom of his craft, along with his comrades. When he glanced backward, all he could see 'was two hands on the wheel and a hand on each machine gun'. The bullets were zipping through the air just inches above his head.

The landing craft juddered to a halt, still a long way from the shore. It was stuck on a sandbar. 'I can't go any further,' yelled the coxswain. 'Ya'll are going to have to get out.'

Lieutenant John Rebarchek shouted the man down. 'You ain't going to drown these men out here.'

The coxswain reversed the engine and managed to get off the bar. He then pushed the craft nearer to shore.

'This is it. I can't make it.'

Rebarchek nodded. 'Pull the pin, drop the ramp!' The men tried but the ramp was stuck and refused to budge.

'To hell with this!'[35] Pike and his comrades leaped over the side into waist-deep water and began pushing through the surf. It was sixty yards to the beach. Bullets were spitting through the air.

Leonard Schroeder's landing craft had fared somewhat better. Leading from the front of the V, it had made it all the way to the shore. The underside of the craft scoured the shingle then crunched to an abrupt halt.

'For God's sake, get off!'[36]

The ramp was shoved downwards and Schroeder jumped into waist-deep water. He was followed by his men, who surged through the waves, dodging mines and barbed wire. Schroeder was in the lead. There was small arms fire. His sights were fixed on the low sea wall. Built out of concrete by the Germans, it was designed to stop tanks from leaving the beach. But to Schroeder's eyes, it offered some sort of shelter.

The water grew shallower, the sand underfoot firmer. A few more paces and Schroeder hit the beach. He had just made history. He was the first Allied soldier to land from the sea.

The beach was gouged with deep craters from the aerial and naval bombardments: it looked as if some giant had stomped through the sand.

'Goddam, we're on French soil!'[37]

The air was filled with grit.

'Bombs, shells . . . rockets whooshing overhead, ack-ack from the German positions . . . an awesome display.'[38]

Schroeder and company were raked with fire that skimmed their heads and splashed into the sea. On Bruce Bradley's craft, a shell smacked into the side. 'The coxswain was gone. The ramp was down. The boat was sinking.'[39]

Schroeder led his lads in a spirited dash across 400 yards of sand. It was not easy, for their clothes were sodden and their waterlogged baggage acted like a dragnet. They eventually reached the low sea wall, where they had a refuge of sorts. In just a couple of minutes, Schroeder's 150 men of F Company were ashore with only a few men down.

Schroeder now took stock of his situation. He had been expecting to be supported by thirty-two amphibious tanks, but they were nowhere to be seen. The planners of the Utah landing had made a disastrous miscalculation of the time it would take them to plough through heavy seas. They were still wallowing through the swell, inching towards land at an agonizingly slow pace.

Off to the right, Schroeder could just make out the men of E Company storming ashore under the leadership of Howard Lees. Among them was Teddy Roosevelt, panting heavily and feeling every one of his fifty-six years. He had perhaps wanted to emulate his father, the former president, who had led the charge of the Rough Riders up Kettle Hill in Cuba. But he was struggling for breath as he 'splashed and floundered through some hundred yards of water while the German salvos fell'. Roosevelt was alarmed to see that E Company was starting to take casualties. 'Men dropped, some silent, some screaming.'[40]

Further along the beach came C Company, many of whom had shaved their heads like Mohawks. 'They yelled like Indians as they ran up the beach.'[41] It felt better arriving in a blaze of noise. As men reached the sea wall they flung themselves into the sand and grasped at the dirt-filled air. Thankful to be still alive, they then poked their heads over the tufted dunes. All were looking for the landmarks they had studied back in England.

It didn't take long to realize that something was seriously wrong. According to the maps and sand-tables used in training, there should have been a windmill and earthen structure known as Mud Fort. But here, there were no landmarks at all. Leonard Schroeder was puzzled, as was Captain Robert Crisson of C Company.

'Dammit, captain,' said one of Crisson's officers, 'there's no Mud Fort down there.'[42]

Roosevelt took a quick scout around the dunes and found 'a house by the seawall where none should have been'.[43] He then crawled on to a higher dune and saw a windmill in the far distance. Only now did the terrible truth sink in: the ferocious swell had pushed them a mile to the south of their intended landing.

This presented a potentially disastrous setback. In their months of training, they had focused all their energies on learning how to capture causeway three, one of the four raised tracks that traversed the flooded meadows behind the dunes. But they had actually landed at causeway two, a mile to the south. This meant that none of their planned objectives could be undertaken. It also meant that all the successive waves, along with the tanks, bulldozers and jeeps, would also land in the wrong place unless they could be urgently alerted to the problem.

Adaptability is everything in warfare; such was the mantra of Colonel James van Fleet, Leonard Schroeder's commanding officer. He landed shortly after Schroeder and was immediately informed that they were in the wrong place. He now had to decide what to do. 'Should we try to shift our entire landing force more than a mile down the beach and follow our original plan? Or should we proceed across the causeways immediately where we had landed?'[44]

The former option carried a clear danger: it would cause chaos for all the follow-up landings. But the latter was also far from ideal, for it would push junior commanders to the limits of their abilities. Their original objectives would be irrelevant and the terrain and targets would be different. In short, they would have to rely on their hard-learned skills to identify and destroy new targets that included bunkers, pillboxes and machine-gun nests.

Van Fleet had played a key role in training his men; now, he took a key role in leading them. 'Go straight inland,' he shouted over the noise of exploding shells. 'We've caught the enemy at a weak point, so let's take advantage of it.'[45] It was a typically pragmatic order from a man who had fought his way through the bloodiest offensives of the First World War. Although General Roosevelt may well have uttered his oft-quoted phrase, 'We'll start the war from here,'[46] it was van Fleet who gave the battlefield command.

The enemy's defensive positions were clearly visible from the top of the dunes. There were five principal strongpoints in Schroeder's zone of beach, three of them behind the dunes and the other two about 700 yards inland. Each consisted of a pillbox surrounded by minefields and barbed wire – easy to defend but extremely dangerous to attack.

Schroeder took the initiative, leading his men on an agonizing belly-crawl through the thick grass that tufted the dunes. This was no-man's-land and progress was slow, for the sand was tangled with barbed wire that had to be blown with Bangalore torpedoes. As Schroeder reached the last of the dunes, he cast a glance back to the beach. He was astonished to see Roosevelt strolling around and 'directing men like the conductor of an orchestra waving his baton'.

Schroeder's target was a German stronghold inside the farm named La Dune. As soon as his men were within range, they let rip with everything they had. To their amazement, the resistance crumpled in seconds. Most of the defenders were still clutching their heads from the pounding of naval shells. They surrendered to Schroeder, 'their hands up, looking terrified'.[47] They were even more terrified when they looked towards the beach, for the sight was little short of astounding. More than sixty landing craft had beached in the five minutes since H-Hour – the moment when the first troops were set ashore – along with tanks, armoured vehicles and specially adapted bulldozers. The tide was out, exposing a watery expanse of sand that was already jammed with military hardware. And this was just the first wave. In its wake came hundreds more tanks and jeeps, along with the Naval Combat Demolition Units and Engineer Battalions – 500 specialists whose task was to destroy the beach obstacles while the tide was still low and then shove the wreckage out of the way. This would enable even greater numbers of landing craft to reach the shore.

While the Germans stared at the beach, Schroeder stared at them. 'They were the first we had ever seen.' He seized their weapons and then took out his trench knife 'and proceeded to cut all their web equipment from their bodies' in order to deprive them of their cartridge and pistol belts. One of the prisoners thought he was going to be stabbed and 'hit the panic button', making a crazed dash towards the beach. Schroeder's men were quick to respond. 'I suppose half the company put bullets into him, thinking he was trying to get away.'[48] Schroeder was surprised to find that many who surrendered were not German, but Czechs and Poles serving under German officers.

He now pushed on inland, killing two Germans who stood in his way. At one point, a shard of flying shrapnel hit his pistol and broke it in two. The gunfire increased in intensity as he pushed through a minefield and he was hit in the arm by two bullets from a machine gun. He felt no pain, for he was numbed by shock. 'The blood was flowing' – it was a serious wound – 'but I continued to lead my men through the minefield towards the village.'[49] One of Schroeder's young lieutenants, Lawrence Hubbard, shouted to those behind him, warning them about some partially concealed mines. As he did so, he stepped on one himself and 'crumpled under the explosion'.[50]

Others were also falling victim to the mines. Captain George Mabry was yelling to a group of seven men when one of them triggered a series of explosions. In seconds, three were killed and four badly injured. Mabry himself had a lucky escape when he inadvertently trod on a mine. 'The explosion slammed me against the ground with a tremendous thud.'[51] He was badly shaken but suffered no injuries.

Howard Lees and his men from E Company had landed at the same time as Leonard Schroeder. After picking their way through the minefield, they saw a glittering prize. Just a few yards further inland was the beginning of causeway one, the raised track that ran like an arrow across the flooded meadows towards Pouppeville. Creeping forward with extreme caution, they advanced on to the causeway. Malvin Pike noticed movement on each side and whispered to the men behind him that 'the Germans were in the water, hiding in the weeds and brush.'[52] They now did the same, shooting at the enemy as they inched through the water.

As they came to the end of the causeway, the Pouppeville church tower was clearly visible. Captain George Mabry was in the lead, unsure as to whether the American airborne troops had already captured the village. He shouted a warning to his men. 'Let's not shoot our own paratroopers.'[53]

He sent Malvin Pike forward towards a low bridge. 'As I approached the undergrowth, I saw a helmet, but as it went down I couldn't tell if it was American or German.'[54] Pike reported back to Captain Mabry on what he had seen. The captain knew exactly what to do. All American troops had been issued with little orange flags to be used to identify themselves. He now put a flag on to a stick and held it over his head. 'An orange flag waved back and forth from a spot on the other side of the bridge.'[55] Soon after, two paratroopers stood up and greeted Pike.

'Fourth Division?'

'Yes.'

They smiled, shook hands and expressed wonder at Pike's newly issued combat gear that looked alarmingly similar to the enemy kit. 'Where in the hell did you get those jackets? We thought you were German paratroopers when we saw you coming across the causeway.'[56]

A few minutes later, they were joined by a third paratrooper, Eugene Brierre. He brought news that the commander of the 101st Airborne Division, Major-General Maxwell Taylor, was in a nearby hedgerow. Brierre told Pike that the general 'would surely be glad'[57] to meet with Captain Mabry.

The captain now went forward and gave the general a crisp salute before warmly shaking his hand. He then motioned to the rest of his men to come forward. Maxwell Taylor was almost overcome with emotion. 'Very soon, the advance guard of the Eighth Infantry appeared, to the cheers of our paratroopers.'[58] It was a historic moment, as everyone knew. Here on the windswept shores of the Cotentin peninsula, the seaborne and airborne assault teams had succeeded in linking up, seizing one of the four causeways so crucial to the day.

Leonard Schroeder was among those aware of the symbolism of the moment. But he was also in considerable pain from the machine-gun bullets that had passed through his arm. Within minutes of the link-up, he fainted from loss of blood and then slipped into unconsciousness. He wouldn't wake up for several hours. When he did come round, he found himself in another world – a tidy canvas medical tent surrounded by doctors.

British commandos head for Sword Beach. Among those aboard
Landing Craft 503 (above right) was Cliff Morris. 'We felt so bad that
we began to wish we were dead.'

12

In Coastal Waters

THE FIRST RAYS of sunshine were mottling the canvas ceiling of Harry Butcher's tent, casting a watery light on to his bed. The canvas smelled of old towels and there was dampness in the air, but for the first time in days the sun was shining through the clouds. It was just as the meteorologist, James Stagg, had forecast.

Butcher's bedside telephone rang sharply at 6.40 a.m. It was Air Chief Marshal Trafford Leigh-Mallory and he wanted to speak to Eisenhower. Butcher, Eisenhower's aide, told him that the Supreme Commander was not yet awake and asked if he could take the message.

'Yes,' said Leigh-Mallory. 'If you've got a scrambler.'

Butcher asked him to call back in a couple of minutes on a secure line. He then grabbed his woollen dressing gown, threw it over his pyjamas and made a dash in his slippers along the cinder path that linked his tent to the communications post. When he picked up the green handset, Leigh-Mallory was already on the other end. He had the latest news from Normandy – an upbeat assessment of everything that had occurred over the previous six hours. 'Only twenty-one of the American C47 [planes] out of the 850 were missing,' he said. 'Only four gliders were unaccounted for.' Better still, one of the returning pilots had watched the paratroopers drop into France and said that they had done so faultlessly. 'It went off smooth, smooth indeed.'

'Grand,' said Butcher in his soft Iowa lilt. 'Grand. I'll tell the boss as soon as he wakes up.' But Leigh-Mallory was not yet finished. With a hint of mischief in his voice he said there was growing evidence that 'the Hun was fooled by our tricks.' Hardly a single Luftwaffe plane had appeared over the skies of Normandy. Rommel, it seemed, had kept 'most of his night fighters over the Pas de Calais area'. The great deception plan, Operation Fortitude, seemed to be paying rich dividends. The Germans clearly thought that the Normandy landings were merely a prelude to something even more spectacular.

Butcher replaced the telephone receiver and considered this news for a moment. It sounded almost too good to be true. The airborne landings appeared to have worked. So had the glider flights. He now strode down the path that led to Eisenhower's caravan and peered through the window to see if the boss was awake. He was happy to be the bearer of good news.

Eisenhower was indeed awake: Butcher could see him reading one of his favourite cowboy novels, 'silhouetted in bed behind a Western'. He knocked and entered, noticing that the Supreme Commander was grinning broadly 'as he lit a cigarette'. He also noticed that the ashtray was overflowing. Eisenhower had been chain-smoking Chesterfields ever since he had left him five hours earlier.

Butcher told him the morning news from Normandy and Eisenhower expressed cautious optimism. He had already received an intelligence report from Admiral Bertram Ramsay, who told him that 'things seemed to be going by plan, and [he] had no bad news at all.'[1] The sinking of USS *Corry* had yet to reach the Southwick House headquarters.

Earlier, Eisenhower had scribbled a note in pencil accepting full responsibility in the event of D-Day being a disaster. 'Our landings in the Cherbourg-Havre area have failed,' he wrote in the note. 'If any blame or fault attaches to the attempt, it is mine alone.'[2] Eisenhower now stuffed it into his jacket pocket in the hope it would no longer be needed.

The initial news of the landings could scarcely have been more upbeat and Eisenhower could be seen visibly to relax. He washed, shaved and, according to Butcher, 'looked in the pink'.[3] The sunshine helped lighten everyone's mood. 'We stood in front of the caravan, enjoying the beautiful, oh, what a beautiful day.'[4] Rome had been captured two days earlier and the 5th Army had triumphed. Butcher could sniff victory in the air.

Not everything was going to plan that morning, however. Out in the English Channel, Lieutenant Commander Heinrich Hoffmann was intending to inflict serious damage on the Allied fleet. His little flotilla of coastal E-boats had burst through the smokescreen enveloping

Force S and let rip with their torpedoes. As they did so, the battleships responded with their own salvo. This landed so close to Hoffmann's craft that 'an enormous column of water enveloped his boat.'[5] For what seemed like minutes, the bridge and command platform were drenched with water.

Most of Hoffmann's torpedoes passed between the *Warspite* and *Ramillies*, missing their target. But the Norwegian destroyer *Svenner* was caught between the two warships and unable to escape the remaining torpedoes. 'A flash of explosion occurred amidships, followed by the sound of detonation and then the burst of fire and smoke that shot high into the air.'[6] So it seemed to the captain, Romuald Nalecz-Tyminski, who was on the bridge at the time. Everything happened in an instant. One minute the crew were on deck, the next they were in the water. From his ship nearby, Able Seaman Sheppard watched them floundering around the stricken ship when 'suddenly her back seemed to break and both the bows and stern, rearing out of the sea, began to edge in towards each other.'[7] To those like Sheppard, who helped pluck the surviving Norwegians from the water, it was a reminder that Operation Overlord was a multinational mission with fighting units from more than a dozen countries, including Norway, Poland, Greece, Czechoslovakia, Belgium, the Netherlands, New Zealand, Australia and France, as well as America, Britain and Canada.

As the *Svenner* went down, Hoffmann found himself under heavy fire from the Allied fleet's big guns. He dispatched an urgent message to headquarters over the wireless: 'Enemy battleships, cruisers with strong destroyers-escort sighted . . . have attacked.'[8] As Allied bombers began diving towards his three vessels, he disengaged from the fight and made a hasty dash back to Le Havre, in order to get more fuel and ammunition. On arrival, he dictated a short report for the naval chief of staff, informing them of the vast fleet approaching Lion-sur-Mer. He added that he had sunk one vessel, perhaps two. He then gulped two cups of coffee, smoked a succession of Woodbines (he had a large stockpile of Allied war booty) and threw back a couple of his self-invented Hoffmann cocktails – four-fifths Napoleon brandy and one-fifth Grand Marnier liqueur. It was the perfect drink after a hard night's work.

★

'Down door; number one.'[9]

'We're off boys, good luck to you. Get into your tanks and follow.'[10]

The amphibious tanks of Force S were already on their way to the shore by the time of Hoffmann's attack, thirty-four floating Shermans whose role was to arrive on Sword Beach just a few minutes before the infantry. The Allies were to land with their heavy weapons first, like a medieval army thrusting its armoured knights into the vanguard. Only when the amphibious tanks were ashore would they send their more vulnerable foot soldiers into battle.

The tanks faced a perilous run-in to the beach. They were to drive off their landing craft at 3,000 yards offshore, plunging into the water and then swimming to the beach with only their inflatable canvas screen to keep them afloat. The idea was for them to wallow so low in the water that the German defenders wouldn't spot them until it was too late.

Sluggish, self-propelled and alarmingly unstable, these tanks had been tested in many different sea conditions, but most of their drivers had never driven them through waters as angry and turbulent as they were on this particular morning.

John Barnes was a twenty-two-year-old corporal with a crest of hair and a razor-sharp moustache: he might have been mistaken for a young Errol Flynn, were it not for the khaki tank uniform. He was dressed in full combat gear, including regulation goggles, nose-clip and air-bottle, as well as a mouthpiece around his chin.

He had rehearsed driving off the landing craft countless times, but only once had the seas been quite as choppy as today, and that had been on a bitter winter's morning in the Moray Firth when snow was blasting horizontal from the sea. It had not been a pleasant experience. Five tanks had sunk and it had been terrifying to see them plunge to the bottom like giant lumps of lead. It was a blessing that only one lad had died.

The worst moment of launching was when the tank lurched off the ramp and slapped into the water like a fat porpoise. If the driver misjudged the timing, the flotation screen would rip. If it ripped, the tank would sink. And if it sank, there was very little chance of escape.

'Don't stall the engine, foot down hard, Fred.'

'Signal is Two Charlie.'

'Mount up.'[11]

As the ramp went down, Barnes could just about make out the distant shore, 'a house on fire, smoke billowing into the sky'. There was dust everywhere. Overhead, Spitfires were dive-bombing the German strongpoints.

The tank edged off the ramp and slumped into the water. It plunged, creaked and bucked, flinging a sheet of freezing spray into the dawn breeze. And then it settled just inches above the water. Barnes would never forget that moment of launching. 'There's spray in your face. You're watching everything that's happening, you're seeing explosions, there's smokescreens being put up . . . As the swell comes, you turn into it and ride it and then come back again.' He had but one thought in his mind: 'I must get to the beach. I must get to the beach.'[12]

The tank belonging to his comrade-in-arms, Corporal Patrick Hennessey, had also launched, but roughly. Hennessey shouted an order to drop the propellers and gave a sigh of relief as he felt them 'bite in the water'. The shoreline was almost invisible, so low were they sitting in the water. 'As a trough appeared in the waves, so the tank slid into the trough and with the engines racing it managed to climb up to the crest of the next wave.'[13] When he looked back through the early morning daylight, he saw 'a stupendous sight . . . ships of every description stretching away to the horizon'.[14]

Hennessey was nineteen, but looked scarcely older than fifteen, a chirpy young boy with big dimples and an even bigger smile. Like every other tank crew, his team had forged an *esprit de corps* over their long months of training. They were an eclectic bunch with equally eclectic surnames: there was a Corporal Gammon, Corporal Bone, Lieutenant Garlicke and Corporal Sweetapple. They sounded more like a regiment heading to the kitchen than one heading to war.

The men had lived together, worked together and knew they would quite possibly die together. For if a tank was hit by a mortar and 'brewed up' – caught fire – there was almost no hope of escape. Nor was there much chance of survival if it sank, even though the tank had an escape hatch in the turret. 'Sounded lovely,' noted Hennessey with more than a touch of sarcasm, 'but if a tank should sink, its heaviest part was the turret. It goes down tracks up.'[15] The men would be trapped underwater and would remain there, alive, until the last pockets of oxygen were exhausted.

For their launch into the English Channel, Hennessey was riding atop the tank, along with the co-driver, Joe Gallagher. His task was to man the bilge pumps that were intended to stop the canvas screen from flooding. Down below, in the claustrophobic driving compartment, young Harry Bone was crouched at the controls, fighting to keep the engine running. 'We all knew that if it stopped, there was no chance of survival.' As they angled away from the landing craft, Hennessey observed the tank of his friend, Noel Denny, coming off the ramp. 'As he was going through the large doorway, the ship rolled and as it rolled the tank lurched to one side and the canvas screen brushed the iron side of the entrance and slashed it.' The tank was unable to reverse, for there were others behind it waiting to launch. The only thing Denny could do was to drive it into the water and hope that it would stay afloat.

Hennessey watched anxiously, praying that his friends would be okay. It was a forlorn hope. 'As it hit the water, the water gushed in through the screen and the tank sank.' Noel Denny managed to fight his way back to the surface, spluttering for breath, but the rest were drowned. Hennessey watched in horror. 'There was nothing anybody could do, it was our first casualty.'[16]

The rest of the tanks were successfully launched to the great relief of their crews, and before long a little battalion of Shermans was ploughing its way through the heavy sea towards the beach of Lion-sur-Mer, still obscured by clouds of drifting smoke.

Lieutenant Commander Hoffmann's dawn strike had caused panic among the captains of Force S, but it was unable to halt the opening act of destruction planned by the architects of D-Day. The naval firepower available to Rear Admiral Arthur George Talbot, commander of the Sword flotilla, was significantly greater than that of the other four Allied fleets. He had twenty-two big vessels at his disposal, including two huge battleships and their accompanying craft, HMS *Roberts*. These were equipped with eighteen fifteen-inch guns that could fire 35,000 pounds of explosive in a single salvo, enough to wipe out all but the strongest bunkers. The rest of the larger ships – five cruisers and fifteen destroyers – were anchored closer to the shoreline. Their task was to target the shore batteries and trenches.

Douglas Reeman was a nineteen-year-old lieutenant aboard a diminutive motor torpedo boat; he thought he had seen everything in his three years at war. He had trailed the Eighth Army along the North African coast and been witness to horrific bloodshed while supporting the invasion of Sicily. But he had never seen a bombardment to match what was planned for Sword Beach and he and his crew of teenage volunteers watched in silent awe as HMS *Warspite*'s massive guns were cranked into the correct angle and primed for action. One by one, the other ships could also be seen inching their lethal firepower towards the coast. For Reeman, it was a sight to savour. 'From our low hull, the cruisers looked enormous with their streaming battle-flags and their turrets already swinging towards the land, high angled and ready to fire.'

He glanced at the skipper of his own craft and was surprised to see he had changed into full dress uniform, trimmed with gold braid. 'Might as well do it proper,' he said proudly. He also ordered the battle ensigns to be flown from the mast – something normally reserved for distinguished guests and burials at sea. Reeman felt a lump in his throat. 'I wanted to cheer. I think we all did.'[17]

It was exactly 5.30 a.m.: HMS *Warspite*, 'the grand old lady'[18] of the Royal Navy, was about to give the greatest performance of her career. First came the opening act, one familiar to gunners on every ship of the fleet: 'the shrill ascending song of the ammunition car speeding upwards from the magazine'.[19] This delivered the shells to the gunners. Then came the thud of the shells being loaded, followed by the loud ram of the pneumatic hammer. And then came a pause – a brief moment of silence. It was as if the venerable old dame was taking a deep breath before letting rip.

'*Fire!*'

The order came from Wing Commander Leslie Glover, who was circling the pale dawn sky in his Spitfire. His task was to direct the aim of the *Warspite*'s gunners on to the German bunkers below

– one of thirty spotter planes flying over the beaches during the course of the landings. Seconds after issuing his command, the warship fired her first fifteen-inch broadside, hurling 11,500 pounds of high explosive at the shoreline. Glover found himself uncomfortably close to the aerial trajectory and his Spitfire suffered 'a most violent bump which practically shook me out of my wits'. As he stared towards the mouth of the River Orne, he saw 'two enormous objects moving rapidly away from me towards the shore'.[20] Inadvertently, he had just flown through the slipstream of *Warspite*'s fifteen-inch shells.

On his high-speed motor torpedo boat, Douglas Reeman was also witness to that opening salvo. It left him exhilarated, terrified and appalled. 'You could see the ripple of flashes along the horizon and had to force yourself not to duck, as the great shells tore overhead with the sounds of tearing canvas.' It was as if the sky itself were being shredded, so deafening was the noise.

He and his crew grasped their heads as the shock waves thudded through their brains. 'It made thought impossible and when we shouted to each other, our voices sounded strange, like divers talking under water.'[21]

A twenty-one-year-old tank officer named Lieutenant David Holbrook had also swung his gaze to the *Warspite*. He saw that she was 'firing swelling clouds of incandescence out of the long trunks of her fifteen-inch guns'. She was also belching noxious black fumes and volcanic orange fire. 'The flames, as long as towers, unrolled into clouds of smoke as big as castles.' Holbrook jammed his fists into his ears, for 'a noise like an express train at full speed followed, as the projectile was thrust through the high air into France. One could see the missile, flying, at times. Each shell weighed nearly a ton.'[22]

It was bad enough to be a spectator, infinitely worse to be a gunner. Each time a broadside was fired, the sudden vacuum sucked the air from men's lungs, causing them to splutter and gasp for breath. Several gunners suffered severe nose-bleeds as capillaries were ruptured. There was the acrid stench of cordite. And the barrels of the guns grew so hot that their paintwork blistered and they had to be hosed down with seawater.

Two hardened Canadian Broadcasting Corporation reporters,

Andrew Cowan and Bill Herbert, thought they had lived through every possible experience since the outbreak of war. But they had never covered anything like this. 'When the guns fired at once, the great 35,000-ton battleship gave a tremendous shudder.' There were shouts from the crew, who needed their help. 'Everything on board that can fall or break loose had to be fastened or battened down.'[23] Anything not tied down was at risk of being flung through the air. Both journalists rammed wads of cotton wool into their ears, lest their brains were pulverized by the roar.

On the *Ramillies*, anchored close to *Warspite*, the violent retorts were starting to wreck the fabric of the ship. 'By now we were causing damage to ourselves below decks, furniture was smashed and heavy pieces of equipment were shaken from bulkheads and thrown across the deck.'[24] More alarmingly, cracks were appearing in the heavy steel stanchions supporting the decks. If the shelling was causing the ship to fall apart, the men on board could only wonder at the destruction they must be causing ashore.

The ships of Force S were not alone in bombarding the beaches. The other four fleets were also hurling vast quantities of explosives towards the little ports that lined the Normandy coast. Force U was pounding the Cotentin peninsula. Force J and Force G were bombing the coastline around Asnelles and Force O was targeting Saint-Laurent and its environs. Few on board the vessels paused to consider that this entire stretch of coast was dotted with bustling little villages like Lion-sur-Mer, Luc-sur-Mer and Vierville-sur-Mer, home to fishermen, farmers, bakers and tradesmen.

Allied Supreme Command had foreseen the danger to local civilians living along the coast, as well as in cities such as Caen, and had dropped thousands of leaflets warning them to flee. *Urgent Message: Leave without Delay! Head for the Fields! You Have Not a Minute to Lose*. But it was impossible to know if anyone had followed this advice.

Eighteen-year-old Pierre Piprel and his older brother, Fernand, had persuaded their mother to remain in Vierville-sur-Mer, even though she was being driven to distraction by the nightly bombardments from the air. Madame Piprel had recently lost her husband; she had no wish to lose her sons as well. But teenage boys are stubborn and fearless and she didn't have the will to argue with them. They would stay in the family home, in spite of the dangers.

Both Piprel boys were already awake at 5 a.m. on 6 June and they went to pay a call on a neighbour, the early rising Monsieur Mary. A garrulous aeronautical expert (and possessor of a forbidden pair of binoculars), he was always the first to know what had been hit in the previous night's raids.

'Nothing,' he said to the brothers on this particular morning. 'Just the usual. Same planes, same bombardment.'

The two of them returned home mildly disappointed. But as they picked their way through the streets, they suddenly caught sight of something intriguing out at sea. The horizon looked different. There were dark patches where no dark patches should be.

'*Ma parole!*' exclaimed Pierre, hardly daring to believe his eyes. '*My word!* Ships!'

The two lads scurried back to Monsieur Mary's house to warn him that something was afoot.

'Come quick, Monsieur Mary! Bring your binoculars. We think there're ships.'

The old engineer was sceptical but he liked to humour the boys and did as they asked. When he looked out to sea, he was stunned into silence. What he saw was a marvel. '*Yes! Yes!*' he said at length. 'The sea's full of ships. They're everywhere.'[25] He broke into an infectious chuckle, for he had been awaiting this moment for years.

His laughter was soon brought to an abrupt end. Quite without warning there was a tremendous explosion as the great guns of HMS *Glasgow* and USS *Texas* launched shells at the beach area around Vierville. It happened in an earth-shattering flash: walls collapsed, homes shuddered to their foundations and tiles shattered into lethal fragments as they were blown off roofs. Pierre and his brother scurried back to their mother in fear of their lives. Their home had had a miraculous escape, for a shell had exploded in the street outside, scouring a deep hole and bringing down the electricity pylon.

Just a short walk from the Piprels' house, on Rue Pavée, five-year-old Fernand Olard was sobbing into his pillow. All night long there had been distant booms and flashes of light that tore through his bedroom curtains. Now, the bangs seemed to be coming from just outside his room. Little Fernand wailed into the darkness but there was never any answer. His mother and father were unable to hear his cries and the two beds where his brothers usually slept were empty, for they had already taken refuge in their parents' room.

Nightly bombing raids had taken place for much of his short life, and the Olard parents had put their children through countless rehearsals so that they would know what to do when the long-expected invasion finally came. Fernand had learned the routine by heart. 'We each had to take our little package of Sunday clothes, along with our pillow, and make our way to their bedroom to get dressed.' Their mother had drummed into them the fact that speed was essential. 'To go faster, we had to use the trapdoor on the landing.'

There were eight Olard children – four girls and four boys – living in the family home. The street was the very picture of old France, with shuttered houses and a giant *publicité* for Dubonnet painted in blue and white on one of the gable walls. It was also extremely close to the sea. Just a stone's throw from their front door was one of the finest beaches in Normandy, five miles of sand and shingle from which the children of Vierville had plucked razor clams in the days before the war. Although Monsieur and Madame Olard didn't breathe a word to their children, they must have known that it was exactly the sort of beach on which the Allies might land. And now, as the bombardment intensified from 5.30 a.m. onwards, they raised the alarm.

Still shivering with fear, little Fernand clambered through the trapdoor and ran into his parents' room, where the rest of his brothers and sisters had already gathered. He had forgotten his clothes and pillow. Once these had been collected and everyone was ready, 'we set off with the pillows on our heads in order to take refuge in the house of our grandparents.' They lived nearby in a stone dwelling as solid as a bunker, with a fireplace so massive it was like a giant shoulder propping up the roof. Monsieur Olard huddled the children into the chimney-breast, reassuring them that it was the safest place to be. He was unaware that, out to sea, the naval guns of Force O were being winched in their direction and that the heavy cruiser HMS *Glasgow* had Vierville in its sights.

The naval spectacle began just minutes after their arrival at the house and they had the misfortune to have front-row seats. 'There was an enormous explosion' that seemed to slam through the foundations. It was accompanied by a clap of thunder and an ear-wrenching crash as the kitchen windows were blown from their frames and a thousand shards of glass were flung across the room. Rubble, bricks and tiles tumbled into a suffocating cloud of dust. The house next door had taken the full force of the blast and had partially collapsed into a pile of masonry that was 'completely blocking the doorways'.[26] It was a blessing that none of the Olard family was hurt.

Help was at hand. A neighbour, Madame Hélène, and her son Louis assisted Fernand's father in passing the children one by one through the shattered kitchen window. They then hurried over to Monsieur Blin's house just down the road: he'd had the foresight to dig a protective trench in the garden.

Little Fernand now cowered in the trench, terrified by the sound of flying shrapnel. As it struck the wooden planks that covered the trench, it made strange crackling noises that he would remember for years afterwards. The big guns continued to fire and the civilians of Vierville found themselves caught in a deadly trap. The mayor's house was hit and a shell exploded on the local *boulangerie*, killing the baker's ten-month-old son, Jacques. Also killed was the family's twenty-year-old helper, Pauline. And still the bombing intensified. The Olard family had long feared the landing would be terrible but they had never realized it would be as bad as this.

They were not alone in their predicament, for very few of their neighbours had taken the Allied warnings seriously. Just a short distance out of town, at the Château de Gruchy, Madame de Loÿs and her sixteen-year-old son, Guy, had just lived through their worst night in months. Madame de Loÿs was chatelaine of her hereditary domain, a pile of architectural whimsy built to the demands of one of her more eccentric forebears, a man with a *folie de grandeur* and a very fat wallet. Not content with turrets and spires, he had excavated fantastical subterranean tunnels that criss-crossed the estate.

Never would he know how useful these tunnels would prove. As the bombs began to shred trees and gouge craters into the lawn, friends, neighbours and Madame de Loÿs herself took refuge in those dripping underground passages. They were a desperate crowd in desperate straits. 'There was a woman in tears, for her husband had just perished in the bombardment, and an infant barely two weeks old.'

The passages were also providing shelter for a number of German soldiers of the 726 Infantry Regiment. Their company commander was Captain Alfred Grunschloss, a bespectacled professor of law with a punctilious adherence to etiquette. He had made the château his command post, much to Madame de Loÿs's displeasure, and remained at his post for much of that night. By 4 a.m., the soldiers were showing signs of panic, 'moving about like madmen, screaming orders down the stairs and running about in every room'. By 5 a.m., as the bombing grew heavier, Captain Grunschloss moved his communications team into the underground sanctuary.

Madame de Loÿs had a natural froideur and had always kept the Germans at arm's length. But now, she couldn't help eavesdropping on Captain Grunschloss's wireless team.

'Did you hear what the telephone operator said?' she whispered to her son. Guy de Loÿs shrugged. Unlike her, he had only a rudimentary understanding of German.

'He said: large enemy fleet eight miles offshore.'

The operator overheard her and displayed a grim face of defeat. '*Deutschland kaput*,' he said. Soon after, the naval bombardment began in earnest. 'The din was infernal, the earth was shuddering under the explosions, the underground passages were shaking from the explosions.' It was not long before the first of the wounded were brought into the shelter. One casualty was grievously injured, lying on a stretcher with his cranial cavity ripped open. Young Guy de Loÿs was both fascinated and appalled. He could 'clearly see, beneath the intact membrane, the palpitating brain'.[27] It was stomach-churning for him, but infinitely worse for the victim. He had to be strapped to the stretcher with tight belts in a vain attempt to keep him from moving.

The naval cannonade seemed to endure for ever and hundreds of families – thousands indeed – were praying for their own survival. But the bombardment was intensifying with every minute that passed. When Fernand Broekx, an inhabitant of Colleville-sur-Mer, looked along the shoreline, he noted a column of acrid black smoke billowing upwards for almost a mile into the sky, while the coast itself was 'nothing more than a gush of flames'.[28]

It felt like the end of the world.

The first American troops to wade ashore on Omaha Beach were jokingly known as the suicide wave. 'We all expected to come back,' said one. Almost none did.

13

Omaha

'So long – good luck.'
   'See you on the beach!'[1]
'Watch out for those French girls!'
'See you in Berlin!'[2]

The young men of A Company were in high spirits as they boarded their landing craft at 4.30 a.m. and prepared to head towards Omaha Beach. Each of the six boats contained thirty-one youths who were to be in the vanguard of the attack. They were a tightly knit band who had trained together for more than a year. Many had even closer ties: thirty of them came from the same home town of Bedford, in Virginia. They felt part of one big family.

In the murky half-light of dawn, Gilbert Murdock shouted across to his friend Robert Bruce, who was clambering into another boat. He then gave a cheery wave to young George Roach, a slight lad of eighteen who was in charge of one of the company's flame-throwers. Roach was grinning broadly. Although the air was moist and chill, it did nothing to diminish the camaraderie of the men of A Company. Nor did the fact that they had been nicknamed the 'suicide wave' on account of being the first to land. One of them went so far as to say it was a badge of honour and 'something that we felt with pride'. Most brushed off the idea of death with the casual abandon of carefree teenagers. 'We all expected to come back.'[3]

The man entrusted with ferrying these young men to the shore was Jimmy Green, an English buccaneer with a thirst for adventure and a keen sense of maritime history. At twenty-three, he was older than many in A Company and his squinted eyes and salt-stiff hair were testimony to his storm-tossed months at sea. Green came from the seafaring port of Bristol, whence Sebastian Cabot had sailed to the New World, and was a keen student of the Anglo-French naval wars. He felt he was making maritime history in ferrying A Company to Omaha Beach and, with a nod and a wink to the pageantry of the occasion, instructed his landing craft to set off in two columns of three, 'like Nelson at Trafalgar'.

Green had spent a year escorting convoys through the treacherous seas of the North Atlantic and a further year with Combined Operations, surviving the catastrophic commando raid on Dieppe. He had also worked alongside the American Rangers and had been most impressed by their cut-throat attitude to warfare: 'a pretty tough group who looked as though they could take care of themselves'.⁴

He was somewhat aghast, therefore, when introduced to the men charged with storming Omaha Beach in the first wave. They were 'a friendly but shy bunch of fresh-faced country lads who must have felt at home in Ivybridge' – a little rural town in Devon – 'where they had trained for the invasion'.⁵ He found them polite and kindly – a group of helpful young men who would run errands for the elderly in their home towns. But they were entirely lacking the warlike spirit of the Rangers.

Their leader was a clean-shaven young chap named Taylor Fellers, a construction foreman in his previous life, who was the sort of community mainstay that could be found in any number of towns in the Blue Ridge foothills of Virginia. Nicknamed Tail-Feathers on account of his prowess in the high school sprint team, he was widely liked and much respected. 'Industrious, competent and thoroughly reliable'⁶ was the opinion of one who knew him well.

Jimmy Green found him 'a very serious, thoughtful officer who seemed a lot older than our sailors, who were in their late teens or early twenties'.⁷ Yet the more he got to know Fellers, the more he felt a nagging sense of anguish – not just for Fellers himself but also for the young men under his command. Their task was a formidable one. They had to capture one of the four ravines that cut a gully upwards through the steep bluffs behind Omaha Beach, a narrow track that provided the only vehicular access to the town of Vierville-sur-Mer. It would have been a tall order even for the finest troops, but far more so for a band of teenagers who, to Jimmy Green's eyes, seemed, at best, 'an inexperienced assault group'.⁸

Allied planners had divided Omaha Beach into seven sections, each with its own codename: Charlie, Dog Green, Dog White, Dog Red, Easy Green, Easy Red and Fox Green. Each section was to be assaulted by a designated company, with Taylor Fellers's men of A Company leading the vanguard on to Dog Green. What made their mission all the more difficult was the fact that Omaha Beach, like Utah, had been heavily fortified with pillboxes, reinforced bunkers and machine-gun posts. There were anti-tank positions, mounted guns and multiple-barrelled mortars, as well as rocket batteries and artillery positions. All were connected by a zigzagging maze of trenches manned by snipers.

The beach itself was waterlogged at high tide and resembled a mine-strewn medieval moat. Next came the twenty-five-foot-high concrete sea wall, built like an enceinte and topped with barbed wire. And then there were the bluffs and cliffs that reared to a height of sixty metres.

Jimmy Green noticed the atmosphere change dramatically as the young men boarded the landing craft and prepared for the run-in to the beach. The jokes and banter came to an abrupt end. 'I think they were realizing that this was it.' Those who did talk were 'quiet and subdued'.

Green's orders were to land the men on the beach at 6.36 a.m., which required his craft to push off from the *Empire Javelin* some two hours earlier. Taylor Fellers's men were to be followed by many more waves of troops arriving at regular intervals after the initial landing.

The craft set off under the cover of darkness and were still five miles from the beach when they happened across a second little flotilla laden with tanks. 'What the hell are these doing here?' asked an incredulous Green. The tanks were meant to land on the shore in advance of the infantry and should, therefore, have been far closer to land.

Fellers was visibly shocked. 'They're supposed to be ahead of us,' he said. This was a crucial part of the landing plan. Without tanks already on the beaches, the young men of A Company would have no artillery support.

'They're not going to make it,' said Green, who checked his watch and realized they were woefully behind schedule. 'They were really ploughing into the waves, going as fast as they could, but they were only doing, what, five knots to our eight, and they were shipping water.' He turned to Fellers with a grim face. 'We've got to go in and leave them behind. Is that all right?'

'Yes,' replied Fellers. 'We've got to be there on time.'[9] He tried to put a brave face on this unexpected mishap, yet he felt a sense of impending disaster. A fundamental part of the plan had gone seriously awry.

A second vital element had also gone wrong, as Green was quick to notice. When the rocket ships fired the first of their salvoes, 'not one came anywhere near the shoreline'. Indeed, most of them splashed into the sea more than a quarter of a mile from the beach. Green was furious. 'A terrific firework display, but absolutely useless and I shook my fist at them.'[10] He had already experienced the poorly planned Dieppe raid. Now, he railed against the architects of D-Day.

He was not alone in his anger. One of the youngsters on Gilbert Murdock's craft spoke for everyone when he gave a cynical shout. 'Well, there go our holes on the beach.'[11] Several nodded grimly, aware that without craters they would have no cover. Many more were too sick to care, vomiting into their helmets on account of the pitching, tossing sea. One young soldier had swallowed so many seasickness tablets that he could scarcely keep himself awake.

Jimmy Green had been told that the American air force would have bombarded the beach, causing additional craters that would provide refuge for the infantry. But when he looked through his binoculars, he could see 'no marks at all'. Indeed, it was 'a virgin beach stretching for three hundred yards with not a sign of any place where the troops could shelter'. He felt depressed at the thought of sending the youths into a trap, a feeling that was accentuated by the drizzling rain and leaden sky. 'It was a grim, depressing sort of morning and the cliffs looked very foreboding and sinister.' As he drew his craft closer to the shoreline, he spotted the first of many pillboxes hidden among the dunes. He thought it would be 'a pretty formidable beach for the troops to take'.[12]

It was almost 6.30 a.m. and they were fast approaching the shoreline. Gilbert Murdock was 'thinking and shivering'.[13] A fine spray had left him soaked and when he looked down at his sodden boots he was alarmed to see that the landing craft was awash. The coxswain had also noticed that the craft was shipping water and ordered the men to bail it out with their helmets.

It was now, as they neared the shore, that they experienced their first mishap. Jimmy Green had just ordered all the landing craft into line when LCA 911 keeled over and started to sink, probably after striking a mine. It was fortunate that the men were wearing life jackets, for most were able to pull themselves from the half-submerged craft.

Only a few hours earlier Green had been given explicit orders: 'Don't pick up anybody from the water. Get to the beach on time.' Now, he shouted across to them: 'I'll be back to pick you up!' He hated abandoning them, even temporarily. 'It really did hurt to go on, but I had to do it.'[14] All his thoughts were focused on reaching the beach.

'Where exactly do you want me to land?' He consulted with Taylor Fellers as the two of them studied the approaching shore. Fellers pointed to the deep ravine that led to the top of the bluffs and said he wanted to land on the right-hand side. 'And I want the other group to land to the left of the pass.'

Jimmy Green nodded, cranked up the engines and began to draw away from the other craft. He was intending to hit the shore at full speed, dodging any obstacles as he thrust the craft forward. A handful of shells landed harmlessly in the water, but there was so little enemy fire that he wondered if the pillboxes and dug-outs were empty. The bluffs drew nearer, the water grew shallow and then there was a loud crunch as the landing craft ground to a halt in the belt of shingle that lay some twenty yards offshore. The ramp went down and Taylor Fellers waded through the breaking surf towards the beach, fording through waist-deep water while his comrades followed closely behind. Green watched them disembark 'in very good order. They didn't need to be ushered out and about. They knew what they had to do.'[15]

Still there was no gunfire. As Green surveyed the scene, he felt a strange sense of the unreal. It was clear that the bluffs and sand dunes were heavily fortified, yet not a single bullet rang out as Taylor Fellers crunched his way up the beach. Indeed nothing moved or stirred. Green had landed the thirty-one men into 'an unearthly silence'.

He had been planning to cover the men with his machine guns. But there was no need, for they were now all ashore and crouched on a ridge of shingle. Unaware that the defence of this little stretch of Omaha was being carefully coordinated, Green prepared to head back to sea in order to rescue the survivors of the stricken LCA 911. But before he did so, he first ordered his radioman to send a message of reassurance to their mother ship, *Empire Javelin*. It was upbeat, truthful and just four words long: 'Landed against light opposition.'[16]

Omaha's defences had proved a walkover.

'*Feuer, Wegner, feuer!*'

Lance-Corporal Lang was screaming at the teenage Karl Wegner, ordering him to let rip with his machine gun. It was now or never: the invading troops were landing on a beach that was almost totally exposed. They could be mown down with very little effort. But Wegner had temporarily frozen, partly out of panic and partly because he had realized the enormity of what he was about to do. 'I saw all those men in olive brown uniforms splashing through the water towards the sand.' They looked young and vulnerable, 'so unprotected in the wide open space of the beach'.[17] He felt deeply disturbed at the idea of cutting them down with his bullets.

Wegner was a nineteen-year-old from Hanover, a boyish young lad who cocked a snook at Nazi regulations by wearing his military beret at a list and posing bare-chested for photographs. Like his teenage compatriot, Franz Gockel, who was at the other end of Omaha Beach, Wegner was stationed in a strongpoint – WN72 – that lay just a few minutes' walk from the town of Vierville-sur-Mer. He had spent the previous few hours cowering in his dug-out, praying that he would survive the ferocious naval bombardment.

When the shelling finally came to an end, he learned that the worst of the damage lay inland. His comrade, Peter Simeth, poked his head out of the bunker and could see 'the black smoke belching out of the fiercely burning village of Trévières'.[18] The beach itself was completely untouched by the Allied shells.

The stress of the bombardment had drained Wegner. In the calm that followed, he dozed for a moment while resting his head on his machine gun. He was woken by a vigorous shake from another of his comrades, Willi Schuster. Still groggy, he asked what was wrong. Schuster pointed towards the sea and Wegner found himself looking at 'ships as far as one could see'. He could also see several lines of landing craft that looked to be stationary in the water. In reality, they were getting into formation. 'Suddenly, they all turned and began to come straight in towards the beach.' Wegner was flushed with fear. 'The sweat rolled down my brow as I watched these boats come closer and closer. My stomach was in knots.'

As they approached, he lived through a hundred nightmares. This, then, was it. Soon, they would be storming towards him. His commanding officer, Lance-Corporal Lang, sensed his fear and took the butt of his pistol 'and crashed it down on the top of my helmet'. This had the desired effect. 'The metallic clang brought me to life and I pulled the trigger up tight.' It was something he had practised on countless occasions, but never against living targets. Now, it had to be done. He watched the landing craft grind into the shore. He saw the first enemy troops begin their advance up the shingle. And then he yanked hard on the trigger. 'The machine gun roared, sending hot lead into the men running along the beach.'

Some collapsed into the sand. 'I knew I hit them.' Others were desperately seeking cover, only to find there was no shelter on that exposed beach. 'The bullets ripped up and down the sand.' It was so easy to kill; it took so little energy. 'My mind rationalized it: this was war. Even so, it left a sour taste in my mouth.' Wegner was shooting down youngsters the same age as him. Yet he knew that they would kill him, if only they could reach his bunker. 'Now was not the time to think of right or wrong, only of survival.'

He pulled on the trigger once again and sent another hail of bullets into the exposed young soldiers on the beach. 'After the first few moments had passed, my mind became automated. I would fire as I had been trained to do, in short bursts 15 to 20cm above the ground.' Each time the gun jammed, he would clear it as fast as possible, aware that every second counted. 'Willi kept the ammunition clean, as dirt would jam the gun, ready to load.' At one point, he paused and looked at the beach. 'I saw Amis [Americans] lying everywhere. Some were dead and others quite alive.'[19]

If this was the long-awaited Allied invasion, it looked set to end in a massacre.

The second wave of troops to land on that stretch of beach were the young men of B Company, who had trained with their buddies in Taylor Fellers's team and had become close friends. One of them, Howard 'Hal' Baumgarten, had originally been in A Company and had only been transferred at the last minute. He was looking forward to being reunited with his friends on the beach.

But he grew increasingly alarmed as his landing craft neared the shore. The wind was stiffening and pitching their craft into the breaking waves, swamping it with freezing water. They were ordered to bail it out with their helmets, an unpleasant task given that it was swirling with vomit. Baumgarten could hear machine-gun fire and the muffled crack of exploding mortars. When he glanced at the shore, he saw a sickening bank of reddish-orange flame billowing skywards. Smoke and dust were drifting across the beach in yellow clouds, casting a chemical pall over the deathly scene. The feeling of optimism had been draining fast: now, it vanished in an instant. 'Suddenly there was silence and the mood of the men became very sombre.'[20] Baumgarten had the impression of being landed into the jaws of death.

He glanced at his Rima watch, a gift from his father. It was 6.15 a.m. The shore was getting closer. He could see the white steeple of the church at Vierville-sur-Mer.

From afar, the noise had sounded like distant thunder. But now, as his landing craft approached the shore, the entire coast was roaring in fury. And then – like a blow from a hammer – his head was spun inside out as an 88mm shell detonated in the adjacent landing craft. It happened in a blink. The wooden hull was shredded to splinters, inflicting catastrophic injuries on the men on board. Some were blown through the air, some torn to shreds. Baumgarten himself was 'showered with wood, metal and body parts. And, of course, blood.'[21] Blood was everywhere, in the air, in the sea, on his face.

He stared through the spray, praying for the hell to be over.

'We can't go in there. We can't see the landmarks. We must pull off.'[22] Panic and confusion mired their approach to the beach. They were almost there. Just a few seconds to go.

'Drop the ramp!'

'Come on, goddam it.'

'Keep your heads down.'

'Let's go!'[23]

Baumgarten jumped into the waist-deep water just as a German machine gun opened up on the ramp. Clarius Riggs was the first to be mown down, killed in a spray of bullets. A strapping six-footer from Pennsylvania, he crashed face-down into the water. Baumgarten saw the surf around him turn red. Next to fall was Robert Ditmar, who lurched forward for ten yards before collapsing on to the beach. He was screaming in shock and agony. 'I'm hit, I'm hit.'[24] He slumped into a tank obstacle and his body made a complete turn. He ended up 'sprawled on the damp sand with his head facing the Germans, his face looking skyward'.[25] He was still screaming, 'Mother! Mom!'[26]

'Keep your heads down!'[27]

'My God!'

'Try to make it in!'[28]

Sergeant Barnes had just reached the beach when he was shot in front of Baumgarten. Four others were bleeding to death in the sand, their bodies twitching and convulsing. Sergeant 'Pilgrim' Robertson had a gaping wound on his forehead. He was stumbling crazily, without helmet, his blond hair streaked with blood. Baumgarten saw him fall to his knees. He reached for his rosary. 'At this moment, the Germans cut him in half with their deadly cross-fire.'[29] Private Kafkalas keeled over as shells and mortars erupted simultaneously.

It was a tableau so macabre, so terrifying in intensity, that it seemed surreal. 'Men with guts hanging out of their wounds and body parts lying along our path.'[30] All around Baumgarten, fountains of sand were being kicked up by exploding shells.

Baumgarten saw a gleam of light on a German helmet up on the bluff. He aimed and fired. 'A miracle.' He had hit the man. His expertise in sharp-shooting had paid off. But German snipers were now aiming at him. He had already been hit by two bullets, one passing clean through the top of his helmet and another hitting the receiver of his M-1 rifle. Now, a monster shell exploded some twenty yards from where he was lying in the sand. It happened in a flash. A cataclysmic bang and a wave of lethal fragments. Baumgarten felt as if he had been hit 'with a baseball bat, only the results were much worse. My upper jaw was shattered, the left cheek was blown open. My upper lip was cut in half. The roof of my mouth was cut up and teeth and gums were laying all over my mouth.'[31]

As blood gushed from the wound, Baumgarten dragged himself back to the water and plunged his head into the freezing surf. He then looked up, blinking, still bleeding profusely. For as far as he could see, to the left and right, his friends and comrades were being cut down. All were trapped in a hellish massacre from which there was no escape. Of his buddies in A Company, there was not a sign. It was as if they had never landed.

The truth of the matter was altogether more sinister. The unearthly silence that had greeted the lads on Jimmy Green's landing craft was carefully orchestrated by the Germans. Karl Wegner and his comrades in WN72 had held their fire until all the troops were ashore. Only then did they fire. As Wegner had let rip with his machine gun, Taylor Fellers and his men were struck by the violent staccato of a dozen machine guns. They were hit from the left, from the right, from above. The guns covered every inch of beach. They didn't stand a chance.

The other landing craft belonging to A Company (the ones that came ashore to the left of the Vierville ravine) had been fired on by the adjacent stronghold, WN71. On Boat Two, Lieutenant Edward Tidrick was horrified to find himself landing on a pristine beach.

'My God!' he cried. 'We're coming in at the right spot, but look at it! No shingle, no wall, no shell holes, no cover. Nothing!'[32]

As he jumped from the ramp, he was shot through the throat.

His friend, Leo Nash, could hear Tidrick trying to give orders, but the blood was foaming and gurgling in his voice box. 'Advance with the wire cutters,'[33] he cried. Seconds later, he was cut down by machine-gun bullets that hit him in an almost perfect straight line, from the crown to the pelvis.

On another landing craft, Gilbert Murdock was watching his lieutenant run down the ramp in readiness for the fight ahead. 'He was immediately cut down by machine-gun fire.' His friend, Rodriguez, was cut in half by bullets. Another mate, Dominguez, crashed over the side into water stained brownish-red with blood. When Murdock himself leaped into the water he sank like lead. The landing craft had grounded on a runnel, not the shore, and the surrounding water was nine feet deep. He clutched his life jacket and 'punched the CO_2 tubes for buoyancy'. It forced him upwards. As he broke the surface, the landing craft smacked into him and swept him forward to the beach.

He reached the shingle amid a sickening clutter of limbs and corpses, but glimpsed a moment of hope as the first of the amphibious tanks roared out of the sea. Within seconds of coming ashore, it was whacked by a German 88 mortar and exploded into an incandescent ball of flame. A second tank also blew up on landing, incinerating its crew. Murdock glanced back to the sea but couldn't see any others. Most of the promised tanks had foundered in the heavy waves.

He began crawling on his belly, tortoise-like, inching his way through the bloody slime. He passed his comrade, Charles McSkimming, who had been hit in the arm and was begging for morphine. Murdock gave him a shot from his first aid kit and then continued furrowing up the sand until he reached one of the sinister beach obstacles, a refuge of sorts from the exploding mortars. He found two others still alive, including his young buddy George Roach. He was trembling from the ferocity of the onslaught.

'*What happened?*' Murdock could hardly form the words in his state of blank incomprehension.

Roach had been watching the unfolding catastrophe from his position behind the tank obstacle and gave Murdock the news in two terse sentences. 'All the officers were dead,' he said. 'All of the non-coms were dead.' The surf was churned with the dead and wounded, some of whom were trying to float in with the tide. Among them was Charles McSkimming, who found the tide lapping around his head just moments after Murdock had given him morphine. Most of those with the strength to haul themselves up the beach were being picked off by German snipers. So were those trying to rescue them. Two hundred and five men had come ashore with A Company's landing craft. Within seven minutes of landing, Murdock reckoned that only thirteen were still alive.

'You're hit,' he muttered to one of those lying next to him.

'You damn fool, so are you.'

Murdock looked down at his leg and saw two spent bullets lodged in his ankle.

The tide was surging in at such a pace that one of the burned-out tanks was already half submerged.

'Look, I'm a good swimmer,' said George Roach, 'and you're not that badly hurt. Let me swim you out to that knocked-out tank in the water out there.'

The two of them slipped into the incoming surf and managed to reach the tank without getting shot again. When they worked their way round to the rear of the vehicle, they found they were not alone. 'We could see three heads bobbing up and down. It was three men from the tank crew with their faces all powder burnt.' It was hard to tell if they were dead or alive.

More shocking was the sight of the tank commander sheltering behind the turret 'with his left leg off at the knee and the bone in the water and the artery in the water'. He was muttering deliriously, saying that 'his men were of no value to him and they wouldn't do what he said.' He somehow persuaded them to swim to the shore before the tank was completely swamped. Murdock watched their vain attempt to reach the beach. 'The last I saw, they were kicking and trying to make the beach, but they didn't.'[34] Murdock himself clung to a jerry-can and floated aimlessly for an eternity before eventually being rescued.

Jimmy Green was horrified when he learned that every lad from his landing craft had been killed. It would haunt him for the rest of his life. 'I was in some way responsible for putting them there,' he said many years later. 'I can still see those fresh-faced boys getting out of the boat.'[35]

The post-battle report would describe the first ten minutes of the Omaha landings with chilling simplicity: 'A Company had ceased to be an assault company and had become a forlorn little rescue party bent on survival.'[36] This was true enough. There was no one to give orders and no sense of purpose. Taylor Fellers's mission had ended in slaughter.

German defenders on Omaha Beach observed the approaching American landing craft from their near-impregnable bunkers. 'Poor swine,' muttered one as the first troops prepared to land.

14

Easy Red

FRANZ GOCKEL WAS crouched in his dug-out at the other end of Omaha Beach when the Allied bombardment struck.

'Boys, this time it's for real.'

Gockel swung his machine gun skywards and checked the ammunition belt. He tried to focus on aiming his weapon, but the bombers were flying too fast and he was forced to throw himself into the dirt as the first of the shells rammed home. 'Dust and smoke enveloped us. The earth shook. Eyes and nose were filled with dust. Sand ground between teeth.'[1] No sooner had the planes disappeared than the naval bombardment began. 'A deafening torrent of smoke and dust rolled towards us, cracking, screaming, whistling and sizzling.'[2]

Six months in France had changed Gockel. He still looked like a boyish conscript, but he had trained hard and learned to operate his machine gun efficiently. He would never be a soldier, that much was clear, but he had the capacity to wreak carnage on any Allied troops landing on his sector of beach. This was just as well, for it was imperative to stop the invading troops as they waded ashore, when still seasick and disorientated. If they managed to reach the bluffs behind the strongpoints, they could knock out the defences of Omaha Beach from the rear.

The Allies were playing for high stakes that morning. If they failed to capture Omaha's eastern end, as Taylor Fellers and his men had failed to capture the western end, then the entire invasion plan would be at risk. The Allied-controlled zone at Utah Beach would be left isolated and exposed, with the next nearest beachhead – at Gold – more than thirty-five miles to the east. Success on D-Day was dependent on Omaha Beach being seized by the Americans.

'Now it's starting!' The cry came from Bernhard Frerking, the battery commander. 'They're landing! Are you all right?'

Gockel looked through his field glasses and realized that the troops would be landing directly into his line of fire. 'The sea had come alive. Assault boats and landing craft rapidly approached the beach.'[3]

As the first American troops waded through the waist-high water towards the Easy Red section of Omaha Beach, they were unaware they were being watched by twenty-eight pairs of eyes. Franz Gockel moved his finger on to the trigger of the machine gun. He was ready for them.

'Poor swine,'[4] muttered Bernhard Frerking.

Jack Ellery was a sergeant with the 116th Infantry; his goal that morning was to land on the Easy Red section of Omaha and capture the track that led up the cliff to the village of Saint-Laurent. Ellery looked younger than his twenty-four years: a fresh-faced marine cadet whose pudgy cheeks and winsome smile were those of a teenager rather than a man. He had joined the army by default, having failed to get into the parachute regiment. Energetic and highly motivated, he described himself as 'clean, bright and lightly oiled',[5] just like the M1 rifle he was carrying. He was confident that his men would take Easy Red beach.

Two thousand yards to his right, Warner Hamlett was to land on Easy Green, in the very centre of the beach. One of eight children from an impoverished family, Hamlett had joined the army as a means of escaping from the suburban dreariness of Danville, Virginia. Now, he was beginning to wonder if he shouldn't have stayed at home. He was far less sanguine than Jack Ellery about pulling through the initial assault. His company commander, Captain Charles Callahan, had made another of those infelicitous addresses to his men as they crossed the Channel, warning them that 'three out of four of us would not come back.' He had added that only the toughest would survive and told them 'to kill everything that stood in our way of our going home'.[6] His words caused dismay and mental anguish. When Hamlett snatched a moment of sleep later that evening, he dreamed of clawing his way up the beach amid a terrifying barrage of flying logs.

The thirty men in his landing craft were under the command of Lieutenant Hillshure, who spent much of his time trying to undo the damage caused by Captain Callahan. He went 'to each man and patted him on the back, trying to provide encouragement'. In an attempt to raise a smile, he spoke in folksy, old-time language. 'Go get them rascals,' he said. Few were in the mood for levity as they were extremely anxious about what lay ahead, 'some cursing, some vomiting'.[7]

Each landing craft that morning was its own little world of thirty frightened men squatting in a knee-deep swill of seawater and vomit. The squall was whipping freezing spray across the bow of each boat, soaking them to their bones.

'Hurry up. Pass the bucket, I have to shit.' Joe Pilck's craft was heading for Easy Green. 'Just do as I did. Shit in your pants.'[8]

The two coxswains on Warner Hamlett's boat had noticed that many of the landing craft were stopping far short of the beach on account of the intense gunfire. Many were also coming in at the wrong place, due to the strong wind and current that was sweeping them off-course, just as it had done at Utah Beach. The coxswains on Jack Ellery's craft did their best to rectify the problem and they also vowed to set the men down on dry land.

When the ramp went down, Ellery's first view would be the massive stronghold of WN62.

Franz Gockel was peering through the embrasure of his concrete-lined bunker, watching the Americans as they leaped through the waves. Crouched some twenty yards away was his young comrade-in-arms, Josef Schröder, and his weapon of destruction, an MG 42 machine gun that fired 1,200 rounds per minute over a distance of 1,000 metres. The men called it their Hitlersäge or Hitler's bone-saw on account of the tearing sound that it made when fired. It was a fearsome weapon. 'It eats up a lot of ammunition,' said one soldier, 'but it eats up a lot of people too.'[9]

The American invaders were getting closer, 'some in knee-deep water, others up to their chest'. Gockel swung into position behind his Polish-made water-cooled machine gun. He was trembling with fear and could hear his own voice repeating a doom-laden phrase inside his head. 'I won't survive this,' it said, 'I won't survive this.'[10]

'Franz, watch out! They're coming!'[11]

The guns in the main part of the strongpoint were already firing and 'the first assault wave troops collapsed after making only a few metres headway.' Now, it was his turn to join the massacre, aiming the machine gun and 'firing straight into the boats with ramps'. The tidal shallows were just 250 metres away and within easy reach of the machine gun. Gockel could scarcely comprehend the bloodshed he was causing. 'So many bodies lay on the beach. And new men just kept coming. We couldn't understand it.'

At one point his machine gun jammed as grit blew into the belt. It was the moment every gunner feared. 'I tore the belt from the feed tray, shook it clean and slapped it back in.' He then resumed gunning down the newly landed troops. 'Soon the beach was covered in Americans caught by our firepower.'

Josef Schröder was also keeping up relentless fire. 'It's hell. It's like hell.' These words kept repeating themselves in his head. But he also knew that this was the law of the jungle: 'It's them or me.' He continued to shoot, 'constantly'.[12]

Very few Americans were making it to the sea wall. Most were splayed on the sand, horrifically injured or too shaken to move. Gockel now used his rifle to pick off individual soldiers, 'getting about 300 hits and at a distance of 100–250 metres'. His comrades were hurling grenades into the densest groups of men. This proved no less deadly, creating 'heavy, heavy losses amongst the Americans'.[13]

When word came through that a group of Americans had reached the sea wall, the team in WN62 unleashed another nasty surprise. 'Our mortars had waited for this moment and now lay down a terrible shelling on them, showering the men with splinters and rocks, inflicting heavy casualties on the men who sought shelter there.'[14]

Some eighty metres inland from Gockel's position, Hein Severloh was manning the observation post of WN62. The strongpoint's commander, Bernhard Frerking, had given him clear instructions to 'open fire when the enemy is knee-deep in the water and is still unable to run quickly'. Severloh had done just that, and he had a panoramic view of the carnage he was causing. 'I saw how the water sprayed up where my machine gun bursts landed, and when the small fountains came closer to the GIs, they threw themselves down. Very soon the first bodies were drifting in the waves of the rising tide. In a short time, all the Americans down there were shot.'

Each burst of fire brought down another group of troops. 'I do not know how many men I shot. I almost emptied an entire infantry landing craft. The sea was red around it and I could hear an American officer shouting hysterically in a loudspeaker.'[15]

The men in WN62 were causing mayhem. 'The beach became strewn with dead, wounded and shelter-seeking soldiers.'[16] It seemed inconceivable that the Americans would gain a foothold anywhere on Omaha Beach, for the bloodshed taking place below Franz Gockel's stronghold was being replicated along every inch of sand.

'Get off the beach!'[17]

The same urgent cry could be heard up and down the shoreline, over the roar of exploding mortars.

Jack Ellery was desperate to do just that, for he had landed in hell. 'Direct fire, plunging and grazing and flanking fire.' He was half aware 'of men falling around me' but his entire focus was on forcing himself through the choking haze 'of sweat, smoke, dust and mist'.[18]

His comrade, Roger Brugger, had landed shortly after him, wading into a maelstrom of lethal fire. WN62's bullets were 'tearing up the sand on either side of me' and shells were slamming into the beach and exploding into fountains of sand. One of his comrades received a direct hit and all Brugger could see were 'three hunks of his body flying through the air'.[19] When he looked around, bodies were sprawled on the sand in various states of mutilation.

'Get off the beach!'

Warner Hamlett could hear his pal, Mervin Matze, yelling to the men as he led a half-crazed dash up the sand. He saw Lieutenant Hillshure crumple to his knees as another shell ruptured the shoreline. He fell 'headlong into the hole caused by the explosion'.

Hamlett hurled himself into a nearby crater. As he did so, a petrified teenager named Gillingham tumbled in after him. His face was 'white with fear' and he seemed 'to be begging for help with his eyes'. Hamlett heard the sickening screech of another incoming shell. He shoved his face deep into the sand as shrapnel burst all around him. When he raised his head, he saw that flying shards had taken off Gillingham's chin, 'including the bone, except for a small piece of flesh'. It was terrible to behold. As Gillingham ran towards the sea wall, he was desperately trying 'to hold his chin in place'.

Hamlett himself was struck by shrapnel. A sharp pain jolted through his spine 'from my neck down to my lower back'. He dragged himself back to a shell-hole where he was joined by O.T. Grimes, 'with blood covering his face where shrapnel had cut and torn his skin'.

Hamlett tested his legs. They still worked. He crawled from his hole and lurched forward, only to be caught by another wave of bullets. None hit him. He ran and he jumped, 'falling down each time' the machine-gun fire came close. In this way, yard by agonizing yard, he made it to the sea wall. The injured Gillingham had also made it, but he was suffering from catastrophic wounds. Hamlett and Bill Hawkes gave him a shot of morphine. He groaned in pain but was unable to speak. 'The entire time he remained conscious and aware he was dying.' It would take thirty minutes for him to expire, with the roar of shells as his final requiem.

Hamlett was joined by a small clutch of men from F Company, who had drifted ashore far from their intended landing. Their leader, Lieutenant Wise, was trying to form them into some sort of coherent unit when a bullet smacked him in the centre of his forehead. Hamlett watched in appalled fascination. 'He continued to instruct his men' – just for a second – 'until he sat down and held his head in the palm of his hand before falling dead.'[20] The bullet had ploughed through his brain before breaking out through the back of his skull.

'Get the men off this fucking boat!'

Just a few yards from the shoreline, Sergeant William Otlowski was yelling at the coxswain as two eight-centimetre mortars landed on each side of their craft. Otlowski knew the next one would land exactly on target.

'Sergeant, stay where you are.'

'To hell with you, Lieutenant.'[21]

Otlowski plunged into the water and swam for the shore. As he did so, a third eight-centimetre smacked into the craft, shredding everyone.

Back on shore, Hamlett's desperate little group were still being targeted by Gockel's men, who were now using firebombs containing a yellowish powder that ignited everything it touched. They were also firing mortars at the sea wall, causing 'shrapnel to rivet the air'. One of Hamlett's buddies, Private Tway, was severely wounded in the back and leg.

As Hamlett looked back across the beach, he thought he could see his brother, Lee, lying face-down in the sand. 'The back of his head looked just like Lee, but I chose not to know. The soldier's clothes had been blown from his body.'[22] It would be several weeks before he learned that his brother had also survived the first wave.

A few hundred yards to Hamlett's right, Harry Bare was one of the few survivors of F Company who had made it to the sea wall. Now, glancing back towards the sea, he saw a massacre. He would remember it for ever, a tableau of death. 'My radioman had his head blown off three yards from me. The beach was covered with bodies, men with no legs, no arms – God, it was awful.'[23]

Barton Davis was a twenty-three-year-old army engineer who had been due to land with the first wave at the centre of Omaha Beach. But his landing craft was swept eastwards by the strong current and he landed on Fox Green, well within range of Gockel's machine gun. His men came under a blitz of fire and Davis was witness to one young infantryman being hit in the jugular vein. 'He was propped up by his buddies who were frantically trying to stop the bleeding. They were stuffing towels in his neck' – all done while under fire – 'and trying pressure points, to no avail.' The lad himself knew it was no use. He 'smiled at his buddies, waved his hand in a gesture of "so long" and died so fast it was as though a hand passed over his face'.

Barton Davis was to witness a world of bloodshed that morning, but nothing came close to seeing a landing craft strike one of the beach obstacles. There was a violent explosion 'and the boat seemed to disintegrate. Bodies – parts of bodies – debris – rifles – everything seemed to mushroom upward and outward like some large flower of indescribable beauty, yet terrible! It was terrible! We were horror-struck watching it.'

There had been forty men in the craft when it struck the mine and it was also laden with fuel and ammunition. 'The water became a cauldron of burning gasoline and oil with black dots of the men trying to swim through it.' Davis watched as 'a headless torso flew a good fifty feet through the air and landed with a sickening thud near us.' It was deeply shocking. 'Some men vomited. All were heartsick.'

Most of those on board were killed instantly, but one, Nick Fina, sank straight to the bottom of the sea, gulping water as he choked to death. 'The next thing he knew, he was being pulled from the water by his 1st Sergeant, full of water – hair, eyebrows, lashes, all burned off, but alive.'[24] He eventually made it to the sea wall, where he slumped into the sand, stunned and traumatized by everything he had experienced.

The first landings on Omaha Beach were an ongoing catastrophe, with wave after wave of men being mown down as they landed. But a few troops had managed to reach the sea wall and they represented the first glimmer of hope that not everything was lost. If they could only scale the bluffs and attack the strongholds from behind, they had a chance of silencing the guns of Hitler's Atlantic Wall.

Jack Ellery was one of those sheltering under the sea wall: he was within a stone's throw of WN62. Now, in a display of extraordinary courage, he gathered four or five men and started to lead them up the bluff.

'About half to two-thirds of the way up, a machine gun opened upon us from the right front.' His little band scraped themselves into the dirt while Ellery himself 'scurried and scratched' his way forward until he was just ten metres from the gun position.

'Then I unloaded all four of my fragmentation grenades' and hurled them into the machine-gun nest. All four exploded, devastatingly, enabling Ellery to continue his dash up the bluff. 'Those other kids were right behind me.'

Ellery knew that if others acted like him, then the catastrophe of Omaha might yet be turned to victory. But he also knew that any advance up the bluffs would have to be led by young officers like himself, for none of the senior ranks had landed in the first waves. He saw one young lad with a broken arm leading seven men up the bluff. He saw another carrying a wounded comrade up the cliffs.

As he clambered ever higher, and saw a handful of others doing the same, he was struck by a thought that would remain with him for years to come. That morning's fighting owed nothing to the much decorated generals and chiefs of staff, but everything to the heroic individuals in the lesser ranks. 'True courage is found in those who believe that there are things in life that are worth fighting for and worth dying for. You can't buy valour and you can't pull heroes off an assembly line.'

Of the generals and colonels who would later claim to have stormed up the beach, Jack Ellery saw not a single one. 'When you talk about combat leadership under fire on the beach at Normandy, I don't see how the credit can go to anyone other than the company grade officers and senior non-commissioned officers' – men like Ellery himself – 'who led the way.'[25]

Now, the fate of Omaha lay in their hands.

PART V
Foothold

The exact time of H-Hour, the moment at which Allied troops were to land, varied for each beach: this was due to tidal variations on the Normandy coast. The Utah landing had been at 6.30 a.m. On Sword Beach, the most easterly, it was scheduled for 7.25 a.m.

The survival rate for troops coming ashore would depend, in part, on training and combat experience. American Rangers and British commandos were motivated and highly capable. Uniquely, Canada's D-Day soldiers on Juno Beach were all volunteers. It was less clear how young and inexperienced conscripts would fare when under fire.

French forces were to play a small but important role in the Sword Beach landings. The 177 men of the 1er Bataillon de Fusiliers Marins commandos were tasked with capturing the vast German bunker complex inside the Riva Bella casino.

Rommel had invested much in the construction of the Atlantic Wall, but rather less in training the soldiers manning it. Many were young conscripts or Osttruppen, and their resilience – especially in service of the Nazis – would be tested under a sustained attack.

Armoured vehicles helped to breach the Atlantic Wall, but many were hit by enemy mortars. 'There was a flash and sixty tons of metal disappeared in front of our eyes,' wrote one British trooper.

15

Gold

Erwin Rommel rose early that Tuesday morning, unaware of the momentous events unfolding in Normandy. He had woken soon after dawn in order to arrange the freshly cut flowers that had been delivered to his home, Villa Lindenhof in south-west Germany, for his wife's birthday. The largest bouquet was from him, naturally enough, and it took centre stage in the drawing room, alongside the carefully wrapped shoes from Paris. The rest of the bunches were being arranged by Frau Rommel's house-guest, Hildegard Kirchheim, who had come to stay with the family for a few days. She was the wife of one of Rommel's officer friends in North Africa. If all went to plan, Lucie Rommel's birthday looked set to be a jolly little occasion.

Villa Lindenhof was the perfect place for a birthday festivity, an enchanting forest dwelling that might have dropped straight from a Teutonic fairy tale. It had steep gabled roofs, a stack of windows and a projecting first-floor observatory room with glazed views over the surrounding beeches and linden trees. It was a place where one could escape, temporarily, from the cares of the world.

Rommel was a man of strict routine, as his aide, Captain Helmut Lang, had discovered over the previous months. He always awoke early at Château La Roche-Guyon, ate the same breakfast each morning (buttered white bread with honey) and had a light lunch. 'A simple field kitchen meal,' he would say to Lang. 'Of course, if you want to throw in a chop, it won't bother me too much.'[1] It was as if the repetitive austerity of army life had become an integral part of his personality, one that was impossible to shake off.

He kept up this routine even when staying at the family home in Herrlingen, although he would allow the rules to be relaxed a little. He would rise in time for the seven o'clock news on the wireless; he would then wash, shave and get dressed before eating a leisurely breakfast: a light broth, perhaps, or a little toast. And then he would chat with his wife and teenage son, Manfred, about life in occupied France.

He had arrived at Villa Lindenhof late on the evening of 4 June after a tiring twelve-hour drive from Château La Roche-Guyon in northern France. He had spent much of the following morning in telephone conversations with the Berghof, arranging his forthcoming meeting with Hitler. It had been set for Thursday, 8 June, much to Rommel's satisfaction. It gave him two whole days to spend with Lucie and Manfred – a veritable luxury for someone who was almost never at home.

He spent his time wisely, regaling the two of them about his visits to the Normandy beaches and walks with his new hunting dog, Treff, in the ancestral grounds of the Duke of Rochefoucauld. He also took photographs of his wife and son: Lucie looking frumpy in an ill-fitting dress and the bespectacled Manfred, aged fifteen, looking gawky and awkward. Rommel was even persuaded to have a picture taken of himself, flanked by Lucie and Frau Kirchheim. The two women managed to contrive a smile for the camera – it was perhaps Manfred behind the lens. But Rommel himself, decked in full military costume, was wearing a deep frown, one that was to deepen yet further as the clock chimed six thirty on the morning of 6 June.

'Herr Feldmarschall Rommel is wanted on the telephone.'[2] It was the housemaid, Karolina, calling to him: she had been doing the early morning chores while he arranged the flowers. Rommel strolled over to the phone and took the receiver. It was Hans Speidel, calling from La Roche-Guyon.

'Well, Speidel, what's up?'

Speidel explained the momentous events of the previous hours: the parachute drops, the beach landings and the sense that no one really knew what was happening. Rommel listened in alarm, his face visibly draining of blood as the scale of the calamity sank in.

'I'm returning,' he snapped to Speidel. 'As fast as I can.'[3]

After making an urgent call to the Berghof, he rushed upstairs and changed into his uniform. 'Get Daniel up here with the car at once,' he barked at his manservant. 'And get Lang to meet me at Freudenstadt.'[4]

And then, after the briefest of farewells to Lucie and Manfred, he clambered into the black Horch and prepared for the long drive back to La Roche-Guyon. Only after he had left did Lucie unwrap her birthday shoes and try them on. They didn't fit.

Captain Lang was waiting for them in Freudenstadt. In order to make the rendezvous on time, he had driven through Stuttgart at over sixty miles an hour with one hand permanently on the horn. Now, as the two men headed towards the French border, Rommel repeatedly urged Daniel the chauffeur to drive faster. 'Tempo, tempo, tempo,' he kept shouting.

Captain Lang had known Rommel for long enough to realize that he was 'quite tense and quite worried'. For the first part of the journey, he said scarcely a word. But eventually he relaxed a little and engaged Lang in a conversation of sorts. 'You see, Lang,' he said, 'I was right all the time. I should have had the Panzer Lehr and the 12th SS under my command near the beaches.'[5]

Both panzer divisions were still under the direct control of high command and General Alfred Jodl (at the Berghof) had declined to release them into the field of battle. Rommel was not alone in being dismayed by his intransigence. The one-legged General Erich Marcks was also demanding that they be sent into battle. His mood had taken a distinct downturn since drinking his chilled birthday Chablis. Now, he had a full-blown Allied invasion on his hands. 'I need every available armoured unit for a counter-attack,'[6] he thundered down the phone. But still Jodl refused to release the panzers.

Over in Château de la Guillerie, senior panzer officers were as frustrated as Marcks. Hubert Meyer was told that his division might be ordered to advance towards the landing beaches 'at a moment's notice', but the expected telephone call from headquarters never came. 'No orders came through from the army command centre, or from the commander of Panzergruppe West.' Meyer couldn't quite believe it. Allied forces were pouring ashore and they were sitting on their hands. 'No alert, nothing.'[7]

Hubert Meyer's wife, Irmgard, had spent the previous hour packing her few belongings: it would soon be time to bid farewell to her charmed life in Château de la Guillerie, as well as to her husband, Hubert. Only now, as she stared blankly out of her bedroom window, did she realize just how serious things were. 'It was a dull day and outside I saw Major-General Witt, quite alone, sitting on a garden seat at a table, his head in his hands, as if he already knew what vast event was hanging over him and the huge responsibility of leading young people into battle, that went with it.'

He may also have been thinking about his own future. He had committed countless atrocities during the long years of war, especially on the Eastern Front, massacring soldiers and civilians alike. Now, he was contemplating defeat. If the invading troops were not routed within the next few hours, the Allied offensive would probably be unstoppable and the war would be lost. Rommel himself had said as much. And that would leave General Witt in a very uncomfortable place.

Irmgard Meyer took a last look around her bedroom and then made her way downstairs to meet the other wives being sent back to Germany. 'Frau Witt and Frau Wuensche were already there, and another young woman whose husband was a *Sturmführer* [SS officer].' The woman was crying bitterly, convinced that she would never see him again. (In this she was correct: he was killed ten days later.) Irmgard Meyer was not the sort of person to shed tears, nor were Frau Witt and Frau Wuensche. 'We had, after all, already experienced some four or five years of war and had said our goodbyes so often before.'[8] They were also aware that they were wives of officers serving in an elite SS regiment in which displays of emotion were not encouraged. She said a crisp farewell to her husband, climbed into the rear seat of the staff car and prepared for the long drive back to Stuttgart. She was saddened by the fact that her holiday in Normandy – with its swimming outings, its fresh asparagus, and its fireside soirées – had been brought to an abrupt end.

As one Normandy adventure came to a close, another was just beginning. The temperature of the sea was hovering around 13 degrees centigrade when a chirpy young Cockney named Wally Blanchard slipped into the shallows offshore from Gold Beach. He was wearing a specialist lightweight kapok vest, but this did little to cut the enveloping chill. The next few hours were going to test both his stamina and his resilience as he undertook an extraordinary undercover operation.

Gold Beach was almost nine miles in length, but its western end was flanked by crumbling cliffs that were impassable to tanks and jeeps. The jutting offshore reefs were also a hazard. Only a short stretch of shoreline was feasible for an amphibious landing, the area between the villages of Le Hamel and La Rivière.

Unfortunately, Rommel had come to exactly the same conclusion and ordered the construction of a string of fortifications. The coastal village of Le Hamel was particularly well defended. In the years before the war, it had boasted seaside villas, hotels and a well-appointed sanatorium. Now, the villas housed machine-gun nests and the sanatorium had been converted into a German bunker.

The underwater obstacles and mines were no less of a problem, for they were specially designed to tear the bottom out of any approaching landing craft. These mines had to be neutralized before the first wave of troops came ashore at Gold. And this is where Wally Blanchard came to the fore: he had trained as a specialist naval frogman whose role was to defuse or blow up the underwater minefield.

It was an unenviable task. Defusing a mine was hard enough on land, but infinitely more hazardous when done underwater, where the unpredictable current could easily hurl a diver against the very objects he was trying to destroy. No less dangerous was the corrosive effect of salt water, which had rendered many of the mines unstable.

A frogman working in such conditions needed many qualities if he was to survive. Stamina was useful, a good pair of lungs essential. Eighteen-year-old Blanchard was blessed with both, and it earned him the job of blasting a series of passages through the underwater minefield off the Jig Green section of Gold Beach.

Like so many of his comrades, Blanchard looked far too young to be participating in D-Day, let alone working as a specialist. When he posed for the camera decked in navy white and blue, he did so with an enigmatic half-smile on his face, as if in an awkward attempt to conceal his shyness.

The pre-war years in Essex had seen him change from boy to man at an unnatural rate of knots. He left school at fourteen, became an apprentice at fifteen and was digging victims out of air-raid rubble at sixteen, while serving as an Air Raid Precautions messenger in London. He then worked the Atlantic convoys and fought with the elite Small Raiding Force, even managing to knife a German sentry through the heart during a raid on Honfleur. 'My first,' he would later say in his heart-of-gold Cockney accent.

But none of these operations was as dangerous as swimming towards Gold Beach in advance of the landing craft in order to blow up unstable underwater mines. As an added layer of complexity, he had to time the explosions to coincide with the pre-dawn bombardment. He was assured that if synchronized correctly, the Germans 'would mistake them for the bombarding ammunition coming in'.

Blanchard was part of a small team that had been ferried to the minefield at 4 a.m. His immediate partner was called Bob – he was never told his surname 'as security was paramount in these matters'.[9] There was also a Captain Jacko and a frogman named Peter who had trained with the commandos. They all slipped into the freezing water and tried to get their bearings in the near darkness. The beachfront villas of Le Hamel were visible as moonlit façades, but the big cruisers of Force G – *Orion*, *Ajax* and *Emerald*, among many others – were lost to the swell and the spray.

Blanchard set to work, trying to identify the various mines and obstructions. It was lonely work and physically gruelling, for the wind was whipping spray from the crests of the waves and flinging it into his eyes. He spent more than an hour swimming from obstacle to obstacle, laying white tape and marker buoys to mark a passage to the shore. His fellow frogmen were marking other passages. They then strapped explosive charges to each of the obstacles to be destroyed.

Not until the aerial bombardment began did they detonate the explosives, clearing a safe run-in for the landing craft. This was the most dangerous part of their work. The kapok vests were said to protect the body from blast concussion in the water, but one of Blanchard's comrades noted that 'if you are in the water within fifty yards of an explosion, it is nearly fatal every time.'[10] They nevertheless succeeded in blowing a large number of mines – and not themselves – thereby reducing the risks for the landing craft.

As Blanchard swam through the shallows, he found his eye

repeatedly drawn to one of the pre-war beach kiosks on the seafront. There was something about it that was not quite right; something that aroused his suspicions. The more he studied it, the more he suspected that it was a pillbox in disguise. He swam a little closer and looked again. To his dismay, he saw 'a heavy machine gun nozzle emerging from the slot'. He had been spotted in the surf and the gun was now being swung towards him.

The German gunner had no reason to suspect that Blanchard was a crack shot. Nor did he know that he was armed with an M1 carbine that worked when wet, emitting 'an excellent, short-range, rapid-firing single shot'.[11] Blanchard steadied himself on the sandy bottom before taking aim. One bullet was all he needed to score a bull's-eye. His crack training with the commandos and American Rangers had just saved his life.

When he glanced back towards the fleet at soon after 7 a.m., he was witness to a sight that gladdened his heart. Hundreds of landing craft were heading for the shore over a wide area. As they approached, the infantrymen spotted Blanchard and his fellow frogmen in their skintight outfits. It was the cue for some good-natured taunts. 'Where did you ballet dancers come from?'[12] they shouted in high-spirited humour.

Blanchard and company had done sterling work in clearing the mines, but there were inevitably some that were missed. One of Blanchard's comrades, Peter Martin, was watching a landing craft at the very moment it struck a concealed obstacle. The resulting explosion was 'like a slow motion cartoon'. As the craft burst into a fireball, 'the men went up as though standing to attention, as though they were going up inside a fountain, and at the top of this fountain the bodies and parts of bodies spread out like drops of water.'[13]

One of the landing craft picked up Blanchard and his fellow frogmen when making its return journey to Force G. Its coxswain issued them with new orders. The Americans, they were told, were being massacred on Omaha Beach. Help was urgently required.

The armoured vehicles emerged on to Gold Beach like watery beasts, dripping with brine and with strands of kelp stuck to their tracks. From the vantage point of Le Hamel, they looked like the stuff of nightmares – grunting, hissing and growling as they thrashed through the surf. Shermans, armoured bulldozers and flail tanks champed at the shingle, grinding it through their tracks and then spitting it into the air. The flail tanks had an air of dark menace: they rode in the vanguard of this amphibious battalion, their steel chains thrashing a passage of safety up the beach.

'*Hang on a minute, Ron!*'

Tank driver Sergeant Vaughan could be heard shouting to his crewmate, Ronald Mole.

'*I can't see anything for the dust!*'

Vaughan stuck his head above the turret and received a shot directly between his eyes. He crumpled back inside the tank like a sack of baggage. 'His right elbow hit me on the neck, his left elbow hit the gun, he sagged and his knees hit me in the kidneys and when I turned I could just see blood running.'

Mole watched in horrified fascination. 'It wasn't splashing, just a gentle run, and there it was on the bottom of the tank, just coagulating in a small pool and getting thicker and thicker.'

The Allied tanks were armed for a fight but they were nonetheless vulnerable to shellfire coming from the big guns of Le Hamel sanatorium. Within minutes of landing, the beach was strewn with the smoke-blackened carcasses of tanks, flails and landing craft. All were belching pungent toxic fumes. Ronald Mole was watching the Churchill tank in front of him when it was struck by a German 88 mortar. 'Suddenly there was a flash and sixty tons of metal just disappeared in front of our eyes. And then down came a sprocket, a piece of track, flames licking the sand.' The entire vehicle 'had literally disappeared in front of our eyes'.[14]

Charlie Wilson, a young trooper with the Essex Yeomanry, was facing his own problems on the beach that morning. He was one of the 'roly-poly team', a group of youths whose job was to drag ashore huge rolls of wire mesh to prevent the monster vehicles getting bogged down in the sand. His landing craft had already survived being struck by two mines on the run-in to shore. Now, as the 'roly-poly' was lowered into the water, it became completely unmanageable and plunged deep into the icy water, dragging Wilson and his comrades with it. As they were drawn inexorably towards the minefield, they had no option but to swim for the beach. Wilson scrambled ashore in a pair of shorts, cold and bedraggled: it was not how he had expected to arrive in France.

Twenty-eight-year-old Robert Palmer was more fortunate. He came ashore as commander of a Sexton self-propelled gun that looked like a tank without a turret. His landing craft had ground to a halt some distance from the shore, but he assumed this would not be a problem since all the vehicles to be offloaded had been waterproofed to a depth of six feet. The signaller gave the thumbs-up and Palmer watched as the half-track in front of him rolled down the ramp and into the shallows. Instead of levelling out as it hit the bottom, it was gulped by the sea and disappeared from view. Not for the first time on D-Day, and not for the last, the landing craft had come to rest on a runnel surrounded by deeper water.

'Dreadful.' It was the only word Palmer could manage. 'You could see the poor devils there, struggling in the water.' He managed to haul out a half-drowned Sergeant Major Harold Broom, along with several others, and then it was his turn to drive off the landing craft. He was rather more fortunate. The coxswain had shifted the craft into shallower water and Palmer managed to engage the tracks of his vehicle with the sand. Within seconds, he was thrusting towards the beach.

Palmer and his crew were serving in the Essex Yeomanry, a regiment originally formed in the eighteenth century to defend England against a French invasion. Now, in a neat reversal of roles, it was spearheading the invasion of France. At a little after 7.40 a.m., Palmer's armoured vehicle was among the first to land on the beach.

His was a close-knit team of seven youngsters who had learned to muck in together during their training sessions on Lord Montagu's estate at Beaulieu. Shortly before embarking for Normandy they had undertaken a joint outing to Bournemouth where they had posed for a group photograph, a keepsake for those who survived the coming battle. They didn't pose in order of rank, as might have been expected, but in ascending order of height.

The Sexton's half-track spun wildly out of control as it hit the shingle: the loss of Charlie Wilson's roly-poly wire matting was causing real problems. But Palmer eventually got the track to bite and they careered up the beach dodging heavy mortar fire. Palmer heard 'lots of crashes and bangs going on all around us, but luckily none of us were hit'.

His orders that morning had come in the form of a battlefield command just six words long: 'Turn right and head towards Bayeux.' This was their goal, the medieval market town that straddled the intersection of several strategically vital roads. But as they advanced inland towards the village of Asnelles-sur-Mer, bringing up the rear of six tanks, they met with an unexpected glitch.

A salvo of mortars arrived from nowhere and struck each of the tanks in turn, turning them to fireballs. It was a salutary lesson in how quickly death could strike. Their Sexton full-track was the only vehicle not to be hit.

'Sergeant!' yelled a captain who had managed to escape from one of the burning tanks. 'Quick! See what's happening? You've got the best gun nearest to that! Put that out of action!'

Palmer clambered out of the vehicle and crept down the country lane towards a line of trees. From this hidden vantage point he got a clear view of the problem through his field glasses. 'There was this enormous monster of a place and it looked like a big, big mushroom.' It was built of reinforced concrete and appeared impregnable. But every bunker had a weak point, as Palmer knew from his training. If he could fire his gun directly through the embrasure, the only opening, he could wipe out everyone inside with a single shot. It was a very tall order and it would mean exposing his half-track to incoming fire as his men calibrated their weapon. But there was no other option.

He now gave them a little pep talk, running through his plan of attack. 'We've got to do something different,' he said, 'and take them by surprise.' His Sexton was a sluggish beast that weighed thirty-five tons, but if driven hard it could travel at more than thirty miles an hour.

'When I say "Go", go. Put your foot down.'

His idea was to emerge into the bunker's line of fire at top speed, then slam the Sexton to an abrupt halt. 'A tap on the head, that's the signal to stop.' The gun was to be swung to 45 degrees offside and fired immediately. If they got the angle correct, they might just put a shell through the embrasure. If they didn't, well, that was the weak point in his plan. They would be sitting ducks.

A mix of bravado and camaraderie overrode any objections. They all nodded in agreement before climbing back into the Sexton. The six knocked-out tanks were still belching acrid smoke. It was time for revenge.

They slammed the engine into high gear and charged forward with the gun already loaded and the safety catch off. It was a dangerous way to advance, but it would save them three or four seconds.

The manoeuvre worked as planned. They cut their engines while still travelling at full tilt and fired 'as soon as we had stopped bouncing, as a tank does when you stop suddenly'. The first shell hit the edge of the aperture, temporarily stunning the defenders inside. Palmer yelled to the gunner: 'A fraction high, a fraction to the left.' A second shot was fired, just seconds after the first. It cut the air like an arrow, passing directly inside the bunker and exploding deep inside, with devastating consequences. None of the young soldiers in the Sexton could quite believe it, least of all Palmer himself. 'If we'd practised it all the morning, we couldn't have got better than that. It was marvellous.'

As they stood around their vehicle, celebrating their success, four terrified Germans 'struggled out of the back of this emplacement with their hands over their ears'. They looked in a terrible state, for they were 'badly knocked about'. Palmer felt a brief moment of compassion. 'Poor devils,' he said under his breath as they were led away into captivity.

Each bunker captured, each strongpoint destroyed, marked a significant step forward, clearing the road ahead and paving the way for reinforcements. Robert Palmer and his men might have rested on their laurels after such a spectacular success, but they had tasted blood and they wanted more. In the hours that followed, they would knock out an even larger German stronghold, using their gunner's steady hand to deliver a series of explosive calling cards.

'Put it in the upstairs right window,' ordered Palmer as another mortar was loaded into the gun. 'Put one through the front door.' The gunner might have been delivering parcels, so accurate were his shots. Panic-stricken Germans could be seen scampering out of the stronghold, some of them 'dropping out of windows upstairs, some coming out from around the back'.

Palmer was in his element. 'Within a very short space of time, we'd been able to knock out four different German gun emplacements.' He took some of the credit, for he was in charge, but he knew he could never have achieved such success on his own. It was all due to training, teamwork and his 'first-class crew'.[15]

Although it was not apparent to the men landing on the beaches, a pattern of fighting was starting to emerge – one that was to shape the course of the day. There were men like those serving under Robert Palmer, who were fighting together as an effective team using skills they had learned over the previous eighteen months. There were also men who were assuming leadership roles, often by default, when the actual leaders had been cut down on the beaches. Jack Ellery was performing just such a role at Omaha, as was James Eads in Sainte-Mère-Église. And there were those who saw improvisation as the order of the day: men like Malcolm Brannen, whose quick thinking and uncommon daring had led to the impromptu killing of Lieutenant General Wilhelm Falley.

But there was one category that stood apart from all the others, one that stood at the extremities of conventional warfare. Wildly unpredictable and seemingly immune to danger, the lone-wolf fighter was the most feared of all, both by the enemy and also by his own men.

Stanley Hollis, from Teesside, was 'a quiet man of simple tastes' and someone who rarely got angry. But on the few occasions when he did lose his temper, he underwent an alarming transformation. 'He seemed to be colder, almost oblivious to what was going on around him.'[16]

This might not have been a danger in itself, were it not for the fact that Hollis was a six-foot-two-inch bruiser built of sinew and muscle, 'tough as nails . . . with fiery red hair and huge hands like shovels'.[17] Those hands, when clenched into fists, became lethal machines that had been put to good use in countless pub brawls.

Hollis's comrades admired their company sergeant, but they also stood in fear of him. His most distinguishing feature was his huge front teeth, wonky, gap-ridden and looking like broken chunks of driftwood. There was good reason for their wonkiness: Hollis was terrified of dentists. This was not because of the pain they inflicted, which didn't bother him one jot, but because he couldn't inflict pain back. As his brother pointed out, 'you couldn't knock the hell out of the dentist'.[18]

A lorry driver when war broke out, Hollis had enlisted almost immediately and survived the evacuation of Dunkirk. He then experienced a whirlwind of adventures in Egypt and Sicily, where he began to gain a reputation for his ruthless daring. There was no one quite like Stanley Hollis on the field of battle. He beheaded one German soldier with a machete, doing so with considerable panache. As the German raised his Schmeisser submachine gun, Hollis swung the blade like some latter-day samurai 'and was surprised to see the man's head roll off'.

Hollis was the first to admit to feeling scared before a battle. 'Fear is a grand thing for a man. It educates you. It teaches you humility.'[19] In his first bayonet charge, he knifed his German adversary directly through his stomach, with the bayonet puncturing his *Gott mit uns* [God with us] belt buckle. The blade went right through the man and came out the other side. Hollis pulled it out and was amazed when the man walked away, covering fully 100 yards before crumpling to the ground.

Now, on the morning of D-Day, Hollis was about to participate in his fourth major combat of the war and he was determined to be more ruthless than ever. 'I had no mercy, no compassion,' he later said. 'If I took a prisoner, it was by coincidence.'

Hollis went ashore with the Green Howards that morning, landing towards the eastern end of Gold Beach. 'Forward the Yanks!' he yelled as his battle-cry. 'And for Chrissakes get off the beach!' He raced across the sand, bullets zipping, and threw himself down at the sea wall. As he did so, his mate, Pat Mullally, crashed down next to him.

'I've been in better places, Paddy,' said Hollis with a smirk.

'So have I, Sarge.'

As the two men glanced around them, Mullally noticed two birds perched on the barbed wire. 'No wonder they're not flying, Sarge,' he said. 'There's no room in the air for them.'

The initial goal for Hollis's D Company was to knock out the powerful Mont Fleury gun battery, a stack of concrete casements built on such a grand scale that its big guns could hit both Gold and Juno beaches. After a cautious advance through a minefield, Hollis and his men crept towards the battery. Its blank concrete walls looked deeply sinister.

'The biggest damn thing I've ever seen,' thought Hollis as he tried to figure the layout of the place. The emplacements had walls as thick as a rampart and there was a labyrinth of communication trenches. 'The whole lot was camouflaged with black and green netting with sacking in a variety of colours.'[20]

As he and one of his comrades, Ronald Lofthouse, surveyed the scene, they spied a disguised pillbox in the near distance. It spelled immediate danger, not just for themselves but for all the men coming up behind. Hollis studied it more closely and was alarmed to see two machine guns moving around in the slits. The Germans had spotted him and were about to open fire.

Most men would have made a hurried withdrawal, slinking away while there was still time. But Hollis was not like most men. He was, said one, 'the perfect example of the hunter and the hunted'. And he was at his most dangerous when playing the latter role.

When it happened, it did so in a flash. Hollis leaped to his feet and sprinted full-pelt towards the pillbox, utterly oblivious of his own safety. The Germans were firing within seconds, pumping out 250 rounds a minute, yet they failed to get a single hit. Hollis had once said that he could always predict 'the men who were going to get it'. He could also predict that it wouldn't be him.

He slammed into the wall of the pillbox, then flattened himself against the concrete, gasping for breath. In those brief few seconds, he was untouchable. But this was no time to pause. He poked his Sten gun straight through the gun slit and pressed the trigger. As he did so, he 'waved the gun around inside like a hose'. It was like watering the garden, except that he was spraying a shower of bullets. As he continued to shoot, all he could hear was screaming and yelling coming from inside. One of his astonished comrades later commented that Hollis 'always wanted to get to close quarters with the enemy'. Now, he could scarcely be closer. He used his free left hand to yank a grenade from his belt. He then 'pulled the pin with his teeth and tossed it in'. His adrenalin was in overdrive. Still oblivious to danger, he jumped on to the roof of the pillbox, put another clip on his Sten and shouted, 'Come out, you bastards.'

His words had the necessary effect. The thick metal door at the rear of the pillbox tentatively opened and a handful of ashen survivors emerged into the daylight. Hollis stared at them blankly. For the rest of his days, he would never be able to explain why he didn't gun them down.

When he glanced back, he saw another group of Germans running towards him. He aimed his Sten gun at them and they also surrendered. He had now bagged twenty prisoners. But more importantly, his extraordinary daring was key to silencing the guns of Mont Fleury. As he and his men advanced towards the main bunker, the Germans fled in panic. Hollis watched them run 'out of the back of the pillboxes and over a wall into a wood'.[21]

His action was so heroic, so foolhardy, that it would earn him the plaudits of his comrades, as well as the first of two nominations for the Victoria Cross that day.

British commandos support the Canadian landings on Juno Beach. The heavily laden soldier on the gangplank has just lost his balance.

16

Juno

S OUTHWICK HOUSE, NEAR Portsmouth, was a wedding cake of
a building, a stucco-fronted mansion with a stack of pillars and
a façade that gleamed like icing. It was gleaming more than usual
on this particular morning as the strengthening sun lit the paintwork
of the eastern gable.

Southwick was the home of Colonel Evelyn Thistlethwaite, a
bewhiskered country squire who had spent the early years of the
war hobnobbing with Portsmouth-based admirals. He invited them
to hunt on his estate and they accepted with alacrity, but they repaid
his generosity with a poachers' sting: a requisitioning order that
stripped the colonel of his hereditary pile and gave them the run
of the place. Soon afterwards, their hunting games took a more
dangerous turn as they plotted how to flush the German quarry
out of Normandy.

Southwick House was the advance command post of SHAEF,
the Supreme Headquarters Allied Expeditionary Force: it was from
here that the final details of the invasion were planned. The house
was also home to a namesake, Shaef, Eisenhower's cat, who had
been gifted to the general a few months earlier by Staff Sergeant
Mickey McKeogh. Sergeant McKeogh hoped that Shaef would help
Eisenhower to relax and this indeed proved the case. He grew so
fond of his black-furred pet that he would later transport him
to France.

But nothing could calm Eisenhower's fragile nerves on that long
and stressful Tuesday: the chirpiness he had displayed on waking
had rapidly dissipated and been replaced by a cloud of doubt. When
McKeogh visited him in his trailer, he found Eisenhower seated
next to his overflowing ashtray. 'His voice and face showed that
tightness we had all been feeling.'

A collective anxiety was to pervade Southwick House for much of the morning. 'Everybody was very sober. It was the soberest day we ever had.' McKeogh felt as if everyone had been struck by the enormity of what was taking place. 'Nobody made any of the little jokes we usually had.'[1]

Eisenhower's personal aide, Harry Butcher, remained by Ike's side for some hours. At one point the two of them were seated in silence in a tented communications post in the grounds of the house: it was so quiet that they could overhear a British officer, Jimmy Gault, listening to a naval transmission. 'It was coming through in glub-glubs and blurp-blurps of scramblese,' said Butcher, who saw that Eisenhower was growing increasingly nervous. 'God,' blurted Ike after several minutes, 'this must be bad, it's so long.' In fact, the naval report brought relatively good news: just two destroyers (USS *Corry* and *Svenner*) were known to have sunk.

Shortly afterwards, Ike paced over to the war room inside nearby Southwick House. This was the nerve centre of the invasion and it was bristling with energy as staff read through the latest information before swiftly incorporating it on to the vast situation map of Normandy. Among the senior officers present was Major-General Kenneth Strong, Eisenhower's intelligence expert, who chuckled with delight as he informed the Supreme Commander that the Germans had been outwitted by the 'tactical surprise' of the Allied landings. His breezy confidence fell on deaf ears. Eisenhower wished for one thing alone: that he could be in France, directing operations from the front line of battle. 'From where he sits,' noted Butcher, 'he can't just step in.'[2] In the absence of having orders to issue – or anything else to do – he began planning his following day's visit to the Allied beachhead.

While General Eisenhower fretted about the troops landing on the Normandy coastline, the BBC transmitted his urgent message to the local inhabitants, warning that those who lived near to the coast were in grave danger of being killed.

This is London calling. I bring you an urgent instruction from the Supreme Commander. The lives of many of you depend upon the speed and thoroughness with which you obey it.

It was particularly addressed to all 'who live within thirty-five kilometres of any part of the coast'.[3] Twenty-year-old Jacques Martin lived rather closer than that: his family's villa was just fifty metres from the beach, so close that in stormy weather its windows were regularly doused with spray. He had not heard the BBC's message, for the naval bombardment had forced him to seek refuge in the covered trench at the rear of the garden, along with his frightened parents and sister.

They had no idea that the largest seaborne invasion in history was heading for their coast; no idea that a thousand Allied binoculars were fixed on the silhouette of their own home, using it as one of the landmarks by which the troops would know where to charge ashore. Jacques Martin and his sibling had fled the house when a large shell exploded on the beach and flung half a ton of sand through Jacques's bedroom window. They were still in their nightclothes.

Leave your towns at once . . . stay off frequented roads . . . Go on foot and take nothing with you which you can't easily carry.

The Martin family had decided some weeks earlier to stay put in Bernières-sur-Mer, even though old Paul Martin (Jacques's father) had long wagered that the Allies would land on this stretch of beach. A grizzled veteran of the Great War, he had kept his family in the town during four long years of Nazi occupation. Nothing was going to move him now.

Those four years had been painful and humiliating, punctuated by a few memorable flashes of dark humour. On one occasion, a local youth named Gaston Godin had dared to shout out 'The Boche [Germans] are fucked'[4] when arriving for a day of forced labour. It had earned him much local admiration, along with a lengthy spell in prison.

Another high point had come when the elderly Georges Guriec handed over his massive wireless to the German authorities, in conformity with orders. In front of an assembled crowd that included the town's senior German officer, he then pulled out a huge axe and began smashing it into a thousand pieces. As an example of public resistance, it was beautifully theatrical and perfectly choreographed.

Bernières had also experienced its share of pain, and the worst incident had occurred just three weeks earlier, when a much loved old pensioner, Monsieur Flambard, had inadvertently stepped on a landmine. One of the town's youth, Georges Regnauld, had the misfortune to see him with both legs blown off – '*dans des souffrances atroces*'[5] – in terrible suffering, screaming and moaning as he died.

The years of occupation had tightened the community of this bustling coastal town as friends and neighbours kept their secrets hidden from the Nazis. No one would have dreamed of informing on Monsieur Witosky, who was transmitting messages to the English via his clandestine radio transmitter. And no one would have revealed who placed an ostentatious floral bouquet on the French war memorial each 11 November, even though everyone knew it was the same Georges Guriec who had smashed his wireless.

Now, on the morning of 6 June, there was yet another show of unity as people offered shelter to friends and neighbours in their home-made dug-outs. They were finding it increasingly hard to breathe, for 'the air was thick with dust and powder',[6] and the shellfire had been growing in intensity for more than an hour. When Jacques Martin peeked out of his shelter at around 6.30 a.m., he got the first of many shocks that morning. The family home was engulfed in flames.

Most of the inhabitants of Bernières had by now woken up to the fact that Allied forces were heading towards their stretch of coast. What they didn't know was that their local beach had been chosen as one of the five main points of assault. Nor did they know that it had been given a codename by Eisenhower's team: Juno.

Georges Regnauld had taken refuge with the Audrée family that morning: their home lay 200 metres from the beach. It was danger-ously close to a German mortar position and Regnauld could hear panic in the soldiers' voices as they shouted guttural commands to each other. For what seemed like an eternity, he lived through 'a hell of fire and steel'.

But then, at around 7.30 a.m., there was a sudden and dramatic change to the infernal din outside. 'A weird noise appeared just by our shelter, making the whole place shake as it went past.' Young Georges dared to poke his head outside and was astounded by what he saw. 'Several Sherman tanks, still dripping wet, arrived, flattening everything in their path.' The first amphibious tanks were rolling into Bernières-sur-Mer.

The tanks were not the only surprise that morning. Behind them came 'a tall, handsome fellow in khaki' – a lone Allied soldier – who tentatively approached Regnauld, his submachine gun pointing at his stomach.

'You're not Boche?' he asked in French.

'No, I'm not Boche. But you're speaking French.'

'*Oui*,' said the man as he broke into a nervous smile and proffered chocolates and cigarettes. 'We're Canadian French.'[7]

Regnauld could scarcely believe what was happening. So this was it. This was the long-awaited *débarquement* – the landing. The Canadian advance guard had landed on Juno Beach.

The two assault companies that landed in the first wave at Bernières were commanded by brothers from Toronto, Charles and Elliot Dalton. At thirty-three years of age, Charles was more than half a decade older than his sibling, but the age gap had done nothing to dampen the deep affection they had for one another – two grinning brothers with rugged faces and swept-back hair. Charles had flashing teeth and a winning smile that spread all the way to his eyes. 'The archetypal dashing young officer,' said one under his command. 'He really had a lot of style.'[8] He was a soldier to the very last button on his epaulettes, having first joined the Queen's Own Rifles Cadet Company at the tender age of fifteen.

Elliot was more earnest, more rounded, more youthful, although he was also a keen soldier. He had followed in his brother's footsteps by joining the same regiment in 1931. They were known by their men as Mark I and Mark II: each was held in equal regard.

'The Dalton brothers were legends,' said one of Charles's comrades. 'You always had confidence in what they were doing and they always had the human touch.' Both shared a common trait: they were 'very down to earth'[9] and never looked down on their men, nor did they ever pull rank.

The brothers had 'developed a strong bond' and were so close to each other, as they were to their dear mother, that Charles had begged his commanding officer to spare Elliot the initial assault. 'Don't send Elliot on the first wave,' he said. 'You know what it will do to our mother if we both die.'[10] But there was nothing the commanding officer could do. It had already been decided that both brothers would be among the first to storm the beach.

All siblings have an in-built spirit of rivalry and these two 'had competed all their lives'. Now, they were facing the greatest competition of all – to survive the run-in to the sea wall and then fight their way into Bernières-sur-Mer. Elliot was the first to admit he was driven by fear. 'You're a phoney if you're not afraid,' he said to his men. 'The only thing that's going to keep you going is that you're afraid of being afraid.' But he intended to use his competitiveness to drive his company forward. 'A pride in your unit makes you afraid to be a coward.'[11] Under his leadership, A Company was there to succeed.

His older brother Charles also confessed to being scared: it was only natural. 'Of course, you're always frightened.' But he also knew not to reveal that fear to his men. 'The important thing is that I give the leadership they're expecting from me, because I have their lives in my hands.'[12] He felt an acute sense of responsibility, perhaps because he had played the role of responsible elder brother for much of his life. It had become a part of who he was.

When the two men parted company in order to prepare for the 3.15 a.m. reveille, they knew in their hearts that they might never see each other again. Charles shook his brother's hand warmly, if a little stiffly. 'See you on the beach!'[13] He said it with forced jollity, but the lump was firmly in his throat. It was hard to be light-hearted at such a moment.

One of the lads serving in Elliot Dalton's A Company was Charlie Martin. He had tried to imagine the landing on countless occasions over the previous weeks, picturing his platoon as part of a vast fleet of assault craft. But now, as his company began the sea-tossed journey towards the beach, reality hit home. The emptiness was profound. 'Suddenly, there was just us – and an awful lot of ocean.'

When he looked to his left and right, all he could see was ten isolated assault craft – five belonging to A Company (his own) and five belonging to B Company. He glanced back at his comrades and realized that they were feeling no less vulnerable. 'We had never felt so alone in our lives.'

It got worse as they neared the shore. 'The boats began to look even tinier as the gaps widened, with more than the length of a football field between each.' He was praying that Allied bombers would knock out the German shore defences, but when he peered

over the ramp of his landing craft, he was alarmed to see 'a formidable fifteen-foot wall with three large heavy cement pill-boxes'.
Worse still, 'the entire beach was open to murderous fire',[14] with
machine guns positioned in such a way as to cover every inch of
foreshore.

Landing on such a heavily fortified coast was one problem, but
Juno Beach presented an additional hazard. Unlike Utah and Omaha,
the men would be coming ashore in a town, Bernières, and would
almost certainly have to fight their way through heavily defended
streets – house-to-house combat in which every door might be
booby-trapped and every attic conceal a sniper. But there was no
time to reflect on the dangers, for the first landing craft were already
entering the coastal shallows. A few seconds later they scrunched
into the gravel and came to a halt in a few inches of water.

'Down ramp.'

'Move! Fast! Don't stop for anything. Go! Go! Go!'

Charles Dalton's B Company faced a tough reception. 'Follow
me!'[15] yelled their commander, only to disappear in twelve feet of
water. By the time he had made it ashore, most of his men had
been hit. Young Doug Hester watched three of his comrades jump
off the ramp into knee-deep water. All were gunned down in an
instant. Hester found himself jumping into seawater that was frothing
and pink, coloured by 'their rising blood'.

He surged forward under fire and caught up with his friend,
John 'Gibby' Gibson, just as a burst went through Gibby's backpack.

'That was close, Dougie,' he said with a grin.

The next burst killed him. 'He fell down spread-eagled in front
of me.'[16] Hester pushed himself forward before collapsing in exhaustion at the sea wall. When he looked back towards the sea, he saw
that many of his comrades were not so fortunate. Jim Wilkins had
jumped off the ramp just after him, landing in a rain of fire. He
felt a terrific blow. 'All of a sudden, something slapped the side of
my right leg.' The next thing he knew, he was flat on his face
in the water. He'd lost his rifle and helmet and he could hear his
friend, Kenny, 'yelling at me to come on'.[17]

B Company had suffered severe losses. When Charles Dalton
glanced back towards the sea, he saw that most of his men were
lying on the sand. 'I thought they'd gone to ground for cover, then

realized they'd been hit.'[18] One of them, John Missions, saw all but six of the soldiers on his landing craft gunned down.

Dalton had by now reached his objective, an enemy pillbox. But when he fired his Sten gun through the aperture, he was met by the bullet of a German automatic pistol. The bullet went straight through his helmet, tracing the outline of his skull and peeling back his scalp, but mercifully avoiding his brain. It sent a cascade of blood down his face. Weakened by the wound, Dalton urged his surviving men to knock out the seafront pillboxes and press on into Bernières.

Teamwork counted for everything that morning. René Tessier and William Chicoski rushed towards one of the casemates, firing all the while with their Sten guns. Their action allowed other men to creep up behind. Once underneath the embrasure, they were halfway to victory. Tessier and Chicoski jumped on to the shoulders of the other men, allowing them to reach the gun slit. 'They stood on our backs and were lobbing grenades through the apertures.'[19] Another member of the team had positioned himself at the rear door of the pillbox, just as he had learned during training. When the Germans tried to make their escape, he tore them apart with his Sten gun.

The wounded Charles Dalton had so far received no news from his brother's company. He had no idea if young Elliot was still alive. In fact, Elliot Dalton's men had experienced a somewhat less chaotic landing, although they had nevertheless come under heavy fire from the German machine guns. Charlie Martin had pitched himself forward from the landing craft, only to see his three friends, Hugh 'Rocky' Rocks, George Dalzell and Gil May, cut down by bullets.

One of the landing craft took a particularly cruel hit, with twenty-eight of the thirty-five men gunned down on the beach. But Elliot Dalton himself survived the run-in and now rallied the survivors at the sea wall, encouraging them to attack the concrete pillboxes. Taking charge of a precarious situation, he led a small band of men along the rubble-strewn seafront towards a fin-de-siècle villa being used as a strongpoint. Three years of training now proved its worth. 'We kicked in the door, tossed in a grenade, charged in quickly, guns blazing, while the defenders were stunned.'[20] There was no time for taking prisoners: the men shot everything that moved.

One by one the shoreline pillboxes were silenced, enabling the bruised survivors to push forward into the streets of Bernières. They now embarked on the most dangerous form of warfare, fighting at close quarters and with danger lurking in every building. Bob Rae was an intelligence officer who had landed with the Queen's Own Rifles: with considerable trepidation, he ushered a few men towards one of the deserted streets that led away from the beach. A burned-out tank provided cover.

'Crouching low, with our Sten automatics at the immediate alert, we ventured a little further away from the protection of the tank.'[21] They hugged the low walls that surrounded the houses and pushed on into town. There was no sign of life: it was as if every civilian had fled. Only when the men of A Company attacked what they believed to be a German communications centre did they learn, to their astonishment, that Bernières was full of people.

'We opened fire and, with that, a big gold ball on the end of a flagpole started to come out of the basement window.' The men kept on firing, assuming it to be a ruse, but next 'an enormous French flag came out of the window'. Elliot Dalton ordered his men to stop shooting. As he did so, 'around seventy French people came out of the cellars with their hands up.' Every one of them was a pensioner. Elliot found himself smiling, for the scene was darkly comic. 'My chance for a VC went down the drain with attacking seventy elderly French people hiding in the basement.'[22]

His flight of good humour was to be abruptly shattered. A runner came to him with the dreadful news that his brother Charles had been killed. He had put up a stiff fight on the beach and displayed great bravery, but the German resistance had proved too strong. Charles had died of his wounds.

Elliot was devastated – it was a gut-wrenching loss – but this was no time to dwell on the tragedy. Men's lives were at stake. He needed to lead. 'While I grieved,' he said, 'I had a job to do and had to carry on.'[23] It was nonetheless a devastating blow. After a lifetime of competing with his brother, he had just won the most bitter of prizes.

To the lads fighting their way through Bernières, it felt as if they were engaged in a desperate guerrilla war in which there was no sense of order. 'Each of the ten boatloads had become an independent fighting unit' and 'none had connection with the other.' Yet the two Daltons had done a magnificent job in training their men and Elliot's order rang clear in the ears of all in A Company. 'Do not stop till you reach the objective. Otherwise, once you're stopped, you are ninety per cent defeated.'[24]

And so forward they went, pushing ever deeper into the rubble-strewn streets of Bernières, amid burning houses and exploding shells. Bob Rae was one of the first into the centre of town and was astonished to discover that 'members of the civilian population were appearing in the streets.' He had assumed the local inhabitants would have fled. Quite the contrary. 'By the time I reached the main square, women and children were emerging from the flimsy shelter afforded by kitchens and cellars.' One elderly man appeared with a bottle of wine. 'He even carried neat little wine glasses for service.' It was a most incongruous sight, given that shops were ablaze and enemy snipers picking off unwary troops.

When he entered the square flanked by the parish church of Notre Dame de la Nativité, he found that other troops had beaten him there. 'A carrier and tank were standing in the shelter of the walls and several children stood around, gazing wide-eyed at these strange vehicles.'[25]

Huge numbers of men and machines were now pouring into Bernières. The Queen's Own Rifles were followed by the French-speaking Régiment de la Chaudière. It was one of their soldiers who had approached young Georges Regnauld and cautiously asked if he was a Boche.

So many tanks were ploughing through the town that they were having problems manoeuvring around the tight corners. Joe Wagar watched one tank 'trying to negotiate a narrow turn in a street, tearing off the corner of a building and not stopping'.

The arrival of the first of the specialist armoured vehicles only increased the chaos, 'rotary chains flailing the sand in front of it to explode the mines'.[26] When John McClean glanced back towards the sea, he was met by an unforgettable sight. 'On the rising tide, hundreds of ships and landing craft made the approach, discharged their cargoes of men and machines, backed off, turned around and headed back to England.'[27]

Elliot Dalton spent much of the morning fighting against stiff

German resistance. 'House fighting was harder than anticipated. They hung in there and were difficult to get out of the houses.'[28] But he and his men flushed through every building until the whole town had been liberated. Soon, they could begin the push inland.

Elliot would continue his fight for several more days, aware that he was doing it not only for himself but also in memory of his beloved brother. He would eventually be wounded and sent back to England to be hospitalized. When the nurse wheeled him to the bed marked Major Dalton, she noticed a patient already lying there with a sheet pulled over his head. She asked what he was doing there, prompting him to sit bolt upright and reply, 'I'm Major Dalton.'[29] It was Elliot's brother Charles: miraculously still alive, having survived the head wound he received on the beach.

All along the five-mile length of Juno Beach, stretching from Graye-sur-Mer to Saint-Aubin-sur-Mer, with the two largest towns, Bernières and Courseulles, situated towards the middle, the Canadians were engaged in similar fighting.

Charles Tubb was a major in the Regina Rifles: he was among the first into Courseulles. He had told his men to 'crash the beach and go like stink'.[30] Leo Gariepy was doing just that, driving one of the nineteen amphibious tanks in his squadron. The voyage to shore was a nightmare of endurance due to the screeching gale and freezing spray, but the terror of the ride was worth it just to see the look of astonishment from the German machine gunners hiding in the dunes. They were 'absolutely stupefied to see a tank emerging from the sea'. Some fled in terror. Many more 'just stood up in their nests and stared, unable to believe their eyes'. In doing so, they made themselves sitting ducks. 'We mowed them down like they were corn on the cobs.'[31]

A few hundred feet offshore, Lieutenant Gerald Ashcroft had spotted a pillbox concealed in one corner of Courseulles harbour. As he studied it through his binoculars, he could see that the soldiers inside were swivelling their gun barrel around. They were training it directly on to his tank-laden landing craft.

He took swift action, pulling hard on the throttle and slamming his craft towards the beach, having advised the driver in the lead tank to hit the sand at full tilt while simultaneously training his gun on to the pillbox. This is what the driver did, and with consummate skill, for he managed to send a shell directly through the narrow aperture. Although he was in a war zone, Ashcroft couldn't resist stepping ashore to inspect the damage.

'It really was an astonishing sight and it showed how effective a solid shot in a pillbox can be.' As he peered through the gloom, 'there was literally nothing left but skin, blood and bits of flesh, all mixed up like a load of mincemeat.' The concrete walls had contained the shot and it 'had ricocheted round and round, tearing everyone inside to pieces'.[32]

The Canadian infantry moved swiftly into Courseulles, flushing out the Germans from their network of underground tunnels. As they did so, the second and third waves started to arrive. Charles Belton was still making his way up the beach when he saw his friend, Bob, lying on the sand and looking as if he didn't have a care in the world.

'Bob, you silly fool, this is no time to rest. Get up on the sand dunes.'

Belton nudged him in the ribs before realizing, to his horror, that his friend was dead. 'I saw a tiny round mark in his forehead.' He'd been hit by a rifle bullet.

It was to be a morning of chilling sights for Charles Belton. As he peered through the slits of a pillbox, he spotted another dead comrade, Walter 'Bull' Klos. He was a veritable bull of a man who weighed 230 pounds and had arms like tree trunks.

He had been hit in the stomach as he ran up the beach: the shell had torn open his uniform 'and there was a handful of intestines hanging out over his belt, as large as my fist'. But even this terrible wound hadn't stopped the Bull. He had launched himself into the pillbox and fallen on the three German occupants like a snarling grizzly bear. 'He'd killed the two with his bare hands' – strangling them to death – 'before he died. We found him sitting astride the third German' – also dead – 'with his hands around the fellow's throat.'[33]

US Rangers aimed to ambush the German defenders at Pointe du Hoc, using ropes and ladders to scale the cliffs. This picture was taken a few days after their dramatic assault.

17

Cliff-top Guns

I T WAS NOW 7.45 a.m., exactly sixty-five minutes since Leonard Schroeder had stormed through the surf on Utah Beach, and the world had all but exploded. Utah, Omaha, Juno and Gold – an entire slice of Normandy coastline was ablaze, with wave after wave of Allied soldiers pouring ashore in a welter of fire. The smaller landing craft used to ferry ashore the first wave had been followed by far larger vessels. Each of these disgorged more than 200 soldiers, along with tanks and armoured vehicles. On Sword Beach, too, the first wave of troops were ashore: the men of the East Yorks had landed some twenty minutes earlier, although it would be another hour before the beach would be stormed by Lord Lovat's elite commandos.

In the meantime, an operation of uncommon daring was taking place some thirty miles to the west, between the seaside towns of Grandcamp and Vierville. The sky was still hunkered into night when James Rudder and his band of adventurers set off for the forbidding cliffs of Pointe du Hoc, a forlorn shoulder of coastline with no villages and only a handful of isolated farms. Here, the relentless sea gale tore through the gorse at the top of the cliff, stunting hawthorns and flattening the tufted grass.

This vertical promontory loomed skywards to the height of a nine-storey building, a crumbling scarp of Jurassic limestone whose upper reaches were lost to a veil of drizzle and spray. But invisibility had not rendered it immune to attack. High-explosive shells from USS *Satterlee* and HMS *Talybont* were thumping into the grassland atop the cliffs, sending a cascade of watery detritus on to the rock-strewn foreshore. Boulders, pebbles and shingle were all being slicked with gleaming clay.

James Rudder had been waiting for this moment for months and training for it for even longer. In terms of complexity, his 225 crack troops were about to undertake a mission that matched John Howard's assault on Bénouville Bridge. For sheer daring, it was on a par with the Merville Battery attack. But Rudder's mission had an added component that rendered it suicidal.

The goal was this: to knock out the big German guns situated on the top of Pointe du Hoc, six 155mm cannon that could lob huge shells a distance of 25,000 metres. They could hit both Utah Beach and Omaha Beach, as well as the cruisers and destroyers at anchor in the coastal waters. 'This mission was deemed vital,' according to General Omar Bradley, who had realized that those six guns 'could fatally wreck our invasion forces'.[1]

The Germans were well aware that there was only one feasible means of knocking out these cliff-top guns and that was by attacking from the land. For this reason, they had fortified the guns from the rear, protecting them with minefields and trenches. James Rudder knew this and it had prompted a more creative approach. He studied aerial reconnaissance photographs and samples of clay before announcing his plan of attack to Max Schneider, a war-toughened colonel in the Rangers. Schneider could scarcely believe what he was being told: he 'just whistled through his teeth'.[2] Others thought Rudder had lost his marbles. 'It can't be done,'[3] snorted an officer from naval intelligence.

Rudder's plan was to give the Germans a surprise they would never forget. Instead of attacking from the land, as they expected, he intended to strike from the sea, scaling the near-vertical cliffs using grapnels, ropes and ladders. Such a dramatic assault was a nod and a wink to Major-General James Wolfe's attack on Quebec almost two centuries earlier, relying on stealth, subterfuge and physical stamina. But it would also require two other ingredients that didn't yet exist. If the plan were to work, it would require the best trained men ever to go into battle. It would also need a battle-field leader of uncommon ability.

Cometh the hour, cometh the man. James Rudder was to be that leader, a thirty-four-year-old football coach who had been drafted into the army three years earlier. A physical powerhouse, he was big-boned, broad of chest and fuelled by a heady cocktail of testosterone and stamina. He was a Texan through and through,

and Texas, it was said, was full of big things: 'big land, big buildings, big oil wells, big cities, big hats and, more importantly, big
men'.[4]

He had an intelligent gaze, quizzical even, as if carefully processing
any information that passed through his hands. And there was
something reassuring about his natural Texan drawl. His voice 'was
as soft as a presiding elder saying Sunday grace over a chicken
dinner'.[5] Yet when he got animated, as he often did, the nerves
were audible in his larynx. 'He had a way of speaking that promised
coming excitement, keeping the men keyed up, expecting formidable
but achievable missions ahead.' Most importantly, he commanded
authority. One of his recruits said he was 'the kind of man that
when he walked into a room, you just naturally wanted to stand
up and salute'.[6] His recruits knew that he would never let them
down. When he was told by his divisional commander that he
wouldn't be allowed to lead the Pointe du Hoc assault on account
of its danger, he said, 'I'm sorry, sir, but I'm going to have to
disobey you. If I don't take it, it may not go.'[7]

Rudder wanted only the finest men in his battalion and he
selected them for their stamina and motivation. His chosen band
could come from any walk of life, just so long as they were prepared
to fight to the death. One of them was a fellow Texan named James
Eikner, a thirty-year-old telephone installer with keen eyes and a
smudge of moustache. His day job involved shimmying up very
high poles: the idea of scaling a cliff held few fears. Another recruit,
Leonard Lomell, was a smooth-faced railway worker with a scoured
parting and winning teeth. He had ridden the freight trains of New
Jersey before volunteering for Rudder's outfit. Now, he was hoping
to get the ride of his life.

Many of Rudder's recruits were unruly misfits. Merril Stinnetti
was a firebrand whose years in the merchant marines had done
nothing to calm his high-wire nerves. A few drinks was all it took
for his simmering anger to burst skywards. 'He'd as soon knock
you off the bar-stool if you looked him wrong,' said one of his
mates, Herman Stein. 'I was sitting right next to him when he
cold-cocked a guy.'

Bill Anderson was another hulk of 'downright blood and guts'
who had been demoted from sergeant to private after a fist-fight.

'A braggart and self-centred,' thought Stein, 'but he had the stuff to back it up.'

William 'L-Rod' Petty was 'the same type of nut',[8] only marginally more dangerous. He looked waifish, 'a pale-faced, unimposing lad with slick blond hair'.[9] Yet his missing front teeth hinted at a violent and unpredictable temperament. Petty had once attacked his abusive father with a mattock, a type of pick-axe, the perfect example of using overwhelming force to crush a weaker opponent. He was twice rejected by Rudder, but got lucky on his third attempt. Rudder intended to focus his aggression and thereby turn him into a deadly killing machine. 'Such a great fighting man,' noted one of his officers, but so unruly 'that I guarded and kept private a whole lot of what I knew about him'.[10]

Petty soon fell in with a gang of hotheads like himself – Bill Colden, Gene 'Rattop' Vershare, Bill Coldsmith and Bill McHugh. Collectively they were known as Petty's bastards. They were determined to prove that they could be bastards – absolute bastards – on the field of battle. Others viewed them with a mixture of awe and respect. Stein thought they were all maniacs, yet he was glad to have such unique fighters onside. 'You can count them on the fingers of one hand,' he said, 'but take them away and you'll never win a war.'[11]

After a training programme that included being dumped in an eighteen-foot tropical sea infested with sharks, the men were shipped from Florida to the Isle of Wight. Here, they were taught to scale the cliffs at the Needles while under live fire. By the time D-Day ticked into place, Rudder's troops felt supremely confident. 'We knew what we were getting into,' said James Eikner. 'We knew we were volunteering for extra hazardous duty, so we went into battle confident that we could overcome any situation.'[12] Herman Stein went one step further: he knew they were on a winning streak. 'The Germans were no match for us.'[13]

They would need every last drop of confidence, for just about everything was to go wrong on that wet and overcast morning. The seas around Pointe du Hoc were so choppy that many of the men found themselves vomiting and bailing water at the same time, a form of multitasking that not even Rudder's training had taught them to do.

One of the landing craft foundered in the mountainous seas,

requiring the survivors to tread water for hours before being rescued. One of the supply boats also sank, while the second, carrying the ammunition, was so close to being swamped that much of the weaponry had to be dumped over the side.

Even more alarming than the heavy sea was the fact that the Royal Navy coxswain was in the process of leading the remaining nine landing craft to the wrong cliff. Aware that he was lost, he asked for directions from an American control craft that was coasting along offshore. 'I say,' he said, 'can you tell me the way to Pointe du Hoc?' The American lieutenant, William Steel, could hardly believe his ears. The coxswain sounded for all the world like a well-spoken British tourist 'standing on a street in New York City saying, "How do you get to Times Square?"'[14]

Lieutenant Steel pointed towards Pointe du Hoc and the British naval officer once again picked up his megaphone. 'Thank you very much,' he said as he swung the landing craft round in the direction of the distant cliffs. It was a fortunate encounter but the damage was already done. The navigational error caused the Rangers to arrive thirty-five minutes behind schedule, giving the German defenders time to recover from the naval bombardment planned in advance by Rudder. By the time his 225 men arrived, the enemy was ready and waiting.

'Get your heads down!'[15]

As the men leaped from their landing craft into thigh-deep water, some of them tumbled into craters so deep that they found themselves plunged underwater. One minute George Kerchner was yelling, 'Okay, let's go,'[16] the next he was sinking to the bottom, gulping mouthfuls of seawater as he fought his way back to the surface. Those who hit the shore as planned were raked with machine-gun fire from a concealed enemy trench.

It was now that their live-ammunition training paid dividends. Leonard Lomell didn't stop running even when shot through his side. The bullet 'didn't hit any organs or bones'[17] – at least it didn't seem to have done – so he pressed home his advance.

William Petty was also running like hell as he tried to avoid the machine gun that was 'kicking the pants out of the cliff'.[18] As he took shelter beneath the bluff, he was astonished to see one of their number, Travis Trevor, strolling up and down the beach as if he were taking a summer stroll. Trevor was a young British commando who had helped train Petty and his comrades. He was a gaunt giant, 'a great big, black-haired son of a gun'[19] with a towering frame that made him a very conspicuous target. Yet he seemed oblivious to danger.

'How in the world do you do that when you're being fired on all the time?' shouted Elmer Vermeer from the safety of a crater. 'I take two short steps and three long ones and they always miss me,' was Trevor's shouted reply.

He spoke too soon. Vermeer found him a little later hiding in a shell crater. 'He'd been hit right through the front of his helmet, and the helmet was stuck on his head with the steel edge poking into his forehead.' It was fortunate that it hadn't been rammed through his brain. Vermeer had to jerk the helmet back and forth to get it off. When he finally succeeded, Trevor let rip with his tongue, screaming abuse in the general direction of the German who had shot at him. 'You dirty son of a bitch.'[20]

One of the Rangers' greatest problems in those opening minutes of combat came when their amphibious vehicles were unable to get a purchase on the shingle beach. It meant that the eighty-foot extending ladders, loaned by the London Fire Brigade and welded securely to the decks, could not reach the cliff-top. This technical drawback did nothing to deter one of Rudder's more acrobatic men, William Stivison, who hoisted one of the ladders vertically into the sky and then scampered to the top. He was completely unfazed by the fact that the ladder was swinging back and forth like a precarious trapeze as the amphibious vehicle bucked and kicked in the heavy swell. In the brief seconds when the ladder was upright, Stivison would straighten his machine gun and 'fire short bursts as he passed over the edge of the cliff'.[21] Seconds later, he would wrap his arms around the rungs of the ladder as it plunged back towards the water.

With the extending ladders out of action, the men were forced to rely on their rope and steel grapnels. These were fired from rocket guns and had been designed to embed themselves into the cliff-top and leave a trail of rope dangling down to the beach. That, at least, was the theory. In reality, most of the ropes were too sodden with spray (and therefore too heavy) to reach the cliff-top. Very few of the grapnels buried themselves into the wet clay at the top of Pointe du Hoc.

William Petty was about to scale one of the dangling ropes when a German machine gun began spitting bullets at his comrade halfway up the cliff. 'He stiffened and swung out. Next, he slid down the rope like an elevator, bounced several times against ledges'[22] before thumping on to the rocks below. Now it was Petty's turn. He grabbed the greasy rope and started to climb, praying that the machine-gun fire wouldn't hit him.

There were other hazards that hadn't been foreseen. One group of Germans was trying to cut the ropes. Others were lobbing grenades over the cliff. And some were firing directly down on the men as they climbed.

'Heads in, butts out!' yelled James Eikner to the men clambering behind him. Eikner had never felt so vulnerable. 'The Germans were taking us under fire like shooting ducks on a tub.'[23]

Rudder's men could easily have been defeated there and then. But with Stivison performing his circus act from the top of the ladder, and the *Satterlee* still plastering the cliff-top with naval shells, the first of the Rangers had just enough cover to get to the top. Those who did make it were struck by a most extraordinary sight – the exposed white buttocks of Ralph 'Preacher' Davis, a student chaplain from Tennessee. The climb up the cliffs had – to use the vernacular – scared the shit out of Davis. As soon as he reached the top he had pulled down his trousers and pants in order to relieve himself. James Eikner couldn't help but smile at the absurdity of it all. He had arrived at the top expecting to find mortars and machine guns; instead, he was confronted by the incongruous sight of Preacher's bottom. 'The war had to stop for a while until Preacher could get organized,'[24] he said.

In truth, Preacher's open-air privy was no place to linger, for gunfire was spurting from all directions. The men might well have been wiped out, had it not been for the hundreds of shell craters that had transformed Pointe du Hoc into a clay-drenched chaos of detritus and concrete.

★

'*Praise the Lord!*'

James Eikner flashed a message signalling that the Rangers were on top of the cliff. He knew they would need every bit of help from the Lord if they were to retain this precarious foothold.

'Let's go!'

'I don't know what to do.'

'Mac, you and Coldsmith take the left flank. Colden, you take the right and move out.'

Petty's bastards were on the move, hungry for action. Gene 'Rattop' Vershare was cursing his carbine as he leaped from crater to crater. 'This thing is no fucking good!' Petty was keeping a sharp eye on the German positions. 'There come seven of the bastards.' They all let rip and watched them drop to the ground. The few Germans they captured alive would live to regret it. 'All right, let's see you bastards goosestep,' yelled Bill 'Mac' McHugh to one small group of captives he was tormenting. '*Ein – Zwei – Drei.*'[25]

A few hundred yards away, one of their comrades, Herman Stein, was part of a fighting pair, having joined Jack Richards in a crater. Richards poked his head above the edge then instantly keeled over, struck by a single bullet. 'The blood was gushing out of his throat.' Stein thumped his fist into the gaping hole, 'trying to stop the flow of blood, but that high blood pressure of his was pumping like mad'. It took just a couple of minutes for him to die. His eyes 'opened in a glassy, far-away look and I knew he was gone'.[26]

The chewed-up terrain meant it was impossible to undertake a coherent attack and the assault soon broke down into a series of individual fire-fights. Each platoon had been given an objective. Now, even when separated, they tried to fulfil their goals. The German defenders were firing with everything they had, using their elaborate system of trenches to maximum effect. George Kerchner found himself in the vanguard and jumped into one of the German trenches, following its zigzagging course towards the main bunker. Two years earlier he had been an ice-cream seller in Baltimore; he'd never imagined the day when he would be flushing Nazis from their front-line defences. It was a whole lot scarier than selling ice-cream soda. 'I never felt so lonesome before and since in all my life. I didn't know whether I was going to come face to face with a German or not.' At one point he stumbled across the corpses of six of his buddies. 'Nearly every one was shot through the head.'[27] They'd been killed by a concealed sniper.

James Rudder had established his command post in a crater close to the cliff edge. He had been shot through the leg but refused to let it trouble him. He ordered the medic to run a swab through the hole – excruciatingly painful without anaesthetic – and then sluice some iodine on to the raw flesh. One of his men, Elmer Vermeer, winced as he watched this impromptu operation. Rudder himself got back to work.

The first German prisoner was caught within minutes of establishing the command post: 'a little freckle-faced kid who looked like an American'. Rudder told a couple of his men to use the lad to lead them into his underground hiding place, where they would surely capture more prisoners. 'They just started him around this corner when the Germans opened up out of the entrance and he fell dead, face down, with his hands still clasped on the top of his head.'[28]

Rudder's men were by now under fire from every direction. Leonard Lomell stumbled across Gilbert Baugh, commander of E Company, just after he'd been hit, 'his hand practically blown off'. He was in profound shock. 'Hey, Captain, we'll send you a medic,'[29] shouted Lomell. Baugh would soon get shot again, this time through the face. When Elmer Vermeer saw him, he was gushing with blood.

Rudder's most urgent priority was to silence the machine gun situated towards the eastern edge of the promontory. This was done in characteristically ebullient fashion. Rudder's communications man, Eikner, had lugged a massive First World War signal lamp up the cliff: it was a precaution in case their radios failed (which they did). He had been much mocked for relying on such antiquated technology, but now it proved its worth. Its telescopic sight and tracking system could be linked to any given ship, allowing Eikner to ask the *Satterlee* for help in knocking out the machine gun. It was not long in coming. *Satterlee's* five-inch shells blasted the entire nest off the cliff, punching it to the beach in an avalanche of rubble, hardware and enemy soldiers.

The *Texas* also began bombarding the cliff-top, with results that were rather less welcome. A huge fourteen-inch shell exploded virtually on top of Rudder's command post, smacking into the ground with unbelievable force. Captain Harwood was so seriously injured that he died soon after. Others were left clutching their heads as they reeled from the shock. Jerking with terror, they found their skin had been dyed bright yellow from the smoke of the coloured shell. 'It was as though they'd been stricken with jaundice. It wasn't only their faces and hands, but the skin beneath their clothes.'[30]

James Rudder told Eikner to re-contact the *Satterlee* to ask for emergency help in evacuating the wounded. The *Satterlee*'s captain immediately launched a rescue boat, but it was unable to approach the shore owing to the intensity of the gunfire. It was the darkest of moments for the Rangers: they were now cut off from both the sea and the land – an embattled group of fighters trapped on the edge of a cliff. They had but two options: to fight or to die.

Rudder's objectives were twofold. Capturing the six big guns on top of the Pointe du Hoc was the principal reason for the mission: these 155mm cannon had the potential to wreak yet more havoc on Omaha Beach. Rudder had assigned each company of men its combat duties long before they arrived at the promontory. Company E was to capture No. 3 gun; Company D, Nos. 4, 5 and 6; and Company F, Nos. 1 and 2.

A secondary task was to seize the coastal road that traversed the cliff-top and linked Vierville with Grandcamp. This was scarcely less important, for its capture would cut the German supply lines and prevent them from getting reinforcements to Omaha Beach.

Leonard Lomell was one of the first to go in search of the guns; by his own admission he was 'too cocky to be fearful or frightened'. He managed to round up twenty-two comrades who shared a similar spirit of bravado. They liked to brag that if they got into a fight, 'they would win, as they always had'.[31] Now, they scampered between craters as they advanced on the gun positions. But when they finally reached them, they got the shock of their lives. The emplacements were empty. The guns were not there.

They felt deflated. Their mission had been in vain. But Lomell smelled a rat. 'They must have an alternate position somewhere,' he said. Either that, or the guns had been hidden. Before searching for them, his comrades first cleared the underground tunnels that were being used by the Germans to deadly effect. 'When we were confronted, we'd drive them out and fight them and they'd run like rabbits, right into their holes.' Lomell's group tracked them down without mercy. 'We never stopped. We kept firing and charging all the way through their buildings area, where they came out of their billets in all states of undress.'

Once the tunnels were cleared, Lomell returned to the principal objective. 'Find the guns!'[32] It was the only thought in his head. His men wasted no time in advancing to the Vierville–Grandcamp road, where they set up a roadblock. It was situated between an orchard and wheat field, close to the hamlet of Au Guay. This advance guard was soon joined by William Petty and his bastards, who vowed to let nothing get through. At one point, they captured six Germans and put them through the goose-stepping routine. Dix 'Dixie' had meanwhile set his sights on a lone German soldier who was sauntering along the country road, apparently unaware of the danger he was in. Dix got a clean hit with his semi-automatic carbine, greatly impressing Petty. 'The prettiest shot I've seen.' Petty himself was crouching behind a low wall with a view over a sweep of road. At one point, eight Germans swung by on bicycles. Petty opened up on them. 'Almost like goin' duck huntin','[33] he said with a grin.

Leonard Lomell was convinced that the Germans had concealed their big guns in order to safeguard them from the Allied aerial bombardment. Now, he and his platoon sergeant, Jack Kahn, decided to scout the area to see if they could find them. It wasn't long before they came across a sunken road with deep track marks in the mud. To Lomell's eyes, 'it looked like something heavy had been over it.'[34] They advanced with caution, aware that the dense hedgerows could be hiding snipers. Every few feet they paused to check the ground ahead, before pressing forward in the direction of a dip in the land. When Lomell next stopped to peer over the hedge, he got a welcome surprise.

'God!' he called to Kahn. 'Here they are!' Concealed in an orchard and half camouflaged by trees, were the big guns they had come to destroy. They were huge, far bigger than Lomell was expecting. 'The wheels went up over our heads. Their muzzles went way up into the air, above our reach.' Alarmingly, they were all pointing towards Utah Beach, some eight miles away. 'Their positions were textbook ready.'

The two of them were preparing to destroy the guns with thermite grenades when Lomell caught sight of movement in a nearby field. Dozens of German soldiers were being addressed by an officer. Lomell could see them quite clearly and decided to act before they were spotted.

'Let's take a chance.'[35]

Jack nodded and handed over his thermite grenade. It was the perfect weapon for sabotage – totally silent on detonation, yet releasing such a furnace of heat that it would turn steel to liquid.

'You cover me. I'm going in there and destroying them.'

Lomell crawled forward and lodged the thermite grenades into the traversing mechanism of two of the cannons. This would melt them and render them useless. He then smashed the sights on the remaining guns, before signalling to Kahn that they should return to the roadblock and collect the rest of the thermite grenades. This they duly did. 'We stuffed them in our jackets and we rushed back and we put the thermite grenades, as many as we could, in traversing mechanisms and elevation mechanisms.'[36] When they detonated, they turned everything to a gooey mess of molten steel – guns, cranks, hinges and breechblocks. It was work well done.

'Hurry up, Len!' Kahn was getting increasingly concerned about being spotted by the German soldiers.

'Hurry up! Hurry up! Let's get the hell out of here!'[37]

They had just started making their escape when there was an explosion of such staggering force that the blast lifted them from the ground and hurled them into the sunken lane. 'We went flying, and ramrods, rocks, dust and everything came down on us.' Shaking with fear, they picked themselves up and 'ran like two scared rabbits as fast as we could back to our men at the roadblock'.[38] They assumed that a nearby ammunition dump had been hit by a stray shell from the *Texas*. In fact, the explosion was the work of their fellow Rangers. Sergeant Frank Rupinski had stumbled across the dump while looking for the guns, and blown it sky-high with explosive charges. The resulting blast had destroyed absolutely everything, including a sizeable chunk of field. One of Rudder's men would later milk a cow that had survived the blast. The animal had been so terrified that its milk had turned sour in its udder. 'It was bitter, like quinine. It had that onion taste and it was awful.'[39]

When James Rudder received word that the guns had been destroyed, he sent a message to the ships offshore, using Eikner's signal lamp. 'Located Pointe-du-Hoc – mission accomplished – need ammunition and reinforcements – many casualties.'

It was an hour before he received a reply. 'No reinforcements available.'[40] All his fellow Rangers had been diverted to Omaha Beach. Rudder's men were now on their own, surrounded and under siege. Even Petty's bastards wondered how they would survive the rest of the day.

An iconic image of bagpiper Bill Millin (foreground) preparing to land on Sword Beach. The central figure, arms akimbo, is Lord Lovat, 'the mad bastard'.

18

The Mad Bastard

Elsie Campbell was in bed when the first Allied troops landed in Normandy. Three days had passed since she picked up the secret signal about 'the Far Shore' and she remained convinced that the invasion was imminent. But she had kept her thoughts to herself, for she knew that very few people 'were aware of impending events'.[1] There was nothing to do but wait and see what happened.

As her shift had ended on the previous evening, so that of her colleague, Pat Blandford, had just begun. Miss Blandford had survived on almost no sleep for the previous forty-eight hours and was worn down by exhaustion. But her weariness was soon to be overtaken by adrenalin, for this particular shift was to be more exciting than most. At some point around dawn, she found her nerves on edge.

'Ma'am, ma'am!' shouted one of the younger girls. 'Something is coming through.'

Pat Blandford rushed over to the signalling machine and immediately realized what was happening. 'The red light on the panel glowed brightly. There it was – the long-awaited code-word which meant so much. They were through at last.' All the tensions of the previous weeks found a sudden release. 'A cheer went up and many young girls shed a tear.' Miss Blandford herself was deeply moved. 'It was a very emotional moment,' she confessed. 'One which I shall never forget.'[2]

Elsie Campbell was still in her lodgings when that dramatic D-Day message came through. She had been awake for much of the night, thinking about the fate of 'all the men, soldiers, sailors and airmen on their way to battle, and what they might face'. Her night had been a short one, for she was due back at Fort Southwick for the morning shift. As the bus hissed and grunted its way over

Portsdown Hill, she saw a sight she would never forget. The waters of Portsmouth Harbour were completely empty. There was not a ship in sight. It was as if a magician had conjured the entire fleet into thin air. 'Only HMS *Victory* was still there.' Miss Campbell allowed her gaze to linger on Nelson's flagship and had a moment of private reflection. 'Was it a hopeful sign?'[3] She prayed that it was.

Everyone who witnessed the empty ports and harbours of southern England was struck by the scale and gravity of what was taking place. Jean Watson worked in secret communications for the Women's Royal Naval Service (WRNS or Wrens): for months, her Southampton naval base had been a whirl of energy. Now, there was nothing but 'an awful deathly silence' that hung over everything. 'Where there had been thousands of troops, armaments and incessant noise, there was nothing. The tents, the troops, the guns, the ships – all were gone.'[4] In common with Miss Campbell and Miss Blandford, Jean Watson knew that life would never be quite the same again.

The previous few hours had been unexpectedly pleasant for the fifteenth Lord Lovat, for he had enjoyed an untroubled slumber as his landing craft pitched its way across the English Channel. He had gone to his makeshift cabin earlier that evening, still musing over the joyous send-off he had arranged in Portsmouth Harbour.

He was acutely aware that he had the chance of writing himself into the history books, not just because of his illustrious pedigree but because he was commanding a class act. His Special Service Brigade was at the very top of its game – so good, indeed, that his men had helped to train James Rudder's Rangers. It was a role that had brought Lovat a quiet satisfaction: the imperial master teaching his once colonial servants how to fight.

His men referred to him as 'the mad bastard',[5] a term of endearment. They admired his flamboyance just as they loved his swaggering confidence. Lord Lovat was a showman and D-Day was to be his greatest act.

Now, as his landing craft approached the French coast, he slipped into his monogrammed shirt and battledress and joined Commander Rupert Curtis on the bridge. Together they watched the early morning light turn the sea from an inky swill to an oyster-shell grey. The whitewashed villas of Lion-sur-Mer were visible as faint smears of pearl, while the shorefront façade of the Grand Hotel lent a few sharp lines to the haze. This stretch of coast had long been popular with the Parisian bourgeoisie, who had dined on the local oysters since the days of Louis Napoleon. But the annual feast had come to an abrupt end in 1940, when the hotels had been requisitioned, the esplanade placed out of bounds and the tidal shallows laid with mines. The oysters had been left unshucked for four years.

Lovat was familiar with the topography of the coastline, for he had been studying it for many months. He also knew the battle plan by heart. The amphibious tanks should have already landed, followed almost immediately by the first wave of troops. These were the young soldiers of the East Yorks. Lovat's commandos were to be the next to land, at 8.40 a.m., on a beach whose gun nests and pillboxes should have been knocked out by the intense aerial bombardment.

As the shoreline sharpened into focus, the commandos rechecked their life jackets and strapped on the last pieces of equipment. The final run-in was scheduled to take forty minutes.

'Good morning, commandos, and the best of British luck.' The message was flashed by Aldis signalling lamp from a nearby battleship. Lovat sent a suitable reply. 'Thanks, we're going to bloody well need it.'[6]

As the wind gave a stiff sigh, Commander Curtis ran up his battle ensign. Lovat was delighted. 'War was becoming personal again.'[7] He said it with more than a hint of relish.

He spoke to his men that morning of the swaggering Elizabethan adventurers, Drake, Essex and Frobisher. He told them how Charles Howard, Lord High Admiral of England, had taunted the Spanish by ordering enemy fire 'to be greeted by a fanfare from his trumpeters'. One of the soldiers suggested that his bagpiper, Bill Millin, should do the same. Millin was feeling too seasick to play anything: as he slid deeper behind the pile of protective rucksacks he was heard to mutter something incoherent about 'farting fire'.[8] No one understood what he was saying, but it was a prosaic riposte to Lovat's lofty eloquence.

The men took a tot of rum. Waterspouts erupted around them as the landing craft broached the shore in tight arrowheads. Lovat stood up to survey the scene. He nodded approvingly when he heard that Hutchie Burt's troop were belting out 'Jerusalem' 'like the fierce Covenanters of old'.[9] On Landing Craft 516, commanded by the thickset New Zealand boxer Denis Glover, an even more extraordinary scene was unfolding. Glover had carried his gramophone on board and was playing 'the robust music of an English hunting song'.[10] Such brass-balls bravado was a vital component in raising men's spirits: Lovat was a master of the psychology of war.

The shore was now so close that they could hear the crash of the breakers. Commander Curtis gunned the engines as he prepared to cut through the shallows.

'*I'm going in!*'

He was answered by other cries from landing craft all around.

'Stand by the ramps!'

'Lower away there!'[11]

The commandos were hitting the beach at Sword.

Each of the five beach landings followed a similar pattern, yet each was intensely different for those racing from the shallows to the sea wall, with every individual poised between life and eternity. Death that morning was a game of chance. For most the landing was petrifying. For a few, it was intoxicating.

Derek Mills-Roberts, standard-bearer of 6 Commando, leaped ashore as the ramp was shot from under him. He was in his element. A second mortar hit its target and Ryan Price's craft 'went up with a roar'.[12] A German shell passed clean through the four petrol tanks on Max Harper Gow's craft. Inexplicably, it failed to explode. On Landing Craft 506, Cliff Morris had spent the previous hour comforting himself with prayer. Now, he felt like 'a duck being held up for a target and all the guns in creation firing'.[13]

There was one sight that would remain with every commando that morning. The shoreline told a sorry tale of the first wave to land, the East Yorkshire Regiment. It had been butchered. Even Lovat took a momentary knock. 'The rising tide slopped round bodies with tin hats that bobbed grotesquely in the waves.'[14]

So much blood was in the water that it formed a viscous slick on men's boots. Hundreds of corpses floated in the shallows, 'bodies stacked like cordwood'. Some had been shredded, others picked off by snipers, yet more had been hit by flying shrapnel and were engaged in a forlorn struggle to haul themselves up the beach, dragging their entrails behind them. Cliff Morris was still reeling from acute seasickness when he jumped ashore. The sight that greeted him turned his stomach to watery soup. 'Bodies lay sprawled all over the beach, some with legs, arms and heads missing, the blood clotting in the sand.' The sound was even worse, like the amplified wail of an animal in pain. 'The moans and screams of those in agony blended with the shriek of bullets and whining of shells.'[15]

Lionel Roebuck was one of the few East Yorks men who had made it to the top of the beach. When he glanced back, he was appalled by the gore that was trailed behind him. 'A scene of utter destruction. Wrecked boats lay broadside on, dead comrades floated face down in the tide, others lay in grotesque positions on the beach.'[16]

The commandos knew better than to hang around at the water's edge. They fanned out as they sprinted up the beach, dodging the heavy fire. Yet they were not immune to danger and Lovat saw many of those close to him gunned down. David Colley was shot through the heart. Sapper Mullen, a talented young artist, was cut down by machine-gun fire; as blood welled from his many wounds, he unwittingly painted his last canvas on the beach. 'Like a broken doll, [he] lay with both legs shattered at the end of a bloody trail.' He died a few hours later.

Little Ginger Cunningham had flaming red hair that made him an easy target. He had his feet shot from under him as he legged it up the beach, but was scooped to safety by big Murdoch McDougall. Ginger was mouthing it off about the 'f---ing Germans' who'd hit *him*, of all people, the smallest lad in the entire commandos. 'To think they could miss a big bugger like you,'[17] he said to McDougall.

Bill Millin leaped off the ramp shortly after Lord Lovat, landing in waist-deep water. 'My kilt floated to the surface and the shock of the freezing cold water knocked all feelings of sickness from me.'[18] The commando in front of him was hit in the face by a lump of flying shrapnel and collapsed into the foaming water. Lovat himself could be seen striding through the shallows with scarcely a care in the world. It was as if he were immune to danger.

Rupert Curtis was watching the unfolding scene from the bridge of his landing craft. It was both incongruous and striking. 'Every minute detail of that scene seemed to take on a microscopic intensity' – and nothing more than the 'sight of Shimi Lovat's tall, immaculate figure striding through the water, rifle in hand'.[19]

As he paced briskly out of the surf, Lovat turned to Millin and initiated one of the more unlikely snatches of conversation to take place on the beach that morning.

'Would you mind giving us a tune?' he said as a line of bullets zipped into the sand.

Millin could not believe his ears. He had just seen a comrade crumple dead into the water. They were all in grave danger of getting hit.

'You must be joking, surely?'

'What was that?' said Lovat.

Millin knew better than to protest. If he was going to die, he might as well do so playing the bagpipes. 'Well, what tune would you have in mind, sir?'

'How about "Road to the Isles"?'

'Now would you want me to walk up and down, sir?'

'Yes. That would be nice. Yes, walk up and down.'

Shellfire was exploding and mortars were thumping into the dunes. There was the stutter of machine guns and acrid smoke was billowing from the shoreline. Yet Bill Millin strolled up and down the beach blasting his pipes for all he was worth. At one point, he felt a hand slap his shoulder. It was his sergeant.

'What are you fucking playing at, you mad bastard? You're attracting all the German attention.'[20] Millin might have retorted, as he did in years to come, that Lord Lovat was the mad bastard, not him. He would later learn from two captured Germans that they didn't shoot him because they couldn't believe their eyes. They thought he was *dumkopf* – simple-minded.

One beachside pillbox was causing such serious trouble that it required prompt and decisive action. Knyvey 'Muscles' Carr, a 'skinny but determined young subaltern',[21] now proved just how determined he was, storming the pillbox single-handed and silencing its guns with a couple of well-placed grenades. Lovat thought he deserved a Victoria Cross for his bravery but he was one of the many whose heroics were forgotten over the weeks and months to come. Not for the first time in war, and not for the last, many in the lower ranks were deprived of richly deserved medals. Only the dead got their name on a public memorial.

His lordship had drilled an urgent dictum into his men: *he who hesitates is lost*. It was one they followed to the letter. Few hesitated on the beach that morning, least of all the men of 6 Commando who 'moved like a knife through enemy butter'. They blasted a passage off the beach, achieving in seconds what the lads of the East Yorks had failed to do over the course of forty minutes. The German defenders didn't stand a chance as two of Lovat's most efficient officers, Alan Pyman and Donald Colquhoun, blew their way through this stretch of the Atlantic Wall, 'mopping up pill-boxes and the immediate strong-points with hand grenades and portable flame-throwers'.

Bren machine guns were used to devastating effect, spraying lead into every beachside redoubt. Lovat chuckled with delight as he glimpsed Derek Mills-Roberts bounding through exploding shells and mortars as if he were invincible. He looked like 'Marshal Ney leading the Old Guard at Waterloo'.[22]

It was not long before the Germans threw in the towel: they were simply outclassed by the commandos. 'Soon a trickle of grey uniforms appeared: bewildered men in shock, their hands clasped behind their back.' They were taken prisoner and then lined up prior to being sent down to an assembly point on the beach.

'Oh, you are the chap with the languages,' said Lovat as he caught sight of Peter Masters, his German translator. Masters had fled his native Vienna in 1938 and sought refuge in England, signing up for 10 Commando, a specialist unit that consisted entirely of foreign nationals. Lovat pointed to a band of captured Germans. 'Ask them where their howitzers are,'[23] he said.

Masters quizzed one of the men, a burly bruiser with a bald pate. But the prisoner simply shrugged his shoulders and declined to answer.

'Look at that arrogant bastard,' sniped one who was watching.

'He doesn't even talk to our man when he's asking him a question.'

But when Masters looked at their pay-books, he saw they were all Russian or Polish. The bald man's name was Johann Kramarczyk, a farmer from Ratibor. He didn't understand a word of German.

Masters now tried to address them in French, thinking they might have learned it at school. But Lord Lovat's French was better than his and he took over the interrogation. Masters was more worldly and cultured than many of his fellow commandos: he had been raised outside the English class system and felt none of the social deference that his comrades displayed towards their aristocratic commander. Yet he nevertheless admired Lovat's impeccable coolness. 'He was very calm. He carried no other weapon other than his Colt 45 in his holster. Instead, he had a walking stick, a slim long stick forked at the top.'[24] It was, in fact, his Scottish wading stick, more usually used when fording fast-flowing Scottish rivers.

The commandos' plans of attack were to commence as soon as they were off the beach. No. 4 Commando was tasked with capturing the formidable German strongpoint built around the seaside casino at Riva Bella, a mile or so to the east of the landing point. Its men were reinforced by 177 French troops commanded by Lieutenant Commander Philippe Kieffer. No. 45 Royal Marine Commando was meanwhile to attack the enemy strongpoint at Lion-sur-Mer. But the bulk of Lord Lovat's men had the urgent goal of linking up with John Howard's beleaguered force at the two captured bridges. No one had any idea if they were alive or dead. If alive, they would most likely be in desperate need of help.

This thrust inland was to be spearheaded by the 500 men of 6 Commando, led by the redoubtable Derek Mills-Roberts. Among those 500 was Cliff Morris and his small unit of troops, whose bravura was matched by their fighting prowess.

Their first few hundred yards were trouble-free. As they edged through the streets of La Brèche, just behind the beach, cheering locals poured on to the pavements and offered them wine and fruit. Cliff Morris detected anguish behind the smiles. 'They seemed very worried as to whether we had come to stay or not.'[25] All knew of the retributions meted out by the Germans after the commandos' abortive raid on Dieppe two years earlier.

As Morris and his men pushed across the inland meadows, they were hit with everything the Germans could fire: shells, mortars, oil bombs and the terrifying *Nebelwerfer* or Moaning Minnie, which indeed 'made a low moaning sound like a cow in labour'.[26] But they gave as good as they got. Morris's captain, Alan Pyman, managed to creep up to one pillbox with his portable flame-thrower, along with a couple of others. They incinerated everyone inside. Mills-Roberts recorded the event with an enthusiasm that verged on glee. 'I know they had been bursting to use it.'[27]

The men stumbled across gruesome sights as they advanced. One of the most noteworthy was 'a leg standing upright in a polished jackboot'.[28] The whereabouts of the second boot, the missing leg and indeed the rest of the German body was a complete mystery.

There were also lightning ambushes that could transform a peaceful scene into a bloody one in seconds. Twenty-six-year-old Pat Porteous thought he had seen everything, having fought a violent hand-to-hand battle with the Germans in Dieppe. It had won him a Victoria Cross. But now, the unpredictability of war hit home. He was chatting with a French civilian in a peaceful little village when he heard a mortar bomb approaching at high speed. He hurled himself to the ground, as trained, but the Frenchman was slower to respond. 'There was an explosion and as I looked up, I saw his head rolling down the road.' Even for one used to war, Porteous admitted it was 'kind of off-putting'.[29]

Thereafter, the morning developed into a series of violent fire-fights as Cliff Morris and his comrades charged across meadows knocking out pillbox after pillbox. He was the first to see that their training was paying dividends, for they had it down to an art. They would lay a smokescreen and then advance in separate groups, each covering the other until their Sten submachine guns were close enough to fire through the aperture. 'Surely there was a better way of doing this,'[30] mused George Jowett, who had a number of close shaves with the enemy. But if there was, no one could think of it. Close combat was the only certain way to knock out a concrete bunker.

The men were not immune from casualties. One of Morris's comrades, young Adams, was shot through the throat and had to be abandoned in a mud-churned field. Morris was sickened to leave his friend to die. 'Not a nice feeling. Our first experience of leaving anyone.'[31] Another in their troop, Bill Coade, was hit full-square by a stick grenade. 'His face was a mass of blood.' Indeed he had been blinded and was 'in a shocking mess'.[32]

The lack of news about John Howard's men gave real impetus to their drive inland. Lord Lovat joined them in Saint-Aubin-d'Arquenay, an unremarkable little village some two miles from the coast. Here, his lordship's run of good fortune almost came to an untimely end. 'A sniper's bullet smacked into the wall beside my head with a crack like a whip.'

That German sniper would soon regret his attempt on Lord Lovat's life. '*Over there, top storey!*' shouted one of Lovat's men. The commandos stormed the building with overwhelming force, tossing grenades through windows and doors. 'Bobby [Holmes] kicked the door down and cut loose with his Tommy gun.'[33] The sniper's last look was one of utter incredulity. Then he was shot to pieces.

The sniper made Lord Lovat more cautious – but only a little. Bill Millin found him still 'striding along as if he was out for a walk around his estate'. At one point his lordship noticed an enemy sniper hiding in a nearby cornfield. After asking for his hunting rifle, he got down on one knee and fired, scoring a perfect hit. It was not so different from stalking deer, except that tracking Germans was altogether more exhilarating. Lovat sent two of his men to fetch the dead body, rather as if they were bagging a hunting trophy.

'Right, piper,' said Lovat to Millin, 'start the pipes again.'[34] He was intending to give John Howard and his men the greeting of their lives.

Assuming, that was, they were still alive.

The rearguard commandos were still slogging their way up the beaches that morning when there occurred another of those scenes that would be remembered for years to come. It was heralded by a low drone that grew increasingly loud, throaty and menacing. A plane was heading for Sword Beach, a Focke-Wulf 190, and inside the cockpit was a German fighter ace whose flamboyant high spirits were matched only by those of Lovat himself. Josef 'Pips' Priller shared a number of traits with his lordship. Both were ruthlessly determined. Both were professionals. Both were showmen. And both men displayed no reticence when it came to self-publicity.

Priller was a legend in the Luftwaffe. Appointed wing commander of the 26th Fighter Wing, he was 'short, chubby-faced, stocky and bronzed', with carefully oiled hair and a 'penetrating intelligence that was often deployed with engaging wit'. When relaxed, he could be charming. Yet Pips had a split personality. He was infamous for his violent temper that was deployed against anyone who stood in his way. He even tongue-lashed his superiors, but his insubordinate behaviour was tolerated because he displayed a 'bull-necked'[35] ferocity when attacking enemy planes.

He had developed his own unique technique for shooting down Allied aircraft, one that was dangerous but highly effective. He would hug the contours of the ground at a very low altitude before ascending like an arrow when he got a whiff of his quarry. He would then sneak from above on to the tail of the lumbering Allied bombers before swooping hard and fast, knocking out two or three of them before plunging back to the ground at breakneck speed. It was a technique so successful that it had won him the Knight's Cross with Oak Leaves and Sword.

Priller might have reaped havoc on the beaches of Normandy were it not for a catastrophic decision taken by his superior, General Werner Junck. Just a few days earlier, Junck had ordered the three squadrons under Priller's command to be transferred away from their airfields at Lille. One was moved to Reims, another to Toulouse and the third to Metz. Junck's reasoning was that they would be closer to the areas being targeted by Allied bombers.

Priller had exploded when he learned this news. 'It's crazy to move the squadrons back in view of the fact that we're expecting an invasion. If anything, they should be moved forward.' In this he was correct: Focke-Wulf planes needed to be stationed close to the action because they had a flying time of less than two hours. But Priller was overruled and by the time of the Allied landings, his Lille squadron had been reduced to two planes – his own and that of his wingman, Sergeant Heinz Wodarczyk.

The two of them had spent the previous night getting drunk on local brandy, leaving Priller with a crashing hangover. He fell into a prize rage when awoken with news of the invasion. 'Now you've really dropped it,' he fumed at the staff officer on the phone. 'I only have two planes. What the hell do I do now?'

'Get up there,' was the blunt reply. 'Do what you can.'

Priller was in despair. A golden opportunity to strike at the Allies from the sky had been squandered. He and Sergeant Wodarczyk were later described as 'weeping as they ran for their planes'. They were perhaps also weeping on account of their sore heads.

Priller was determined to wreak as much damage on the Allied landings as possible, even though his mission was little short of suicidal. 'We can't afford to break up,' he warned Wodarczyk. 'We'll have to go into the invasion area alone and I doubt we're going to come back.'

The Luftwaffe communications were so pitiful that he was given no details about the landings. He knew only that they were taking place 'somewhere around Caen'. But it did not take him long to spot the invasion once airborne.

'Jesus,' he said over the radio to Wodarczyk. 'Look at it! Look at this show!' As he circled through the breaking cloud, he was dumbfounded by the scale of what was taking place on the beaches below: 'the whole fleet of ships, landing craft going back and forth, soldiers on the beaches'. In happier times, it would have been 'a fighter pilot's dream'.

The sky, too, was filled with Allied aircraft. Indeed there were so many of them that Priller knew he needed to attack hard and fast if he was to survive. He decided to make just one pass over the beach – he was flying over Sword – and then head back to the aerodrome at full speed. To this end, he plunged his craft into a stomach-churning dive, swooping downwards at a top speed of 400 miles per hour, down to an altitude that he later claimed (not very convincingly) to have been not more than ten feet from the ground: 'so low that he could even see the faces of the men on the beaches'. He blitzed the shoreline with bullets before pulling the nose of his plane hard out of its dive in order to get himself airborne again.

It was a moment to be savoured. As the BMW engine thrust into gear, the entire plane shuddered as it climbed at a gravity-defying fifteen metres a second. Priller was soon back in the clouds, closely trailed by Wodarczyk. The two of them then headed directly to Poix-nord airfield, just to the north of Paris, as they had agreed in advance.

Priller was staggered to find the airfield completely deserted. Göring's much vaunted air force was nowhere in sight. 'There were no planes on the field. There was no equipment on the field.' He searched through all the aerodromes and cabins and eventually located an elderly Luftwaffe major sitting alone in a hut furnished with one table, two chairs and two telephones, neither of which appeared to be working. The major seemed to know nothing whatsoever about the invasion, nor did he display any signs of alarm. 'Get ready,' blasted Priller at the top of his voice. 'Get gasoline, get supplies, get food.'

'Yes, Colonel. Yes, Colonel.'

Priller got a call through to his second fighter corps and raged down the phone. 'I'm alone,' he screamed, 'and I can't do anything at all.' Still suffering from his hangover, he slammed down the receiver 'and collapsed into one of the chairs, absolutely tongue-tied with fury'.

Matters were scarcely helped by the fact that he had run out of cigarettes. It was fortunate that he had a box of black cigars in the cockpit of his plane and he now chain-smoked his way through the lot, a less than ideal cure for a hangover. As he did so, he lounged in a chair 'wishing to God he could find himself a drink'.[36]

While Lord Lovat and the soldiers of 6 Commando were surging inland, a sharp fire-fight was under way at the seafront casino in Riva Bella. This architectural oddity had the air of an oversize villa with a stack of tiled roofs and a multi-tiered belvedere that acted as a beacon for those at sea. But much of the building had been destroyed when the Germans transformed it into a fortified bunker. Where once it had robbed men of their fortunes, now it was designed to rob them of their lives.

The capture of the casino had been assigned to No. 4 Commando, with much of the responsibility being shouldered by Lieutenant Commander Philippe Kieffer and his French troop of 177 fighting stalwarts. They had piqued Lord Lovat's curiosity when he first met them. 'The sailor types were curiously tattooed,' he noticed. 'One brown-eyed fellow – I suspect he had served a prison sentence – bore the legend *Pas de Chance* [Tough Luck] enscrolled upon his forehead.' That was the only name he answered to. Some were veterans of Bir Hakeim and bore the scars of the desert battle two years earlier. Others had fled to England after the French fleet capitulated to the Vichy regime.

They were tough and dependable and came with a splash of Gallic panache. 'They sang *Sambre et Meuse*' – a patriotic military march from the time of the Franco-Prussian war – 'and their eyes were bright, for they were going home.' Led by the ebullient Kieffer, whose six-foot frame was as ramrod straight as that of General de Gaulle, they intended to live up to their motto: *L'audace et toujours de l'audace*. It was a paraphrase of Georges Danton's famous 1792 speech to the French legislative assembly: 'Audacity, more audacity and always audacity and the Fatherland will be saved.'

Lord Lovat's eve-of-battle address, delivered in French, had been greeted with wild acclaim. 'You'll be the first French soldiers in uniform to smash the bastards' faces,' he said. 'Tomorrow morning, we'll get them.'[37]

Kieffer's men landed under such withering fire that they were temporarily pinned down on the beach. Among them was René Rossey, a seventeen-year-old soldier, who was one of the many to be saved by the unexpected. 'When Lovat's piper walked up and down the beach, piping his lungs out, the Germans seemed stunned, as if they'd seen a ghost.' Rossey glanced up from his ditch in the sand and realized that the enemy had briefly stopped firing. He seized the moment, making a dash 'to the barbed wire at the top of the fence',[38] as did many of his comrades. But thirty were seriously wounded and had to be abandoned.

Kieffer himself had shrapnel embedded deep in his thigh, but he had no intention of retiring from the fight. He was on home soil for the first time in years and he intended to savour every minute. His men now engaged in ferocious house-to-house fighting as they advanced towards the casino, astonished to discover that La Brèche was full of civilians. Maurice Chauvet looked into one garden and saw an old lady doing her best to shield five little children. She gave a plaintive cry. 'When will the bombardment end?'[39] He could give no answer.

Further along the same street, Chauvet saw two teenagers manoeuvring a badly injured man to safety, seemingly oblivious to the bullets flying through the air. Kieffer himself was stopped by an elderly warhorse, Marcel Lefèvre, who had thundered his way through the Great War and now wanted a crack at this new conflict. He guided the French soldiers towards the casino, picking a path through the encircling minefield.

In the ensuing struggle, men were pitted against machine guns. It was terrible for those involved and equally terrible for the towns-folk trapped nearby. Gaston Decroix, a pensioner, had moved himself and his wife to Riva Bella because he thought it would offer them some sort of safety. Now, he was regretting his decision. The two of them were cowering inside their house, but it was shaking violently under the force of the explosions. When he later spoke of his experiences, they remained so vivid that he found himself recounting them in the present tense. 'Plaster falls onto Christiane's bed upstairs, a mortar lands in the courtyard, the roof tiles slide off the garage roof and perhaps off the house itself – we don't dare go outside and expose ourselves to the risk of the falling bombs.'[40]

The battle for the casino looked set to end in stalemate when Kieffer learned that the first of the amphibious tanks were clattering down the main street. Flagging down a Sherman, much as he might have hailed a London taxi, he leaped on to the turret and person-ally directed its fire through the windows of the casino. After a dozen shells had been pumped inside, his men stormed the place using hand grenades and bayonets – a vicious skirmish that ended in German surrender. Kieffer and his men had won their first battle on French soil. *L'audace et toujours de l'audace.* The casino, and much of the surrounding coastline, had been liberated.

PART VI
Towards Noon

The Atlantic Wall was designed to thwart a seaborne landing and all its guns faced the English Channel. Allied planners had realized that if troops survived the initial onslaught and got off the beaches, they could outflank the strongpoints from the rear. If so, they had a real chance of overwhelming them.

Allied warships had enough fire-power to transform the struggle for the beaches. Omaha Beach alone had an eighteen-strong bombardment fleet. But the use of big naval guns risked hitting troops with friendly fire: on Omaha, it was uncertain if and when Admiral Carleton Bryant would order his vessels to enter the fray.

Rommel's military strategy was to hit hard and fast, counter-attacking the Allies while they were still on the beaches. To execute this he needed the 12th SS Panzer Division and Panzer Lehr. But as noon approached, no one could be certain if Hitler would release them. The Führer still believed, as he had for some time, that there would be a second and larger Allied landing at the Pas de Calais.

Twenty miles east of Omaha, British commandos had an urgent goal that morning: to link up with the glider-borne force that had captured the Bénouville and Ranville bridges, thereby securing the eastern route out of the beachhead. It was impossible to know if these troops were still holding these vital bridges, or if the men themselves were still alive.

An exhausted American medic on Omaha Beach at around midday. Saving lives on the shoreline was harrowing and dangerous.

19

Deadlock on Omaha

BERCHTESGADEN WAS ENJOYING a glorious June morning, one perfectly poised between spring and summer. The air smelled fresh as it swept off the high slopes of the Obersalzberg and the twirls of alpine ragwort were nodding in the sunshine. In the mountain valley, the twin spires of St Peter and Johannes cast truncated shadows across the cobblestones below.

Hitler awoke late: the exact time is contested. His loyal adjutant, Otto Günsche, said that he saw the Führer enter the great hall of the Berghof as early as 8 a.m. He even claimed to have heard Hitler say to two of his generals: 'Gentlemen, this is the invasion. I have said all along that this is where it would come.'[1] But Karl von Puttkamer insisted that the Berghof's clocks had already struck nine when General Rudolf Schmundt went to wake the Führer. He added that Hitler had been fast asleep and emerged from his bedroom in his dressing gown: only then did he order his key generals to make their way up to the Berghof from the village below. While he awaited their arrival, he got dressed in his customary black trousers, field grey tunic, white shirt and brown tie. The Iron Cross, First Class, was pinned to his left breast.

Puttkamer found the Führer 'quiet and composed', as were all the Berghof staff that morning. Unlike Otto Günsche, Puttkamer said that Hitler was telling everyone 'that this was not the main invasion'. Yet it was a sign of his anxiety, perhaps, that he 'kept repeating this over and over again'. None of the assembled company agreed. 'He was rather isolated in this opinion,'[2] said Puttkamer with his customary tact.

It so happened that the Führer had arranged to meet the new Hungarian premier, Döme Sztojay, at noon that day. The meeting was to take place in Schloss Klessheim, a baroque wedding cake of a palace in Salzburg, just twelve miles or so from the Berghof. Hitler often used this castle for state dignitaries, for it was a jewel-box of Italianate luxury, from its crystal-drop chandeliers to its Venetian Old Masters. Having made the short journey to the schloss, he paused momentarily in one of the ante-rooms in order to receive the latest update from Normandy. General Warlimont was surprised to find the Führer so upbeat. 'He was brimming over with confidence and in his usual manner he gave the impression of a man who hadn't a worry in the world, neither for himself nor for Germany.'

'Well, it has begun,'[3] he snapped with glee, before bursting into the adjacent conference room to greet Sztojay, eschewing the normal protocol. Earlier he had told Goebbels that he was 'absolutely certain' the Allied troops would be repulsed. 'If we repel the invasion,' he said, 'then the scene in the war will be completely transformed.'[4]

Others were not so sure. Puttkamer was gravely concerned by the news from Normandy and 'had the distinct feeling that things would not work out this time unless the Allies were thrown back into the sea immediately'. General Warlimont agreed. When he studied the latest reports from Normandy, he felt 'the situation seemed to be quite grave.'[5] He assumed that Hitler had already released the two panzer divisions stationed near Paris and that they were even now heading towards the landing beaches. But this was not the case: it was only when his meeting with the Hungarian delegation was concluded that Hitler gave the necessary orders.

Among the other dignitaries assembled at Schloss Klessheim was Hermann Göring, Reichsmarschall of the Luftwaffe. As Hitler unrolled a map of Normandy and spread it across the marble table, he turned to Göring with a look of triumph. 'They're landing *here* and *here*,' he said, stabbing his finger at the map. 'Just where we expected.'[6] But if the landings were indeed taking place where Hitler expected (which is open to question), the manner in which they were unfolding was to prove alarmingly unpredictable – and nowhere more so than in the shallow waters off Omaha Beach.

General Omar Bradley was pacing the spray-soaked bridge of USS *Augusta*, anchored some ten miles off Omaha Beach. He had squeezed a wedge of cotton wool into each ear in a vain attempt to muffle the thunderous roar of the ship's big guns; he also had a swathe of bandage on his nose. It was covering a huge boil that the ship's doctors had lanced just a few hours earlier.

Bradley was General Eisenhower's principal American commander on D-Day – a salt-of-the-earth Midwesterner who took blows and punches squarely on the chin. There were some who whispered that he had been over-promoted, while others noted that he lacked the folksy charm of his friend Eisenhower. Less than twenty-four hours earlier, he had gathered his officers and delivered a pre-battle address that was decidedly misplaced. 'Gentlemen,' he told his audience, 'this is going to be the greatest show on earth. You are honoured by having grandstand seats.' One of those assembled officers had the temerity to correct him, albeit in jovial fashion. 'Hell goddamn! We're not in the grandstand! We're down on the gridiron.'[7]

General Bradley was one of the few to find himself in the grand-stand that morning and it was so unnerving that he was close to breaking point. His anxiety was due in large part to the total absence of news from Omaha Beach. Not a single wireless report had been picked up on the ship's radio and whenever Bradley turned his binoculars to the distant shoreline, he saw nothing but scuds of yellow smoke.

The role of the senior commander can be a lonely one. Stuck on the bridge of the *Augusta*, at a far remove from the action, Bradley confessed to being consumed by 'grave personal anxiety and frustration'. When he began to receive the first fragmentary reports from the beach, they only served to increase that anxiety. 'We could piece together only an incoherent account of sinkings, swampings, heavy enemy fire and chaos on the beach.'[8] He sensed that things were going badly, 'that our forces had suffered an irre-versible catastrophe' and that 'there was little hope we could force the beach.'[9]

This was not so far from the truth. As Bradley blinked into his binoculars for the umpteenth time that morning, young Wally Blanchard was getting a rather closer view of the unfolding massacre. Blanchard was the Cockney frogman who had done such sterling work in clearing the underwater mines on Gold Beach. No sooner had he completed that perilous task than he was ordered to lend a hand on neighbouring Omaha.

He was quick to realize that he was entering a twilight zone of carnage and chaos. As his little craft approached the shoreline he was caught in such a deluge of fire that he had no option but to fling himself overboard, not in search of mines but safety. 'Practically the first thing I became aware of was a lot of objects in the water and the peculiar colour of the water and the froth.' The sea was foaming with blood.

Over the din of battle, Blanchard was appalled by 'the cries and the screams, and an awful lot of young men, bodies, nudging you in the water'. On several occasions he had to plunge deep below the surface as gunfire clipped around his head, 'pinging and clanging like rain'. When he surfaced and looked to the shore, he saw corpses and body parts being sluiced in with the tide, along with a churning mass of detritus: deflated life jackets, abandoned wireless sets and sodden ration packs. The surf was so thick with diesel oil that it slapped noisily at the shingle, sluicing everything with a sticky film.

For the survivors of Omaha Beach, this apocalyptic vision was to acquire a searing intensity that time would never diminish. Years would pass, decades, yet a part of Wally Blanchard would be for ever on Omaha. 'People scream, they shout. They call out for mothers and Lord knows what.'[10]

For some, the tableau of slaughter would haunt them to the grave. Even sleep brought no respite. William Marshall was a young American engineer fighting to stay alive as he clawed his way up the beach. 'As I came around the end of a stalled tank, I found myself staring horrified into the chest cavity of a mutilated corpse. It was cut diagonally in two, from the left armpit to the bottom of the right ribcage.'

Marshall would try to forget, try to move on, yet still the images would remain, and always in vivid Technicolor. 'The upper part, along with the viscera, was nowhere to be seen; the lower part was lying prone before me, naked except for the brown GI shoes that identified it as being recently part of a US soldier.'[11]

In such extreme situations the passage of time that D-Day morning became a flexible thread, one that stretched and slackened according to the intensity of events happening all around. As Cliff Morris and his commandos fought their way towards Bénouville Bridge, they felt the morning flash by on the wing of an arrow. But for others

– especially those on Omaha – every second was counted out in screams of pain.

The sickly morning sun had yet to break through the cloud when General Bradley started to receive concrete news of the unfolding disaster on the shoreline. It came from ashen-faced coxswains who had survived the run-in to the shore. They brought a sharpened focus to the blur that Bradley had seen through his binoculars, recounting tales of six-foot breakers that pounded their landing craft and a tidal rip that had driven them far from their appointed zones. On the eastern sector of beach, the Channel waters had proved particularly merciless, swallowing twenty-seven of the twenty-nine amphibious tanks launched at sea.

'A nightmare.' That was Bradley's overriding thought as he watched hundreds of landing craft circling in the distant shallows, unable to land because the beach was so choked with junk. What was to be done? What orders should he give? If ever there was time for leadership, it was now.

'Privately, I considered evacuating the beach-head and directing the follow-up troops to Utah Beach or the British beaches.' But he knew that evacuation was logistically impossible and that a diversion of troops would wreck the entire invasion plan. It would also condemn those already on the beach to certain death. 'I agonized over the withdrawal decision, praying that our men could hang on.'[12]

It was in this moment of desperation that Bradley chose to deploy two of the most formidable weapons in his arsenal, both of which came equipped with high-explosive charges. Norman Cota and Charles Canham were to be dispatched to Omaha Beach with the unenviable task of saving the landing from catastrophe. Cota was a brigadier general, Canham a colonel, but their ranks were only partly relevant to everything that was to follow. More crucially, both were tried and tested leaders accustomed to getting their way.

Colonel Canham was the more unusual of the two. He had the pinched facial features of a physician and a look so sinister as to be almost contrived. His steel-rimmed glasses accentuated the narrowness of his eyes (he looked uncannily like Himmler) and magnified his uncompromising gaze. Those caught in that gaze were left with the uncomfortable feeling that they'd been trapped, like a rabbit caught in headlamps. Canham's most remarkable feature was his clipped moustache – more angular than Hitler's yet no less striking. His men were frankly terrified of him. 'A fiery old guy who spat fire and brimstone,' thought Felix Branham, who added that he was 'so tough that we used to call ourselves Colonel Canham's Concentration Camp'.[13] Another of his recruits, Robert Slaughter, thought him 'a tough son of a bitch: tall and lanky, he had a thin little moustache like the villain in a movie'.[14] A third said he resembled the cowboy actor Andy Clyde – 'one hell of a man'[15] in almost every respect – except that he lacked Clyde's charm and humour. If anyone could break the deadlock at Omaha, it would be him.

The second in this duo, Norman 'Dutch' Cota, was cut from very different cloth. Fifty-one years of age and with thinning hair and leaden jowls, he was an old man leading a young man's game. There was something of the outlaw about Cota: he champed on an unlit cigar even when under fire, and had perfected the art of swinging a pistol on his index finger. He was contemptuous of the Germans, even their snipers, and openly flaunted his disdain. He 'walked upright, unflinchingly, daring the enemy to bring him down'.[16] In this respect, he was not unlike Lord Lovat. And Cota shared an additional trait with his lordship, one that was wholly absent from Colonel Canham's toolbox of tricks. This was the ability to bond with the men serving under him, to chat convivially, to inspire them. He was 'a bona-fide friend of the common soldier and familiar to virtually all members of the division'.[17] He drove them hard, trained them to the hilt. And then he led from the front. Cota's men were known as the Bastard Brigade. He was the Bastard-in-Chief.

Cota's participation in the Allied invasions of North Africa and Sicily had been rewarded with a role in planning the assault on Omaha Beach. It had also led him into confrontation with Supreme Headquarters. Cota had argued that the Omaha landing was so fraught with danger that it should be carried out at night. Darkness would give his troops 'the advantage of surprise and concealment inherent in a night operation'.[18] He was overruled. Supreme Headquarters assured him there would be very little opposition from the German gun batteries due to the aerial and naval bombardments.

Cota remained unconvinced and warned his men to be prepared

for anything and everything. 'You're going to find confusion. The landing craft aren't going in on schedule or people aren't going to be landed in the right place. Some won't be landed at all. We must improvise, carry on, not lose our heads.'[19] How prescient were those words to prove. As confusion spiralled into catastrophe, improvisation alone could save the day.

Norman Cota and Charles Canham rode to the beach in the same landing craft, accompanied by ten officers and fourteen others. The majority of them were carrying the heavy backpack wirelesses so necessary for directing naval gunfire at German strongpoints. There was a moment of high tension as the craft scraped a mined obstacle. 'Kiss everything goodbye,'[20] yelled one of the men in panic. Inexplicably, the mine failed to explode.

Cota was taking a huge gamble in placing all his officers in the same craft. A single German shell could have brought a swift end to the hope of breaking the Omaha deadlock. The craft did indeed come under sustained fire that killed three of Cota's men. But Colonel Canham seemed undaunted by danger, charging up the shingle like some fiery Chicago gangster, with a .45 pistol in one hand and an automatic rifle in the other. 'Get your ass out of there!' he screamed at the men lying paralysed on the shingle. 'What are you doing there, laying there like that? Get up! Get across the rest of this goddamn beach!'

At one point, Canham's rifle was shot clean out of his hand: unfazed, he continued his advance up the beach, firing with the pistol. 'The bravest guy,' thought one of those running in his shadow. Others thought he was completely crazy. One officer had taken cover in an abandoned German pillbox right at the edge of the beach. From his position of safety, he yelled a warning at Canham. 'Colonel, if you don't take cover, you're going to get killed!'

'Colonel,' Canham screamed back, 'get your goddamn ass out of that goddamn pillbox and get these men off this goddamn beach!'

His words proved an inspiration to the men following in his wake. 'Goldarn,' thought Robert Slaughter, 'if that guy can do that, then, hell, I can too.'[21]

Norman Cota joined Canham at the sea wall just a minute or so after his dash up the beach and made a rapid assessment of the chaotic situation. This immediate stretch of beach – Dog White – was divided into self-contained sections, each separated by wooden groynes. Some eighty or so men lay in each section, crouched in the lee of the five-foot sea wall. Inert and dazed, they were overcome by such paralysis that not even shellfire caused them to move.

'Hopelessly jumbled,' noted Jack Shea, Cota's aide-de-camp. 'Crowded against the sea wall, sprawled there seeking protection from enemy rifle and machine gun fire.'[22] It was a deeply worrying sight.

Corpses lay all around, intermingled with mutilated body parts, and the tide-narrowed beach was cluttered with the jetsam of war: crippled trucks, jeeps and half-tracks along with burned-out landing craft still belching noxious fumes.

Cota and Canham conferred. The Germans were starting to target the sea wall with mortar fire, placing the haggard survivors of the first and second waves in even greater danger. It was imperative to get the men off the beach and up the bluffs, even though this meant wading through the mined marshland that lay between the beach and the cliffs.

'We've got to get them off the beach,' insisted Cota. 'We've got to get them moving.'[23]

Canham was shot through the left wrist in these first few minutes on the beach, but refused point-blank Cota's suggestion of evacuation. He was intending to lead his men up the heights. Cota was also rallying the men around him, personally supervising the firing of a tubed Bangalore torpedo that blasted a gap through the barbed-wire defences. The first man through was cut down by a ripple of German machine-gun fire.

'Medic,' he howled. 'Medic, I'm hit. Help me!' Jack Shea watched the man succumb to his wounds. 'He moaned, cried for a few minutes, finally he died after sobbing "Mama" several times.'

Cota knew that soldiers can easily be demoralized by witnessing such distraught scenes, so he ensured that he was next through the wire. His first action was to install an automatic rifle close to the sea wall so as to provide covering fire for the fighting advance up the bluff. A dense cloud of toxic smoke was rolling in from the beach, providing the attackers with a battlefield advantage. 'It seemed to be hindering enemy observation,' noted Shea, 'and there was a chance that we could break through off the beach and reach the base of the bluff.'

As the smoke turned the sky to darkness, an oil-filled incendiary shell struck a flame-thrower that was strapped to the back of a young American soldier who had yet to land. The explosion that followed packed a volcanic punch. Jack Shea saw him 'burst into a huge wave of flames' as the flame-thrower erupted. 'His body stiffened with such convulsive reaction that he was catapulted clear off the deck, completely clearing the starboard bulkhead and plunging into the water.'[24] The entire landing craft was engulfed in acrid smoke, giving Cota's men further cover as they picked their way towards the bluffs.

Cota seemed completely fearless as he returned to the beach and jostled through enemy gunfire, chewing on his unlit cigar and exhorting the men to advance. Alone among them, he walked upright, yelling, gesticulating wildly and bawling orders to the shattered survivors of the first wave.

A few hundred yards along the beach, a young Ranger named John Raaen was astonished to see this rambunctious, seemingly imperturbable figure. Realizing he was someone with authority, he made his way towards him accompanied by a band of fellow Rangers. As he approached Cota, he defied the enemy gunfire and clipped a salute.

'Captain Raaen, Fifth Ranger Infantry Battalion, sir!'

'*Raaen* – you must be Jack Raaen's son. I'm General Cota. What's the situation here?'

Raaen told him that the Rangers had landed almost intact, along with their commander, Lieutenant Colonel Max Schneider, who was further along the beach.

'You men are Rangers!' exclaimed Cota with evident glee. 'I know you won't let me down!' He then bounded off to greet Schneider in person.

'Are you Colonel Schneider of the Rangers?'

'Yes, sir!'

'Colonel, you are going to have to lead the way. We are bogged down. We've got to get these men off this goddamned beach.' He then turned to the men around him and shouted four words of such resonance that they would later be adopted as the motto of these fighting heroes: 'Rangers! Lead the way!'[25]

Within seconds, John Raaen and his comrades blew more gaps in the barbed wire and began advancing towards the bluffs. One of their number, Victor Fast, lost his helmet in the process. 'I crawled around to find a helmet from a dead buddy, only to find it half full of head.'[26] Somewhat queasily, he scouted around for another.

Colonel Canham was also leading from the front, despite his battle injuries. His arm was in a makeshift splint and tied to his neck with a sling and his battledress was smeared with blood. Worse still, shrapnel had gone through both his cheeks. 'He spouted blood as he talked,' said one, 'but he didn't seem to mind it.'[27] He had by now advanced to the foot of the bluff where he established a temporary command post. Shellfire continued to burst all around him, flinging high-velocity shrapnel in all directions. These shards were lethal, as Jack Shea was to witness. 'One of the fragments striking a man in the small of the back, almost completely severed the upper portion of his body from his trunk.'[28]

A mortar shell landed just short of Cota, killing the two men next to him and seriously injuring his radio operator. Two other men were flung through the air. One landed twenty feet up the bluff, the other seventy-five feet below. Yet Cota himself emerged completely unscathed.

The Rangers had taken Cota at his word and were already beginning to scramble up the crumbling bluffs, knocking out trenches and machine-gun nests as they advanced. Individual bravery counted for everything that morning. Harry Parley had landed in the first wave of infantry and was in a bad state, 'soaking wet, shivering, but trying like hell to keep control'. He had seen half his friends blown to shreds and 'could feel the cold fingers of fear grip me'. Yet he was to perform one of those countless unsung actions that swung the balance on Omaha that morning. A burst of machine-gun fire alerted him to the presence of two concealed bunkers. 'I crawled forward, circled wide and came down between the bunkers and destroyed both with grenades in the gun-slots.'[29] In the process, his metal canteen was dented by six bullets, saving him from certain death.

John Raaen was now in the vanguard, pushing through the dry brush that had been set alight during the bombardment. 'The smoke was so bad that we found ourselves gasping for breath but gulping in smoke.'[30] It was indeed so thick that they had to strap on their gas masks.

As the Rangers advanced, bedraggled Germans began to emerge from foxholes with their hands up. It was the first sign that Hitler's Atlantic Wall was starting to crumble. Once disarmed, they were handed over to Victor Fast (now with a helmet), whose principal role was as German translator and interpreter. Fast picked the youngest prisoner and demanded information on minefields and machine-gun posts. But first, he issued a warning as to what would happen if any of his information were to be proved incorrect. 'I'll turn you over to my Jewish buddy here standing next to me, Herb Epstein, and he'll take you behind that bush over there – you get what I mean?'

The German youngster was shivering with fear, and not without reason. Epstein looked like a prize thug, with a bulbous neck and fists like pork knuckle. 'He had not shaved for a day, he was big and burly.' He was also armed to the hilt, with 'a 45 on his hips and a Ranger knife in his boot and an automatic Thompson machine gun'. Even Fast was slightly in awe of him. 'He looked mean enough to scare the living daylight out of anybody.'[31]

Capitulating German soldiers faced not just Herb Epstein's fists, but the additional hazard of being targeted by their own side. Jack Shea watched one of his comrades leading five prisoners down to the shoreline. As they neared the promenade, 'the two leading prisoners crumbled under a burst of machine gun fire that was obviously of German origin.' Three others fell to their knees as if pleading with the next machine-gun operator not to shoot them. It was to no avail. 'The next burst caught the first kneeling German full in the chest and as he crumbled, the remaining two took to the cover of the sea wall with their American captors.'[32]

The American Rangers took no chances as they advanced up the bluffs. One company commander, George Whittington, stumbled across a German machine-gun position and surprised its three occupants. Carl Weast was witness to what happened next. 'When one of the three Germans turned and saw Whit[tington], a fierce looking fellow, he repeated the words *bitte, bitte, bitte*. Whit shot the three of them, turned and asked, "I wonder what *bitte* means."'[33]

Inch by terrifying inch they scaled the mud-sluiced heights, taking horrific casualties as they advanced. The leadership of Canham and Cota had broken the stalemate on the beach and small parties were starting to make it to the cliff-top. Yet the assault was hopelessly behind schedule. It was now almost 9 a.m. and according to the battle plan, the four vehicular tracks – known to the military planners as 'draws' – should soon be open to Allied tanks and jeeps. But none of them had yet been captured and the beach was a logjam of charred wreckage and burned-out tanks. Two and a half hours after the first wave landed, the battle for Omaha still hung in the balance.

The Allies' powerful naval guns transformed the battle for the beaches. USS Nevada *fires deadly salvoes at Utah Beach.*

20

Cracks in the Wall

CROUCHED INSIDE THE radio room of USS *Shubrick*, his head-phones clamped to his ears, twenty-four-year-old Edward Duffy was sucking on a lemon drop and trying to make sense of the crackled reports of events taking place onshore. 'The voices over my phones were now describing the scene of fire, smoke, explosions and destruction, and the dead American bodies float-ing by.'

Duffy felt at a strange remove from the action. His own horizon was limited to a few feet: he was squatting in a metal shoebox of a room crammed with gyro-compasses, sound-powered telephones and a primitive computer for controlling the gun batteries. On the desk in front of him were all the essentials: two packets of cigarettes, a Zippo lighter (a gift from his sister, Agnes) and a one-pound box of lemon drops. He also had a 'D' cell red flashlight to be used if the ship sank and he found himself in the water.

For several hours, Edward Duffy and his six radiomen had been casting anxious glances at each other as the deep boom of mortars grew louder and closer. 'We could hear the projectiles exploding in the water around us. We were below the main deck at just about water level, so the sounds of the explosions reverberated within the steel hull.'[1]

At exactly 9.50 a.m., Duffy's headphones crackled into life. An urgent message was being transmitted from USS *Texas*, the ship overseeing naval operations for the western half of Omaha Beach. The message was intended for all ships in the vicinity. 'Get on them, men! Get on them! They are raising hell with the men on the beach and we can't have any more of that! We must stop it!'[2] The message came from Admiral Carleton Bryant, who had received enough reports from the shore to realize that the situation was precarious indeed. Although small numbers of men had reached the cliff-top, it was imperative for the naval vessels to join the fray since they alone had guns powerful enough to knock out the German strongpoints.

Within minutes of receiving Bryant's message, all the captains stationed closest to Omaha swung into action, manoeuvring their ships into water so shallow that their keels could be felt to shudder as they scoured the muddy bottom. Lieutenant Commander Ralph 'Rebel' Ramey was one of the first commanders to open fire, training USS *McCook*'s guns on to the German batteries.

With his jug ears and lantern jaw, Ramey had the look of a stand-up comic. Genial and big-hearted, he 'sprinkled his conversation with country aphorisms'[3] and laboured good humour. The youths serving under him thought him a dead ringer for Will Rogers, the vaudeville comedian whose witty aphorisms had made him a household name in America. ('I am not a member of an organized political party. I am a Democrat.'[4]) But on this particular morning, Ramey put his wit to one side and focused instead on destroying the enemy. He kept up such relentless fire on one German gun battery that he destroyed the entire strata of rock supporting its concrete foundations. As the cliff crumbled and collapsed, so the strongpoint plunged down the cliff in a chute of rock, dirt and men.

If all had gone to plan that morning, Ramey would have been in constant contact with the fire control shore parties. Their role was to use wireless communication to direct and coordinate the naval gunfire. But most had been killed on the beach and the few still alive found that their wirelesses no longer worked. The reliance on technology, so central to Supreme Headquarters' battle plan, was dead in the water.

Now, in an attempt to increase the accuracy of his guns, Ramey nudged his destroyer perilously close to the shore and kept up constant fire from a position just 1,300 yards from the beach. His finest gunner that morning was Gerald Grove, an Iowa farmer who 'had the best pair of eyes on the ship'.

'*Grove!*' yelled Ramey for the hundredth time. 'Do you see anything?'[5]

Grove could indeed see something. A few flashes were coming

from a stone house tucked into a gulch close to the beach. Range was established and *McCook's* guns went into action, blasting the entire area. The resulting destruction was witnessed by the journalist Martin Sommers, who was covering D-Day for the *Saturday Evening Post.* 'Finally, a direct hit – a gun tumbles stern over teakettle from the wreckage.' Sommers was surprised that Grove displayed none of the elation of those around him. Blank-faced and aloof, he looked 'as though he would feel much more at home milking cows back on the farm than spotting enemy guns in battle from the bridge of a pitching can'.[6]

At one point that morning, Captain Ramey achieved a quite remarkable feat. As he blasted the bluffs, a thin line of haggard Germans could be seen emerging from their strongpoint waving the white flag of surrender. For the next hour, the Germans attempted to contact the *McCook* using a flashing semaphore light. Ramey soon tired of trying to decipher their messages and resumed fire. This time, the Germans made themselves understood. 'Ceize fire!'[7] was the misspelled message they flashed. It was perhaps the first time in the history of warfare that infantrymen had surrendered to a battleship.

USS *McCook* was by no means the only ship to take the offensive. Still crouched inside the radio room of USS *Shubrick*, Edward Duffy had just received news that a German officer on shore was supplying his fellow gunners with the coordinates of Allied targets. Duffy calculated the range of the German officer's location and let rip, as he put it, with 'a four-gun salute'. He scored a direct hit 'and the tension was relieved because we had gotten one of the bastards ourselves'. For the next hour or so, the *Shubrick* blasted away at the shore, engaged in what Duffy called 'Dodge City shootouts'. Although the Germans were 'good shootists',[8] they were not as good as him.

Along the entire stretch of Omaha Beach, from Pointe du Hoc in the west to Colleville in the east, Allied ships were hurling vast quantities of explosives at the exposed bluffs. USS *Carmick, Thompson, Texas, Frankford, Emmons, Doyle, Harding* and *Baldwin* – along with many others – kept up a sustained barrage of highly destructive five-inch shells. The *Shubrick* and *McCook* fired almost 1,500 shells that morning. Other vessels dispatched even more. Young Felix

Podolak was helping to arm the guns on USS *Butler* when he realized they were getting dangerously overheated.

'We had to hook up one-and-half-inch fire hoses to hydrants to spray water on our gun mount.' Even this did little to reduce the temperature. They were firing so many shells that 'the barrels were running red hot.'[9]

Karl Wegner, the teenage German soldier stationed in WN72, had the misfortune to be in the very area under attack from the *Shubrick* and *McCook*. He was also close to the bluffs that Norman Cota and Charles Canham had chosen for their dramatic assault.

The American destroyers soon began firing directly at WN72, pounding away at the concrete bunker. One burst exploded directly on to the embrasure. 'A chunk of cement struck Lang in the face. He swung violently around and hit the floor.' Wegner's friend, Willi Schuster, rushed to his aid and swathed his face in bandages. As soon as he was patched up, Lang went back to the damaged viewing slit and held his battered field glasses to his eyes.

'Another huge force of boats approaching.'

The atmosphere inside the bunker had become increasingly tense ever since the first sighting of the Allied fleet. Now, everyone's nerves were dancing on a high-wire. A noise outside suggested that someone had reached the rear entrance of the bunker. The bandaged Lang raced over to the metal door and covered it with his loaded pistol. As he did so, he heard a shout.

'*Nicht Schiessen! Ich bin Deutscher!* Don't shoot! I'm German!'

Lang peered outside and saw a wounded German comrade, 'bruised and bloody about the face, with a deep gash on his right leg'. Lang opened the door and pulled him in. He then bandaged the soldier's wounds and asked why he was exposing himself to such gunfire. The young invalid, Helmuth, recounted an alarming story. He said that his bunker was manned by Volksdeutsche – Alsatians and Poles – whose loyalty to Hitler had long been in question. When the Americans made a concerted effort to capture the stronghold, these Volksdeutsche told their German leader of their intention to surrender. The leader 'became infuriated and threatened to execute anyone who did not fight', a threat that caused them to take matters into their own hands. A single bullet was all it required. Once the officer was dead they turned their fury on Helmuth, the only other German in the bunker. He was badly beaten before fleeing for his life and seeking refuge with Wegner, Lang and Schuster.

Lance Corporal Lang was disgusted with what he was told. He picked up the field telephone and tried to call the adjacent stronghold, but the wires had been cut. He therefore decided to take justice into his own hands, asking for covering fire so that he could have his revenge on these detested Volksdeutsche. He was going to pitch grenades through the embrasure of their bunker. Wegner watched Lang make a crazed dash towards the strongpoint and witnessed the explosion triggered by the grenades. But Lang's mini-offensive was to have an equally violent ending. 'Fate was not with him that time. Fire from one of the landing craft cut him in two.' Wegner was horrified. 'This was the first person we knew who had been killed – and right before our eyes.'

The three who still remained in the stronghold now found themselves in a desperate situation – isolated, vulnerable and low on ammunition. It was bad enough that the Americans were advancing off the beach. Even worse was the fact that Germans were now killing each other.

Wegner and Schuster peered out through the firing-slot. 'We could see smoke belching from some of our strongpoints, while others had fallen silent. We had no way to contact those that still resisted or to get further orders, since our field telephone was out.' They felt they were doomed.

'I guess you're in command now,' said Schuster.

'In command of what?'

Wegner was momentarily puzzled until he realized that he was the most senior of the three of them in the bunker. All three had lost the will to fight and fired their guns in desultory fashion, aiming only at soldiers coming directly towards them. 'My thought was simple: do not shoot at me and I won't shoot at you.' All of them wanted to leave, but abandoning their bunker would place them at the mercy of the much feared Kettenhund, or Chained Dogs, the German military police who were under orders to shoot anyone who abandoned their post.

In the end, the matter was decided for them. Schuster was about to reload his machine gun when he noticed that the belt only had 50 rounds instead of the usual 200. When Wegner told him to fetch some more, he said there were none left. Wegner was staggered. 'I looked at him in disbelief, then realized we were standing on a pile of empty ammunition cans, belts and spent shell casings.' A 50-round belt was all that was left from 15,000 rounds.

No less alarming was the sound of fighting coming from the bluffs behind them. It suggested that some American troops had already broken through the Atlantic Wall. If so, they were in a most dangerous predicament.

Wegner now took his first important decision as commander: they would flee the bunker and try to join the troops stationed inland. They would take the MG42 and the remaining ammunition. It did not amount to much: sixty-two rounds and two grenades, which they intended to detonate as they left the stronghold to give them cover.

'We all crowded in the entryway. I took a deep breath and nodded to them. Both grenades flew out at the same time, explosions followed.' Wegner sprang out of the doorway, closely followed by Schuster and Helmuth. In leaving the bunker, the men now had not one enemy but two: the Americans and the German military police.

They came under heavy fire as soon as they were outside. They dived into a slit trench and tried to catch their breath. Wegner glanced grimly at his two friends. 'Both looked as scared as I felt. I asked if they were unhurt. Out of breath they nodded.' Schuster momentarily poked his head above the trench. 'Abruptly a cascade of rifle fire landed around us. I saw Willi's helmet fly off and his body snap back.' It was a miracle that the bullet glanced off him, leaving him unharmed.

The men now found themselves in the unnerving position of following the Americans up the bluff. They managed to reach the top and took cover in a drainage ditch that ran alongside the country road to Vierville. They were unaware that their goal – the village – was the same as that of Cota and Canham. At one point, they came across a cluster of dead soldiers, shot from the air by an Allied plane. Soon after, they stumbled across more dead. 'For a while it felt as if we were the only ones alive.'

They eventually came across a platoon leader who told Wegner they should join his group. But he added a word of caution. 'He told me to be wary of the Chained Dogs, because they might accuse me of cowardice and desertion.'[10]

Wegner was in total despair. He had fought until he had run out of ammunition; he had seen his commanding officer cut down by gunfire. And now he was at risk of being shot for desertion.

These were the dangers of being on the losing side.

All along the western end of Omaha Beach, men were nearing the tops of the bluffs – exhausted and slicked with clay but just about alive. For many, it was a moment of sheer relief. They had survived against all the odds, thrusting through Hitler's Atlantic Wall with a combination of brute force and dogged persistence.

Cota and Canham had landed with almost a dozen radio operators and these now proved invaluable. As one group inched their way up the Vierville draw that led to the cliff-top, they came under sniper fire from the church steeple in Vierville. Colonel Schneider sent a radio message to USS *Harding* (codename Blondi) asking for naval support. It was fortunate that the vessel had on board a master gunner named Walter Vollrath. He now gave a lesson in accurate firing. Among those watching the results was William Gentry. 'Vollrath's first shot took off the tip of the steeple, his second, the tower in the steeple; the third, the bottom of the tower and part of the church roof and the fourth and fifth shots completed the destruction of the entire church.'

'Fine shooting, Blondi,' was the message from the squadron commander. Gentry was no less impressed. 'It really was a beautiful sight to see.'[11] Vollrath alone had a momentary sense of guilt. 'I felt like quite a heathen knocking down the church.'[12]

The men at the top of the cliffs hoped that their troubles would soon be at an end, but it was not to be. Carl Weast and his group were crossing a field when they came under intense bombardment. One of his comrades took a direct hit from a mortar shell. He was blown 'all to hell', a death shocking in its violence. He was reduced to 'a pile of entrails and shredded GI clothing'. Curiosity got the better of Weast and he went over to have a closer look. 'This guy was a mess. I mean, you couldn't even recognize where the hell his head was.'[13]

The mortar explosions stopped the Rangers in their tracks. They were in real danger of being pushed back over the cliff. And this is where Norman Cota once again proved his worth. He rallied the men and personally led them on a charge across the field, 'instructing them to fire at the hedgerows and houses as they advanced'. Leading from the front, he proved that nowhere was a no-go area just as long as you had enough fire-power. 'The machine-gun fire stopped as soon as the troops started to move across the open fields towards them.'[14] They soon found themselves on the country lane that led to Vierville-sur-Mer, where the snipers inside the church had just been knocked out by the guns of USS *Harding*.

Cota and Canham had a rendezvous at the crossroads outside Vierville and agreed on a new plan of action. Their leadership had enabled them to get the men off the beach. Now, they had to lead them into Vierville and beyond.

Squatting inside his beachside bunker at the eastern end of Omaha, young Franz Gockel was unaware that American troops were scaling the cliffs. He and his comrade, Siegfried Kusta, were completely isolated, with their worldview limited to what they could see through the embrasure of their concrete redoubt. It was a sight of pure devastation, with more and more craft heading in their direction.

The two of them had lost contact with their commanding officer, Bernhard Frerking, and his orderly, Hein Severloh. The latter was hiding out in a small foxhole, but he made frequent trips to the nearby observation post with its sweeping panorama of the beach. When Severloh looked through his field glasses, he was appalled by the scene of human butchery. A 'ribbon of bloody slime' stretched some 300 metres along the beach in front of WN62. 'There were hundreds and hundreds of lifeless bodies of American soldiers – in places piled on top of each other.' It was a sickening sight. 'Wounded moved around in the bloody, watery slime, mostly creeping, trying to get to the upper beach to get some cover.'[15]

For several hours that morning, his comrades had held the upper hand. But as the sun started to burn off the morning cloud, Severloh sensed they were no longer immune to danger. American soldiers were starting to fight back.

First to be hit was one of the strongpoint's technical sergeants. He approached Severloh through their trench system, his face drained of colour. 'There was dark blood running from two holes in his throat.'[16] Severloh was next to be hit – a blow that struck so violently it was like being smacked in the eye with a horsewhip. A well-placed bullet had hit the front sight of his machine gun, slamming it deep into his eye.

Closer to the beach, Gockel and Kusta were under such a sustained assault that they decided to retreat. Under covering fire from their comrades, they made a dash for the upper position, where Gockel devoured a half ration of bread and a mess-tin of milk. He was wondering what had happened to his friend, Heinrich Kriftwirth, when the young lad appeared from nowhere, 'covered with dirt, creeping towards us with a torn uniform'. Kriftwirth explained how he had been caught in the shock wave of a naval shell that had 'thrown him against the concrete wall, and he had remained uncon-scious in a corner for a long time'.

It was clear they were all in grave danger. When Gockel peered out through the rear entrance, he could see Americans scaling the bluffs. They were knocking out strongpoints one by one. They had captured 'those positions to the west and east of us which had suffered heaviest damage and casualties through air attacks and naval gunfire'.[17] This enabled them to advance more rapidly and it also placed Gockel and company in even greater danger. If they did not flee soon, they would find themselves surrounded.

Still in his foxhole, Hein Severloh had come to the same conclu-sion. He could see Americans pushing off the beach in ever greater numbers, 'climbing the sloping heights in long columns'. When he looked back towards the observation post, he realized it was under attack. He ran over to see what had happened to his two comrades, Bernhard Frerking and Lieutenant Grass. The latter was seriously wounded and could only move if supported, while Frerking was trying to work out how long it would be until they were encircled. 'It's now time for all of us to get out and abandon our position up here,' he shouted.

Severloh passed on his message to the two besieged radio oper-ators, Herbert Schulz and Kurt Wernecke. 'You jump out first and start out carefully to the rear. I'll jump out next.'

Frerking displayed the same decency as commander as he had done in civilian life, ensuring that his men headed for safety before him.

'You go next, Hein,' he said to Severloh. 'Take care.' Severloh noticed he used the familiar '*du*' for the first time. He suddenly felt sad, as if he knew he would never see Frerking again. 'A feeling of sympathy, warmth and attachment welled up again quickly in me and, simultaneously, a deep melancholy.'[18] He took a final glance at his old friend then grabbed his machine gun and leaped from the trench.

Gockel was also planning his escape. Grenades were starting to hit his position, flinging shrapnel through the air. He was alarmed to see that a group of American soldiers 'had entered our network of trenches and were suddenly only twenty metres from us'. He ducked. Another grenade exploded, injuring him in the hand. One of his comrades congratulated him on getting the perfect *Heimatschuss* – a 'home-for-sure' wound.

But if Gockel was ever to make it home to Germany, he first needed to escape from the beach. Crawling through the network of trenches and then scampering up the bluffs, he began to make his way towards Colleville-sur-Mer. He was unaware that the Americans were already there. He was also unaware that General Bradley, still pacing the bridge of USS *Augusta*, had just received a message that would finally calm his shattered nerves. 'Troops formerly pinned down on beaches Easy Red, Easy Green, Fox Red advancing up heights behind beaches.'[19]

Omaha was almost won.

British soldiers advance inland, dodging concealed German snipers. A key objective was the relief of John Howard's beleaguered force at Bénouville Bridge.

21

Race to the Bridge

As one area of beachhead became increasingly stable, another found itself in danger. Although parachutists of the 6th Airborne Division had been dropped into the eastern end of the landing zone during the night, they had been widely scattered and were unable to fight as a coherent force. The countryside around Bénouville Bridge was particularly vulnerable to a German counterattack and John Howard's beleaguered men were at grave risk of capture or death. There was only one man who could save them from potential catastrophe and that was the illustrious Lord Lovat – 'the Mad Bastard' – who had vowed to arrive at the bridge on the dot of noon.

Not only was his lordship a man of his word, but he also knew that in relieving Howard's men he would earn himself a place in the history books. The British have always enjoyed tales of victory against impossible odds and this particular disaster-in-the-making had all the requisite ingredients: an enfeebled group cut off from the outside world; a hostile enemy that has them surrounded; the certainty of a gruesome death unless the relief force arrives in time.

Lord Lovat's childhood had been built upon such tales: Major Baden-Powell's irregular forces smashing the siege of Mafeking; Sir Alfred Gaselee's heroic relief of the Peking legations; Sir Garnet Wolseley marching his redcoats towards Khartoum. The latter was a colourful example of what could go wrong if you didn't reach your destination in time. Sir Garnet arrived to discover General Gordon's severed head stuck on the end of a pike.

Lovat always kept half an eye on the narrative and this one ticked all the boxes. When he finally came to write his version of events he would prove himself a master storyteller, recounting a tale splashed with high drama. He would make two memorable utterances when he finally reached John Howard's embattled men at Bénouville. The first was uniquely British: he apologized for being late. The second was rather more grandiloquent. He told Howard they were writing themselves into history for ever.

But not everything unfolded in quite the fashion that his lordship recorded in his memoirs. There was to be a lost narrative of that morning's adventures, one no less exhilarating than its Victorian counterparts. It would even come with its own memorable quote – not as eloquent as his lordship's, nor as self-congratulatory, but every bit as resonant.

The curtain-raiser for the drama began at the bridge itself, where Howard's troops were isolated, desperate and exhausted. They had received no news of the landings on Sword Beach, five miles distant, because wireless communication had proved impossible. The only sign of something afoot came when several stray mortars smacked into the ground close to Howard's field headquarters, causing a tremendous explosion. 'Blimey, sir,' said one of the Cockney lads in his troop. 'They're firing jeeps.'[1] Howard smiled, but it was a nervous smile. He knew that his men were trapped. Harry Clark spoke for all when he said 'the situation was getting more desperate by the minute'.[2] Howard himself was more succinct. Close to 'total annihilation'[3] was how he expressed it.

But the greatest test of their stamina was yet to come. The Germans were determined to do one of two things that morning: either recapture the bridge from Howard's men or else destroy the structure. The former option was preferable, but the latter was a great deal easier. It would also prove a game-changer, for if they destroyed the bridge they would have trapped the Allies inside their beachhead. It was indeed a golden prize.

The first hint of trouble came at first light, when young Harry Clark spied an enemy gunboat sneaking up the Caen Canal. Although shrouded in mist, he could see it was heavily armed with 'a wicked-looking gun mounted on the forward deck'. Its intent was clear: it was coming to blow up the bridge. But Clark's comrade-in-arms, Private Cheesely, was on his own lethal mission that morning. He had dragged the PIAT gun into his hiding place on the bank of the canal and now, as he watched the gunboat draw closer, he prepared to stop the Germans in their tracks.

When it happened, it did so in a flash and a bang. Cheesely fired the mortar and it spun through the morning mist, smashing into the hull just below the wheelhouse and exploding deep inside. The vessel slewed through 180 degrees like a drunkard and ploughed headlong into the nettle-covered bank. Private Cheesely could not have scored a more perfect bull's-eye.

Harry Clark watched in glee 'as two very scared Germans appeared from below deck'. Caught in the gun-sights of a dozen or more of Howard's men, they had no option but to surrender. It was an early morning surprise that led to an outburst of indignation, but Clark was not taking any lectures from prisoners of war. He smacked one of them hard with his rifle 'and he immediately became meek'.[4] As a means of silencing Germans, it proved most effective.

Quick action had thwarted the German gunboat attack, but Howard's men were not yet out of trouble. At around 10 a.m. a lone German Dornier aeroplane appeared from nowhere, flying straight out of the weak morning sun. It was alarmingly close to the ground, 'hedgehopping, with one damn great bomb slung underneath'.[5] The bomb did nothing to hinder its ability to cause havoc, for it suddenly leaped into the sky and then came swooping towards the bridge with a menacing growl, unleashing its high-explosive munition as it dive-bombed the structure. There was enough explosive to blow the bridge sky-high, but the unbelievable happened. The bomb hit the superstructure, bounced off a metal girder and splashed harmlessly into the canal.

'My God,' exclaimed Howard. 'It was a dud.'[6]

Parr whistled through his teeth. 'Our biggest stroke of luck. It would have blown the whole damn lot to pieces, and taken everything with it.'[7]

Two German attacks had failed, but their third was rather more disturbing. For some hours, Howard's men had felt as if they were being spied on by a thousand hidden eyes. Trees, bushes, hedges – all seemed to be alive with gun-sights and field glasses. This was indeed the case. German snipers had sneaked forward under the mantle of darkness and concealed themselves in trees and abandoned houses. From these mini-redoubts, they now began to pick off Howard's men one by one, aware that in a war of attrition they would surely win.

Denis Edwards was an unwilling witness to this deadly game. The first indication of the snipers' presence was a distant 'crack' as they fired. 'Almost instantaneously, one of our lads would crash to the ground.'[8] What made it more alarming was the fact that the snipers were constantly on the move, making it impossible to return fire.

Wally Parr was enraged by such guerrilla tactics and came up with a solution of sorts, one that was noisy, theatrical and highly effective. He had been scouting through a German gun-pit when he found what appeared to be the latest model of anti-tank gun. 'Gorgeous,' he said. 'There was a telescopic sight and elevating angle . . . the gun swung up and down, it traversed left and right.' It looked so lethal that one of his comrades warned him not to fire it without Howard's authority.

'Please, sir, permission to fire the anti-tank gun. Please, sir!'

Howard was momentarily distracted. 'Okay, Parr – but just be careful where you aim it.'

Parr was rarely careful, nor was his friend, Charlie Gardner.

'Hang about,' said Gardner. 'I've found something.'

'What you got, Charlie?'

'There's a button here.'

'Press it and see what happens.'

The next thing Parr knew, the power of the retort had flung him through a backwards somersault and left him with a rattled brain. 'I thought both my eardrums had gone.' The shell took off in the general direction of Caen, leaving Charlie Gardner shaking with fear.

'I want nothing more to do with it,' he said. 'It's all yours.'[9]

Parr was delighted and now set to work, taking out snipers' nests with his monster gun. If the Germans wanted a war of attrition, then they could have one. He spent the rest of that morning engaged in a very personal vendetta against the enemy snipers, one that he undertook with characteristic glee. Even Howard had to suppress a smile when he heard Parr shouting *Number One Gun*, 'as if he had a whole barrage of cannons at his disposal'.

At one point he spotted a group of Germans hiding out on top of the nearby water tower. They were using its elevated position as an observation post for sharpshooters on the ground. But their hideout was now firmly in Parr's sights.

'*Fire!*'

Howard heard the shout for the umpteenth time. It was followed by 'the most God-awful blast'. When he looked up, he saw the huge tower burst into an elevated waterfall as a shell went smack through the middle. The water sprayed far and wide and the German observers were forced to make a hasty (and very wet) descent. 'A very happy Wally Parr,' noted John Howard, 'in control of the biggest gun he'd ever fired.'[10]

Parr himself put it more succinctly. 'It gave me the greatest personal delight to sit behind a captured German gun, firing German ammunition up German arseholes. I thoroughly enjoyed every minute of it.'[11]

Wally Parr's action brought some welcome relief from the snipers, but it was clear to everyone in Howard's troop that they could not retain their position for much longer. They had vowed to hold the bridge until the commandos arrived, but the hours passed and they never came.

'Where were the commandos?'[12] It was the question on everyone's lips. John Howard was by now extremely nervous, for he knew it was only a matter of time before his exhausted forces would be overwhelmed.

'I kept checking my watch constantly . . . I said to myself under my breath, "Come on lads – where are the bloody Commandos?"'[13]

John Howard's question was not an easy one to answer, for the commandos were spread over a wide stretch of countryside. All of them knew they were in a race against the clock. They had to reach Bénouville Bridge – and they had to reach it fast.

It was fortunate that Lord Lovat's men were among the most competitive troops taking part in the invasion that day and a good number of them were determined to be in the vanguard. One of the first off the starting block was Peter Masters, the Vienna-born corporal serving in 10 Commando: cycling towards the village of Bénouville, he reached the outskirts at around 10.30 a.m. that morning, far in advance of Lord Lovat. He was less than half a mile from the bridge.

But that final stretch was to prove a half-mile from hell. A burst of machine-gun fire flung one of his fellow commandos from his bike: he was shot through the head. Another commando was also hit and collapsed into the dirt. Masters slammed on the brakes before he too was killed. As he came to a standstill, he watched the front wheel of the second lad's bike spinning idly in the air.

He and his comrades had to pass through the village if they were to reach Howard's men at the bridge, but it was clear that many of the houses were in enemy hands. There was no possibility of blasting their way through until someone had scouted ahead.

Masters himself was selected for this suicidal role. 'There's something you can do, Corporal Masters,' said his troop commander. 'Go into this village and see what's going on.' In particular, he was told to find the hiding place of the sniper who had killed the two cycling commandos. It was an unenviable task. Masters felt as if he were 'mounting the scaffold of the guillotine', for there was precious little cover in the main street of the village. 'All hell seemed to be loose, with odd bursts of fire in every direction.'

As he set off down the main street, he suddenly recalled a scene from *Gunga Din*, starring Cary Grant and Victor McLaglen. As the two of them stumbled into a group of Indian guerrillas and looked certain to be killed, Cary Grant shouted out a witty line. 'You are all under arrest!' It saved his skin. Masters now decided to do the same as he strode down the main street, putting his fluent German to good use.

'*Ergebt Euch alle! Alle 'raus! Surrender, all of you! Come out!* You are completely surrounded – you don't have a chance. Throw away your weapons and come out with your hands up if you want to go on living. The war is over for you!'[14]

No one emerged from the houses, nor did anyone shoot at him. He even spotted yellow recognition scarves in a few of the upstairs windows, a clear sign that some of the houses had been occupied by the parachutists. But no one dared show their faces, for Bénouville had become a no-man's-land, a village between two front lines. It was deathly and eerily silent.

Not until he reached the far side of the village did he come under fire. By then, his comrades were also advancing up the main street and they were taking no chances, shooting, dodging and inching their way through the village. They successfully reached the far side and it looked certain that they would claim the prize of being the first to reach Howard's men at Bénouville Bridge.

But no. This was to be a day of astonishing happenings, and none more so than their discovery that a five-strong band of street fighters was ahead of them. A little group of commandos had surged inland from Sword Beach, travelling at an extraordinary rate of knots.

Most vocal of the five was Stanley 'Scotty' Scott, a chippy London bruiser from Tottenham. Scott was described as 'armour-plated', a pugnacious warhorse whose flattened nose looked as if it had been punched once too often in a pub brawl. 'With Stan Scott,' said one, 'what you see is what you get.'[15] He had served in the Middle East before signing up for the commandos, where his hard talk and tough action left a deep impression on his comrades. 'The sight of Stan Scott in Para smock, Commando beret and blackened face, leading an assault section charging forwards firing from the hip and shouting "Get the bastards" is a sight to behold.'[16]

Scott liked to be first, especially in combat, and saw no reason why his No. 3 Troop could not be first to Bénouville Bridge. To this end, he gathered a core of his hardest-hitters – Campbell, Ozzy Osbourne and Jimmy Synnott among them – and made a dash for the bridge in a welter of fire. They were equipped with bicycles, like Peter Masters, but Scott's men intended to pedal harder and faster than any of their fellow commandos as they enacted their very own version of the Tour de France. 'There was five of us, a little detached party, like yellow jerseys going first.'

They moved swiftly inland after a bruising beach landing. 'Blokes going down left and right,' said Scott, who was almost blown apart. 'The first thing we did was pull off all the reeds and mud from the chain, then mounted up and rode away to our first objective, the canal bridge.'

They were the first into Bénouville, arriving some time before Masters and company, and cycled down the main street at such speed that they avoided the enemy fire. As they reached the furthest end of the village, close to the parish church, they suddenly found themselves riding across the finishing line. For it was here, shielded from German snipers, that they became the first troops to link up with the airborne forces.

The encounter was very different to the one made famous by Lord Lovat. There were no apologies for being late, no skirl of the bagpipes. A lone British paratrooper was seated on the ground with his shattered leg propped up on a chair. He looked Scotty up and down and said, 'Where the fuck have you been?'

Scott's response was similarly profane. He gave 'the usual British greeting, "Bollocks!"'[17] and then prepared to cycle like crazy towards the bridge. 'Get on your bikes and go like the clappers!' he shouted to his men.

The final approach was the most hazardous of all, for the last seventy-five yards were exposed and alive with gunfire. 'Rounds hitting from all sides, there was rounds ricocheting off and splatting and hitting.' Four of his troop sailed through the gunfire, with Scott in the lead, but the fifth got caught in crossfire. 'Campbell was just the unlucky one. He got clobbered. He got hit through the neck, fell down in one big lump, him, the bike and all that.'

Scott spun across the bridge at high speed before taking refuge behind a burned-out German vehicle. 'I suddenly realized there was a strong smell of roasting pork, looked in and saw three incinerated occupants.'

His thrust towards the bridge had been little short of remarkable, but it was witnessed by only a handful of John Howard's men. 'There was none of the bagpipe-playing and cheering and all that crap,'[18] said Scott. The subdued reception enabled Lord Lovat to steal their thunder. As ever with his lordship, he was to create a visual scene that would be forever remembered by those who witnessed it. Denis Edwards was still hiding out in the outskirts of Bénouville when everything fell silent. Even the air turned mute. And then he heard a shout.

'It's them! It's the commandos!'

He and his company erupted into spontaneous cheers, blotting out the skirl of music. But as the commandos drew nearer, they fell into silence as they listened to 'the high-pitched and uneven wailing of bagpipes'.[19] It was Lovat himself who had once again demanded the pipes. As his men closed in on Bénouville, he turned to Bill Millin with a smile.

'Right, piper,' he said, 'start the pipes again.'[20]

Millin asked what he should play and Lovat requested 'Blue

Bonnets over the Border'. Even Millin thought it incongruous. Houses were aflame and mortars bursting on to the roadside, yet here he was piping the Jacobite anthem that had celebrated Bonnie Prince Charlie's march on England.

The sight of the commandos gave renewed confidence to men who had feared they were soon to be annihilated. They shouted, they cheered, they threw caution to the wind. 'Now you Jerry bastards,' they yelled. 'You've got a real fight on your hands.'[21]

Wally Parr was still firing mortars from his gun-pit next to the bridge when he heard a cry from John Howard.

'Quiet!' said Howard. 'Quiet!'

Parr poked his head outside and heard the pipes. His heart skipped a beat. After all the stresses and terrors of the previous twelve hours it was time to let rip. 'We went potty,' he said. 'We fired everything we could. We were cheering and shouting and shooting like mad.'

He still hadn't sighted Lovat's commandos, but that was about to change. As they approached the crossroads that led to the bridge, they came into view.

'Come and look at this lot!'

Parr rushed outside in time to see the unmistakable figure of Lord Lovat. 'He was wearing a roll-neck white or cream pullover, a green beret and a pack on his back.' To his right, precisely three paces in front, Bill Millin was blowing his bagpipes for all he was worth.

Parr was overcome with emotion. He leaped into the road and stopped six feet away from Lovat.

Lovat 'held out his hand as a way of greeting'. Parr clipped his hand into a salute, feeling somewhat bashful. 'I suddenly thought, What the hell am I doing here?' But Lovat was a model of politesse. He saluted back before turning his gaze to the bridge while Bill Millin took a much needed rest from his pipes.

'We're very pleased to see you, sir,' said Parr.

'Well done, well done,'[22] replied Lovat. He then asked for the whereabouts of John Howard.

Howard appeared seconds later and held out his hand, addressing Lovat with evident relief. 'We are very pleased to see you, old boy,' he said.

'Aye,' replied Lovat, 'we are pleased to see you.' And then he glanced at his watch and uttered his famous words: 'Sorry, we are two and a half minutes late.'[23]

He shook Howard's hand once again, only gripping it slightly tighter this time. 'Today, history is being made,' he said.

Howard would have liked to utter something equally memorable, but he was too dog-tired. 'About bloody time!'[24] he said with a grin. They were the only words he could muster.

All the isolated soldiers in Bénouville celebrated the arrival of the commandos, though not always in the same fashion. John Butler, a Canadian paratrooper with the Airborne Division, learned of their arrival when he entered a little backstreet café in order to beg some water for his parched throat.

'Not water!' roared the proprietor. 'I have something better!' A moment later he emerged from his cellar with 'an armful of dirty bottles which turned out to be magnums of champagne'. He had buried them in the summer of 1940 and vowed not to drink them until the Germans had been vanquished.

Butler slugged a first glass and then a second. 'He started to fill my glass again, thought better of it and gave me the bottle.' Butler drained the dregs and then launched himself into a second magnum. But the jollity came to an abrupt end when he and his troop were given orders to flush the last remaining snipers from the abandoned buildings of Bénouville.

Butler no longer feared anything. 'After two quarts of champagne on an empty stomach, I was fighting drunk.' As his pals scampered from doorway to doorway, dodging through the midday shadows, he took more direct action. 'I just strolled down the centre of the street blazing away at windows, doors and roofs with my Sten gun.'[25] Miraculously, he emerged at the far end of the street unscathed. It gave the lie to the old advice not to drink on the job.

PART VII
Afternoon

American troops on Omaha Beach were many hours behind schedule and still struggling up the steep cliffs. On the other four beaches, soldiers were moving steadily inland. But in the countryside around Utah Beach, American paratroopers spent much of the afternoon rebuffing German counter-attacks.

One of the fiercest battles occurred at Neuville-au-Plain, close to Sainte-Mère-Église. German troops from the 91st Luftlande-Infanterie-Division launched a surprise attack, aware that if they could recapture the town – and the N13 highway – the destruction of the entire western landing zone might yet be achievable.

Another key military objective that afternoon was Caen, a major city at the intersection of many main roads. In preparation for an assault on the city by ground troops, the Allied plan called for the bombing of bridges and railway lines to stop the Germans bringing up reinforcements. But Caen was home to 60,000 civilians. Although many families had dug makeshift shelters in their gardens, the raids over previous months in Normandy had already caused 34,000 casualties. Warnings of new raids had been issued by the Allies, yet it seemed all too possible that many inhabitants would not have fled by the time of the bombing mission.

Caen's roads and railways were a key target for Allied bombers. But the city also had 60,000 inhabitants, who found themselves trapped in a deadly bombardment.

22

The Bombing of Caen

S IR HENRY MORRIS-JONES, Member of Parliament for Denbigh, had not allowed rumours of the Allied invasion to disrupt his working day. He was still fuming over his discovery that 14,000 ration books had been stolen from the Food Office warehouse in Hertfordshire. Now, in the House of Commons, he wanted to know from the minister responsible if the books had been recovered. He also demanded 'more drastic punishment of those found guilty of this form of sabotage on the war effort'.

The answers he received were far from satisfactory. Not only had the ration books not been recovered, but even more had been stolen. As for punishment of the culprits, the parliamentary secretary said it was a matter 'for the courts and not for the Ministry of Food'.[1]

Sir Henry Morris-Jones persisted in his questioning but the House was not in the mood for routine business on such an eventful day. When Harold Nicolson, the member for Leicester West, entered the chamber at ten minutes to noon, parliamentary questions had been brought to an early close. The place was abuzz with rumour and everyone was awaiting the arrival of the Prime Minister. It was said that Churchill was on his way to the House in order to make a statement about the Normandy landings.

Those seated closest to the Speaker's Chair were the first to glimpse the unmistakable bulk of the Prime Minister as he entered the chamber. The room fell suddenly silent. 'An unusual scene,' mused Nicolson as he glanced at his watch. Three minutes to noon. All faces were turned towards Churchill; all eyes stared at him as if trying to read his face. Nicolson thought he looked 'as white as a sheet' and braced himself for what was to come. 'We feared that he was about to announce some terrible disaster.'[2]

The Prime Minister was clutching two large files of typescript, both of which he placed on the dispatch box. The Speaker got to his feet and called for order. 'With the permission of the House,' he said, 'there will be a short interval to allow a statement by the Prime Minister.'

Churchill rose heavily, pausing for a moment as he cleared his throat. When he finally began his discourse, he spoke not of the landings in Normandy; rather, he informed the House of the rapidly changing situation in Italy. Rome had been liberated two days earlier, he said: 'a memorable and glorious event, which rewards the intense fighting of the last five months in Italy'.[3] To Nicolson's ears, it was as if he were warming to the occasion, speaking with 'a rise of the voice and that familiar bending of the two knees'.[4] It was indeed a powerful performance, but it was not what the members were hoping to hear. They wanted news from Normandy.

Churchill paused for a moment, as if playing with his audience. He placed his first folder of notes back on the dispatch box and slowly picked up the second. 'I have also to announce to the House,' he said in a solemn tone, 'that during the night and the early hours of this morning, the first of the series of landings in force upon the European continent has taken place.'[5]

Silence. Everyone was listening 'in hushed awe',[6] or so it seemed to Nicolson. The Prime Minister spoke of the 'immense armada' and gave news of the 'massed airborne landings' and the destruction of German shore batteries. For fully seven minutes he provided them with the latest information – as much as he could – before ending on a rousing note of optimism. 'Nothing that equipment, science or forethought could do has been neglected,' he said, 'and the whole process of opening this great new front will be pursued with the utmost resolution, both by the commanders and by the United States and British governments whom they serve.'

As his speech came to an end, Harold Nicolson glanced around the chamber. There was total silence as everyone digested the information. And then suddenly, spontaneously, the entire chamber burst into rapturous applause. As the noise of clapping finally died away, the Speaker rose to his feet and added a few extra words. 'We are living through momentous times,'[7] he said.

It was a fitting epitaph to the Prime Minister's speech. There was nothing more to add.

★

On the far side of the English Channel, the noonday sunshine was fast burning off the cloud cover and the mercury was on the rise. On the ground, men who had been freezing a few hours earlier were now sweltering under the weight of their packs. But not everywhere on that stretch of coastline was enveloped in sun. There were still large areas where the cloud stubbornly persisted, hanging in dense clots at around 1,000 feet above sea level.

Those cloud-studded skies belonged to the Allies that afternoon, a high-altitude battlefield that stretched to infinity. This was the fighter pilots' playground, an aerial empire of some 15,000 square miles in which the Luftwaffe was almost invisible. A few German aces would get airborne that day, including Josef Priller and Helmut Eberspächer, but for much of the afternoon the battle for the skies was a one-sided affair.

The young Allied fighter pilots fought with cocksure audacity and on this particular day they showcased their brio with a mastery that bordered on arrogance – the Americans in their P47 Thunderbolts or P38 Lightnings and the British in their nimble, one-seater Typhoons. The RAF pilots referred to themselves as 'the Brylcreem Boys' on account of their greased hair: they were swaggerers like James Kyle, just twenty-one years of age, who had a swing to his gait and talked a good talk. Supremely confident of his own skills, he was no less sure of his Typhoon's ability to perform aeronautical acrobatics. He described it as 'a deadly accurate attack plane' and it was certainly accurate when he was behind the controls.

He had got the taste for this aerial blood-sport in the weeks preceding D-Day, when his thirty-strong squadron perfected the art of extreme flying – attacking 'the Hun' from a height of thirty feet. 'We bombed and strafed at will, flying at tree-top level, hedge-hopping, avoiding protruding hazards.' Piloting a plane at such low altitudes was exhilarating and gave an instant adrenalin pump to the heart, with the additional kick of knowing that one false manoeuvre spelled certain death. Kyle had the audacity to practise his low-level aeronautics on the country lanes of Normandy. 'We could have read the signposts,' he said with glee, 'had we slowed down.' No fear of crashing, no twinge of nerves. 'I could fly the aircraft to its limitations. I knew what I could do with it.' To prove the point, he flew through the high-tension electricity cables between

Northampton and Bedford, passing through 330,000 volts without so much as an electric shock.

For Kyle, D-Day was just another routine operation: the target that day happened to be the German high command headquarters in Bayeux. His squadron swept inland at 500 feet on account of the low-lying cloud, then paid a leisurely visit to the property, 'bombing and strafing at will'. There was no challenge from the Luftwaffe and only light flak from the ground. They left an RAF calling card to be remembered: a packet of explosives so huge that it reduced the château to 'a smouldering waste'.[8] And then they departed as they arrived – at 300 mph. It was one of the many targets successfully destroyed that day. Kyle was soon back at RAF Needs Oar Point, an airfield on the Solent, where the mission was relived with glee.

Soon after Kyle's mission, a monster fleet of fifty-six Liberator heavy bombers headed due south across the English Channel with an escort of seven squadrons of Mustang fighter aircraft. Their target was Caen, the largest city on this stretch of coast.

Caen lay just eight miles to the south of Sword Beach, and its network of roads, bridges and railways was of vital importance to the German army. It was imperative for it to be destroyed in order to stop the enemy from rushing reinforcements to the coast. There was but one drawback to the Allied plan of destruction: Caen's civilian population numbered 60,000 and very few had taken heed of the leaflets dropped from the sky, urging them to seek refuge in the countryside. Even fewer had any notion of the horror that was approaching from the north at almost 200 mph. The lead pilots of that fleet of Liberators could already make out the squat-shouldered castle in the city centre. It soon loomed large in their plane's glass-plated nose. Caen was in their sights and there were just a few minutes to go. It was 1.30 p.m.

Bernard Goupil had been hungry for more than an hour. Given the choice, he would have knocked off for lunch long ago. But his team worked in shifts and he had to await the return of his boss, Louis Asseline, before he could go home.

Monsieur Goupil was a thirty-nine-year-old insurance broker who had been coopted into working for Caen's Défense Passive.

His job was to care for civilians left homeless or wounded by the Allied bombing raids. He worked at one of the branch offices on Rue des Carmes, in the austere surroundings of a former boarding school.

He was a man with a cool head. His was a world of numerical order, one in which things added up, columns tallied and income was always offset by expenditure. Yet ever since being woken by the sound of coastal gunfire that morning, all sense of order had disappeared.

Caen had received official news of the Allied landings at a little after 8.30 a.m., when the local radio station had announced that 'Allied troops have begun to land in the north of France.' By then, it was already clear that something was afoot. When Madame Hélène Hurel had stepped outside soon after daybreak, she noticed that people greeted each other 'with a bit of a smile, despite their anxiety'.[9] There were already ominous signs of things to come. Electricity, water, gas and telephones had all been cut.

A second unwelcome surprise had come shortly afterwards, when thousands of Allied leaflets were dropped on the town exhorting people to leave their homes. Few took the warnings seriously: in common with those who lived on the coast, they had nowhere to go. Monsieur Goupil was one of the many who chose to ignore the leaflets. He would stay put with his family.

His boss returned to the office soon after one o'clock and told Goupil he was free to go. Goupil strapped on his helmet and white armband and left without further ado, heading for the home that he shared with his wife, Lilly, and their five children. As he cycled through the sunlit streets, he could hardly fail to notice that the skies had cleared over the previous few hours. Where before there had been thick cloud, now there was an ever expanding patch of blue. Summer was at long last returning to Normandy.

Monsieur Goupil might have paused to reflect on that change in the weather, for it was to be feared as much as it was to be welcomed. In time of war, clear skies were a bomber pilot's dream.

Madame Goupil had spent the morning scraping together a meal, but it was hard to make an appetizing lunch from boiled Jerusalem artichokes. Lunch was served without ceremony and the children wolfed down the food. They were still scraping their plates when

Monsieur Goupil heard a low throbbing in the sky. It sounded like a vast cloud of bees approaching from the north. It was just a whisker after 1.30 p.m. He felt a chill run through his bones. Such a noise could only come from warplanes. He rushed out into the garden and turned his head to the sky. It was worse than he feared.

'The bombers are coming!' he yelled. 'Towards *us*.'

He dashed back inside, aware that there was not a moment to lose. He had to get his children into the trench at the end of the garden. But there was no time even for that. Just seconds after seeing the planes, he heard 'sinister whistling sounds' coming from high in the sky.

'It's the bombs, isn't it?' His wife's face was white with panic.

Before he could answer, Caen was shaken by a series of explosions so violent that it felt as if the core of the earth were buckling. 'Our poor little dining room shook violently, the chandelier crashed onto the table and the front door of the house was torn from its hinges by the force of the blast.'[10] Marie-Noelle, the youngest of the Goupil children, was screaming in fear. The older ones had pushed themselves tight against the wall in the hope that the fabric of the house might yet save them.

'Get to the shelters! Get to the shelters!'[11]

Those caught outside in the streets could be heard shouting in desperation. One old lady was screeching in anguish, prompting an angry response from someone nearby. 'That's enough shrieking now. If you don't stop immediately, I'll slap you.'[12]

In the home of the Quaire family, Madame Quaire felt her unborn baby kicking violently as the first bombs began to explode. 'Quick, quick, everyone downstairs.' Her husband was shouting to everyone in the house. The elderly grandmother was dragged into the cellar and then they all sat there, 'tightly pressed against each other under the stairs, listening to the bombs falling closer and closer'. The house rattled, the children cried and there was 'another bomb, even closer, and everything went black'. Sheer terror. 'For a second or two we thought we were dead, stupefied by the noise, the fear, the dark and the dust.'[13] Madame Quaire began to haemorrhage.

Just across town, in the Saint-Jean district, fourteen-year-old Denise Harel was cowering in the bathroom of the apartment she shared with her older cousin, Thérèse. Also with them was Babeth, one of

Thérèse's friends. The noise outside was infernal. Thérèse gave a weak smile, hoping to raise the spirits of the other two girls. As she did so, there was a blast of such violence that the bathroom floor fell away beneath them. Down they tumbled amid a vast chute of masonry, beams and roof tiles. A bomb had scored a direct hit on the neighbouring house, wrecking everything that surrounded it.

'My God! My God! Have mercy!'

Babeth wondered if she was still alive. She had crashed into the cellar and landed under a vast pile of masonry, trapped but conscious. Denise was alive too, but also pinned down by debris. She begged Thérèse to help her out of the rubble, but Thérèse remained curiously silent, 'her right arm around my waist'.[14] Denise's blouse was growing wet but she couldn't tell if it was water or blood.

In the centre of town, Geneviève Vion was in the midst of doing household chores when her entire neighbourhood was kicked to oblivion. She and her husband lived above the famous Passage Bellivet, a covered shopping market known for its fin-de-siècle glass ceiling. Now, that ceiling crashed to the ground in a lethal cascade. Madame Vion was still reeling from the force of the blast. 'All the windows of our shops were blown out, and inside the house a thick cloud of dust poured from the walls and ceilings.'[15]

When she peered outside, she saw that the Monoprix supermarket, just thirty metres away, was a raging inferno. She feared for those trapped inside. A few firemen had rushed to the front of the building but they faced a hopeless task. The mains water pump had been shattered in the bombardment and spluttered up nothing more than a few muddy drops.

The bombing raid was like a catastrophic earthquake. As the planes flew over the historic quarter of Caen, they dropped 156 tonnes of explosives. The pilots were aiming for the city's roads and bridges, but it was hard for them to pinpoint such targets with any accuracy. Nor did they succeed in killing enemy soldiers. The local inhabitants outnumbered the German garrison by more than two hundred to one and stood a far greater chance of being hit.

The raid on Caen lasted less than twenty minutes, yet it took a good deal longer for the dust to settle. When Bernard Goupil dared to peek outside his shattered home, he saw that 'a dense cloud of smoke and dust was covering the city and day had turned to night.'[16] In a surreal scene, the sky was filled with millions of feathers, the stuffing of pillows and eiderdowns shredded in the bombing.

Across the city, those not trapped in the rubble were beginning to emerge from their homes. They blinked at the sky, tentative at first lest the aircraft pay them another visit.

'That's it,' said the pregnant Madame Quaire, whose haemorrhaging seemed to have stopped. 'It's the end. We've got to get out.'[17] As she and her family crawled into the street, she noticed an armchair suspended in the telegraph wires.

Others were still trapped in the rubble and in desperate need of help. Among them were Babeth, Denise and Thérèse, all buried under debris.

Thérèse's husband Joseph had survived the bombing raid and was engaged in a desperate mission to dig out the three girls when a team from the civil defence force came to his aid.

'There's a young girl, fourteen years old, who's still alive,' he cried. 'Pull her out as fast as possible.' The distress could be heard in his voice. 'There's also my wife, poor Thérèse.'

The men used shovels to dig away the rubble, desperate to reach the girls before they were asphyxiated.

'*Courage!* Almost there!'

Babeth was the first to be released, weak but miraculously alive: she had survived the ordeal of being entombed under tons of masonry. But the rescuers faced real difficulty extracting Denise because of floor joists that had fallen on to her back.

'A saw! Quick! A saw!'

They began to cut the wood, but as they did so large chunks of stonework began to slide down on top of her.

'*Dépêchez-vous!* Hurry up! I can hardly breathe!'

Although trapped, Denise tried to revive her cousin, but without success. She cried again to the rescuers but each time she was choked with dirt. She was sobbing and moaning. '*Je souffre.* I'm suffering.'

After three hours of digging, her head and back were finally freed from the rubble, followed by her arms and the rest of her body. It was astonishing that she didn't have any broken bones. She felt 'dizzy, disfigured and stained by my cousin's blood, my head heavy, one eye completely closed and a numb arm'.[18]

She was lifted on to a stretcher and transported to a first aid post. She was extraordinarily lucky to be alive, as was Babeth. But Denise's cousin, Thérèse, had not pulled through. She was one of Caen's many innocent victims. The exact number of civilians killed in that lunchtime raid would never be known, but it included many of the 800 who perished in the first forty-eight hours of the Allied invasion.

Similar scenes were being played out across the city – hundreds of individual tragedies that added up to something truly terrible. When Bernard Goupil made his way back to Rue des Carmes, he was greeted by a sight of utter devastation. 'Many of the buildings had been torn apart or had collapsed, the streets were covered in debris, and lighting cables, not used since the beginning of the occupation, had been left hanging.'

The Saint-Jean district of the city had been the worst hit. Rue Saint-Jean itself had ceased to exist. The famous Place de la Mare was a tangle of stone, concrete and broken beams. The destruction itself was bad enough. What made it more sickening was the fact that most of the buildings had been full of people.

The damage was completely random. Some homes were pulverized, while neighbouring properties were completely unscathed. Most buildings around Rue des Jacobins were hollow shells, their shattered interiors exposed to the daylight. Yet the offices of the newspaper *Ouest-France* were untouched.

As Goupil approached Place Courtonne, he noticed that the huge Odon building was open to the sky and its five-storey neighbour had completely disappeared. He stared at it for a moment, deeply shocked. 'Is it possible that this huge pile of stones is all that remains?'

He also felt a heavy heart at the inevitable death toll. 'How many unfortunate people were caught unawares while eating their meal, just like us?'[19] He wondered how many were still trapped under the rubble.

As he picked his way through streets that were scarcely recognizable, he chanced upon his old friend Jean Yver, professor of law. Professor Yver had a stretcher tied to the back of his bicycle. With an air of desperation, he asked Goupil how he could best help trapped civilians. It was not an easy question to answer.

The Bon Sauveur Hospital started to receive its first patients soon after the bombing came to an end. It was well staffed with doctors and nurses, yet it had never had to deal with such a large-scale emergency.

Among the volunteer stretcher-bearers was André Heinz, a member of the resistance, who found himself digging the injured from ruined buildings. Once freed from the rubble, they were loaded on to stretchers and transported to the Bon Sauveur, where Heinz's sister was working as a nurse. Since Caen's other two hospitals had been hit, Heinz felt the need to place some sort of recognition symbol on the building. 'Painting red crosses would take too long and finding the paint itself was a problem.' He briefly considered using the long red carpets laid out in churches for wedding ceremonies, 'but could not find the key or anyone who would help us'. In the end, he came up with a simpler solution. 'My sister decided to take four of the big sheets that had been used in the operating theatre and were already smeared with blood. We dipped them into pails of blood that stood there' – the result of countless amputations – 'and went to spread them in the hospital garden.'

A lone Allied plane flew overhead as they were spreading out the fourth arm of the cross. 'We thought it was going to strafe us and we were tempted to abandon the job.' But it was a reconnaissance plane and Heinz was relieved to see it was 'waggling its wings to let us know it had seen the red cross'.[20]

The blood soon turned dark brown, requiring Heinz to repeat the procedure with fresh blood. This time, he added mercurochrome in order to stain the sheets more efficiently. Once he was finished, the surgeon asked him to empty the buckets of blood. 'As I was throwing the blood from one of the pails, a severed hand fell out.' Heinz almost vomited on the spot. He would later remark that 'it took me years before I could admire again any of Dürer's or Rodin's studies of hands.'[21]

The tally of wounded civilians multiplied dramatically as the afternoon wore on. The Bon Sauveur doctors were used to terrible injuries, for there had been bombing raids for many months, yet they were deeply shocked by the state of some who were placed in their care. Dr Chaperon had already undertaken five operations when a sixth patient was rushed into the theatre. 'An atrocious sight,' he later said. 'A young man of eighteen skewered onto a piece of wood.'[22] It was almost a metre in length and over four centimetres thick.

Many of the seriously injured never made it to the hospital. Antoine Magonette's brother, Jean-Marie, had been crushed by a stone wall. He was rushed to Bon Sauveur on a makeshift stretcher, but died from internal injuries en route. His brother later recalled that he breathed his last, having made peace with his maker and with 'a smile on his lips, holding the hand of his confessor and friend, Father Yard'.

Magonette was instructed to take his brother's body to the hospital's mortuary, a large room with whitewashed walls 'that smelled strongly of chlorine'. Here, he was witness to a most incongruous sight. 'The dead were laid out on the ground, side by side, like well-behaved children.'[23] The first victims had been wrapped in canvas sheeting, but there were soon so many bodies that hospital orderlies abandoned wrapping them and simply tied a number around their necks. Antoine's brother was laid out with a new batch of corpses. He was number four.

It was a day of horror for everyone who lived in Caen, but particularly for Bernard Goupil, who was charged with trying to identify the corpses brought to his defence post.

He had to examine their heads and note any recognizable features. 'Some of them [were] horribly mutilated, with faces covered in dirt and blood. Some of the bodies had limbs that were crushed or torn. What a terrible sight!' Monsieur Goupil was praying that he wouldn't 'suddenly be confronted with the face of someone dear to me'.

One female victim was so badly mutilated that she was beyond identification. Goupil removed her wedding ring in the hope that the name of a loved one might be engraved inside, but to no avail. 'I was reduced to noting the address where her body had been found, with a report on her clothes and the colour of her hair.'

He paused for a moment to take stock of the carnage that lay around him. It was almost too much to bear. 'What an upheaval to our lives – and all in just a few hours.'

Just the previous day, he had been cycling through the country-side and being greeted by friendly faces. Now he was 'in the midst of the dead, being brought here in their dozens'.[24]

He tried to cope with the shock by thinking rationally: it was an insurance broker's way of coping with loss. Others in Caen found it harder to contain their anger. Antoine Magonette felt extremely bitter about losing his brother in the bombing raid, and all the more so when he was told that the town had been bombed by aircraft called Liberators.

'*Quel nom!*'[25] he said sardonically.

His eventual liberation was not to come for another thirty-three days. In the intervening time, the city of Caen was to find itself in a deadly trap.

Amphibious tanks, with canvas flotation screens still in place, support British troops advancing up Rue de Riva-Bella in Ouistreham. Built-up areas were a German snipers' dream.

23

Counter-Attack

I T WAS A little after 2.30 p.m. when the German intelligence officer Friedrich Hayn set off from his staff headquarters in Saint-Lô. He wanted to see for himself the extent of the Allied invasion. The timing of his trip had been chosen by his staff driver, who noticed that the airborne raids seemed to slacken each day at around 3 p.m., which was 4 p.m. across the Channel. 'They are now having their tea in England,' he said to Hayn, displaying a useful knowledge of British customs.

As his staff car sped across the Normandy countryside, Hayn was stunned by the scale of the devastation. 'Every moment of our way we came across a charred, battered and bent skeleton of some vehicle. Most of them were lying on their rear axle, looking like some large squatting animal.' Field guns, armoured vehicles and tanks had all been targeted and the roads were strewn with detritus. 'A smouldering panzer with the paint boiling on hot steel, or a crackling, hissing and puffing ammunition car.' In among the metal debris were mangled corpses in uniform and the half-shredded carcasses of cows, stiff and bloated with their legs sticking rigidly skywards.

Hayn couldn't believe that the mighty German army had taken such a battering. The Allies were taking full advantage of their air supremacy to smash the Wehrmacht before it even reached the beaches.

His staff driver would live to regret his comment about English tea breaks, for the sky was soon filled with fighter-bombers, 'swarming about in the sky like hornets'. Hayn was terrified by 'the gargling sound of rocket projectiles' and even more alarmed by the 'bursts of fire' that swept along every road. He soon had a first-hand encounter with a pilot from the same school of daring as James Kyle, who now performed his aerial gymnastics right over Hayn's head. 'One moment the plane seemed to drop out of the sun, the next it soared up into the sky like a rocket.' There seemed to be no escape from this infernal fighter. 'The pilot always kept his finger on the button of his 2cm gun, ready to fire at anything moving.' Hayn managed to survive unscathed, aware that he'd had a lucky escape. Yet the attack left him despairing. 'Where, now, was our Luftwaffe?' The question kept repeating itself in his head. 'Could there ever have been a better chance to strike at the massed enemy forces with paralyzing effect?' But there was not a German plane to be seen.

As he drove eastwards from Saint-Lô, he was witness to the mass exodus of civilians who had realized, far too late, that fleeing their homes was their best hope of saving their lives. Thousands were on the move, carrying their families and goods on two-wheeled carts covered with white sheets. 'Men who kept a gloomy eye on the sky were sitting on them, together with sobbing women and frightened children.'[1]

D-Day had now been under way for the better part of fourteen hours and a vast military machine was thrusting inland – tanks, jeeps and armoured bulldozers, as well as hundreds of mechanized 'funnies' belching thick diesel from their thunderous engines. Their like had never before been seen on the country lanes of Normandy: Crab tanks with flailing chains were thrashing their way through minefields while ditch-filling Fascine tanks were tossing giant logs into the enemy's defensive trenches. Armoured bulldozers were shunting aside concrete obstacles while Crocodile flame-throwers squelched jets of petrol-fuelled fire into bunkers that continued to resist.

But mostly it was tanks: a vast army of Shermans, Centaurs and Churchills that was ploughing through metalled roads and churning the Normandy mud, shredding a passage through thickets and spinneys. By early afternoon the Allied advance was no mere pinprick: the landing forces were pushing forward along a front that stretched more than fifty miles. The stench of diesel hung thickly on the air from Ouistreham in the east to Sainte-Mère-Église in the west. Above and beyond the immediate battlefield, a pall of smoke was staining the sky above Caen. The five beachheads had not yet linked up, but if and when they did, the Allies would control a formidable slice of territory.

The situation on the ground was indeed more optimistic than some of the Overlord planners had originally predicted. On the eastern flank, Lord Lovat's commandos had successfully linked up with John Howard's paratroopers and secured the bridges over the River Orne and the Caen Canal. On neighbouring Juno, the Canadians were moving swiftly inland having knocked out the German strongpoint at Saint-Aubin-sur-Mer. They had also captured the resort of Bernières-sur-Mer, leaving only the coastal fortress at Langrune still in enemy hands.

The British troops on Gold Beach were also driving inland after overcoming stiff resistance. WN33 was cleared late morning, while the monstrous Le Hamel bunker was being targeted by two companies from the Hampshires. By early afternoon they were ready to launch a rearguard attack.

Even the defences of Omaha Beach were busted. Franz Gockel and Karl Wegner had not been alone in fleeing their strongholds. When the German radio operator Alfred Sturm attempted to call a beachside bunker from his position inland, he was met with a sorry tale of abandoned positions and unmanned guns. One particularly desperate message was to stick in his mind: it came from a young German defender whose bunker was under attack. 'The artillery has entered our strongpoint. I'm on my own.' There was a brief pause before the youth gave his valedictory farewell. 'Live well, comrades!'[2]

Omaha had proved a costly victory for the Allies, but neighbouring Utah had been won with comparative ease. As wave after wave of men pounded ashore in the footsteps of Leonard Schroeder, fewer than 200 were gunned down by the German defenders. Every loss was a tragedy; every death a cause of grief. Yet it could have been far worse. In the live-ammunition rehearsal for the landing at Slapton Sands in Devon – Exercise Tiger – no fewer than 749 American servicemen had accidentally perished. It was a disaster of such magnitude that any survivor who revealed the truth was threatened with a court martial for years to come.

Now, on D-Day afternoon, there was a feeling of cautious

optimism among senior officials at Supreme Headquarters in Southwick House, even though very few battle reports had been received. Admiral Bertram Ramsay, mastermind of the naval operation, was in particularly ebullient form. In a briefing with journalists, he (somewhat oddly) compared the attack on the Atlantic Wall to the cutting of a slice of pie. 'The crust is broken,' he said, 'and now we must go through with it.'

Shortly after Ramsay's briefing, General Montgomery chatted with journalists on the neatly clipped lawn in front of his lodgings, close to Southwick House. He was as chirpy and upbeat as usual. 'Things are going nicely,' he beamed, 'otherwise I should not be enjoying my garden.'[3]

Alone among senior staff, Eisenhower remained cautious. True, he had dictated a short message to the Combined Chiefs of Staff in London, informing them that the invasion seemed to be going smoothly. Yet his famously broad grin masked a genuine anxiety. He was alarmed that so few reports had been received from the beachhead, especially given the vast numbers of wireless sets issued to the men. He had no idea that most of these sets were slopping around in the shallows of the English Channel, waterlogged and useless. Nor could he know that many of their operators had been gunned down on the beaches.

Something of his state of mind that D-Day afternoon can be gleaned from the tongue-lashing he was to give General Bradley on the following day. 'Why the devil didn't you let us know what was going on?' he snapped. 'Nothing came through until late afternoon – not a damned word. I didn't know what had happened to you.'

'We radioed you every scrap of information we had,'[4] said Bradley weakly but honestly. Only later did it transpire that his hourly dispatches, sent from USS *Augusta*, lay piled up in Montgomery's radio room, undeciphered and unread because of a lack of staff.

Eisenhower might have been better off tuning in to the BBC, which scored a coup of sorts that afternoon with a so-called 'live report' from the battlefront. It was not live, as such, for it was broadcast some hours after it was recorded. Yet the correspondent who made it, William Helmore, was a consummate performer who had cut his broadcasting teeth reporting on the Schneider Trophy, a hair-raising race between seaplanes and flying boats. Now, there was an even bigger trophy up for grabs – occupied Europe – and Helmore was to give the performance of his life.

'I'm calling you from a Mitchell bomber,' he told his listeners. 'I'm speaking now at ten thousand feet.' With the background roar of engines and the crackle of static, his report was a little master-piece of 'live' reporting. 'We're going to have a look at the invasion . . . Now I'm looking down, down, through a thin patch of white cloud.' The sky, he said, was 'full of aircraft of all kinds, coming and going . . . the heavy bombers are out, fighters have been passing us . . . we've just had some whacking big bombers swarming by here.'

What made his report all the more compelling was the fact that he was participating in a live bombing mission. 'We're going across to bomb a target which is a railway bridge,' he told his listeners, 'which I hope we shall succeed in dropping four one-thousand-pound bombs on.' And off they went, bombing their way on to the radio. Lest he sounded too confident, he ended on a note of caution. 'I can see a very beautiful scene,' he said, 'but it is a rather nervous scene, though I feel it holds in it the seeds of history.'[5]

William Helmore was right to describe the scene on the ground as 'nervous'. Many soldiers were concerned that they would not be able to hold on to their territorial gains. In the hinterland behind Utah Beach, the key objective that afternoon was to retain control of the town of Sainte-Mère-Église, wrested from the Germans some ten hours earlier. Without the use of the N13 that ran through the town, all German forces to the north were effectively cut off.

The stakes could scarcely have been higher for both sides, as the Germans were well aware. If they failed to recapture the town, it was hard to see how they could prevent a massive build-up of American supplies. But if they could retake it – and reopen the N13 – they could dramatically turn the tables. The thousands of American paratroopers who had landed in the fields to the west would be completely isolated.

The stage was set for an epic struggle whose intensity and violence would reflect the personalities of the men involved. In a scene reminiscent of Custer's Last Stand, a small group of American paratroopers on the outskirts of town were to find themselves isolated, alone and massively outnumbered.

The northern defences of Sainte-Mère-Église had been entrusted to Benjamin Vandervoort, the brook-no-nonsense battalion commander who had broken his ankle on landing. Neither the fracture itself, nor the accompanying pain, had diminished his relish for the fight ahead. Like a true gambler, he seemed to enjoy the fact that the odds were stacked against him.

His views were shared by the men entrusted with holding that road to the north. They were led by Turner Turnbull, a hardened combat veteran whose half-Choctaw, half-Scottish ancestry had scored two key traits into his personality. One was stubbornness, inherited perhaps from his Scottish mother. The other was pride, a trait that must surely have come from his paternal forebears. His distinguished great-grandparents had been forced to walk the infamous Trail of Tears when evicted from their ancestral lands, while his father had been the youngest Choctaw chief ever to be elected by popular vote (so young, indeed, that federal law forbade him from serving). Not for nothing was young Turnbull known by everyone as Chief.

There was a third factor in Turnbull's childhood that had left him with a fierce sense of independence. He had been orphaned at the age of fifteen, a blow that had required resilience and courage for him to survive the harsh world of adolescence. He grew into adulthood with a rod-like backbone, enabling him to fight with distinction in Sicily, where he was shot in the abdomen and hospitalized for four months. It could have been his ticket out of the army; instead, he volunteered for the D-Day invasion. And now he was being sent to its outer fringes, to the lonely hamlet of Neuville-au-Plain that lay one and a half miles to the north of Sainte-Mère-Église. His role, and that of the forty-three men with him, was to block any German advance.

This little outpost was frontier territory, wild, dangerous and unpredictable. Turnbull sniffed the lie of the land and prepared to use its natural features to his advantage. He concealed one squad of ten men in an orchard close to the roadside. The rest were dug in behind a hedgerow, along with a 2.36-inch bazooka. With luck, it could knock out a tank.

For some hours all was quiet. The skies had been brightening ever since midday and it had turned into one of those bucolic summer afternoons that made Normandy so picturesque. At around 1 p.m., Vandervoort had ventured out to Neuville-au-Plain in a jeep, passing en route a Frenchman clattering along on a bicycle. When he arrived at the outpost, Turnbull told him that the same cyclist had just given him some unexpected news. A large group of German prisoners was being marched towards Neuville, having been captured by American paratroopers.

Turnbull had scarcely finished speaking when the long column hove into view. There was more than a battalion of them, and they were accompanied by two tracked army vehicles. Both he and Vandervoort could clearly identify the field-grey colour of the German uniform, as well as a few soldiers in paratrooper uniform. The latter were cheerfully waving the orange recognition flag that had been issued before leaving England. Vandervoort smelled a rat. 'It looked just too good to be true.'

His suspicions turned out to be correct. He told Turnbull to fire a warning burst from his machine gun, deliberately aiming to miss. The reaction was instant and revealed the Germans' true intent: the prisoners were nothing of the sort. They now deployed themselves on either side of the road and began firing their self-propelled guns directly at Turnbull and Vandervoort. One shot knocked out the bazooka, another just missed the machine gun. Turnbull and his men were in deep trouble.

It soon became clear that they were facing a 'whole damned battalion of Krauts'[6] – it was the 91st Luftlande Division – who had been ordered to force open the road to Sainte-Mère-Église. Against them, Turnbull had fewer than four dozen men. He was outnumbered by at least five to one.

Vandervoort had to make a snap decision: abandon Neuville or defend it at all costs. There was never much doubt as to which option he would choose. He ordered Turnbull to dig in and hang on while he made a spirited dash back to Sainte-Mère-Église in order to call up reinforcements. He jumped into his jeep and careered into town, screeching to a halt at his battlefield headquarters and ordering Captain Clyde Russell and his men of E Company to join Turnbull at his outpost. He warned them not to become embroiled in a head-to-head battle. Rather, they were to fight like guerrillas, picking off the Germans one by one.

Among these reinforcements was Otis Sampson, a tough-nut paratrooper in a band of hardened veterans. In later years he liked to recount the story of how one of his comrades had been stricken with malaria just days before D-Day. The sickly individual 'insisted he would make the jump if he had to crawl out of the door on his hands and knees'. This, said Sampson, 'was the kind of man that made up our unit'. He and his comrades had served in Sicily and Italy, where they terrified the enemy by shaving their heads 'Iroquoi Indian style, with just a narrow strip of hair running from back to front'. Many had done the same for their Normandy adventure. Such a haircut must have bemused the Choctaw chief, Turner Turnbull.

As they swooped north towards Neuville, they spied German soldiers creeping forward and attempting to surround Turnbull's outpost. Sampson and his men launched an immediate counter-attack. 'We hit hard and fast.' They pounded the German positions with everything they had and 'moved the mortar continuously so as not to give Jerry a target'. It was guerrilla warfare at its most effective. The Germans began crossing the road as fast as possible, one by one. Sampson timed them. 'I judged when another would cross and had another round put in the tube.' Bang. He scored a bull's-eye each time. 'The timing was perfect.'[7]

Fighting alongside Sampson was John Fitzgerald, a paratrooper with the 101st Airborne Division who had got hopelessly separated from his comrades and now found himself serving with men he had never met. It did not take him long to see the danger posed by the advancing Germans. 'They were quickly gaining command of the entire area and were shelling it with artillery and chemical mortars. The mortars would announce themselves with a spine-chilling scream. A few seconds later, they would land, spreading shovel-sized fragments of shrapnel.' Travelling at high velocity, these could decapitate a man in an instant.

The Germans soon sighted the machine gun manned by Fitzgerald and his comrade-in-arms and began pouring in heavy concentrations of 88mm artillery fire. It was of an intensity he had never before experienced. 'We could not raise our heads, much less return fire.

Rounds were coming in, one after the other, most landed within feet of us.' Fitzgerald was half terrified, half exhilarated. 'The impact of the shells threw up mounds of dirt and mud. The ground trembled and my eardrums felt as if they would burst. Dirt was filling my shirt and it was beginning to get into my eyes and mouth.' He had a deep respect for the accuracy and punch of the Germans' 88mm gun, saying that 'there were more soldiers converted to Christianity by this 88 than by Peter and Paul combined.' He was only half joking. That big gun also taught him to fear the enemy. 'I could not hold a razor steady enough to shave for the next few days.'[8]

Chief Turnbull's situation was grave indeed. What had begun as a skirmish had developed into a fire-fight to the death. His own men were still dug into their positions in Neuville, while the men of E Company were battling their way towards them.

Colonel Vandervoort was so concerned not to lose control of the N13 that he ordered yet more reinforcements to the north side of town. Many of these men were to excel themselves under extreme pressure, even though they appeared at first glance to be ill-equipped for the fight. Waverly Wray was one such hero. A slow-spoken young gentleman 'from the Old South' (he was from Mississippi), Wray carried the Bible with him at all times 'and read it in his fox-hole in the evening, when he had the chance'. Indeed, he had such a 'devout religious faith in the goodness of God that [it] kept him from drinking, smoking or even using language stronger than "Dad-burn" or "Dad-brown"'. He could virtually recite the Old Testament by heart: its uncompromising God seemed to chime with his own concepts of vengeance. An eye for an eye. A tooth for a tooth. 'He was armed,' said one, 'with the conviction that he fought on the side of the Lord.'

As the battle for Neuville raged all around, Wray set off on a desperate lone-wolf mission, just as Stanley Hollis had done at Gold Beach. He disappeared for hours. When Vandervoort next saw him, he looked like he had stepped out of hell, 'with his cartridge belt half-torn from his middle and with two large nicks in his right ear'. He had clearly been involved in quite a scrap. 'Dry blood was caked on his neck, shoulder and right breast on his jump jacket.' Vandervoort gave him a cheery greeting. 'They have been getting kind of close to you, haven't they, Waverly.' Wray gave a wide grin. 'Not as close as I've been getting to them.'[9]

Chief Turnbull's little band held out for another three hours, until about 5 p.m. It was a superb act of defiance that effectively stopped the Germans at the gates of Sainte-Mère-Église. He had started his defence with one officer and forty-three men; by the time he got back to the town, there was only himself and fourteen men left alive. As they beat their tactical retreat, Otis Sampson could hear the Germans taunting them. 'It reminded me of an unfinished ball game, and they were yelling for us to come back and finish it.' But Sampson knew there was no need. 'Our mission,' he said, 'had been accomplished.'[10]

By the time they had retreated, the defences of Sainte-Mère-Église had been massively strengthened. 'We still held the town,' said Fitzgerald, 'and there was talk of tanks coming up from the beaches to help us.'[11]

Turnbull's defence was magnificent, but it came at a cost. One of the defenders, Charles Sammon, helped a few of the walking wounded into a makeshift farmhouse-hospital. He was greeted by a sight he would never forget: 'a couple of German doctors working alongside a couple of American airborne doctors on what had once been a dining room table. They were sawing off arms, legs, etcetera, and throwing the discarded limbs into a pile.'[12]

Such was the reality of war. Yet Vandervoort knew it was worth it. He described Chief Turnbull's stand as truly heroic, 'a small unit performance that has seldom been equaled'.[13] Turnbull himself would pay the ultimate price for his up-front leadership. He would be killed by a round of artillery on the very next day.

The Allies were not alone in fielding soldiers who were prepared to put their lives on the line. The Germans, too, had countless troops willing to fight to the death. Many of those stationed close to the Cotentin peninsula spent that afternoon battling their way towards Sainte-Mère-Église in a desperate attempt to throw the Americans back into the sea. They knew that if they could not do this by nightfall, they would probably be unable to do it at all.

Among those spoiling for a fight was a hard-drinking young corporal named Anton Wuensch, a stocky twenty-three-year-old from Silesia with a barbed wit and instantly recognizable features. This was due, in part, to his bulbous nose and deep-set eyes. But it was also because of an ugly scar 'running through his left eyebrow and down onto his left eyelid'. He was popular with his men – a seven-strong mortar unit – on account of having a seemingly inexhaustible supply of the local *digestif*. Each evening, they would gather at his foxhole and drink until late into the night.

Wuensch's unit was stationed at the Vire estuary, just seven miles from Sainte-Mère-Église. They had been on high alert ever since being woken by the pre-dawn bombardment. 'We must really throw them back into the sea,' said Wuensch to his men as they prepared to advance towards the landing zone. 'There are no reserves behind us.'

As they moved northwards towards the town, they found their progress hampered by Allied fighter planes that seemed to jump out of the sky from nowhere. They also encountered other unexpected surprises. 'Look!' whispered one of Wuensch's comrades as he pointed towards a tree. 'There's an American sniper.' Wuensch observed the man intently before crouching down with his rifle and preparing to have a crack.

'All right, my boy,' he muttered under his breath. 'Now I'm going to get you.'

He raised his rifle, took aim and squeezed the trigger – once, twice and then a third time. It was the final shot that hit its mark. He 'saw the sniper throw up his arms and fall backwards out of the tree'. They all cheered and then ran across to inspect their victim. He was dark-haired, handsome and very young. 'His eyes were open and blood was trickling down from his mouth.' When they looked more clearly, they noticed that the bullet had passed 'through the back and out through the left breast'.

Wuensch 'felt nothing' at first, as befitted his cocksure veneer. He watched in silence as his men went through the young soldier's pockets. The ever hungry Fritz Wendt filched his K-rations while others flicked through the pictures of the man's wife. As they did so, Wuensch felt a sense of revulsion. The gruesomeness of the scene was compounded by the blood still welling from the man's mouth. He would later confess to feeling as if 'he was looking down at a dog that had been run over'.

As they approached the village of Saint-Côme-du-Mont, less than five miles from Sainte-Mère-Église, they ran into serious trouble. A group of American paratroopers had occupied a ridge above the village, blocking the way forward. Wuensch and company needed to eliminate them if they were to push northwards into town. They were in the process of preparing their mortar when one of Wuensch's gunners suddenly crashed to the ground. He had been shot through the head. Seconds later, a second gunner was also shot dead. When a third member of the team tried to take his revenge, he, too, was hit. He 'threw up his arms and with a frightful scream fell back dead'.

Wuensch was shocked by the deaths, yet he refused to retreat. 'Let's keep busy,' he yelled. But just a few seconds later another of his men was shot, causing a sudden loss of nerve. 'Leo – Franz – what's happening to us? What's happening?' He was worried that he would be next. 'Let's knock off,' he said.

It was his first confession of doubt. For years, he had thought of himself as invincible and had assumed that he and his men would sweep the Allies briskly back into the sea. Now, he was not so sure.

'Let's move back again and surround them,' whispered one of his sergeants. If they could attack from the rear, they still had a chance to break the American line.

They crept towards the ridge from a different angle, manoeuvring their mortar as quickly as they could. Others had crept forward to join them, so that Wuensch now had almost two dozen men at his disposal, as well as a second mortar. He was in the process of leading them towards the N13 when the ground in front of him was kicked skywards in an explosion of dirt. He was smacked by a full burst of machine-gun fire and felt as if he had been hit 'by a red hot iron'. The bullets passed clean through the thighs of both legs, shredding the flesh and shattering the bone. He fell flat on his face and lay on the road, screaming in pain. His feet were bloodless and numb.

Fritz Wendt went to his aid. 'What's happened?' he said. 'What's this?'

'*Legs, legs!*'

Wuensch was howling in agony.

Wendt drew his knife and cut away the trousers. More bullets started hitting the road, so he dragged Wuensch over to a tree, trailing his useless legs behind him in a welter of blood. Wuensch was wide-eyed with panic as he stared at the blood gurgling out of him. He felt as if he was 'burning up from his own blood, as though it was lava'. In a daze of pain, he saw that both his feet were back to front. His legs had been skewed through 180 degrees.

One of his men, Lance Corporal Richter, tried to perform first aid.

'Am I going to die?'

'You? Die?' Richter tried to make light of the wounds, but he was all too aware of their seriousness. Wuensch's legs had been almost severed from his body.

It was several hours before the stretcher-bearers arrived and lugged him across the fields to a Volkswagen ambulance.

'So they got you too, did they?' He was half aware of a voice coming from a misty figure leaning over him. The next thing he knew, a doctor was removing the bandages from his legs and giving him a shot of morphine.

'Am I going to die?' asked Wuensch again.

'Nothing much wrong with you,' said the doctor as he slapped him hard across the face to see if the morphine was working. He then turned to a German soldier standing nearby and said, 'Hold him.' The soldier did as ordered, pinning Wuensch's shoulders in a vice-like grip.

'This is going to hurt a bit,' said the doctor as he grabbed one of Wuensch's shattered legs. He then wrenched it back through 180 degrees.

Wuensch screamed. He howled in agony. He heard the crunching of the bones as they twisted inside his leg. And then the doctor did the same to the second leg, twisting the shattered bones into their correct position.

'Oh for God's sake,' he said when finished. 'It can't hurt that much.'

Wuensch's last memory of D-Day was slugging a large shot of Calvados. He was only half conscious. He had a blurred vision of the fire-fight, of the American paratroopers, of the road leading north to Sainte-Mère-Église. 'We've certainly missed it this time,'[14] he shouted out to no one in particular. And then he passed out.

German gunners hide out in a concealed foxhole. Often positioned at crossroads, they hindered the American advance inland from Omaha.

24

Victory at Omaha

AMBULANCES HAD BEEN arriving at Portsmouth's Queen Alexandra Hospital ever since noon, sweeping up the formal driveway whose herbaceous borders had yet to recover from the previous day's storm. The hospital was a red-brick mansion built in the classical style, with a palatial façade, a stack of chimneys and two imposing wings. It might have been the domain of some Edwardian squire, such was the grandeur of the place. Rather, it had been purpose-built as a military hospital, the largest and best in the Portsmouth area.

Sixteen-year-old Naina Beaven was to find her world turned upside down on that fateful D-Day afternoon. A young nurse at the hospital, she had been buried away in the accounts department when her nursing commandant, Miss Hobbs, told her she was urgently required in the wards. The accounts could wait for another day: right now, men's lives were at stake. Puzzled and not a little alarmed, Miss Beaven rushed out to see what was wrong.

The hospital was a veritable rabbit warren of corridors and it took her some minutes to reach the hospital wards. 'All the corridors were laid end to end with stretchers. Lorries were coming up from the dockyard so quickly that there wasn't room for all the wounded.' It was mid-afternoon and the place was full to bursting with injured soldiers who had been brought back to England. Only the most seriously wounded were given beds. The rest had to make do with the floor.

For a teenage girl only recently out of nursing school, the sight of so many injured young men was deeply shocking. But Miss Beaven had a steady nerve and practical hands. When told to start cleaning the injured, she set to work without further ado. 'Many of them were filthy' – they had soiled themselves – 'so the main

357

thing to do was to clean them and bed-bath them.' She was too inexperienced to tend to their wounds and was told that if she cut away a battledress 'and found something bad' then she should call for the sister.

Miss Beaven was struck by two things. First, the men spoke not a word: it was as if they had lost their tongues. Second, they looked utterly drained by what they had been through, 'so completely exhausted they didn't care one jot what happened to them'. She tried to exchange a few words of encouragement, but they simply stared back at her blank-eyed. 'As I worked with these poor exhausted soldiers, I was thinking, How long will this go on? If I could come back tomorrow and the next day, would I still be doing this?' She had a horrible suspicion that the answer would be yes.

She was still scrubbing them down when she was told to go and report to the staff matron, along with her friend, Win. The matron in question was forthright and blunt-of-tongue, conforming to all the matronly stereotypes. 'You know we have a lot of German prisoners,' she snapped at the two girls. Miss Beaven nodded meekly: she and Win had just been told that Queen Alexandra's was also receiving wounded Germans.

'Well, a lot of people won't work with them,' said matron. 'They are either walking out or refusing to work with them. Will you do what you're doing, for *them*?'

Miss Beaven was tongue-tied. In truth, she didn't know what to say. Neither did Win. Their silence irritated the matron, who had no time for vacillation. 'Hurry up and make up your minds,' she scolded, 'because if you're not going to do it, I'll try somebody else.'

Win turned to her friend and said her mind was made up. 'Oh come on, Naina. My Eddie is out there and if somebody said they wouldn't clean him up, Mum would feel terrible.'

Her words had the desired effect. Miss Beaven agreed to help, partly because she couldn't bear the thought of the senior nurse telling people that 'one of my girls wouldn't even give a prisoner a cup of water.' She was nevertheless filled with trepidation at the thought of going to nurse the enemy. She suggested to Win that they stay side by side 'and protect each other' if anything untoward were to happen.

The two of them walked across to the large Nissen hut in which the wounded prisoners were being held. Miss Beaven noticed that the hut was guarded by four armed soldiers, 'two on the outer doors who had rifles and two on the inner door with pistols'. The soldiers searched the two girls, checked their papers and then turned them over to the sister in charge.

'You know what you are here for, don't you?' she said briskly. 'Get on with it.'

Miss Beaven stepped into the gloom and got her first glimpse of the enemy. It was a moment she would never forget. 'They were filthy dirty, absolutely stinking dirty, very white, unhealthy, unwhole-some looking people.' A childhood filled with propaganda had done much to dehumanize all Germans. Now, her worst fears and preju-dices were confirmed. 'They had the dirty pallor of tramps, a horrible, yellowy-grey unhealthy look.' The atmosphere, and stench, were even worse than in the British-occupied wards. All the men had a faraway look in their eyes, the glazed emptiness of the vanquished, and no one spoke. 'I hardly heard a word, just the odd grunt or the odd word; nobody had any brightness or any life.'

As she set to work scrubbing their filthy skin, she kept having to remind herself that 'one of the rules of the Red Cross is that you are there to help everybody.' A few of the men seemed grateful to be washed. Some even offered her a weak smile when she gave them milk or water. She couldn't get over how young they were. 'Some of them were only kids, they weren't really much older than me.' Some, indeed, were younger.

As she passed her afternoon in a never-ending cycle of undressing the injured, she felt sure she was doing the right thing. She would later feel proud to have overcome her prejudices. 'I'm really glad I didn't refuse to help these men,'[1] she said.

If the medical situation in Portsmouth was more or less under control, the same could not be said for the situation across the English Channel where battlefront doctors were toiling in situations of extreme duress. Treadwell Ireland had first set foot on Omaha Beach some five hours earlier, coming ashore in the same landing craft as Ernest Hemingway. 'He was the only guy in a trench-coat. He was also wearing binoculars, which everyone else got rid of so the German snipers wouldn't think you were important.'[2]

A thirty-year-old physician with the Third Auxiliary Surgical Group, Ireland was part of a seven-strong experimental medical team whose task was to perform surgery on the battlefield. Only the boldest men had been considered for the job: it was, as one put it, 'a stout-hearted, high-spirited, red-blooded outfit'.[3] It was best suited to those with a death wish.

In his first few hours on the beach, surgery was out of the question. Ireland and his fellow medics were pinned down on the sand and under constant machine-gun fire. 'We all crawled east, towards Easy Red Beach. Eventually, we found ourselves below one of the reinforced concrete blockhouses.' Although he didn't know it at the time, this was WN62, the stronghold of Franz Gockel and his comrades. As the American troops advanced, so the Germans had fled for their lives, bringing a safety of sorts to this stretch of beach. By mid-afternoon, it was deemed safe for Ireland and his team to enter the stronghold. 'We took possession with a whoop and a holler,' but soon discovered that their optimism was misplaced. Their makeshift infirmary was squalid, filthy and had almost no natural light.

Their principal handicap was a lack of medical supplies: they had lost much of their equipment in the landing and had little except morphine, plasma and dressings, along with some penicillin. They nevertheless set to work in the near darkness, stitching wounds, extracting shrapnel and staunching blood. One limp soldier was carried in with 'a sucking chest wound' that was suffocating him. Each time he tried to breathe there was a sickening gurgling sound. The team rushed into action, performing emergency and life-saving surgery in the most extreme circumstances. 'While Finley inserted a needle into the man's chest to allow the excess air to escape and then gave plasma, one medic held a blanket over the opening to the pillbox and another held a lighted candle so we all could see.'[4]

This complex procedure was made all the harder by the fact that Ireland and his team of medics came under aerial attack from a lone Messerschmitt at that exact moment, with a huge bomb falling next to the entrance of the bunker. The blast was so powerful that it knocked Ireland off his feet 'and sent great clouds of sand billowing into the pillbox'. It could scarcely have happened at a worse moment. 'The wounded man moaned. The medics cursed. Plasma bottles were upset, sand seeped under dressings, blankets were blown away.'

The bunker was soon overflowing with casualties carried down from the cliff-tops above. There were men with suppurating wounds, with severe burns, with lacerated skin. There were no beds, nor even many stretchers. The wounded were simply piled up on the filthy concrete floor. 'For the most part they lay there very still. Some had rude splints; others had bulky, bloody dressings; the majority had neither splints nor dressings.' Their gaping wounds were half concealed by 'layers of ill-smelling, gas-impregnated clothes and heavy sticky combat layers'. Flies – large and noisy summer bluebottles – penetrated even the darkest corner of the bunker.

Ireland had always been expecting the worst, but this was the stuff of nightmares. 'Prostrate forms were everywhere. Dead and dying lay next to those who still might live.' Some were screaming, some moaning. A few simply whimpered in pain. 'The pillbox became the focal point of all the suffering on the invasion beach.'[5] Amid the horror, there were moments that were almost surreal. One dying soldier clutched at Ireland and heaved himself upright before collapsing into his arms murmuring that 'life would have been very pleasant with my wife'.[6] He then sang a line of 'I'll Be Seeing You', softly and serenely, before falling back dead.

If the situation inside WN62 was ghastly, it was even worse on the Easy Green sector of beach, just 1,500 yards to the west. Here, twenty-year-old medic Alfred Eigenberg lacked even the most rudimentary supplies and found himself using whatever expedients he could, 'such as crude splints and medical procedures not known in any text'. Although homespun, they worked. They included 'pinning a thigh that had been laid open from groin to kneecap with common safety pins' and 'tying off a large artery in the foot with the man's shoelaces'.

While some were saved, many more were not. Eigenberg's worst case was that of a teenage soldier whose helmet had been half-shredded into his brain. 'We did everything we could to get the helmet off and stop the bleeding, but we couldn't move it.' The gruesome sight shocked even the medics and came to haunt Eigenberg for the rest of his life. Even many years later, he could 'still remember his screams as they carried him away'.[7]

Head wounds were always terrible, especially if caused by shrapnel. One injured Ranger was put in the care of a young American medic named Vincent DelGiudice, who noticed blood dripping from under the man's helmet. When he eased the helmet from his head, he saw that a shard of shrapnel had cracked open his cranium. 'As the helmet came off, his brain oozed out of the laceration that was created.' DelGuidice was horrified. 'I grabbed an 8 x 8 sterile gauze, put it over his head and in my naiveté tried to push the brain back into his skull.' He then administered a shot of morphine and shouted over to the medical officer, Dr Walsh. The doctor took one look at the fellow and said 'there was nothing more that I could do for him and that he would probably die very shortly.'[8] He was correct: the Ranger was dead within the hour.

While Alfred Eigenberg and his medics struggled to save injured men down on the beach, the first battle-weary troops were starting to filter into Vierville-sur-Mer, one of the larger villages atop the bluffs. As they picked through the rubble-strewn streets, they were greeted by a sight that left them blinking in disbelief. General Norman 'Dutch' Cota, the fifty-one-year-old bruiser who had first ordered them up the cliffs, was standing in the centre of town 'calmly twirling his pistol on his finger'. He looked like an outlaw cowboy who had ridden in from the Wild West. 'Where the hell have you been, boys?'[9] were his first words of greeting.

His men faced little opposition as they filtered through Vierville, for the German defenders had slipped away and the Americans were able rapidly to consolidate their hold on the place. There were a few terrible sights to be confronted as they made their way through the streets. One young sergeant stumbled across a fellow American whose belly had been ripped open by shrapnel. 'Help me! Help me!' he was hollering at the top of his voice, but there was little the sergeant could do. 'His intestines were kind of hanging and running out through his fingers.'[10] He died shortly afterwards.

For these exhausted men, the capture of Vierville felt like a second Yorktown. It may have been a one-horse, one-cart sort of place, but it was a key prize and it had only fallen into their hands after a desperate fight up the bluffs.

While some of the men dug themselves into defensive positions, a few Rangers continued their drive westwards along the coastal road that led towards Pointe du Hoc. Their D-Day assignment was to relieve James Rudder's beleaguered men still holding out in their precarious cliff-top foxholes. But they soon found their passage blocked. The Germans had dug themselves in on both sides of the road and were spitting fire at anyone who dared to approach.

It was the first hint of the troubles that were to plague Allied forces for weeks to come. Normandy's characteristic *bocage* terrain, a landscape of submerged lanes and tangled hedgerows, was a defenders' dream and an attackers' nightmare. 'Like nothing any of us had ever seen before,' thought John Raaen, one of those in that advance band of Rangers. The hedges were 'old, gnarled and heavy, with huge roots holding the mounds together'. They were to prove a formidable obstacle on the road to Pointe du Hoc. 'The Germans dug holes in the back side of these natural barriers and hollowed out small machine-gun nests and fighting positions.'[11]

News that the coastal road was firmly in enemy hands came close to spoiling Norman Cota's day. He immediately set off to see the German defences for himself. The Rangers were astonished when they saw him approach. 'Up the road from Vierville, alone and smoking a cigar, came General Cota.' He looked as if he were taking a stroll through the backlands of his native Massachusetts.

He asked what was holding them up.

'*Snipers*,' hissed one of the men.

'Snipers? There aren't any snipers here!'

A shot rang out and just missed his head. 'Well maybe there are.' He ordered the men to dig in for the evening, creating the outermost frontier of the Omaha beachhead, while he headed back to the beach in order to help knock out the remaining coastal bunkers. It was not long before the last German troops holding the Vierville draw were flushed from their positions. It was a defining moment of the day, for it enabled tanks and armoured vehicles to join the battle on the coastal heights.

Cota was in his element as he tramped up and down the draw chewing heavily on yet another cigar.

'Come down here you sons-of-bitches,'[12] he roared at two terrified German prisoners as he once again twirled his .45 into its now familiar spin.

Not surprisingly, they did exactly as ordered.

★

The defence of Vierville was entrusted to Colonel Canham, the Himmler lookalike with frightening eyes and a terrifying tongue. His day had hitherto been taken up with a series of attacks on German strongpoints. Now, he switched roles from attack to defence. It was imperative that his men hold on to Vierville, for if it was lost to a German counter-attack then the entire western end of Omaha Beach could also be lost.

Although his men were in control of the village, the situation was far from stable. One of the Rangers, Carl Weast, was crouched at a crossroads on the edge of the village when a German dispatch rider came spinning towards them on his bicycle. Seeing the soldiers, but not realizing they were American, he dismounted and walked towards them. Not until he was twenty yards away did he realize that he had walked into a trap.

He should have surrendered, or at the very least kept stock-still. But his nerves were such that he started fumbling in his pockets and giving the impression that he was reaching for his pistol. It was an error that cost him dear. Weast and his men were on to him in seconds and 'he must have been hit with about nine or ten rounds real quick.' The man collapsed on to the road, bleeding profusely but just about alive. 'The blood gathered under his face and he was breathing into it,' producing a sickening slurping sound. 'It was nerve-wracking as hell,' said Weast, and so unpleasant that one of his comrades decided to put the man out of his misery. 'He went over to the guy and he put a bullet through the back of his head.'

Colonel Canham had displayed considerable panache in fighting his way into Vierville; now, he needed a command post to match that panache. There was never any question as to which property he would choose. Château de Vaumicel was a sprawling country mansion with a conical turret and a stack of chimneys. It was the sort of creaking pile that would once have belonged to a hereditary Normandy landowner. Canham had no claim on hereditary rights, but he had become a landowner of sorts and decided to make the château his own. There was only one drawback, as Weast was quick to point out. 'It was full of Germans.'

Weast feared that he and his comrades would have to fight their way from room to room, flushing enemy soldiers from the salons, cellars and panelled corridors. But as he studied the façade through his field glasses, he saw that the German occupants were in the process of checking out. 'Lo and behold, these Germans came out of the château and they formed up in a column of twos and they got an old two-wheeled horse buggy with wounded in it, and they were pulling it with manpower, two guys shoving and two guys pulling.' Alarmingly but excitingly, they were heading directly towards Weast and his buddy Blacky Morgan, who was crouched in the same ditch with his automatic rifle.

'So we wait until they get real close, I'm saying maybe ten yards, and we step out into the road with our weapons pointed at them.' Not for the first time that day, the temptation was to shoot. 'With this sort of situation,' said Weast, 'what the hell do you do with prisoners?' But he was still feeling queasy from the shooting of the cyclist, whose corpse was lying nearby in a heap of blood-drenched rags. He and Blacky Morgan took the Germans prisoner, escorting them to a holding area in a nearby orchard.

By late afternoon, Colonel Canham was safely installed in the château, a grandiose headquarters for a fiefdom that stretched just a few hundred yards in either direction. Carl Weast had never liked Canham, but he didn't envy his predicament as commander that afternoon. 'Word had gotten round that nothing more was coming in from the beaches and what had come in was either sunk or stalled on the beach, so you can damn well imagine the mental anguish this poor bastard was enduring.'[13]

Fear and exhaustion had sapped the last drop of energy from most of the men who had survived the climb up the Omaha cliff-tops. They had fought since dawn, dragging their kit up the bluffs and then fighting again when they reached the top. Most were in desperate need of rest, but there were a hardy few who showed such reserves of strength that their comrades could only look on in wonder.

One such battlefield giant was Jimmie 'Punk' Monteith, a twenty-six-year-old mechanical engineer who had landed on the beach that morning equipped with sparkling eyes, a quiff of hair and a deep reserve of courage. Hitherto, he had displayed no outward signs of being a hero-in-waiting and his curriculum vitae made no mention of his concrete nerves.

But now, those nerves went on display for all to see. As his company attempted to capture Grand Hameau, at the eastern end of the Omaha beachhead, they found themselves advancing headlong into a nest of machine guns.

'The Germans yelled to us to surrender,' recalled one in Monteith's company, but surrender was not a word in young Jimmie's lexicon. His answer, when it came, was delivered with mathematical precision. He 'moved toward the sound of voices and launched a rifle grenade at them from twenty yards'. In one thunderous explosion, he knocked out their first machine-gun position. When two more machine guns opened up, he crawled forward on his belly, sneaking up on the gun and hand-delivering a couple of grenades. A fourth machine-gun position now opened up. This time, a covert attack was impossible. Undaunted, he 'crossed a two-hundred-yard stretch of open field under fire to launch rifle grenades'. Another gun was silenced.

But Jimmie Monteith was living on borrowed time. Bravery came with a price that day and he was to pay dearly for his heroism. As he attempted to knock out the final machine gun, he was cut down by a burst of fire. The soldiers under his command were distraught to see him fall at Grand Hameau's final fence. He was, said one, 'a man I had the utmost admiration and respect for'.[14]

General Eisenhower agreed. When he learned of Monteith's actions, he awarded him a posthumous Medal of Honor. It was the very least he deserved. Jimmie Monteith's actions enabled the rest of his company to force their way into Grand Hameau. A much valued life had been lost, but the Omaha beachhead had been made a great deal more secure, with fortified defensive positions at both its eastern and western ends.

The treacherous cliff-tops fell into American hands inch by agonizing inch. Each house that was cleansed, each strongpoint attacked, required a surfeit of bravery by men who had been living on borrowed time since dawn. Joe Dawson and John Spalding were among the boldest of the bold, a duo of stalwarts who had scaled the cliffs together before launching a twin-pronged assault on the strategically vital village of Colleville. This, like Grand Hameau, was situated at the eastern end of Omaha.

Fighting from house to house was dangerous and claimed many

lives, but they eventually swept the village of enemy soldiers. Once this was done, their most urgent task was to contact the battleships anchored offshore, alerting them to the news that Colleville had been captured. The Allied ships had already blasted enemy soldiers out of Vierville, firing five-inch 38-calibre shells into German positions. It was only a matter of time before they would turn their guns on Colleville.

Joe Dawson tried to get a wireless message through, but there was never any response. Again and again he tried, increasingly anxious, but still the wireless merely crackled and coughed. None of the radio sets was working and there was no contact with the ships. He and his men were caught in a deadly trap.

On board USS *Harding*, Commander George Palmer had received precious little news from the shore. His gunners had already fired hundreds of rounds on to the bluffs, hitting dozens of German targets. He encouraged them to fire at anything that moved.

The *Harding's* executive officer, William Gentry, described Palmer as full of 'autistic energy and nervous tension'.[15] Now, the commander intended to focus all that energy on destroying Colleville. He had no idea that the village was already in American hands.

The ship's guns were cranked into position and primed for firing. Below decks, in the magazine, Horace Flack was preparing his ears for yet another thunderous attack. Life below decks was 'like being inside a drum',[16] for the roar of the guns reverberated through the ship each time they fired.

The firing order came from Commander Palmer. 'Open fire again for two minutes on Colleville church . . . spread fire around area.'[17] It was a sight to behold when she finally let rip, unleashing seventy-three rounds in her first salvo and following it with two further salvos, all of them fired from a distance of less than 4,000 yards. No one on board realized that they were aiming directly at Joe Dawson and his comrades.

These haggard soldiers were to find themselves hit by a devastating barrage of fire. 'It swept the town from one end to the other,' pulverizing homes and spinning men into the air. There was no escape from the naval shells. When the dust finally settled, the full extent of the destruction was revealed. The Allied bombardment had caused 'a severe number of casualties and a most tragic loss'. Sixty-four men who had survived the battle for Colleville had been killed by friendly fire.

Joe Dawson was beside himself with rage. 'I was angered by it,' he fumed, 'angered beyond all measure.'[18] It was such a terrible waste of human life.

PART VIII
Win or Lose

As troops pushed inland, two vast temporary and portable Mulberry Harbours were being towed in sections across the English Channel. These were essential if the Allies were to land the 2 million troops stationed in England, along with huge quantities of supplies, weapons and tanks.

One of these prefabricated harbours was destined for Omaha Beach, the other for Arromanches: this latter town became a key afternoon target for the British troops who landed on Gold. Overlord also called for the capture of Caen and Bayeux, together with their roads, railways and infrastructure: by mid-afternoon, it seemed doubtful if such ambitious goals could be met.

Meanwhile, the Germans were quick to spot a potentially fatal weakness in the Allied beachhead – a four-mile gap separating Sword Beach and Juno Beach. The 20th Panzer Division sought to exploit this gap, moving swiftly north towards the coast. If successful, Rommel's panzers could cut the eastern end of the beachhead into two isolated zones.

German forces also sought to stop the Allies wresting control of the high ground to the east of Bénouville and Ranville bridges. As the Allied commandos rapidly advanced, the Germans faced a stiff fight if they were to prevent these elite troops from moving into commanding defensive positions.

When the French living in the coastal zone realized that this was indeed the invasion, and not just a raid, many fled inland. It would be many weeks before they could return to their bombed-out towns and villages.

Wireless operators were trained to direct naval gunfire from the front line of battle, but their sets often malfunctioned. By the afternoon, many operators were overcome by exhaustion.

25

Frontier Fighting

THE LATE AFTERNOON sunshine was sapping the energies of the men pushing relentlessly through the fields. They found themselves sweating profusely under the weight of their equipment, weapons and packs. Some, to the incredulity of their commanding officers, paused to brew up mugs of tea on their portable stoves. But most did not halt for many hours and it was not until mid-afternoon that one young private, Dennis Bowen, stopped for long enough to take his first swig of water.

The great thrust inland from Gold Beach took the form of three sweeping arrows, one of which was thrusting inland to the Bayeux–Caen highway and another pushing towards the city of Bayeux itself. A third arrow was advancing along the coast, with the goal of capturing the towns of Arromanches and Port-en-Bessin.

Arromanches was one of the key targets in this sector of beach-head, for its offshore waters had been selected for the first of the planned Mulberry Harbours. If the town was not prised from enemy troops, this giant floating harbour could not be installed. That, in turn, meant that millions of tons of stockpiled military hardware could not be delivered to Normandy.

The advance on Arromanches proved tough going and by the time Lieutenant Edward Wright and his soldiers from the Royal Hampshires reached the outskirts of town they were feeling bloodied and bruised. Wright's battalion had lost 200 men, some killed, some badly injured. Those who limped into the outskirts of Arromanches were told to dig themselves in while they awaited reinforcements.

While they were doing this they witnessed a scene that might have dropped straight from an Ealing comedy. As the men scooped a ditch through the garden of one of the larger villas on the edge of town, Lieutenant Wright found himself being dressed down by a female voice of such haughtiness that it could only have belonged to an upper-class English matriarch – one who had inexplicably avoided being interned by the Germans.

'I demand to speak to the officer in charge,' snapped the lady in question.

Wright asked why, only to find himself at the end of an angrily wagging finger.

'Your men are digging up my flowerbeds and making a whole mess of the place,' she said, 'and it's quite unnecessary. I demand that they stop.'

Wright could scarcely believe his ears. He had spent the last nine hours fighting a bloody advance towards Arromanches and now he was being admonished for damaging a flowerbed. Amused and bemused in equal measure, he expressed his astonishment at the lady's outburst. But this only poured fuel on to her fire: she gave him a second dressing down.

In different circumstances, or in a different world, Wright might have meekly obeyed. She, after all, was his social superior. But after his experiences that day he simply lost his rag. 'I told her very curtly that I was not going to have any of this nonsense and I asked if her house had a cellar.' When she nodded, he offered her a most helpful piece of advice. 'If you don't want to be shot, go down there until I tell you if you can come out.'[1]

She stormed off in a fit of pique and disappeared underground, just as he had suggested. Within a few hours, Wright and his men continued their advance into Arromanches, leaving behind one crushed flowerbed and one disgruntled English lady. Only much later did Wright realize that he had forgotten to inform her that she could leave her hiding place.

For many young men fighting their way inland from Gold Beach, that June afternoon was one of constant fear. Ambush and death could lie around any corner. But for a few, the fighting was a time of sheer exhilaration. Donald Gardner, a twenty-three-year-old sergeant in 47 Royal Marine Commando, belonged to that select group for whom D-Day was the adrenalin-rush of their lives. Gone was the rulebook, gone were the petty strictures of life back in England. He and his comrades were young, hot-blooded and hungry for action. Bristling with weaponry and carrying backpacks filled with menace, they felt invincible – and none more so than Gardner himself. A tough pugilist with an angry scowl and a disdain for death, he was quite open about his intentions of killing as many Germans as possible. He had his reasons: his best friend, Don Skipp, had been killed in an air raid.

'I was bloody minded,' he admitted, 'and was determined to avenge Don's death.' His advance towards Port-en-Bessin was to involve considerable bloodshed.

Armed like bandits and with their faces smeared with black grease, he and his six angry comrades could have been raised from the depths of hell. When Gardner looked at himself in the mirror, he confessed to looking 'fearful and awesome'. He was borrowing an old trick of psychological warfare: scare the living daylights out of your enemy.

Now, as his gang raced headlong along the coast to Port-en-Bessin, they did so in a welter of fire and blood, using overwhelming force to destroy each enemy machine-gun post they encountered. High explosives and smoke grenades were tossed into pillboxes, then Gardner and his band would advance 'firing from the hip' like fugitive outlaws. The more violent their behaviour, the more confident they felt. When one German tried to make his escape, Gardner fired his tommy gun straight into the man's back, hitting a grenade in his backpack.

'Good shot!' roared one of the lads.

It was indeed, for 'it blew his head off'. They rushed forward in order to steal the man's weaponry. What they found was worse than any abattoir. 'The bloke's head and bits were plastered over the gun, bits of flesh etc. We flicked it off, collected bullets, loaded ourselves up.' A further four Germans were shot before they pushed onwards into the trajectory of the late afternoon sun.

'I wasn't scared of anything,' bragged Gardner. Indeed he was in his element. His little gang had been close mates for years. 'We lived together and played together.' Now, they killed together.

One of them, McKenna, had a sniper's accuracy when firing his rifle. He spent the afternoon tracking down unsuspecting Germans. One enemy soldier saw the glint of this rifle and tried to flee on horseback.

'Bet you can't get him,' wagered one of the band.

Bang. 'McKenna upped and got him,' said Gardner.

They were not interested in taking prisoners, although at one point they found themselves inadvertently capturing several dozen in one swoop. 'If a bloke as much as coughed, he would have got a bullet through his neck.'

Gardner himself was nonchalant about death. 'One either lived or didn't live.' He always preferred shooting to asking questions. 'We took no chances.'

As they neared their goal late that afternoon, they grew even more bullish about killing Germans. 'Our simple aim was to get where we were going and knock them off. We were so confident that we were sure we'd get through anything.'[2]

By 7 p.m. they were in possession of Hill 72 that overlooked Port-en-Bessin. Their late arrival at the beach had delayed their advance along the coast, meaning that they could not attack the port that night. But Gardner vowed that it would be in their hands by the following day. It was – and he was awarded a Military Medal for his part in its capture.

The central thrust inland from Gold had been no less relentless. It was led by the men of the Green Howards, with a machine-gun battalion of the Cheshire Regiment accompanying them in the vanguard. Among its officers was a flamboyant young captain with a suitably flamboyant name: Peter Lawrence de Carteret Martin was a blond-haired, blue-eyed twenty-four-year-old from colonial India whose youthful good looks belied the fact that he had accumulated a world of experience on the battlefield. He had fought through France in 1940, survived Dunkirk and rampaged his way through Cyprus, Palestine, Iraq and Syria. He had twice been captured by the Germans (at El Alamein) and twice made his escape. He had also helped spearhead the Allied landings in Sicily, being one of the first into Messina. His military curriculum vitae read like a bullet-point list of all the great battles of the war in the west. But he was not yet ready to hang up his rifle. As a company commander in the Cheshire Regiment, he was intent on thrusting deep into Normandy that day. By late afternoon, his troop was five miles inland at a village called

Esquay-sur-Seulles. Here, they were told to dig in while they awaited supplies.

But Captain Martin had tasted action and was keen for more. After convincing himself that 'reconnaissance was seldom wasted', he proposed to the staff driver of his jeep that they push yet deeper into enemy territory. The driver advanced cautiously into Rucqueville, which was 'absolutely dead quiet', prompting Captain Martin to suggest that they head for the main Caen–Bayeux highway. In successfully doing so, they had reached one of the most important goals of that afternoon. The road, like the town before, was completely deserted. 'Not a sign of a soul or anything.'

Captain Martin was by now in highly dangerous territory. The farmland here was completely uncharted, as far as the enemy defences were concerned, and carried a high risk of ambush. Yet he was an irrepressible adventurer and knew from the explorers of old that there was treasure to be found in unexplored lands. With this in mind, he turned to his driver with a mischievous smile.

'What about popping down to Bayeux and liberating it?' He was only half joking.

The driver might have been forgiven for declining to take part in such a dangerous jaunt, but he knew his place in the military hierarchy and displayed dutiful deference to someone of superior rank.

'Good idea, sir,' he said with a nervous smile, and then slammed his foot hard on the accelerator. He, like Captain Martin himself, was hoping that the men of the 56th Brigade would have already reached the outskirts of town.

But it was not to be. As they approached the first buildings of Bayeux, they were halted in their tracks. 'A Frenchman standing on a corner whistled through his teeth and said, "*Boche! Boche!*" and pointed down the road.'[3] Bayeux was still firmly in German hands. Even Captain Martin decided that discretion was the better part of valour. He ordered his driver to perform a swift U-turn, an order that was obeyed with unusual alacrity. As the two of them retreated to Esquay-sur-Seulles, they were machine-gunned from the air by one of the hundreds of American fighters flying overhead. 'We managed to get into the ditch just in time and the only damage to the jeep was a bullet through one of the tyres.'

It was fortunate that the driver had packed a spare. 'We did the quickest wheel change that I think has ever been done outside of a Grand Prix meeting and got back to join the headquarters.'[4] The liberation of Bayeux would have to wait a few more hours.

The biggest problem of the day was with wireless communications: it very nearly proved fatal, not just to Gold Beach but to the entire military operation. Such was the opinion of an observation officer named Richard Gosling, an eccentric Old Etonian who had been one of the first men ashore at Gold. He had always treated modern technology with a healthy degree of scepticism: it was the reason why he had landed with a Victorian firearm tucked into his belt. 'I had a wonderful old revolver which had belonged to my Uncle Seymour in the Boer War.' He fired several shots with this relic, but did not hang around long enough to discover if it worked the same deadly magic as it had done in the Transvaal.

Gosling may have had a penchant for vintage weapons but he was no Luddite. He had a degree in mechanical science from Cambridge University and knew only too well that technology could be a boon (at its best) and a disaster (at its worst). And now he sensed a disaster in the making. For the better part of the day he had been struggling with his portable 68 Wireless Set and accompanying telescopic aerial. He desperately needed to relay messages between troops inland and the gunners on board the battleships at anchor offshore. With correct coordinates, they could knock out the smaller concrete bunkers that were proving murderous to the advancing infantry.

But as with so many wireless operators that afternoon, Gosling found that his radio stubbornly refused to work. 'We were trying all the time, on three wireless sets, to send messages, shouting, calling, trying to get through to regimental headquarters.' He kept changing frequencies, adjusting his headphones and shouting even louder into the static. He had the sort of plummy baritone that befitted his Eton and Cambridge upbringing, yet no amount of fine elocution could help him now. 'We had these wretched headphones and all you could hear was this high-pitched whistling from ships and from tanks and a lot of it coming from the German wireless sets and airplanes and naval craft.'

It was deeply frustrating. He and his team had been assured that technology was the key to victory on D-Day; that the hundreds of radio sets issued to observation officers on each of the five beaches would prove the clincher in any finely poised battle situation. Yet the very opposite was the case. Seawater and the damp maritime air played havoc with such highly sensitive equipment and radio communications were to prove all but impossible. Gosling flung down his headphones in despair. 'We were never rehearsed to expect this,' he said. 'We thought we had radios and could talk to anyone, but we couldn't at all. We got no news of how the battle was progressing.'[5] It was a disastrous situation.

But on the rare occasions when the communications did work, they were used to deadly effect. Young Harry Siggins was a telegraphist aboard HMS *Ajax*, anchored off Gold Beach. He had just started eating a corned beef sandwich when a wireless message came through from an RAF spotter plane flying above the countryside inland from the coast.

'Enemy pillboxes, grid reference so-and-so and so-and-so.' Such was the message he received. He passed the reference to the gunner, who immediately fired a ranging salvo.

'You're too high, you're too high, come back fifty, come back a hundred.'

Siggins once again relayed the message and the gunner fired a second shot.

'Now up twenty, now up twenty.'

He prepared to fire again, this time with the exact coordinates.

'A turret ready! B turret ready! X turret ready, sir! Y turret ready. Firing gongs: Gong! Gong! Gong! Gong!'

There was a deafening roar. '*Phrmmmm!* Off the shells went.'

Seconds later, Siggins received a new message from the spotter plane.

'That's it! That's it! Give them the lot! Give them the lot! Give them the lot! Marvellous! They're running, they're running, they're coming out.'

With the aid of the transmissions from the spotter plane, Siggins found himself spending his afternoon in an exhilarating turkey shoot. Pillboxes, bunkers and groups of enemy soldiers were all targeted by the ship's big guns.

'There's tanks! There's tanks! Tanks in a field. They're in a hedge. Take this bearing.'

These may well have been the tanks of a young lieutenant colonel named Karl Meyer, who had just launched an abortive panzer attack on the advancing troops close to Bazenville.

Siggins noted the bearing and the guns roared once again.

'You've straddled them. You've straddled them now. Now, twenty this way and thirty that.'

If they were indeed Meyer's tanks, then the shots hit with devastating effect. Meyer himself was killed and his force was annihilated. His afternoon offensive ground to a bloody halt.

When there was finally a pause, Harry Siggins returned to his half-eaten corned beef sandwich. He couldn't determine if it was because of battle-hunger or the exhilaration of causing so much destruction, but the meat seemed to have transformed itself into something altogether more delicious. 'Ah,' he said to his comrades in the wireless room. 'It tastes like chicken!'[6]

Few German soldiers stationed inland had any grasp of the seriousness of the situation that late afternoon. The elite SS tank commander Kurt 'Panzer' Meyer was to display his characteristic arrogance when brought news of what was taking place. 'Little fish,' he snapped. 'We'll throw them back into the sea in the morning.'[7]

But one of his SS comrades, Peter Hansmann, was rather more cautious. Equipped with an eight-wheeled armoured car, a pair of field glasses and a desire to see the landings with his own eyes, he had spent much of that day in search of information. And now, standing on the high ground above Juno Beach, he got the shock of his life. 'An endless front of ships, extending from the cliffs of Arromanches to the horizon east of the Orne estuary, all coming towards us!' In that moment, he suddenly felt the precariousness of the German army in France. 'I wish I could call all the Generals up to Adolf Hitler and say: "Get here quickly – before it's too late! Anything that can still fight; get it here! The fastest, strongest divisions here! The Air Force – where are they now? Get here! The Navy . . . where are they? They must get here."'[8]

He was right to panic, for the Canadians at Juno Beach had been pouring ashore in huge numbers and in their wake came an eye-boggling number of jeeps and tanks. Leading from the front was Elliot Dalton, one of the pair of competitive brothers who had thundered ashore that morning. Unlike brother Charles, Elliot had escaped being injured on the beach and was now storming inland with his men from the Queen's Own Rifles. Their goal was a mound of high ground known prosaically as Hill 70, close to the village of Anguerny. Whoever controlled this hill controlled the surrounding countryside.

Pushing inland with Dalton was Bob Rae, one of his intelligence officers, who was equipped with a stash of weaponry and 'an unusually keen pair of eyes'. But Rae didn't need keen eyes to tell him that the Canadians were sweeping all before them. 'Our two main axes of advance were clogged with soldiers on foot, carriers, tanks, half-tracks, self-propelled guns and many weird and wonderful vehicles.' The Germans had put up a strong defence in the coastal towns, but once their front line was smashed the troops inland were capitulating after short fire-fights.

Rae had observed many shocking sights since landing that morning, but none was as shocking as beholding wave after wave of captured Germans. 'Very unprepossessing examples of the so-called Master Race. Dirty, dusty, ragged and dejected, with unkempt hair and unshaven faces.' He thought that many of them looked like half-starved children, until he realized that that was exactly what they were. 'Short or lean hungry scarecrows with here and there the fresh, downy cheeks of boys, 14 and 15.'[9]

Over a wide front the Canadians were pushing inland and one by one a succession of villages fell into their hands: Banville, Reviers, Creully and Basly. There were dangers lurking in the fast-ripening fields of wheat and Bob Rae's unit found safety in speed. 'Our driver needed no urging,' he said, 'and we fairly screamed across the open ground with Captain Weir's luxuriant moustache streaming behind in the slipstream.' When the first of the armoured vehicles finally reached Hill 70, they found themselves in a duck-shoot with the enemy. 'It was just like a shooting gallery,' thought Robert Grant. 'They were going across in front of us. It was a great initiation – they weren't firing at us – we were firing at them.'[10] When the dust finally settled, the men found that Hill 70 was theirs for the taking.

On reaching the top, they took in the sweeping panorama. From their vantage point they could see as far as Carpiquet airfield, some five miles to the south, with its landing strip, hangars and outbuildings.

Had they looked more closely through their field glasses, they might have witnessed one of the more remarkable sights of that day. Thrusting towards the inland horizon, flattening wheat and crushing hedgerows, were three tanks of the 1st Hussars, hell-bent on breaking through to Carpiquet. In the lead tank, commanding from the front, was a grinning twenty-three-year-old from Ontario named Bill McCormack. He had joined the armoured division because 'he liked to be on the move'.¹¹ Now, he was moving into territory that was firmly in enemy hands. After blasting a passage through Creully, he headed further south, towards Camilly and onwards to Bretteville-l'Orgueilleuse. Here, McCormack and his crew got the chance to demonstrate how to deal with enemy vehicles. As a German scout car came bowling around a corner, McCormack's gunner raked it with machine-gun fire, while the tank's driver slammed the Sherman into the front of the vehicle, crushing it against a stone wall and causing it to burst into a fireball. The driver was instantly killed, ending his life sprawled over the windshield. His two passengers were thrown from the car and in a desperate state. One was twitching violently in the dirt as his muscles went into spasms. The other had been shot in the legs and both his feet were on fire. They were left on the road as a grim calling card from this advance guard of Canadians.

McCormack and his pioneers now pushed on even further south, swinging their tanks on to the Caen to Bayeux highway. In doing so, they were just a few miles from where Captain Peter Lawrence de Carteret Martin was engaged in his own little frontier adventure.

'*Come up! Come up!*'

McCormack repeatedly tried to call up support, realizing that he had a unique opportunity to capture Carpiquet airfield. But he was so far in advance of the wireless operators that his signal was never picked up. With the greatest reluctance, he realized that they had no choice other than to retreat from their forward position. His achievement had been nothing short of outstanding. He had pushed his tanks deeper into France than any other unit.

To those Germans who witnessed such bravado – men like the SS officer Peter Hansmann – it only confirmed their sense of doom.

Their last hope now lay in a bold German counter-attack. Despite the huge numbers of Allied troops already ashore, there were many weaknesses in the front line. One of these weaknesses was the gap between the Sword and Juno beachheads. If properly exploited, it could slice the Allied front in two.

It was time to send in the 20th Panzer Division.

The brilliant panzer commander Colonel Hermann von Oppeln-Bronikowski led the critical D-Day counter-attack. Charming and debonair, he thought Hitler's senior staff to be incompetent amateurs.

26

Panzer Attack

COLONEL LEOPOLD AUGUST Hermann von Oppeln-Bronikowski was having a bad day. His experiences as a panzer commander on the Eastern Front had taught him the value of speed. Strike hard and fast, that was how to fight with tanks. But speed was proving impossible right now, at the very time when it was most needed.

The colonel was one of the great panzer leaders of Nazi Germany, 'an exuberant, dashing, gay individual' with a noble Prussian pedigree that stretched back to the age of chivalry. War was in his blood: his dynasty had fought their way through central Europe for the better part of half a millennium and their coat of arms was bedecked with martial paraphernalia. At its centrepiece was a vicious-looking trapping hook that had been the family's weapon of choice against the Saracens.

Colonel von Oppeln-Bronikowski was known by everyone for his 'well-chiselled features, black hair, keen eyes and, frankly, enjoying the war for the thrills that he got'. He certainly looked the part, with impeccably oiled hair and an engaging smile. He also had 'the amazing ability of always looking clean and well pressed, even in the midst of a battle'. He had represented the Fatherland at the infamous 1936 Olympic Games (he won a gold medal in equestrian dressage) and had subsequently proved a genius at tank warfare, personally destroying twenty-five Russian tanks on the Eastern Front. Now, his regiment's precision guns had the ability to wreak carnage on the newly landed Allies.

But his morning offensive had been stalled by the OKW (Supreme Command) staff in Bavaria, much to his fury. He considered Hitler's senior staff to be incompetent amateurs who 'knew nothing of the problems of infantry or of panzers'. Nor, for that matter, did he 'give a damn about Hitler'.[1] Like so many noble-born Prussians in the military, he viewed the Führer as an ignorant upstart with little grasp of modern warfare. And now, when clear direction was most needed, the colonel found himself receiving wildly conflicting orders as to what to do with the 127 Panzer IV tanks of his panzer division. First, he was told to throw them against the British airborne forces around Bénouville Bridge, an operation that took considerable time to put into effect. No sooner were they on the move than the order was countermanded. The situation on the coast was deteriorating so fast that he was told to wheel his tanks northwards, with the aim of driving a wedge between the British troops on Sword Beach and the Canadians on Juno.

His panzers were to receive no additional support for their counter-attack. The Panzer Lehr division, stationed seventy-five miles outside Paris, was not to receive its marching orders until later that day. The 12th SS Panzer Division was similarly paralysed. Major-General Fritz Witt and his officers had spent much of the day at Château de la Guillerie awaiting instructions from Bavaria.

It therefore fell to Colonel von Oppeln-Bronikowski to reverse the fast-growing catastrophe. The stakes could scarcely have been higher, as General Erich Marcks, commander of the 84th Corps, was quick to point out when he addressed the colonel that afternoon. 'Oppeln,' he said, 'the future of Germany may very well rest on your shoulders. If you don't push the British back into the sea, we've lost the war.' Oppeln-Bronikowski snapped a crisp response. 'General, I intend to attack immediately.'[2]

But attacking the beachhead was no easy matter. To do so, his tanks first had to cross the River Orne. This in itself presented a major logistical feat, for the nearest bridges had either been destroyed or were in the hands of the British. The colonel had no option but to lead his column of tanks towards Caen in the hope that one or more of its bridges was still intact. And this is where his difficulties began.

Among those riding alongside him was a nineteen-year-old corporal, Werner Kortenhaus. Hitherto, Kortenhaus's attitude to the Allied landings had typified the headstrong arrogance of the panzer elite. There would be a sharp fight followed by a long bout of victorious celebration. 'We were pretty convinced that by the evening we would be back in our quarters.' But as his tank rumbled towards Caen, he got his first inkling that they were facing a formidable enemy. 'When we finally reached the top of the rise, we saw huge black clouds in the distance, over the city.' Caen was still aflame from the earlier bombing raid.

Kortenhaus was unexpectedly shaken. 'In that moment, I had the feeling that we were now actually in the war. It was then that I realized that there was no chance of being back in our quarters that night.'[3] He also realized how naïve he had been. If the Allies were prepared to sacrifice a city as big as Caen, they clearly had no intention of being driven back into the sea.

As the gigantic armoured convoy snaked its way through the city's outskirts, the scale of the destruction became all too evident. Entire buildings had been shattered by 1,000-pound bombs, blocking the streets with massive chunks of concrete. Crushed vehicles had been pitched into crazy angles and the ruins of shops were festooned with telephone wires. The dead lay mangled and exposed: many had yet to be taken away.

The convoy of tanks was soon joined by General Edgar Feuchtinger, commander of the 21st Panzer Division, who pitched up 'in his special bulletproof glass-domed combat car' equipped with machine guns and a radio. Feuchtinger had fought his way through the Great War and much of the current one and had participated in many highly destructive missions. Yet even he was taken aback by the scale of devastation in Caen. 'The town was a sight of sheer hell,' he said. 'Dead were lying everywhere, German soldiers, French civilians, uniformed German women auxiliaries.'[4] Oppeln-Bronikowski was no less shocked. As he surveyed the damage, he shook his head in despair. 'A complete shambles.'[5] They were the only words he could muster.

One of his junior staffers, Captain Herr, scouted ahead and discovered that a single bridge across the River Orne was still intact. But it was being 'ceaselessly bombed by fighter bombers' and anything that attempted to cross it risked being strafed from the air.

Captain Herr had two key qualities: cool-headedness and pragmatism. His first thought was to weigh up the odds of surviving the bridge crossing. 'I got out my watch and timed the intervals at which the bombers flew over.' His second was to study the flight pattern of each Allied plane. 'Once each machine had dropped its bomb-load, it pulled up in order to allow the next to make a run.' That gap between bomb-drops gave him the window of opportunity he needed. 'As coldly as if I had been timing athletics, I sent my tanks over the bridge.'

Survival was a matter of timing. *'On your marks! Ready! Go!'* His bellowed order was followed by a terrific roar as the engine of each tank clanked into gear. The vehicle would then lurch across the bridge in a choking swirl of dust and diesel fumes. All the while, Herr kept his eyes fixed on the falling bombs that followed each fly-pass. 'Amazingly, the bombs fell right and left, into the river, but none hit the bridge.'[6]

While Captain Herr painstakingly manoeuvred his fleet of tanks across the river, Colonel von Oppeln-Bronikowski was brought news that a second bridge across the River Orne was still intact at the village of Colombelles. Impatient for action and increasingly concerned about the time it would take for the entire column to cross that one bridge in Caen, he led his vehicles around the outskirts of the city towards Colombelles. It was safer than Captain Herr's approach, but no less time-consuming and it delayed the counter-attack yet further. The afternoon was well advanced by the time his armoured convoy regrouped, more or less unscathed, on the far side of Caen. Now, he had to thrust his mechanized army north-wards, across the rolling farmland that lay between Caen and the coast.

The convoy had scarcely left the ruins of Caen when he was witness to a most unexpected sight. A Wehrmacht paymaster and two German soldiers were stumbling along the road, 'drunk as pigs, their faces dirty and swaying from side to side'. As they lurched along, retreating from the coast, they didn't even notice the approaching tanks. Oppeln-Bronikowski cut the engine of his vehicle for a moment and was astonished to hear that they were singing *'Deutschland Über Alles'* 'at the top of their voices'. He found the scene both pitiful and 'tragically humorous': he felt sure that half of his men would have happily joined these drunken clowns, since most felt 'utter depression'[7] at fighting a war that was clearly lost.

Scarcely five miles now lay between his armoured convoy and the sea, but those five miles held a unique geological feature. Between the villages of Périers and Biéville, the chalky bedrock thrust itself upwards into a smoothly contoured escarpment that afforded a fine panorama over the surrounding pastureland, orchards and coastline. Colonel Oppeln-Bronikowski was only too aware of the value of such high ground. It was every tank-man's dream.

Before pushing forward, he gathered his forces in a glade near the hamlet of Lébisey, some three miles to the north of Caen. Here, he discussed tactics with his captains. Here, too, he was joined by the stiff-jointed General Erich Marcks. Such was the gravity of the situation that Marcks wanted to be there in person, yet he was in a highly agitated state. 'His normally composed features were twitching. He had only one thought in mind, to get into action, to attack.'[8] At a little after 5 p.m., he gave the nod to Oppeln-Bronikowski: the great panzer counter-attack could at long last commence.

As the tanks fired their engines, the air was once again filled with the stench of diesel. One by one their low-slung silhouettes emerged from the wooded glade, knocking unripe apples from the branches and crushing them into the dirt. The thrust towards the coast was to be twin-pronged. Oppeln-Bronikowski himself was to take twenty-five tanks towards the heights of Biéville, some two miles from their current position, while his most trusted captain, Wilhelm von Gottberg, would lead a further thirty-five tanks towards the high ground at Périers. From these two commanding positions, they would be able to wreak havoc on the Allied forces below.

Gottberg was a wise choice to lead the advance: although only twenty-nine years of age, he (like Oppeln-Bronikowski) was the scion of a distinguished Prussian military dynasty and had considerable experience of tank warfare. Oppeln-Bronikowski valued him so highly that he had persuaded him to cancel his overdue furlough (he should have been visiting his mother in Berlin) and remain in Normandy. 'Don't go, Gottberg,' he had said just a few days earlier. 'I think our time will soon be up.'[9]

Advancing with Oppeln-Bronikowski's battle group was Captain Herr, who had so carefully timed his tanks across the bridge at Caen. As they churned their way towards the high ground, they flattened the near-ripe corn and sent whirls of dust into the air, a telltale sign for Allied soldiers that something big was coming their way. It was not long before Captain Herr sighted a stationary column of Sherman tanks less than 600 metres away. He felt a sudden frisson of fear. 'It was really spooky. They just stood there and nothing moved.'[10] There was no one in sight. It was as if the entire position had been abandoned.

The truth was somewhat different. The soldiers of the Staffordshire Yeomanry were lying in wait and studying the advance of the panzers through their field glasses. So, too, were the troops manning the British anti-tank guns dug in between Périers and Biéville. The original goal of all these troops had been the city of Caen, but they had been delayed in getting off the beach and then halted altogether by the German counter-attack. Caen would have to wait for another day: checking the advance of the panzers was the most urgent priority.

Wilhelm von Gottberg was the first to move forward, thrusting his thirty-five tanks towards the ridge at Périers. He soon found his advance stalled. A thwacking explosion rocked his vehicles long before he got close to the high ground, triggering a series of powerful blasts. When it was safe to peer outside, he was aghast to see that ten of his tanks had been knocked out. He felt a deep sense of helplessness: there was nothing he could do other than 'curse the shortsightedness'[11] of his own command.

Colonel von Oppeln-Bronikowski was also grinding his way forward, aware that he and Captain Herr needed to get as close as possible to the Allied lines. Their Panzer IV tanks were equipped with 75mm long-barrel guns that were deadly when fired at a nearby target. But their maximum range was no more than a mile and a half, rendering them quite useless against the British long-range anti-tank guns.

The colonel sent five of his tanks ahead: they were to scout up a small incline in order to check the lie of the land. It proved a fatal error, for they were silhouetted against the sky, presenting the perfect target. 'The moment they reached the ridge, they were suddenly hit, one after the other, by British anti-tank fire.' Oppeln-Bronikowski had a soldier's respect for the enemy and would later admit that 'the British gunners were better by more than six hundred yards at firing.'[12]

He continued his advance with greater caution, but soon found himself facing a bruising assault from the British anti-tank guns. The Staffordshire troops opened up with everything they had, shredding metal and gouging craters. One shell exploded right next to Captain Herr's tank, ripping away the protective skirt that covered the tracks. 'It just swirled up and literally flew through the air.' Herr felt his second frisson of terror. 'I personally had always been frightened of being burned to death in the cockpit of my tank, so I lengthened the lead of my microphone so that I could sit behind the turret.' It was not a wise decision, but it was born of experience. 'I'd had such appalling experiences earlier, when I had to extract the [shrunken] bodies of comrades from tanks that had been burned out and put them in coffins that were as little as three-quarters of a metre long.'

It was not long before this fate came close. A second shell burst on to his tank, flinging a deadly wave of shrapnel through the air. He felt a searing pain in his lower half. 'I fell to the ground and had to feel around my knees with my hands to check that I still had my legs. Blood was pouring out of me.' He would survive, but he was seriously injured.

Colonel von Oppeln-Bronikowski knew he was outnumbered and outgunned. He also knew there was no hope of recapturing the high ground that lay between him and the coast. Dismayed and dejected, he turned to the blood-soaked Captain Herr and asked for advice. Herr shrugged. 'If you don't know, then how on earth should I know?'

Herr was in the process of radioing one of his comrades, Lieutenant Lehman, when the line was rocked by a thunderous boom. A shell had scored a direct hit on the seven-centimetre-thick glass observation window in the turret of Lehman's Panzer IV tank. 'The black forage cap that Lehman always wore was hurled out and landed on my tank in the shock waves of the explosion.' Herr peered through the dense black smoke 'and saw that the whole dome had been blown away – it was an appalling situation'.[13] Of Lieutenant Lehman, there was no trace.

As the enemy fire increased in intensity, Oppeln-Bronikowski's great panzer advance was stalled and then stopped. Only a tiny unit of grenadier-adventurers would fight their way through to the beach that afternoon. In their vanguard was Walter Hermes, a nineteen-year-old army messenger with the 192nd Regiment: small, dark-haired and wiry, he was equipped with a low-slung 350cc Terrot motorcycle and a snarling disdain for the enemy. 'We'll soon throw these British back into the sea,'[14] he snapped to his comrades. After scouting the coastal dunes and dodging Allied soldiers, he stumbled across a few German defenders still hiding out in a bunker. They represented the last shattered remnants of the Atlantic Wall, a forlorn group of survivors who had yet to be spotted by the Allies. It was clear that further resistance was hopeless without the support of the panzers. It was also clear that the panzers would never come. Colonel von Oppeln-Bronikowski's tank offensive had been permanently stalled by the brawn of the Staffordshire Yeomanry.

As the first shadows of evening tarnished the clear sky, the colonel began digging his tanks into the fields around Lébisey, leaving only their turrets poking above ground level. For him, on a personal level, digging those impromptu earthworks was the defining moment of the war – the moment at which his role changed from attack to defence.

An hour or so later, he witnessed German officers retreating from the front line with twenty or thirty men apiece. They were haggard and dejected and had defeat in their eyes. He was aghast at the spectacle of his fellow fighters throwing in the towel. He suddenly felt like a broken man.

'I never thought I'd see the day this would happen,' he later admitted. It was his D-Day epiphany. 'I knew then that the war was really finished.'[15]

Colonel von Oppeln-Bronikowski was not alone in feeling a profound sense of gloom. Just over a mile from his newly dug tank positions, Hans Sauer was wondering if he would survive the rest of the day. He had spent the last five hours cowering in an underground bunker in fear of his life. Ever since lunchtime, WN17 – known to Allied forces as Strongpoint Hillman – had been under siege by the young men of the Suffolk Regiment.

Sauer was twenty years of age, a heavily jowled young cartographer from North Rhine-Westphalia with a badly injured knee (that saved him from serving on the Eastern Front). Until now, he had considered himself fortunate to have escaped being sent to

Russia, but as shells and mortars began slamming into the concrete roof of his bunker, he grew increasingly anxious. It was not that he didn't have confidence in the structure: he had worked for Krupps before the war and had first-hand experience of the skill of the company's technicians. Rather, it was the fact that his job was to squat beneath the steel cupola and peer through the long-range periscope in order to observe what was taking place outside.

What he saw that afternoon made for a terrifying sight. Enemy soldiers could be seen advancing on every side, crawling on their bellies through the churned mud.

Among those soldiers was twenty-eight-year-old George Rayson, a baker by profession who, four and a half years earlier, had listened with excitement to Neville Chamberlain's declaration of war against Germany. It was, he thought, 'the best thing we could do'.[16] Now, he wasn't so sure. He had been through a lifetime of unwelcome adventures since wading ashore, the worst of which was getting trapped underneath his landing craft when he jumped off the ramp. His lungs were half filled with seawater by the time he choked his way ashore. When he eventually emerged from the shallows, his nose was broken and he was drenched in blood. Even now, hours later, he was caked in dried blood.

Yet his adventures were by no means over. He was one of a band of young men charged with capturing Hillman, the most formidable of the inland strongpoints on this stretch of coast. It was more heavily fortified than Morris, which had capitulated at 1 p.m., and Daimler, which had also been seized. There was good reason for the extra fortifications. WN17 was the headquarters of the 736th Infantry Regiment, under the command of Colonel Ludwig Krug. The colonel had placed his trust in the stronghold's formidable network of tunnels and redoubts. He had no intention of surrendering his headquarters to the enemy.

'The size of a bloody football pitch.' That was Rayson's first thought as he peered through his field glasses at the mass of trenches and machine-gun nests. 'It looked as though they'd piled up dirt and then built this place in the middle.' As he sized it up, he grew increasingly alarmed about the fight ahead. 'There were about twenty gun emplacements on the top, machine guns, and round it triple Dannert wire [reinforced barbed wire] and a thirty-foot minefield.'[17] Worse still, although as yet unknown to Rayson, its concrete walls were nine feet thick and it was defended by 300 highly motivated fighters.

Rayson's teenage comrade-in-arms, Leslie Perry, was more concerned by the lack of craters, which his troop had been intending to use for cover as they advanced. Perry had been assured that the American air force and the Royal Navy would have pummelled the ground with heavy mortars. But the Americans had bombed little more than the surrounding fields, while the Royal Navy signaller had been killed on landing and was thus unable to direct the naval gunfire. There was to be no further bombardment: Perry was told that Hillman 'was to be taken using just infantry and sappers',[18] the latter having been trained to breach exactly such fortifications.

The men had practised long and hard for this moment and now prepared for the well-planned attack. Three engineers crept forward and cleared a six-foot path through the minefield while two more used a Bangalore torpedo to blow a hole in the perimeter wire. One of the Suffolk lads, Jim Hunter, more than lived up to his surname by launching a pre-emptive one-man assault on his German quarry. 'I've bloody well had enough of this,' he yelled. 'I'm going to have a go.' His words were still hanging in the air when he grabbed his Bren gun and advanced into a hail of bullets. 'There was bullets spattering all around me but I was so annoyed I just didn't care.'[19] As he leaped into a zigzag-shaped trench to avoid flying shrapnel, he ran headlong into a German soldier. They both fired simultaneously, a deadly duel in a deadly trench. The German bullet plunged clean through Hunter's helmet, creasing the top of his head but leaving him unharmed. His own bullet was more fatal. He hit the German squarely in the chest.

'*Come on, Rayson!*'

It was the company commander bawling at him. The main assault was under way. Time to move forward. Rayson leaped into action, only to find himself running headlong into machine-gun fire. 'The first two blokes got killed – a corporal and a private soldier.' Rayson flung himself into a deep trench, landing right behind a corporal who had just been shot through the face. It was not a pleasant sight. 'Cor, his head. Just a mass of blood, brains and bone.' Rayson tried to peek over the top of the trench but it was too deep. Aware that his mates were somewhere up front, he zigzagged forward until he caught up with them.

'What you all stopped for?'

One of them pointed tellingly to the end of the trench.

'Round the corner, Captain Ryley, Lieutenant Tooley, Corporal Stares, they're all dead.' The three of them had over-hastily swung around the corner and been hit by a burst of machine-gun fire.

As Rayson and the others crouched there wondering what to do next, a handful of stick bombs exploded into the dirt. Rayson lobbed some explosives back, unsure how they were meant to press home the attack.

'*You've got to get out as fast as you can!*'[20]

There was sudden panic. A runner was yelling at them, telling them to call off the attack. The frontal assault was being postponed until the arrival of heavy armour.

Among the first of the German defenders to see the Allied tanks was Hans Sauer, who spied them through his long-range periscope. 'They were advancing very slowly, very cautiously.' It was happening before his very eyes, a most disconcerting experience. 'One advances, stops, waits. Another advances. They seemed extremely cautious, looking everywhere before moving forwards as much as a metre.'[21] He released his eye from the periscope and rushed down the narrow metal staircase in order to report what he'd seen. As he did so, there was an explosion of such force that it seemed to wrench at his brain. A shell had crashed through the Krupps steel cupola, shattering its dome. Sauer was fortunate not to have been killed.

Allied trooper John Barnes was advancing in one of those tanks and wrestling with the gun controls as he tried to crank his biggest gun into an angle low enough to fire into the slit trenches. But it proved impossible and he eventually abandoned his efforts, leaving the crew to deal with the problem in more homespun fashion. They lobbed grenades into the trenches in the hope that the German defenders would be ripped to shreds.

Barnes couldn't help reflecting on how brutal war had become. 'It wasn't like it was before: "Play up and play the game." You didn't care who was in there – they got it this time.'[22] Although the infantry and artillery fought with great tenacity, it was to require hours of brutal combat in the trenches and underground corridors before Hillman's main bunkers could finally be entered.

As the attackers penetrated the interior of the stronghold at around 8.15 p.m., its commandant, Colonel Ludwig Krug, telephoned his commander, General Wilhelm Richter. 'Herr General,' he said, 'the enemy are on top of my bunker. They are demanding my surrender. I have no means of resisting and no contact with my own men. What am I to do?'

There was a long pause down the line. General Richter had received nothing but bad news all day. 'Herr Oberst,' he replied, 'I can no longer give you any orders. You must act on your own judgment. *Auf Wiedersehen.*'[23] Richter's valedictory words to Colonel Krug would be oft-quoted in the years to come. They seemed to encapsulate the fate of the entire German army.

Krug managed to hold out for the rest of the night and it was not until the following morning that he finally threw in the towel, along with Hans Sauer and the others.

One of George Rayson's comrades, Arthur Blizzard, led the troops into the heart of the stronghold. 'I saw a big metal cupboard in the corner and opened the door and it was crammed with bottles from the top to the bottom. And when I picked one up, it was five-star brandy.' He was amazed. 'I said, "Look at this, Alec." He said, "Is it all right?"'

Blizzard put the bottle to his lips and tasted it. It was more than all right. 'After me and him had drunk the first bottle, I said, "We feel better now, don't we?" And he said, "Yeah."'

Grinning widely and with their heads swimming with brandy fumes, Blizzard suddenly noticed a door in the corner of the room. 'And I pulled the iron bolt back and opened the door and there they all stood. Sixty-odd Germans, I counted.'[24]

He had to pinch himself to check it wasn't the alcohol. But no, it was for real. Part of the garrison had remained hidden away in the pitch darkness of this subterranean hell. Arthur Blizzard felt obliged to take them all prisoner, although he would have been happier leaving them in their underground dungeon. It seemed like a fitting place for them to end their occupation of Normandy.

Hundreds of Allied gliders arrived at dusk, bringing weaponry and reinforcements. They raised the spirits of exhausted soldiers on the ground. 'One of the most thrilling sights I have ever seen,' said one.

27

Twilight

THE SUN WAS in slow decline, lengthening shadows and casting the meadows in a soft and buttery light. Those long hours of late afternoon were unfolding in dramatic fashion for the small group of commandos who had reached Bénouville Bridge in advance of Lord Lovat.

Stan 'Scotty' Scott and his band of fighters had more than earned their laurels by dint of their morning's exertions, but they had no intention of halting at the banks of the River Orne. They were intent on driving far deeper into enemy territory in order to achieve that day's vital goal, securing the high ground that lay to the east of the bridges.

This was a military imperative – so important, indeed, that it had been entrusted to the elite commandos by Supreme Headquarters. Before the day's end, it was essential for them to throw an impenetrable cordon around the left flank of the beachhead in order to prevent any German lunge westwards during the night. If the commandos' mission failed, the landing zone would be desperately exposed.

Lord Lovat himself had been instrumental in planning the defensive strategy for the evening of D-Day: it required capturing the hilly ground that rose up from the River Orne. 'As I see it,' he explained, 'the high ground across the river controls the battle.' The Overlord generals agreed and gave Lovat the nod. He, in turn, passed on this news to his men with a phrase that might have come straight from a Hollywood movie. 'Dig in, lie low and don't shoot till you see the whites of their eyes.'[1]

It was entirely appropriate that Stan Scott and his soldiers from 3 Commando should find themselves in the front line of fighting. They, after all, had been in the vanguard since dawn. But they were to suffer some serious setbacks that afternoon – and none more so than when they were bowling towards the village of Le Plein.

'There was a gun, a dirty great Russian thing on wheels with a shield, and when we came around that bloody corner, wallop, we got hit.' Seven of Scott's band took the full-force of the attack. 'Dixie Dean got it in the guts . . . I couldn't do a thing for him; he was just looking at me.' Les Hill got a bullet through his head. 'Westley got hit in the wrist. Paddy Harnett got it in the arse. And Bud Arnott, he lost a foot.' In one burst of fire, Scott's team had been decimated. It was a devastating blow to this band of close-knit comrades. It was also a reminder of the dangers of being in the front line: the first to advance were the first to be hit.

Scott did what he could to help the injured, for he was carrying the first aid kit in his pack, but most required professional medical attention. Dixie Dean was the most seriously wounded. 'He was wearing one of these stupid bloody combat jackets, brown canvas things. I ripped all that open and he was just one mass of jelly, he must have taken the big part of the burst.' Scott gave him a shot of morphine but he knew it was futile. 'I couldn't do anything; it was useless. He couldn't talk, he had blood coming out of his nostrils, blood coming out of his mouth. I laid him down and thought, Oh Christ.' He died shortly afterwards.

Les Hill was also gravely wounded from the shot in the head. He came stumbling towards Scott 'like a man in a dream, all blood coming down, and he had a Thompson and he was dragging that down the road and I looked at him and I thought, Well, he ain't going to go far.' Scott once again went over to help, but the others called him off. 'Let him go, Scotty.'

Westley was in better shape, although smeared with blood. 'He had a shattered wrist. It had gone.' His fighting days were over.

Even in times of crisis there were flashes of dark humour, even though the situation hardly warranted it. Scott's mate Paddy Harnett was worried that he had taken a bullet in the groin, right between his legs. 'All he kept saying was, "Scotty, is my wedding tackle all right? Scotty, is my wedding tackle all right?" And I said, "For Christ's sake, Paddy, you've got it through the arse, you haven't got it through anything else."'

The German ambush temporarily blunted the assault on Le Plein, but it failed to stop the uninjured men in Scott's band. Indeed it drove them to fight with even greater resolve. 'Flash Freeman had a two-inch mortar – he was using it like a piece of bleedin' light artillery.' Tucker Jenkins was also in his element, dodging through the village with a tommy gun when a German soldier stepped out of a door. Jenkins's finger was already on the trigger. 'I hear three rounds, bloom-whoof, and Tucker's hit him.' Both men watched the soldier crumple into the doorway, fatally wounded. 'Oh good,' said Jenkins with characteristic nonchalance. Another of Scott's band, Ozzy Osbourne, had meanwhile swept through the local Post Office and flushed out the last remaining Germans. The building was then converted into a much needed first aid post.

As the group advanced towards a T-junction, they paused for a moment while they waited for Scott, who was bringing up the rear. When he saw them lingering in such an exposed position, he was suddenly reminded of the words of his father, Old Man Scottie, who had fought his way through the Great War. 'Never stay on a T-junction' – that was the wise advice of the old man. Scott yelled at the men to take shelter on a nearby track. 'Hadn't gone halfway up that track when, wrrrr-whoosh, straight on the T-junction. Jerry's shelling it.' The spot where they had been standing just seconds earlier erupted into a ball of fire and dirt.

Not everyone had such lucky escapes that afternoon. As Scott's band approached the driveway to a château, one of his commanding officers, a man named Croker, sauntered over to a parked jeep and helped himself to a spare helmet lying on the back seat. 'I'll be all right now,' he said as he clamped it firmly to his head. He spoke too soon, as Scott was to witness. 'Wrrrr-bang. Hit. Half his head gone. Same with Billy Ryall – lost half his arm.'[2]

Scott and his troops were not alone in advancing out of the low-lying Orne valley. By late afternoon, commando units were pushing eastwards through the streets of Ranville, Amfreville and the many other villages that dotted the far bank of the river. Their objective, so simple on paper, rapidly developed into a battle of wills between themselves and the stubborn German defenders.

Among those driving towards the high ground at Le Plein was Derek Mills-Roberts, the foul-mouthed solicitor-turned-colonel who terrified his men. Twelve hours of fighting had not dinted his enthusiasm for action. He was still striding around bellowing orders, his Irish blackthorn staff bolted between his thuggish fists. By late afternoon, his mouth was so filled with expletives that no amount of salt water could sluice them away. Post-war sensibilities would require publishers to blank out or tone down the profanities, but one of Mills-Roberts's commands (with original language restored) went as follows: 'Get these fucking fuckers into fucking cover fucking quick.' One of the commandos who witnessed the scene, Donald Gilchrist, noted that Mills-Roberts's robust command was eagerly obeyed. 'There was fast fucking movement.'[3]

Mills-Roberts sent his signalman forward on the road to Le Plein in order to see if the village had already been penetrated from the opposite direction. Signalling was always a dangerous occupation and this occasion was no exception. There was a shot and the signaller had (as Mills-Roberts eloquently expressed it) 'his hair neatly parted'. Intrigued, he went to inspect the man's head injury more closely. 'This extraordinary scalp wound had lifted a flap of scalp and hair from his skull.' Yet it had failed to penetrate the bone.

The signaller himself took it all in his stride: it was simply one of the hazards of the job. 'He cautiously flattened [it] down before getting on with his work.'[4]

The landscape of the river valley around Bénouville had changed dramatically in the course of sixteen hours' fighting and the devastation seemed to stretch as far as the eye could see: it was as if the entire world had been dragged through hell. 'The whole area was pitted with shell and mortar holes and the air reeked of smoke and cordite.' Such was the scene that greeted the young commando, Cliff Morris, as he made his way through the valley. 'Everything was confusion, the area was still under heavy fire and all movement was made at the double, or crawling, as Jerry snipers were taking a heavy toll and both Jerry and Airborne dead and wounded lay sprawled in the road and in the trenches.'[5]

At the same time as Derek Mills-Roberts and his forces pushed forward into Le Plein, Morris's unit from 6 Commando was heading for an even more remote outpost, the village of Bréville, which lay another half-mile to the east. This had been earmarked as the outermost edge of the left flank and was to serve as the frontier of

the Allied beachhead on D-Day. It certainly felt like frontier territory, in which every farm and cowshed seemed to be housing a
German mortar team.

Morris and his young comrades had experienced many dangers
since fighting their way ashore at Sword Beach, losing a number
of comrades on the way. Now, they had a yet more dangerous task:
to capture and hold the village of Bréville. There were already
ominous signs that it was a thrust too far, for two major hurdles
stood in the way. The first was a heavily buttressed stone farm being
used as a German military headquarters. The second was a huge
enemy artillery battery, equipped with machine guns, Spandaus and
large mortars. Eradicating these two obstacles would have been a
tall order for any group of soldiers, but all the more so for men
who were drained of energy after near-constant fighting for the
better part of twelve hours.

The unit divided into two groups. Cliff Morris and his team
were tasked with attacking the fortified farm, while the others were
to assault the mortar position, with Alan Pyman at their helm.
There was no time to be lost: the twin attacks were to be carried
out with immediate effect.

Morris's group began slithering their way through the dirt until
they were just thirty yards from the farm building. In happier times,
it would have been an idyllic place to stay, a fine three-storey farmhouse shaded by an apple orchard and surrounded by a three-foot
wall. But on this particular afternoon, an ominous silence hung
over the farm, as if there were some dark menace in the long
shadows. Morris could sense the hidden eyes of dozens of German
defenders.

He and his pals had gained enough combat experience that day
to know that speed and overwhelming fire offered them their only
hope of victory. One of their number, Doug Underhill, was already
training his Bren gun on to the façade. His task was to send forth
a barrage of covering fire as Morris and company stormed through
the exposed arched gateway.

There was a moment's pause before the action began. Everyone
checked their guns. The adrenalin kicked in. And then it began.

'Go!'

The order was shouted by Clarke 'Spots' Leaphard. A split second later, Underhill began spraying the farm with a barrage of lead. As he did so, Morris and friends pitched themselves into the fray with a sudden surge of energy. 'We all made a mad dash for it' – so mad, indeed, that within seconds they were kicking down the side door of the house and bursting into the building. As an example of breaking and entering, few burglars could have done it better.

It was one thing to enter a building, quite another to clear it of enemy troops. The men had no idea if Germans were hiding inside, nor if they had planted booby traps behind doors and furniture. Morris flushed his way through the deserted cellars before joining one of his comrades-in-arms, Tom Ward, on the upper floors. The place was strangely empty. It was as if everyone had been spirited away. When Morris glanced out of the window, he spied a solitary figure sneaking away through a small gate at the rear. The Germans had fled rather than staying to fight the commandos.

As the men swept through each room of the farm, they were struck by the chaotic fashion in which the soldiers had left. 'Everything was a shambles.' The discarded uniforms revealed that it had been occupied by high-ranking officers, while the half-filled suitcases in the bedroom suggested that the Germans had been given an unwelcome surprise. One suitcase aroused particular curiosity, for it contained 'a number of women's silks, dresses, underclothes, shoes and loads of other female attire'.[6] The farm had clearly served as something more than a straightforward command post.

Its capture was a milestone of sorts, one of many achieved by the Allies that Tuesday afternoon. Yet each painstakingly captured building was also a reminder that it was a very long way to Berlin.

Cliff Morris had received no word from his comrades in the second group of commandos, led by Alan Pyman. It was clear they had attacked the enemy mortar position, for the thud of exploding shells had been all too audible. But now there came a yet more alarming sound. 'The next thing we heard were shouts and cries in English . . . into the yard burst some dishevelled figures, all swearing and grimy, some limping, stumbling, some being half-dragged and carried and others crawling.' It was a most pitiable spectacle.

'Dicky's dead.' These were the first words Morris heard. It was a bitter blow, for he was one of the most popular members of the troop. The survivors spilled a tale of woe as they recounted their disastrous attack on the enemy position. Young Dicky had been advancing towards the German guns when a sniper snapped him through the neck. It was the signal for a ferocious German counter-attack. Spandau machine guns and mortars opened up with such intensity that almost everyone was hit, many of them seriously.

Captain Alan Pyman was among the dead, a grievous loss for everyone, as he was universally popular and highly respected. 'A good soldier and a real gentleman,' thought Morris, 'and never seen without a smile.' The attack was so relentless that only four of the commandos stumbled back to the farm without injuries.

But even here they were not safe, for no sooner had they told of their setback than the farmyard itself came under fire. Clarke Leaphard called across to his best gunner, 'Taffy' John, and told him to fire a six-strong salvo of two-inch mortars into the German position. The men 'watched the bombs soar right up in the air, for he fired at a high angle, then watched them fall and counted the small dull explosions, six of them, all correct'.

'That's quietened them,' said Taffy with a broad grin. He had spoken too soon. An enemy battery of 88mm guns 'which had remained silent and secret until now, opened up with a roar'. The men had been on the receiving end of a great deal of mortar fire since landing on Sword Beach, but nothing matched this latest attack. 'It took all the smiles from our faces.'

It soon did more than that. 'The shells were bursting in the treetops,' sending lethal fragments of shattered wood through the air. Morris's friend Tom Ward 'fell down hit bad', while Goodyear had a mortar shell punched through his back and 'fell into a trench screaming'. Morris ran over to see what he could do. In truth, there was little to be done. 'He was in a very bad way and covered in blood.' But when the medic, Bob Myles, tried to give him a shot of morphine, Goodyear refused, saying that 'somebody may need it more than him'. Dead and dying men lay all around and in the midst of it all sat a sergeant major, 'looking very glum and cursing Jerry to eternity'.

The truth of the matter was that Cliff Morris and his comrades had overreached themselves. Their front-line outpost was danger-ously exposed and at grave risk of being overrun before dusk. They were pondering their predicament when their radioman, Bob Aldenshaw, picked up orders to fall back to Le Plein, which had been secured by Derek Mills-Roberts and his men. This was to be the Allied front line that night – tenuous, fragile and alarmingly close to the German machine guns.

Evacuating the farm with so many wounded was a logistical nightmare, especially as it was decided that 'no one was to be left if at all possible'. The only feasible route of retreat was along the sole country lane, but this would expose them to German snipers lurking in the roadside farmhouses. The men took it in their stride, withdrawing in the same fashion as they had advanced, 'firing as we went, aiming at the doors and windows in the neighbouring houses so that Jerry would not know what was happening'. Taffy John kept up an accompanying torrent of fire from his Bren gun, enabling the injured to stumble back into Le Plein. When they finally arrived, these shell-shocked survivors had an emotional reunion with their fellow commandos.

There was to be one final twist to that long and arduous day, one that came as a bolt from the blue. 'We had only been here a few minutes when all was excitement.' The French inhabitants of Le Plein burst out of their houses screaming and yelling at the tops of their voices. They were pointing at the sky and panic was written across their faces.

'*Avion! Boche avion!*'

It took only a few seconds to realize what was taking place. The Luftwaffe had been absent for much of the day, but now it had taken to the skies in huge numbers and had spotted the commandos in their exposed front-line positions. The troops on the ground stared at the approaching planes in gut-wrenching anguish: they were coming at high speed and very low altitude. 'The sky,' said Morris, 'was black with planes.'[7]

He was not alone in being terrified. The war correspondent Noel Monks was in nearby Hermanville when he heard 'the drone of what seemed to be many hundreds of aeroplane engines'. He feared the worst: 'the Luftwaffe was coming in force to wipe out the bridgehead.'[8]

But Monks, in common with the French locals, had made a crucial mistake – one that only became clear as the huge formation wheeled overhead. Cliff Morris was among the first to see that these were not enemy planes, but friendly ones. They were British and Canadian – Allied – and they were bringing in a whole new wave of the Airborne Division. Troops were being dropped in such huge numbers that everyone on the ground was overcome with emotion.

'Parachutes could be seen floating earthwards, then they started to come down and land.' Morris fought back a tear. 'What a sight!' he exclaimed. 'I shall never forget it.'[9]

Monks felt a similar excitement. 'One of the most thrilling sights I have ever seen,' he said. 'They came over us so low we felt our cheers would have been heard in the noiseless gliders as they slipped their tows.'[10]

To men who were wounded, hungry and half-broken by exhaustion, this was the very tonic they needed. They all began to cheer, 'for it had given us new life'.[11]

Morris took a mental snapshot of the scene, aware that nothing in his life would ever quite match the thrill of this moment. He had fought for the better part of thirteen hours and had seen his friends blown to shreds. And yet that twilight hour on D-Day had seen a miracle ushered in from the sky.

It was a grand finale to an epic day.

*Searchlights of American vessels anchored off the Normandy coast,
scanning for German planes. Darkness brought little respite for front-line
Allied soldiers, who came under continual fire.*

28

Night

THEY CAME IN swarms, scores of gliders that tipped the land-scape into darkness as they passed across the moon. It was the largest glider-borne force in the history of warfare and it was carrying a vast supply of ammunition, mortars, jeeps and armoured cars, as well as two battalions of 1,000 men each. There were more than 250 gliders in total, along with their towing aircraft, and they were accompanied by no fewer than fifteen squadrons of RAF fighters.

The biggest gliders were the Hamilcars, veritable monsters with a wingspan the length of four London double-deckers. They were laden with Tetrarch tanks, so essential for the battle ahead. One of the Hamilcars had an alarmingly explosive cargo: 17,500 pounds of petrol to keep the tanks in action throughout the days ahead.

Wing Commander Desmond Scott was one of those taking part in that aerial armada: he had never experienced anything quite like it: 'a stream of tugs and gliders that reached out southwards from Selsey Bill as far as the eye could see. Hundreds of four-engined bombers were strung in a narrow stream, each pulling a large Hamilcar glider.'[1]

Their journey had begun two hours earlier when they left their English bases with a roar so loud that few would ever forget it. Irene Gray was washing dishes in her home in Southampton when she heard the unmistakable drone of aircraft. Even after four and a half years of war, the sound put her nerves on edge. 'You didn't know if it was one of ours or one of theirs.' On any normal day, the noise gradually subsided as the planes got airborne, but on this particular evening the growl grew so loud that she had to abandon the washing-up and clamp her hands over her ears. 'It increased in intensity to such a pitch that it was absolutely deafening, and I mean deafening.' She rushed outside to see what on earth was taking place, only to find that her neighbours had also gathered outside. All were looking to the sky, which 'was literally black with aircraft towing gliders'. Irene got the shock of her life. 'They were very, very low. Wave after wave.'[2]

This huge aerial convoy passed over the streets of Southampton. It passed over the beaches of southern England. It passed over the English Channel. And as it did so, it passed over the head of Lieutenant Commander Patrick Bayly on board HMS *Mauritius*. He had seen many stunning sights during seven years of naval duty, but he had never seen anything quite like this. 'There, spread from horizon to horizon, were hundreds of planes towing gliders . . . The whole RAF, it looked like, came low over our heads, went over the beach and dropped them all, God knows how many, on the front line. It really was the most remarkable sight I've ever seen.'[3]

It was equally remarkable for the men crammed inside the gliders, for as they became airborne they had an aerial view of the military hardware parked up across southern England. 'Field after field of tanks, and then another field of guns, then another field of lorries.'[4] It was as if the entire south coast had been turned into a giant storage park. No less noteworthy was the logjam of ships, landing craft and Rhino rafts riding the Channel waves as they waited to offload their cargo in Normandy. Each individual Rhino carried up to fifty armoured lorries and they seemed to stretch all the way back to England.

'*Brace! Brace!*'

In James Cramer's glider, the pilot yelled to the men behind, warning them that they were about to hit the ground. The landing zones had been cleared by paratroopers that afternoon, but landing a glider without mishap was nevertheless an exercise fraught with danger. Cramer shoved his head between his knees and prayed hard. 'We landed with a crash of splintered wood and we got out quick,' diving into the field amid a hail of flying detritus. Everyone was running at full tilt to get away from the gliders, and none more so than the men in the Hamilcar filled with petrol.

James Cramer and his comrades bounded across a hedgerow and found themselves running headlong into Major-General Sir Richard Nelson Gale, commander of the 6th Airborne Division, who had landed by parachute earlier that day. He looked them up and down before allowing his gravelly face to crease into a rare smile. 'Welcome to France, gentlemen,'[5] he said.

Gliders were landing everywhere that evening, at least that is how it felt to the soldiers on the ground. It was not just the eastern end of the beachhead that received massive reinforcements. At the western end, close to Sainte-Mère-Église, hundreds more gliders delivered a huge array of military hardware and personnel to the embattled American airborne forces. The first group alone managed to land sixty-four armoured vehicles.

Paratrooper Sam Gibbons had been dropped into Normandy earlier that day: he had been promised delivery of a jeep in that twilight fleet of gliders. To his utter astonishment, the glider carrying his jeep 'landed right on time and right at the designated spot'. It was an extraordinary moment. 'The glider nose opened and my jeep rolled out. I called the driver's name; he recognized me and drove right over.'[6]

Not everything went quite so smoothly. Many of the sharpened anti-glider poles had yet to be removed by the American paratroopers, causing countless accidents as the planes came in to land. Otis Sampson had to run like hell to avoid one glider that misjudged its landing zone. 'I dived over the four-foot bank as the huge glider skidded across the ground and into the trunks of the large trees boarding the road.' There was a sickening crunch followed by an equally sickening silence. 'The tail end of the glider was sticking up at a 45-degree angle.' Sampson dashed over to see if he could help. As he did so, 'a hole started to appear on the right side of the glider'. He rubbed his eyes in disbelief, amazed that anyone could have survived such a crash. 'The men were kicking out an exit. Like bees out of a hive, they came out of that hole, jumped on the ground, ran for the trees.'[7]

As wave after wave of gliders came in to land, there was a detectable change of mood among the men on the ground. Tiredness, depression and despair slowly gave way to elation and relief. A miracle had happened: they were no longer alone.

Field Marshal Rommel had spent the greater part of that day in his black Horch staff car, being driven at high speed back to Château

La Roche-Guyon. His driver, Daniel, kept his foot clamped to the accelerator, but it nevertheless took ten hours and fifteen minutes to cover the route from Rommel's home in Herrlingen. His adjutant, Helmut Lang, sat beside him in the back seat and witnessed first-hand his agitated state. Rommel kept 'driving the gloved fist of his right hand, again and again, into his left hand'.

He bemoaned the fact that the panzer divisions had not been under his direct command. Never one for modesty, he told Lang that he had been right all along. 'I should have had both those divisions under my command to hit them right on the beaches.' He then smacked his gloved fist once again and muttered under his breath, 'My friendly enemy Montgomery.'

His garbled conversation during that car journey revealed much about his state of mind. He was anxious and agitated, but most of all he was angry – angry at the short-sightedness of the generals based in Berchtesgaden. Those long hours in the car also gave him time to prepare himself mentally for the defeat that was surely coming his way. He told Lang of his contempt for the Luftwaffe, whose absence from the skies had made his task of defending the coastline well-nigh impossible. 'Lang, just imagine,' he said, 'the invasion had begun and we didn't even know about it. No reconnaissance aircraft – and this is the way they want me to win the war.' He contended that if Göring's pilots had got airborne, 'no landing would ever have occurred'.

Lang had known Rommel for several years but he had never seen him in such a state of anxiety. At one point he suddenly became upbeat, suggesting that the battle was not yet lost. 'My God,' he said, 'if Feuchtinger [commander of the 21st Panzer Division] can only make it, we might just be able to throw them back in three days.' But almost in the same breath, he expressed his belief that Germany was doomed. 'If I was commander of the Allied forces right now,' he said, 'I could finish the war off in fourteen days.'[8]

German Supreme Command in distant Berchtesgaden had not grasped the danger of what was taking place in Normandy until around 5 p.m., when General Jodl issued a breezy order that 'the enemy in the bridgehead be destroyed by the evening of June 6'. In case that left any room for doubt, he reiterated that 'the bridgehead must be cleared today.'[9] He made it sound like a minor mopping-up exercise.

Such an order was impossible to fulfil, as Rommel knew only too well. So did his junior officers. Seventeen hours earlier, Helmut Liebeskind had been one of the first Germans to sight the British gliders approaching Bénouville Bridge. Now, as D-Day drew to a close, Liebeskind felt a deep sense of gloom. 'That night we sat down in the company of the commanding officer and sundry others and started to analyze the events of the day.' All agreed that the Allies were unbeatable. 'We saw no possibility of throwing them out.' In common with Rommel, they blamed the Luftwaffe for their woes. 'We were bitterly disappointed by the total non-appearance of the German air force,' said Liebeskind. 'If we had had the support of the air force, things would have been different.'[10]

Rommel's Horch finally swung into the driveway of La Roche-Guyon at 9.15 p.m. Lang was the first out of the car. He bounded up the front steps of the château and burst into the main entrance hall. 'As I did so, I was conscious of loud music coming out of General Speidel's office. It sounded like the strains of Wagnerian opera.' Speidel emerged at that very moment and found himself greeted by an astonished Lang. 'General,' he blurted, 'the invasion, it's begun, and you're able to listen to Wagner?'

Speidel looked at him with a half-smile. 'My dear Lang, do you honestly believe that my listening to Wagner will make any difference whatsoever to the course of the invasion?'

Rommel had by now entered the hall: he and Speidel briefly disappeared into the operations room in order to check the situation map. When Rommel cast his eye over the coastal zone, with the Allied beachheads clearly marked, he was shocked. 'That's one hell of a mess,'[11] he said.

Shortly afterwards, the two of them made their way to the dining room, where all the other members of staff had gathered. Speidel and Admiral Ruge had already eaten, but Rommel and Lang were hungry and ordered a platter of cold meats. By the time they had finished, it was almost 11 p.m. At some point during the meal, Rommel was brought confirmation that Colonel von Oppeln-Bronikowski's tank offensive – belatedly boosted by the tanks of the 21st Panzer Division – had been definitively driven back by the Allies. He gave a nonchalant shrug of his shoulders and then spread his fingers wide: Lang felt as if he were trying to say, 'What's the use?' The depression was audible in his voice. 'Well, Lang,' he said, 'you must be tired. Why don't you go to bed and get a good sleep.'

But Lang was too agitated to sleep. An overriding sense of gloom had descended over the turrets and towers of La Roche-Guyon, one that not even the strains of Wagner could lift. 'One thing everybody knew that night,' said Lang, 'was that the landings had been a success.' The Allies had smashed the coastal defences and established a beachhead, 'and nobody knew it better than Field Marshal Rommel that the writing was on the wall.'

Lang recalled Rommel's prescient words, uttered just a few months earlier. 'If we don't throw them back into the sea within the first twenty-four hours, we are lost. When this happens, the day will be the longest day and perhaps the final day.'[12]

For many Allied soldiers, that short summer night was spent in shallow foxholes scratched from the chalky loam. The vast full moon might have provided comfort against the darkness; instead, it felt like the carbide beam of a spotlight, a great bolt of light that lit their hideouts and turned shadows into ogres. Sleep came with difficulty, for there were enemies in the hedgerows and snipers in the trees. It was worst for those on the front line. Derek Mills-Roberts's commandos had scraped trenches into the garden of their Le Plein farmhouse, yet they found themselves uncomfortably close to their German enemy. Cliff Morris and his two comrades had dug a shelter of sorts that was six feet long, five feet deep and eighteen inches wide. But it was damp and filthy and offered only rudimentary protection from the nocturnal shrapnel.

'Mortars kept banging away, heavy fire broke out in front of us and flares blazed up at regular intervals.' It was truly the stuff of nightmares. 'Jerry fired at everything that moved, shadows and all,' and it was made worse by the fact that they had to take turns to man the forward observation post, 'a very creepy business'. The post lay beyond the walls of the farmyard and to reach it involved a dangerous belly-crawl through no-man's-land. Once those frontier guards were in situ, 'no one was allowed to speak, for Jerry was only a matter of a few yards away and his snipers were working overtime.' Coming at the end of a seemingly infinite day, it came close to breaking their spirit. Morris and his comrades had already survived more than sixteen hours on the front line. Now, their night was also to be spent at the very extremities of the beachhead, with their lives hanging by a thread. 'The night dragged by, cold, quiet and eerie.'[13] They were exhausted and desperate to sleep, yet they nevertheless prayed for the welcoming light of dawn.

Many troops were famished when they finally came to a halt, for they had eaten next to nothing since vomiting their grease-slicked breakfasts at dawn. John Madden, a Canadian paratrooper, felt ravenously hungry that evening and gulped a hearty feast of meat stew, two eggs and a hunk of rough brown bread. Long before it was digested, the day's exertions dealt him a blow of fatigue. He was so exhausted he could scarcely move. 'My boots were caked with cow dung and mud. My face was still black where sweat had not washed away the camouflage cream. My badges of rank and unit flashes were hidden beneath layers of dust. My clothes sagged and slouched as I did. We were very, very tired.'[14]

Private Zane Schlemmer had swallowed so many Benzedrine tablets that he was hallucinating wildly in the darkness. It was not a pleasant experience. 'The cows out in the fields were white and black and brown and very dark, and with the spots on these cows and with the hallucinations I'm having from this Benzedrine, I swear there were people coming in.'[15] So terrified was he of the shadowy German giants lumbering through his imagination that he spent the night with a grenade clamped to his hand, its detonating pin removed.

Others had more primeval needs that night. Eighteen-year-old Dennis Bowen was astonished to learn that his officer, Corporal Stephenson, was sowing his oats in the local farmhouse. 'If anyone wants me,' he said to the lads with breezy nonchalance, 'I shall be in there.'[16]

Some found that the day's adrenalin still pulsed through their veins, long after they were given leave to stand down. Unwilling to stop – and perhaps unable – these martial diehards forged onwards with the battle, even though it was almost midnight. Among these remarkable warriors was Harry Pinnegar, a twenty-six-year-old private with the Gloucester Regiment. He had assumed leadership of his platoon after everyone more senior had been killed. Now, under the light of that huge June moon, he cocked a snook at the Germans by leading his ragged band into the heart of Bayeux. He even took temporary possession of the city's cathedral, in which Harold Godwinson (later King Harold II) had once sworn fealty to William of Normandy. Pinnegar's achievement would never be recognized, to his immense dismay. 'In the history books it says that Bayeux was taken on D-plus-one, but my platoon, my section, was in Bayeux Cathedral at seven minutes to midnight on D-Day. That is history because that is true. We were in there on the night of D-Day.'[17]

There were to be many incongruous sights that historic night, but perhaps the strangest of all was taking place inland from Gold Beach. Major Peter Martin had landed that morning with his kit and weaponry, and he had also lugged ashore his sister's wind-up gramophone. Now, in the warm midnight air, he opened its cover and slipped on his favourite disc, 'Paper Doll', by the Mills Brothers. Here was a song to lift men's spirits; here was a means to escape from the horrors of the day. 'Everyone was in tremendous form,' said Major Martin, and not just because of the music. One of the men had milked a cow 'and we had a super brew of hot chocolate.'[18] Elsewhere on that Normandy coast, men were hiding in fear of their lives. But in this particular field, far from German earshot, the Mills Brothers crooned, the trombones blared and the dense strings of the double bass twanged deep and loud into the moonlight.

Many men that night were nursing wounds, both physical and mental. Howard Baumgarten had lost half his jaw when landing in the first wave at Omaha, yet he had struggled into Vierville, where he was shot in the foot. A further bullet slammed through his helmet and 'blood came streaming again over my left ear and down onto my face'. He pumped himself with morphine in an attempt to dull the pain, but eventually collapsed on to the road from exhaustion and loss of blood. When an army ambulance drove past, he had to fire a bullet to force it to stop. The medics asked what they could do to help, only to hear a wail of anguish. 'Anything to get out of here.'[19] Soon after, Baumgarten lapsed into unconsciousness. It would be another fifteen hours before he was transferred to a hospital ship.

Other youngsters were coming to terms with wounds that would never heal. Robert Miller had been racing up Omaha Beach 'when a big white flash enveloped me'. At first he thought his legs had been blown off, 'since I had no sensation of movement in them'.[20] He later discovered that his legs were intact but his spinal cord was not. Miller's first steps on French soil were also his last.

Late that night, when most of the men were trying to catch some rest, the American war reporter Ernie Pyle took a solitary moonlit walk along Omaha Beach. It was a time of rare silence, a time to catch up on the momentous events of the day. The shoreline was a picture of devastation. 'There were tanks that had only just made the beach before being knocked out. There were jeeps that had been burned to a dull grey. There were big derricks on caterpillar treads that didn't quite make it.' Pyle saw smashed bulldozers, broken half-tracks and charred landing craft washed up at crazy angles, like wreckage raised dripping from the deep. Interspersed among them were more personal items: 'toothbrushes and razors, and snapshots of families back home staring up at you from the sand'.

There were also more poignant reminders of the dreadful events of that day. 'As I ploughed out over the wet sand of the beach on that first day ashore, I walked around what seemed to be a couple of pieces of driftwood sticking out of the sand.' He realized with a start that they weren't driftwood. They were the stone-rigid feet of a fallen soldier. 'He was completely covered by the shifting sands except for his feet. The toes of his GI shoes pointed toward the land he had come so far to see, and which he saw so briefly.'[21] Pyle had witnessed a surfeit of horror in the long hours since dawn, yet this particular human tragedy almost broke him. It was the saddest of sights on the saddest of days.

A brighter world would eventually arise from the darkness and young lads would grow into old men. Yet here on the moonlit strand, the detritus of war was mingled with a very human form. That anonymous soldier was one of the many whose stories would remain unknown and untold, lost for ever to the drifting sands of Normandy.

Afterword

THE 156,000 ALLIED troops who landed on D-Day were successful in carving out a beachhead, but it was neither as large nor as secure as intended. If all had gone to plan, the liberated zone would have covered fifty miles of Normandy coast and included four of the landing beaches (Omaha, Gold, Juno and Sword). Perfectly executed, D-Day would also have seen the full capture of the cities of Bayeux and Caen. A further liberated zone was to have stretched eight miles inland from Utah Beach, encompassing Sainte-Mère-Église and a dozen or more nearby villages.

The reality after twenty-four hours was somewhat different: the Allies occupied little more than a precarious ribbon of coastline, with eleven miles of enemy territory between Utah and Omaha and three miles of still vulnerable no-man's-land between Juno and Sword. Only the Gold and Juno beachheads had managed to link up.

Nor had the Allies penetrated far inland. At Juno, the Canadians had managed to advance six miles from the coast, but the American-controlled enclave at Omaha was just 2,000 yards deep. At Pointe du Hoc, the Ranger assault battalions were desperately clinging to their cliff-top position despite heavy casualties.

Those who planned the Allied landings always knew there would be a high cost in human life on that first day of combat. No definitive roster of the dead and wounded was ever compiled for 6 June itself, but subsequent research suggests that there were approximately 8,200 casualties on the right flank – Omaha, Utah and the Cotentin peninsula – and a further 3,000 British and Canadian casualties on the three other beaches. The number of German dead and injured remains unknown: estimates range from 4,000 to 9,000.

The death toll of French civilians is rarely mentioned, despite their many trials in the wake of the invasion. An estimated 3,000 men, women and children died in the forty-eight hours that followed the Allied landings.

This bloodshed was the price to be paid for the coastal bombardment, which aided the landing of massive quantities of military hardware. On Utah Beach, 1,742 vehicles were brought ashore before nightfall, while a further 6,000 vehicles were landed in the British sector, including 900 tanks and armoured vehicles. This was woefully short of the planned totals. The British alone were meant to have landed 10,000 vehicles. But although the beachhead was small, it enabled the Allies to pour in huge quantities of men and machines over the days that followed. Three weeks after D-Day, by the end of June, 850,000 men, 148,000 vehicles and 570,000 tons of supplies had been landed in Normandy. Five days after that, the number of troops would top 1 million.[1]

Securing the beachhead was just the beginning: it was followed by a ferocious battle for the rest of Normandy over the next eleven weeks as German panzer divisions fought with skill and determination. Although Bayeux was liberated on 7 June, the vital intersection city of Caen remained stubbornly in enemy hands. The Panzer Lehr division advanced rapidly towards the city, bringing 3,000 tanks and armoured vehicles. They joined forces with the 21st SS Panzer Division and the 12th SS Panzer and formed a near-impregnable belt around the outskirts. Caen would not be liberated until 21 July, by which time it was in ruins.

Smaller Normandy villages became the focus of vicious battles. At Tilly-sur-Seulles, the Panzer Lehr fought with tenacity; at Villers-Bocage, the British advance was brutally halted by German Tigers. The charred ruins of the town, which lay just thirteen miles from the coast, were not captured until 4 August.

On the right flank of the landing zone, the American drive towards Cherbourg proved equally taxing. They launched their attack on 22 June, but it took four days of intense fighting before the city's Germans finally capitulated, by which time the port's facilities had been systematically destroyed.

The great Allied break-out from Normandy began in the third week of July, a multi-stage operation with the British and Canadians driving south-eastwards beyond Caen and the US Third Army pushing through German lines at Saint-Lô. Almost simultaneously, Hitler was severely wounded in the attempted assassination at his Wolf's Lair field headquarters. The 'July plot' and its aftermath sent shock waves through the army high command. Among those implicated was Field Marshal Rommel, who had been injured in an Allied air attack three days earlier.

Rommel was given the choice to defend himself before a kangaroo court or commit suicide. He chose the latter after assurances that his family would be spared and he would be buried with full military honours. After denying any involvement in the plot – a source of controversy to this day – he swallowed cyanide.

As the Germans retreated in the wake of the great Allied advance, much of Army Group B and Panzer Group West were trapped at Falaise, in Calvados, where they suffered massive losses. Just a few days later the Allies reached Paris, which was liberated on 25 August.

It would take a further six months before Allied forces crossed the Rhine, with many hard-fought battles on the way. The collapse of the last German counter-offensive in the Ardennes – the so-called Battle of the Bulge that ended in January 1945 – paved the road to victory. The first Allied forces crossed the Rhine at Remagen on 7 March 1945, by which time the Red Army was fast approaching Berlin. The city was liberated on 2 May.

In all, D-Day would be followed by 335 days of fighting before Germany's unconditional surrender on 7 May 1945 brought the war in Europe to a close.

Acknowledgements

E VERY BOOK HAS a point of departure – the moment when initial enthusiasm is transformed into words on a page. In the case of this particular book, there were two points of departure and they were separated in time by more than four decades. I was just seven years old – it was 1973 – when my parents first took me to the Normandy beaches.

Amid the tufted sand dunes of the Allied landing beaches, I clambered through the ruins of gigantic concrete bunkers, their backs broken, their roofs staved in, their gloomy interiors half swamped by drifting sand. This was a land of giants – at least it was in the imagination of a child – and it was endlessly absorbing. I returned to England with a gnarled twist of barbed wire, a rusting vestige of Field Marshal Rommel's Atlantic Wall.

Years later in 1994, while working as a journalist for one of Britain's national newspapers, I interviewed French civilians for a commemoration of the fiftieth anniversary of D-Day: the most memorable of these interviews was a long afternoon spent with the cyclist-spy Guillaume Mercader. Further journalistic assignments followed in 2004 and 2014. But it was only as the seventy-fifth anniversary loomed that a hitherto half-formed project began to coalesce into this present book.

D-Day: The Soldiers' Story could not have been written without the advice, support and expertise of archivists in a number of different countries. In England, I am most grateful to Andrew Whitmarsh of Portsmouth's D-Day Museum for generously allowing me access to the archives at the very time when the museum was embarking on a wholesale redevelopment. These archives include (among many others) the research papers of Russell Miller's excellent *Nothing Less than Victory: The Oral History of D-Day* (1993). I am grateful indeed to the author for taking the time to meet with me and for allowing me to quote from his research material.

The largest repository of British veterans' interviews is housed in the Imperial War Museum, where I spent many long hours. Thank you to the excellent archivists who helped to locate documents, diaries and audio-tapes. Another excellent source of information was the Second World War Experience Centre in West Yorkshire. I am grateful to Anne Wickes for her help while I was working there.

A warm thank you to the staff at the Liddell Hart Centre for Military Archives in London for their help and for granting permission to quote extracts from the handwritten diary of Cliff Morris of 6 Commando. I am also grateful to Pen and Sword Books for allowing me to quote from *The Pegasus Diaries: The Private Papers of Major John Howard DSO* and *The Devil's Own Luck: Pegasus Bridge to the Baltic 1944–45* by Denis Edwards. Thank you, too, to Sheil Land Associates for permitting me to quote from John Keegan's *Six Armies in Normandy*. Mention must also be made of Bob Hunt, who runs the excellent Portsdown Tunnels website: http://www.portsdown-tunnels.org.uk.

In America I am deeply grateful to Toni Kiser, Assistant Director for Collections Management of the National World War II Museum in New Orleans, where I spent many long days researching the book. The museum's huge archive collection, much of it collected by the late Stephen Ambrose, is a unique resource, and I am gratified to have been welcomed into the offices for the duration of my visit. Also in New Orleans, I am grateful for the help I received from John Biguenet of Loyola University.

A big thank you, too, to Sara Harrington, Head of Arts and Archives at Ohio University Libraries, for giving me unrestricted access to the monumental Cornelius Ryan archive. Ryan interviewed hundreds of veterans for his 1959 book, *The Longest Day*, including many German soldiers and commanders: a large number of these personal testimonies were not used in his finished book. An equal thank you to the Cornelius Ryan estate for allowing me to quote extracts from this extensive collection.

Thank you to the ever helpful archivists and staff of the National Archives in Washington DC for helping to locate hard-to-find documents. Also in America, I must make a special mention of author Vince Milano for generously allowing me to quote extracts from his interviews with the young German soldier, Karl Wegner. 'Karl,' he said, 'would be honoured to know that his story is going to be in your book.' I am no less honoured at having been allowed to use it.

I am delighted to have corresponded with Julian 'Bud' Rice, whose extraordinary role in the US paratroop landings at Sainte-Mère-Église is featured in this book. A warm thank you, also, to Thomas S. Colones, for his assistance with the story of Malcolm Brannen, as well as for sharing the many video interviews he has made with American veterans.

I am deeply grateful to Kevin McKernon for his help with the accounts of survivors from USS *Corry*. Mr McKernon is an expert on the sinking of the ship and runs the excellent website http://www.uss-corry-dd463.com.

For help with the story of the Canadian landings, thank you to Marie Eve Vaillancourt who, at the time of my researches, was working as History Department Manager at Centre Juno Beach. Thank you, also, to Mark Zuehlke, authority on the Canadians on D-Day and author of many excellent books and articles.

Still in Canada, I would particularly like to thank George Vanderburgh, the publisher of *We Were There*, Jean Portugal's magnificent seven-volume compendium of interviews with 750 Canadian veterans, published by the Battered Silicon Dispatch Box. Mr Vanderburgh told me: 'I am confident that the shade of Jean Portugal would be pleased that her writings be shared with as many readers as possible.' I hope so – and I am grateful to him for making them available to me.

In France, sincere thanks are due to Marie-Claude Berthelot, historian and archivist at the excellent Memorial de Caen. Not only did she locate much valuable French archival material, but she also made scores of photographic copies of this documentation. Thank you also to Jean-François Couriol, secretary-general of the Centre d'Études René-Nodot pour la Mémoire de la Résistance et de la Déportation for allowing me to quote from interviews with André Héricy and Robert le Nevez.

A particular thank you to French journalist Annick Cojean, who originally interviewed Eva Eifler in 1994, and to *Le Monde* for allowing me to quote extracts in my book. Also, to Sonia Stolper for helping with contacts in the world of French journalism; and to the staff of Paris's Bibliothèque Nationale, who tracked down some rare and little-known volumes.

A serendipitous encounter in a Cherbourg restaurant led to an unexpected resource. Marie-Claude Philippart proved a fount of knowledge about D-Day from a French perspective: it transpired that she had worked in the Caen archives and was generous enough to present me with a veritable mini-library of locally published French books about the landings, as viewed by Normandy civilians. Thank you, too, for the help received from the webmaster of the excellent French-language Omaha beach website – http://omaha-vierville.com – who wishes to remain anonymous.

The Normandy branch of Atout, the French national tourist board, has been unfailingly helpful with travel and logistics: special thanks to Fran Lambert, press officer, for her constant support. Thank you also to Frank Barrett and Wendy Driver of the *Mail on Sunday*. I am also extremely grateful to Sue Ockwell and Noel Josephides for their generous hospitality in Saint-Vaast-la-Hougue and for introducing me to their venerable neighbour, Yvonne Marie.

I have visited all the Normandy beach museums during the course of the research and met many curators: thank you to one and all for sparing your time and sharing your knowledge. Thank you, also, to Ulm Activities for flying me over the Normandy beaches.

For German source material outside the Ryan collection, thank you to Michael Strong for allowing me to quote from his book *Steiner's War: The Merville Battery*; to staff of the Bundesarchiv, Berlin, and to the Bundesarchiv-Militärarchiv in Freiberg. A special mention must go to my late German father-in-law, Wolfram Aïchele, who was serving as a Morse code operator in the 77th Infantry Division on D-Day. His candid accounts of life in the Wehrmacht while serving on the front line in Normandy provided a counterpoint to the Allied view of the landings.

I have received the support and advice of a number of people in London and elsewhere. Special mention goes to Roland Philipps; to Jan Henrik Jebsen; to the staff of the British Library; the ever helpful librarians of the London Library, where much of this book was written; and to John McNally for kindly reading the typescript.

I thank my literary agent, Georgia Garrett, for first seeing the book's potential; my Swiss-French publisher, Vera Michalski-Hoffman, for her unfailing loyalty and for acquiring the French rights long before I had finished the book; and my American editor, Stephen Morrison, for his sharp eye and excellent editorial advice.

A sincere thank you is due to Nick Davies, my editor at John Murray, for his invaluable editorial input, along with the ever helpful advice of Joe Zigmond. Thank you indeed to the whole John Murray team: Caroline Westmore, Sara Marafini, Yassine Belkacemi, Emma Petfield, Diana Talyanina, Megan Schaffer, Morag Lyall, Howard Davies, Douglas Matthews and Juliet Brightmore.

Lastly, an unreserved thank you to my family: this D-Day project has been, in no small part, a family affair. To my mother-in-law, Barbara Aïchele, for assisting with German research; to my daughters Héloïse and Aurélia, who have borne my obsessiveness with patience; to my eldest daughter, Madeleine, who translated all the French texts into English; to my wife, Alexandra, who likewise translated all the German texts. She was the first to read the manuscript – my literary guinea-pig – and the first to give me advice. I am profoundly grateful.

There were many bright moments while writing this book: walking the empty Normandy beaches in the first light of dawn was one of the highlights. But even on the most sparkling of days, it was impossible not to be aware of the scenes of heroism and human tragedy that unfolded here all those years before. This was where lives were lost – and freedom won. My final thank you, heartfelt and unreserved, is to all who served.

Photographic Sources

Notes and Sources

Abbreviations

DDMA	D–Day Museum Archive Collection (Portsmouth)
IWM	Imperial War Museum archives
LHCMA	Liddell Hart Centre for Military Archives
MdeC	Memorial de Caen archives
NA	National Archives (UK)
NARA	National Archives and Records Administration (USA)
NWWIIM	National World War Two Museum (archives department)
OUCR	Cornelius Ryan Collection of World War Two Papers, Ohio University
SWWEC	Second World War Experience Centre

Preface

1. Cited in John Costello and Terry Hughes, *The Battle of the Atlantic*, HarperCollins, 1977, p. 281.
2. Cited in General Sir Frederick Morgan, *Peace and War*, p. 156.

Prologue

1. This account of Eva Bojack, née Eifler, is drawn from two principal sources: '*L'Allemande Eva Bojack découvre que les messages en morse annoncent l'invasion*', interview by Annick Cojean, *Le Monde Société*, 5 June 2014; and also '*Eva face à l'invasion*', interview by Georges Bernage, *39–45 Magazine*, n.d.

Chapter 1: Behind Enemy Lines

1. George Lane, Obituary, *The Times*, 7 April 2010.
2. Ian Dear, *Ten Commando*, p. 49.
3. Russell Miller, *Nothing Less than Victory*, p. 73.
4. Ibid. See also George Lane's interview in Janusz Piekalkiewicz, *Secret Agents, Spies and Saboteurs: Famous Undercover Missions of World War II*, pp. 392–7, and Peter Masters, *Striking Back*, pp. 122–6.
5. NA: WO 106/4343, *Tarbrush: Reconnaissance of underwater obstacles on French coast*.
6. Miller, *Nothing Less than Victory*, p. 74. See also Luke Salkeld, 'Rommel saved me from being shot as a spy – and even served me cigarettes and beer', *Daily Mail*, 20 November 2014.
7. Miller, *Nothing Less than Victory*, p. 74.
8. Ibid., and author interview quoted in Dear, *Ten Commando*, p. 89, and IWM: 13307, George Lane oral interview.
9. Miller, *Nothing Less than Victory*, p. 75.
10. Hilary St George Saunders, *The Green Beret*, p. 264.
11. Miller, *Nothing Less than Victory*, p. 75.
12. Dear, *Ten Commando*, p. 89.
13. Ibid.
14. IWM: 13307, George Lane, oral interview.
15. Miller, *Nothing Less than Victory*, p. 76.
16. IWM: 13307, George Lane, oral interview.
17. Miller, *Nothing Less than Victory*, p. 76.
18. Dear, *Ten Commando*, p. 90.
19. IWM: 13307, George Lane, oral interview.
20. Miller, *Nothing Less than Victory*, p. 77.
21. IWM: 13307, George Lane, oral interview.
22. Miller, *Nothing Less than Victory*, p. 78.
23. IWM: 13307, George Lane, oral interview.
24. Miller, *Nothing Less than Victory*, p. 78.
25. OUCR: Rommel papers.
26. Hans Speidel and Ian Duncan Colvin, *We Defended Normandy*, p. 55.
27. OUCR: Rommel papers.
28. OUCR: Lutz Koch, *Erwin Rommel: Die Wandlung Eines Grossen Soldaten*, typescript translation.
29. OUCR: Werner Pluskat, interview.

Chapter 2: Atlantic Wall

1. Miller, *Nothing Less than Victory*, pp. 238–40. See also Hubert Meyer, *The 12th SS*, vol. 1.
2. Miller, *Nothing Less than Victory*, pp. 238–40.
3. Max Hastings, *Overlord*, p. 66.
4. Speidel and Colvin, *We Defended Normandy*, p. 76.
5. Miller, *Nothing Less than Victory*, p. 238.
6. SWWEC: DBR0159-44C, Franz Gockel, letter to parents, 1 May 1944.
7. Franz Gockel, *La Porte de l'enfer*, p. 69.
8. SWWEC: DBR0159-44C, Gockel, letter to parents, 7 December 1943.
9. Gockel, *La Porte de l'enfer*, p. 66.
10. Ibid.
11. SWWEC: DBR0159-44C, Gockel, letter to parents, 23 April 1944.
12. Gockel, *La Porte de l'enfer*, p. 58.
13. *Un Officier Allemand à Omaha Beach: extraits et adaptation d'interview donnée à John Marks et de correspondance avec Stewart Bryant*: cited at http://omaha-vierville.com/WebOmahaVierville1944/indexcolleville.htm.
14. Guillaume Mercader, author interview, May 1994.
15. NWWIIM: Guillaume Mercader, lecture typescript of speech, 7 July 1987; also Mercader file in OUCR.
16. NWWIIM: Guillaume Mercader, lecture typescript of speech, 7 July 1987.
17. Guillaume Mercader, author interview, May 1994.
18. NWWIIM: Guillaume Mercader, lecture typescript of speech, 7 July 1987.

Chapter 3: The Weather Report

1. Doris Buttle, interview: www.portsdown-tunnels.org.uk/palmerston_forts/fort_southwick/2_ughq_wwii_p4.html
2. Elsie Horton (née Campbell), interview: BBC People's War, www.bbc.co.uk/history/ww2peopleswar/stories/38/a2366138.shtml
3. Doris Buttle, interview: www.portsdown-tunnels.org.uk/palmerston_forts/fort_southwick/2_ughq_wwii_p4.html
4. Alison Edye, interview: www.portsdown-tunnels.org.uk/palmerston_forts/fort_southwick/2_ughq_wwii_p4.html
5. June Tollfree, interview: www.portsdown-tunnels.org.uk/palmerston_forts/fort_southwick/2_ughq_wwii_p4.html
6. Sarah Wilson, interview: www.portsdown-tunnels.org.uk/palmerston_forts/fort_southwick/2_ughq_wwii_p4.html

7. Elsie Horton (née Campbell), interview: BBC People's War, www.bbc.co.uk/history/ww2peopleswar/stories/38/a2366138.shtml

8. NWWIIM: Howard Vander Beek, *Aboard the LCC 60*, unpublished typescript.

9. Ibid.

10. OUCR: Bennie Glisson, typescript interview.

11. Emil Vestuti, interview: http://www.uss-corry-dd463.com/d-day_u-boat_photos/d-day_accounts.htm

12. Lloyd 'Red' Brantley written account, http://www.uss-corry-dd463.com/d-day_u-boat_photos/d-day_Brantley.htm

13. NWWIIM: Robert Beeman, unpublished typescript.

14. Ibid.

15. Lloyd Brantley, interview: http://www.uss-corry-dd463.com/d-day_u-boat_photos/d-day_accounts.ht

16. Mort Rubin, interview: http://www.uss-corry-dd463.com/d-day_u-boat_photos/d-day_accounts.htm

17. NWWIIM: Howard Vander Beek, *Aboard the LCC 60*, unpublished typescript.

18. OUCR: Stübe, interview typescript.

19. Ibid.

20. Robert J. Kershaw, *D-Day*, p. 88. The author cites the German weather report from *Verbindungsmeteorloge OB West* 4/5.6.1944.

21. http://www.lrb.co.uk/v16/n10/lawrence-hogben/diary

22. OUCR: Helmuth Lang, interview typescript.

23. Goronwy Rees interview in Bailey, *Forgotten Voices of D-Day*, p. 19.

24. https://www.rmets.org/sites/default/files/presentations/06092013-foden.pdf

25. http://www.lrb.co.uk/v16/n10/lawrence-hogben/diary

26. Brian Audric, *The Meteorological Office Dunstable and the IDA Unit in World War II*, Royal Meteorological Society, 2000. https://www.rmets.org/sites/default/files/pdf/histo2a.pdf

27. https://www.rmets.org/sites/default/files/presentations/06092013-foden.pdf

28. James Martin Stagg, *Forecast for Overlord*, p. 100.

29. http://www.lrb.co.uk/v16/n10/lawrence-hogben/diary

30. Stagg, *Forecast for Overlord*, p. 102.

31. Ibid., p. 108.

32. Ibid., p. 115.

33. Ibid.

Chapter 4: Codebreaking

1. John Keegan, *Six Armies in Normandy*, pp. 11–12.
2. Edward Wallace, interview in Roderick Bailey, *Forgotten Voices*, p. 62.
3. Denis Edwards, *The Devil's Own Luck*, p. 27.
4. Ibid.
5. Ibid., p. 33.
6. Ibid., p. 19.
7. IWM: 11073, Walter 'Wally' Parr, oral interview.
8. Edwards, *The Devil's Own Luck*, p. 19.
9. Ibid., p. 21.
10. Ibid., p. 22.
11. Ibid., p. 33.
12. Ibid.
13. NWWIIM: Guillaume Mercader, lecture typescript of speech, 7 July 1987; also Mercader file in OUCR.
14. Annick Cojean, '*André Héricy, du maquis de Saint-Clair sabote la ligne Caen–Laval*', *Le Monde Société*, 4 June 2014. *http://www.lemonde.fr/societe/article/2014/06/04/les-veterans-du-jour-j-3-18_4432192_3224.html*
15. Ibid.
16. *André Héricy et Philippe Durel*, Centre d'études René-Nodot pour la Mémoire de la Résistance et de la Déportation: https://sites.google.com/site/maquisdesaintclair/andre-hericy-et-philippe-durel. See also Robert le Nevez, interview, https://sites.google.com/site/maquisdesaintclair/06-robert-le-nevez
17. https://sites.google.com/site/maquisdesaintclair/andre-hericy-et-philippe-durel
18. Ibid.
19. OUCR: Helmuth Meyer, typescript interview.
20. Heinz Herbst worked with the Long-Range Reconnaissance Unit in Lambersart. Miller, *Nothing Less than Victory*, p. 94.
21. OUCR: Helmuth Meyer, typescript interview.
22. Eisenhower's exact words are a source of much controversy. For a full analysis, see Tim Rives, 'Just What Did Ike Say When He Launched the D-Day Invasion 70 Years Ago?', *Prologue*, Spring 2014. (Rives was Deputy Director of the Eisenhower Presidential Library.) https://www.archives.gov/files/publications/prologue/2014/spring/d-day.pdf
23. Kay Summersby, *Eisenhower Was My Boss*, p. 133.

24. 'General Eisenhower's Trailer Headquarters', *Commercial Motor*, 3 November 1944. http://archive.commercialmotor.com/article/3rd-november-1944/30/general-eisenhowers-trailer-headquarters

25. Cited in Carlo d'Este, *Eisenhower*, p. 213.

26. Summersby, *Eisenhower Was My Boss*, p. 22.

27. Article in *National Post*, 28 April 2016: http://news.nationalpost.com/full-comment/scott-van-wynsberghe-the-man-who-kept-eisenhowers-diary-but-couldnt-keep-his-secrets

28. D'Este, *Eisenhower*, p. 310.

29. Cited in Rick Atkinson, *The Guns at Last Light*, p. 15.

30. D'Este, *Eisenhower*, p. 198.

31. Article in *Seattle Times*, 28 May 1995: http://community.seattletimes.nwsource.com/archive/?date=19950528&slug=2123420

32. Kay Summersby, *Past Forgetting*, p. 169.

33. Summersby, *Eisenhower Was My Boss*, p. 135.

34. Harry Cecil Butcher, *Three Years with Eisenhower*, p. 486.

35. Summersby, *Past Forgetting*, p. 170.

36. *André Héricy et Philippe Durel*, Centre d'études René-Nodot: Mémoire de la Résistance et de la Déportation: https://sites.google.com/site/maquisdesaintclair/andre-hericy-et-philippe-durel, and Annick Cojean, '*André Héricy, du maquis de Saint-Clair sabote la ligne Caen–Laval*', *Le Monde Société*, 4 June 2014. *http://www.lemonde.fr/societe/article/2014/06/04/les-veterans-du-jour-j-3-18_4432192_3224.html*

Chapter 5: The Midnight Hour

1. SWWEC: 2002-1754, Harry Clark, typescript interview.

2. OUCR: Walter 'Wally' Parr, interview.

3. SWWEC: DBR0052– 39D, Douglas V. Allen, typescript interview by Peter Liddle. See also NWWIIM: John Howard, interview, and John Howard, 'Dropping in on Pegasus', *Illustrated London News*, June 1984.

4. SWWEC: DBR0052–39D, Douglas V. Allen, *The Memoirs of a Gliderborne Soldier*, unpublished typescript.

5. John Howard and Penny Bates, *The Pegasus Diaries*, p. 115.

6. SWWEC: 2002-1754, Harry Clark, typescript interview.

7. Edwards, *The Devil's Own Luck*, p. 32.

8. Ibid.

9. Howard and Bates, *The Pegasus Diaries*, p. 115.

10. Edwards, *The Devil's Own Luck*, p. 35.

11. Ibid., p.35.

12. Albert Gregory, manuscript account, on Pegasus archive: http://www.pegasusarchive.org/normandy/albert_gregory.htm

13. Edwards, *The Devil's Own Luck*, p. 40.

14. SWWEC: 2002-1754, Harry Clark, typescript interview.

15. Edwards, *The Devil's Own Luck*, p. 40.

16. IWM: 11073, Walter 'Wally' Parr, oral interview.

17. Edwards, *The Devil's Own Luck*, p. 41.

18. IWM: 11073, Walter 'Wally' Parr, oral interview.

19. Stephen E. Ambrose, *Pegasus Bridge*, p. 70.

20. Miller, *Nothing Less than Victory*, p. 87ff.

21. Stephen Ambrose, Introduction to Hans von Luck, *Panzer Commander*.

22. Von Luck, *Panzer Commander*, p. 136.

23. Ibid.

24. Miller, *Nothing Less than Victory*, p. 236.

25. Von Luck, *Panzer Commander*, p. 137.

26. Ibid., p. 136.

27. Edwards, *The Devil's Own Luck*, p. 41.

28. Ibid.

29. IWM: 11061, John Howard, oral interview.

30. IWM: 11077, Richard Smith, oral interview.

31. Howard and Bates, *The Pegasus Diaries*, p. 129.

32. Miller, *Nothing Less than Victory*, p. 220.

33. Ibid., p. 221.

34. Kate Connolly, 'I Saw the British and Hid in a Bush', *Daily Telegraph*, 5 June 2004: http://www.telegraph.co.uk/news/1463647/I-saw-the-British-and-hid-in-a-bush.html

35. Edwards, *The Devil's Own Luck*, p. 42.

36. Ambrose, *Pegasus Bridge*, p. 92.

37. IWM: 11073, Walter 'Wally' Parr, oral interview.

38. IWM: 11478, William Gray, oral interview.

39. IWM: 11073, Walter 'Wally' Parr, oral interview.

40. Ibid.

41. Edwards, *The Devil's Own Luck*, p. 42.

42. Miller, *Nothing Less than Victory*, p. 221.

43. Kate Connolly, 'I Saw the British and Hid in a Bush', *Daily Telegraph*, 5 June 2004: http://www.telegraph.co.uk/news/1463647/I-saw-the-British-and-hid-in-a-bush.html

44. IWM: 11478, William Gray, oral interview.

45. IWM: 11073, Walter 'Wally' Parr, oral interview.

46. IWM: 11077, Richard Smith, oral interview.

47. IWM: 11061, John Howard, oral interview.
48. Howard and Bates, *The Pegasus Diaries*, p. 122.
49. IWM: 11073, Walter 'Wally' Parr, oral interview.
50. Ibid.
51. Cited in Ambrose, *Pegasus Bridge*, p. 81.
52. Ibid., p. 75.
53. Ibid., p. 76.
54. Edwards, *The Devil's Own Luck*, p. 43.
55. Howard and Bates, *The Pegasus Diaries*, p. 125.
56. IWM: 11073, Walter 'Wally' Parr, oral interview.
57. Edwards, *The Devil's Own Luck*, p. 44.
58. Howard and Bates, *The Pegasus Diaries*, p. 127.
59. Ibid.
60. Von Luck, *Panzer Commander*, p. 137.
61. Edwards, *The Devil's Own Luck*, p. 44.
62. IWM: 11073, Walter 'Wally' Parr, oral interview.
63. Howard and Bates, *The Pegasus Diaries*, pp. 127–8.
64. IWM: 11357, Harry Clarke, oral interview.
65. Howard and Bates, *The Pegasus Diaries*, p. 126.

Chapter 6: At German Headquarters

1. OUCR: Friedrich Hayn, *Die Invasion*, typescript translation.
2. Alan Jefferson, *Assault on the Guns of Merville*, p. 86.
3. OUCR: Hayn, *Die Invasion*, typescript translation.
4. Ibid.
5. OUCR: Max Pemsel, interview typescript.
6. OUCR: Hayn, *Die Invasion*, typescript translation.
7. Ibid.
8. Paul Carell, *Invasion*, p. 30.
9. OUCR: Friedrich Hayn, interview typescript.
10. Carell, *Invasion*, p. 30.
11. OUCR: Hayn, *Die Invasion*, typescript translation.
12. OUCR: Leodegard Freyberg, interview typescript.
13. OUCR: Hans Speidel, *The Battle in Normandy*, manuscript.
14. OUCR: Max Pemsel and Hans von Salmuth, interview typescripts.
15. OUCR: Hayn, *Die Invasion*, typescript translation.
16. OUCR: the unfolding events are based on transcripts of the 7th and 15th Army telephone logs.
17. Carell, *Invasion*, p. 40.

18. Ibid.
19. OUCR: Walter Ohmsen, interview typescript.
20. Ibid.
21. Carell, *Invasion*, p. 41. There is confusion as to whether his name is Krieg (Ryan interview) or Grieg (Carell). I have chosen Krieg as the most likely.
22. Ibid., p. 42.
23. OUCR: Walter Ohmsen, interview typescript.
24. Ibid.
25. *Royal Engineer Journal*, vol. CVIII–CIX, April–December 1994–5.
26. Ibid.
27. Miller, *Nothing Less than Victory*, p. 209.
28. Ronald J. Drez, *Voices of D-Day*, p. 123.
29. *Royal Engineer Journal*, vol. CVIII–CIX, April–December 1994–5.
30. Drez, *Voices of D-Day*, p. 120.
31. Ibid., p. 123.
32. Ibid., p. 121.
33. Ibid.
34. Ibid., p. 122.
35. Ibid., p. 124.
36. Major John Couch Adams 'Tim' Roseveare, see http://www.pegasusarchive.org/normandy/tim_roseveare.htm
37. *Royal Engineer Journal*, vol. CVIII–CIX, April–December 1994–5.
38. Drez, *Voices of D-Day*, p. 122.
39. Alexander McKee, *Caen*, p. 39.
40. *Royal Engineer Journal*, vol. CVIII–CIX, April–December 1994–5.
41. Drez, *Voices of D-Day*, p. 124.
42. Ibid.
43. Ibid., p. 123.
44. Ibid., p. 125.
45. *Royal Engineer Journal*, vol. CVIII–CIX, April–December 1994–5.

Chapter 7: Landing by Moonlight

1. Speech by Raymond Paris, *Témoignage les 5–6 juin 1944 à Sainte-Mère-Église*, https://www.youtube.com/watch?v=QfWpRoty1js&t=395s
2. Raymond Paris, interview in Miller, *Nothing Less than Victory*, p. 225.
3. Alexandre Renaud, *Sainte-Mère-Église*, p. 36.
4. Rudi Escher, interview in Miller, *Nothing Less than Victory*, p. 228.
5. Raymond Paris, interview in Miller, *Nothing Less than Victory*, p. 225.

6. Renaud, *Sainte-Mère-Église*, p. 36.
7. Raymond Paris, interview in Miller, *Nothing Less than Victory*, p. 226.
8. Renaud, *Sainte-Mère-Église*, p. 37.
9. Raymond Paris, interview in Miller, *Nothing Less than Victory*, p. 226.
10. Julian 'Bud' Rice, written account: http://www.6juin1944.com/veterans/rice.php. See also http://www.usafe.af.mil/News/Features/Display/Article/749508/wwii-veterans-tell-70-year-old-story/ and http://www.smithsonianmag.com/videos/category/history/what-it-was-like-to-parachute-into-enemy-fir/
11. Julian 'Bud' Rice, written account: http://www.6juin1944.com/veterans/rice.php.
12. The paratroopers belonged to the 3rd Battalion of the 505th Parachute Infantry Regiment.
13. Joseph Balkoski, *Utah Beach*, p. 147.
14. MdeC: 02810, Bill Tucker, typescript account.
15. Ibid.
16. Julian 'Bud' Rice, written account: http://www.6juin1944.com/veterans/rice.php
17. MdeC: 02810, Bill Tucker, typescript account.
18. Julian 'Bud' Rice, written account: http://www.6juin1944.com/veterans/rice.php
19. MdeC: 02810, Bill Tucker, typescript account.
20. Julian Rice, 'D-Day Pilot Shares Memories of the Invasion', interview, 5 June 2014, http://www.nbcnews.com/storyline/d--day-70th-anniversary/d-day-pilot-shares-memories-invasion-tom-brokaw-n122951
21. Julian 'Bud' Rice, written account: http:// www.6juin1944.com/veterans/rice.php
22. MdeC: 02810, Bill Tucker, typescript account.
23. Julian 'Bud' Rice, written account: http://www.6juin1944.com/veterans/rice.php
24. Leslie Palmer Cruise, *Normandy, June 1944*, typescript account: http://www.6juin1944.com/veterans/cruise.php
25. MdeC: 02810, Bill Tucker, typescript account.
26. Leslie Palmer Cruise, *Normandy, June 1944*, typescript account: http://www.6juin1944.com/veterans/cruise.php
27. MdeC: 02810, Bill Tucker, typescript account.
28. NWWIIM: Ken Russell, typescript account.
29. Lieutenant Colonel Edward C. Krause, account from NARA but available online: http://www.americandday.org/Veterans/Krause_Edward_C.html

30. Bill Glauber, 'Reminders of D-Day are Part of Everyday Life in Normandy', *Baltimore Sun*, 26 May 2002.

31. John Hanc, 'French Town is a Living D-Day Memorial', *New York Times*, 23 October 2014, https://www.nytimes.com/2014/10/26/arts/artsspecial/french-town-is-a-living-d-day-memorial.html

32. *Sainte-Mère-Église, les civils se souviennent du débarquement*: Midi en France (TV) https://www.youtube.com/watch?v=C3u45murEGY&t=1s

33. Raymond Paris, interview in Miller, *Nothing Less than Victory*, p. 226.

34. As cited in Helmut von Keusgen, *Sainte-Mère-Église und Merderet*.

35. Rudi Escher, interview in Miller, *Nothing Less than Victory*, p. 228.

36. Raymond Paris, interview in ibid., p. 226.

37. Renaud, *Sainte-Mère-Église*, p. 37.

38. Raymond Paris, interview in Miller, *Nothing Less than Victory*, p. 226.

39. Rudi Escher, interview in ibid., p. 229.

Chapter 8: Sainte-Mère-Église

1. MdeC: TE277, Marcelle Hamel, typescript account.

2. Denise Lecourtois, http://www.6juin1944.com/veterans/lecourtois.php

3. MdeC: TE277, Marcelle Hamel, typescript account.

4. OUCR: François Lemonnier-Gruhier, *Parachutés le 6 juin*.

5. NWWIIM: Ronald Snyder, typescript interview.

6. NWWIIM: James Eads, typescript interview.

7. Frank A. Bilich, cited in Michel de Trez, *The Way We Were: Colonel Vandervoort*, D-Day Publishing, 2004, p. 35.

8. OUCR: Benjamin Vandervoort, typescript interview.

9. OUCR: Lyle Putnam, typescript interview and notes.

10. NWWIIM: Benjamin Vandervoort Debriefing Papers, 13 August 1944.

11. Leslie Palmer Cruise, *Normandy, June 1944*, typescript account: http://www.6juin1944.com/veterans/cruise.php

12. NWWIIM: Tom Porcella, typescript interview.

13. NARA: Edward Krause, debriefing paper, 13 August 1944.

14. Cited in Phil Nordyke, *Four Stars of Valor*, p. 150.

15. MdeC: 02810, Bill Tucker, typescript account.

16. Cited in Balkoski, *Utah Beach*, p. 147.

Chapter 9: Night Assault

1. LHCMA: Cliff Morris, *United We Conqered (sic) or The Diary of a Commando Soldier*, unpublished handwritten manuscript.
2. DDMA: DD/2008/54/2, Rupert Curtis, typescript.
3. LHCMA: Cliff Morris, *United We Conqered (sic) or The Diary of a Commando Soldier*, unpublished handwritten manuscript.
4. Dr J.H. Patterson in Simon Lovat, *March Past*, Appendix II, p. 367f.
5. LHCMA: Cliff Morris, *United We Conqered (sic) or The Diary of a Commando Soldier*, unpublished handwritten manuscript.
6. Ibid.
7. Iain Moncreiffe, introduction to Lovat, *March Past*, p. 9.
8. Lovat, *March Past*, p. 296.
9. Ibid., p. 135.
10. LHCMA: Cliff Morris, *United We Conqered (sic) or The Diary of a Commando Soldier*, unpublished handwritten manuscript.
11. Ibid.
12. Iain Moncreiffe, introduction to Lovat, *March Past*, p. 9.
13. DDMA: DD/2008/54/2, Rupert Curtis, typescript.
14. LHCMA: Derek Mills-Roberts, *Clash by Night: A Commando Chronicle* (author's hand-corrected proof).
15. LHCMA: Cliff Morris, *United We Conqered (sic) or The Diary of a Commando Soldier*, unpublished handwritten manuscript.
16. Bailey, *Forgotten Voices*, p. 87.
17. Lovat, *March Past*, p. 368.
18. LHCMA: Mills-Roberts, *Clash by Night* (author's hand-corrected proof).
19. Lovat, *March Past*, p. 305.
20. DDMA: DD/2008/54/2, Rupert Curtis, typescript.
21. MdeC: 02893, Lionel Roebuck, *The Five Yorkshire Tykes*, unpublished typescript.
22. Ibid.
23. Michael Strong, *Steiner's War*, p. 27. See also the detailed article in *Stern* magazine, 'Ich schämte mich, sie zu erschießen', 3 June 2004. For a full appraisal of the battle and the controversies surrounding the capture of the Merville Battery, see Neil Barber, *The Day the Devils Dropped In*, Appendix 5, p. 210ff.
24. Jefferson, *Assault on the Guns of Merville*, p. 93.
25. Ibid., p. 83.
26. Ibid., p. 84.

27. Strong, *Steiner's War*, p. 25.
28. Ibid., p. 38.
29. Ibid.
30. *Das Reich* article, July 1944, cited in Strong, *Steiner's War*, p. 65.
31. Strong, *Steiner's War*, p. 65.
32. OUCR: Alan Mower, interview.
33. OUCR: Sidney Capon, interview.
34. OUCR: Sidney Capon, handwritten account.
35. IWM: 13723, Alan Jefferson, interview.
36. Terence Otway, interview in Miller, *Nothing Less than Victory*, p. 211.
37. IWM: 13723, Alan Jefferson, interview.
38. Stuart Tootal, *The Manner of Men*, p. 139.
39. SWWEC (tape 383): Terence Otway, interview.
40. IWM: 13723, Alan Jefferson, interview.
41. Miller, *Nothing Less than Victory*, p. 211.
42. IWM: 12133, Terence Otway, interview.
43. Ibid.
44. IWM: 13723, Alan Jefferson, interview.
45. OUCR: Alan Mower, interview.
46. Ibid.
47. IWM: 13723, Alan Jefferson, interview.
48. Jefferson, *Assault on the Guns of Merville*, p. 110.
49. Sidney Capon, interview in Bailey, *Forgotten Voices*, p. 173.
50. Ibid., p. 174.
51. IWM: 13723, Alan Jefferson, interview.
52. www.pegasusarchive.org and Barber, *The Day the Devils Dropped In*, p. 92.
53. Miller, *Nothing Less than Victory*, p. 216.
54. Ibid., p. 218.
55. OUCR: Alan Mower, interview.
56. Barney Ross and Sidney Capon, interviews in Bailey, *Forgotten Voices*, p. 175.
57. Strong, *Steiner's War*, p. 47.
58. Sidney Capon, interview in Bailey, *Forgotten Voices*, p. 175.
59. OUCR: Alan Mower, interview.
60. Ibid.
61. Ibid.
62. Barney Ross, interview in Bailey, *Forgotten Voices*, p. 174.
63. *Das Reich* article, July 1944, cited in Strong, *Steiner's War*, p. 67.

64. Raimund Steiner, interview in *Stern* magazine, '*Ich schämte mich, sie zu erschießen*', 3 June 2004.

65. Raimund Steiner, interview in Jefferson, *Assault on the Guns of Merville*, pp. 110–11.

66. Raimund Steiner, interview in *Stern* magazine, '*Ich schämte mich, sie zu erschießen*', 3 June 2004.

67. Ibid.

68. Miller, *Nothing Less than Victory*, p. 216.

69. Hugo Pond, interview in Bailey, *Forgotten Voices*, p. 176.

70. www.pegasusarchive.org and Barber, *The Day the Devils Dropped In*, p. 90.

71. SWWEC (tape 383): Terence Otway, interview.

72. Barney Ross, interview in Bailey, *Forgotten Voices*, p. 174.

73. Barber, *The Day the Devils Dropped In*, p. 95.

Chapter 10: First Light

1. OUCR: Karl von Puttkamer, typescript interview.

2. Ibid.

3. OUCR: General Walter Warlimont, typescript interview.

4. Carell, *Invasion*, p. 50.

5. Malcolm Brannen's D-Day recollections can be found at http://www.6juin1944.com/veterans/brannen.php

6. See E.R. Hooton, *Eagle in Flames*, pp. 283–5 and p. 290. The exact number of sorties is disputed: Hooton's figures are founded on extensive archival research.

7. http://www.telegraph.co.uk/news/newstopics/howaboutthat/9578931/Lost-Lancaster-crew-identified-after-68-years-by-wireless-operators-wedding-ring.html See also 'Last Defence of the Reich, FW190 to the End of the War', *Aviation Classic*, 26 November 2014.

8. The story of the plane's discovery – and Eberspächer's role in shooting it down – was covered in detail in two newspaper articles: http://www.telegraph.co.uk/news/newstopics/howaboutthat/9578931/Lost-Lancaster-crew-identified-after-68-years-by-wireless-operators-wedding-ring.html and http://www.dailymail.co.uk/news/article-2211250/Wreckage-Lancaster-bomber-crashed-D-Day-killing-crew-identified.html

9. Irmgard Meyer, account in Miller, *Nothing Less than Victory*, p. 239.

10. Hubert Meyer, account in ibid., p. 238.

11. Ibid.

12. Irmgard Meyer, account in ibid., p. 239.

13. OUCR: Werner Pluskat, interview. See also the video interview with Pluskat on Belgian television, 5 June 1962, http://www.ina.fr/video/CAF93012581. Pluskat's movements that night have been subject to controversy ever since Hein Severloh claimed that the major was not at his post at the time of the landings. Since Pluskat's post was inland (in Eterham), Severloh's statement in no way contradicts Pluskat's written and oral testimony.

14. OUCR: Lieutenant Commander Heinrich Hoffmann, typescript interview.

Chapter 11: On Utah Beach

1. NWWIIM: Al Corry, typescript account.
2. Bowman, *Air War D-Day*, p. 56.
3. SWWEC: T2236, Captain Scott-Bowden, interview.
4. Samuel Morison, *The Invasion of France and Germany, 1944–1945 (History of United States Naval Operations in World War II)*, p. 93.
5. NWWIIM: Ross Olsen, typescript interview.
6. Morison, *Invasion of France and Germany*, p. 93.
7. Leonard Schroeder, interview in Franz-Olivier Giesbert, *Les Héros du 6 juin*.
8. NWWIIM: Malvin R. Pike, typescript interview.
9. Cited in Balkoski, *Utah Beach*, p. 180.
10. Ibid., p. 187.
11. NWWIIM: Malvin R. Pike, typescript interview.
12. NWWIIM: Howard Vander Beek, *Aboard the LCC 60*, unpublished typescript.
13. NWWIIM: Sims Gauthier, typescript interview.
14. NWWIIM: Samuel N. Grundfast, interview.
15. NWWIIM: Howard Vander Beek, *Aboard the LCC 60*, unpublished typescript.
16. NWWIIM: Cyrus Aydlett, typescript interview.
17. NWWIIM: Howard Vander Beek, *Aboard the LCC 60*, unpublished typescript.
18. NWWIIM: Sims Gauthier, typescript interview.
19. NWWIIM: Howard Vander Beek, *Aboard the LCC 60*, unpublished typescript.
20. Francis McKernon, interview: http://www.uss-corry-dd463.com/d--day_u-boat_photos/d-day_McKernon.htm

21. NWWIIM: Robert Beeman, typescript account, along with correspondence with Stephen Ambrose.

22. OUCR: George Hoffman, interview.

23. Francis McKernon, interview: http://www.uss-corry-dd463.com/d--day_u-boat_photos/d-day_McKernon.htm

24. OUCR: Benny Glisson, interview.

25. Ibid.

26. NWWIIM: Grant Gullickson, typescript account.

27. Ernie McKay, interview: http://www.uss-corry-dd463.com/d-day_u--boat_photos/d-day_McKay.htm

28. Testimony of Emil Vestuti, http://www.uss-corry-dd463.com/d-day_u--boat_photos/d-day_Vestuti.htm

29. Francis McKernon, interview: http://www.uss-corry-dd463.com/d--day_u-boat_photos/d-day_McKernon.htm

30. Mort Rubin, interview: http://www.uss-corry-dd463.com/d-day_u--boat_photos/d-day_Rubin.htm

31. Ibid.

32. Francis McKernon, interview: http://www.uss-corry-dd463.com/d--day_u-boat_photos/d-day_McKernon.htm

33. OUCR: Benny Glisson, interview.

34. NWWIIM: Grant Gullickson, typescript account.

35. NWWIIM: Malvin R. Pike, typescript account.

36. Bailey, *Forgotten Voices*, p. 287.

37. Roland Ruppenthal, *Utah Beach to Cherbourg, 6 June–27 June 1944*

38. NWWIIM: Bruce Bradley, typescript account.

39. Ibid.

40. Balkoski, *Utah Beach*, p. 190.

41. Ibid., p. 191.

42. Ibid., p. 192.

43. Ibid.

44. NWWIIM: Howard Vander Beek, *Aboard the LCC 60*, unpublished typescript.

45. Ibid.

46. NWWIIM: Malvin R. Pike, typescript account.

47. Leonard Schroeder, interview in Giesbert, *Les Héros du 6 juin*.

48. OUCR: Leonard Schroeder, interview.

49. Leonard Schroeder, interview in Giesbert, *Les Héros du 6 juin*.

50. Balkoski, *Utah Beach*, p. 197.

51. Ibid.

52. NWWIIM: Malvin R. Pike, typescript account.

53. Balkoski, *Utah Beach*, p. 197.
54. NWWIIM: Malvin R. Pike, typescript account.
55. Balkoski, *Utah Beach*, p. 243.
56. NWWIIM: Malvin R. Pike and Eugene Brierre, typescript accounts.
57. Balkoski, *Utah Beach*, p. 243.
58. Maxwell Taylor, *Swords and Plowshares*, p. 81.

Chapter 12: In Coastal Waters

1. Butcher, *My Three Years with Eisenhower*, p. 486.
2. Cited in Alan Axelrod, *Eisenhower on Leadership*, p. 209.
3. Butcher, *My Three Years with Eisenhower*, p. 486.
4. Ibid., p. 487.
5. OUCR: Heinrich Hoffmann, typescript interview.
6. NWWIIM: Nalecz-Tyminski, typescript account.
7. DDMA: PORMG 2014/58/103, Able Seaman Sheppard, account.
8. OUCR: Heinrich Hoffmann, typescript interview.
9. IWM: LBY93/2156, Patrick Hennessey, *Young Man in a Tank*.
10. Miller, *Nothing Less Than Victory*, p. 308.
11. IWM: 13390, John Barnes, audio interview.
12. Ibid.
13. IWM: LBY93/2156, Patrick Hennessey, *Young Man in a Tank*.
14. http://www.pegasusarchive.org/normandy/rep1318hussars.htm
15. IWM: 17678, Patrick Hennessey, audio interview, and IWM: LBY93/2156, Hennessey, *Young Man in a Tank*.
16. SWWEC: Patrick Hennessey, typescript interview.
17. Douglas Reeman, *D-Day: A Personal Reminiscence*, p. 12.
18. Craig L. Symonds, *Neptune*, p. 265.
19. Admiral Morton Deyo, cited in ibid., p. 264.
20. Paul Winter, *D-Day Documents*; see also TNA ADM 53/120730 for the *Warspite*'s ship's log.
21. Reeman, *D-Day: A Personal Reminiscence*, p. 13.
22. David Holbrook and Geoffrey Halson, *Flesh Wounds*, p. 119: the novel was drawn directly from Holbrook's own battle experiences, as indicated in the foreword.
23. Winter, *D-Day Documents*, p. 87.
24. Ibid.
25. Piprel account cited in Marie-France Coquart and Philippe Huet, *Le Jour le plus fou*; see also http://omaha-vierville.com/WebOmahaVierville1944/2323-MemoiresPiprel.html

26. Fernand Olard's account: http://omaha-vierville.com/WebOmahaVierville1944/index2omaha.htm

27. The de Loÿs account is cited in Coquart and Huet, *Le Jour le plus fou*. See also http://omaha-vierville.com/WebOmahaVierville1944/index2omaha.htm

28. Cited in Mary Louise Roberts, *D-Day through French Eyes*, p. 73.

Chapter 13: Omaha

1. OUCR: Barton Davis, typescript interview.

2. NWWIIM: Harry Bare, typescript account.

3. IWM: 26677, Jimmy Green, oral interview.

4. Ibid.

5. Jimmy Green account: Green wrote his account in response to Stephen Ambrose's 'flight of fancy', which claims Green's craft was 'vaporized', along with all the men on board. 'A bare minimum of research was all that was required to find out how Taylor Fellers died and where he was buried,' he said. Green was not the first veteran to be irritated by Ambrose's sometimes cavalier approach to the facts. http://www.bbc.co.uk/history/ww2peopleswar/stories/68/a1929468.shtml

6. http://www.newsadvance.com/news/local/bedford-boys-taylor-fellers/article_ea93e4e0-e2a3-11e3-ac52-0017a43b2370.html

7. Jimmy Green, interview: http://www.bbc.co.uk/history/ww2peopleswar/stories/68/a1929468.shtml See also: http://www.newsadvance.com/news/local/bedford-boys-taylor-fellers/article_ea93e4e0-e2a3-11e3-ac52-0017a43b2370.html

8. IWM: 26677, Jimmy Green, oral interview.

9. Ibid.

10. IWM: 26677, Jimmy Green, oral interview.

11. NWWIIM: Gilbert Murdock, typescript interview.

12. IWM: 26677, Jimmy Green, oral interview.

13. NWWIIM: Gilbert Murdock, typescript interview.

14. IWM: 26677, Jimmy Green, oral interview.

15. Alex Kershaw, *The Bedford Boys*, p. 127.

16. Jimmy Green's BBC account cited above.

17. Vince Milano and Bruce Conner, *Normandiefront*, p. 78.

18. Ibid.

19. All from ibid., pp. 78–83.

20. Harold Baumgarten, *D-Day Survivor*, p. 59.

21. Ibid., p. 65.

22. S.L.A. Marshall, 'First Wave at Omaha Beach', *Atlantic Magazine*, November 1960.
23. Ibid.
24. Robin Neillands, *The Battle of Normandy*, p. 184.
25. NWWIIM: Al Little, typescript account.
26. NWWIIM: Harold Baumgarten, typescript account.
27. Neillands, *The Battle of Normandy*, p. 184.
28. S.L.A. Marshall, 'First Wave at Omaha Beach', *Atlantic Magazine*, November 1960.
29. NWWIIM: Harold Baumgarten, typescript account.
30. Baumgarten, *D-Day Survivor*, p. 66.
31. NWWIIM: Harold Baumgarten, typescript account.
32. S.L.A. Marshall, 'First Wave at Omaha Beach', *Atlantic Magazine*, November 1960.
33. Ibid.
34. NWWIIM: Gilbert Murdock, typescript interview.
35. IWM: 26677, Jimmy Green, oral interview.
36. NWWIIM: Company A Battlefield Report, typescript.

Chapter 14: Easy Red

1. NWWIIM: Franz Gockel, typescript.
2. SWWEC: Gockel, letter to parents, 10 June 1944.
3. SWWEC: DBR0159-44C, Gockel, typescript account.
4. Ibid.
5. NWWIIM: Jack Ellery, typescript.
6. NWWIIM: Warner Hamlett, typescript.
7. Ibid.
8. MWWIIM: Joe Pilck, typescript.
9. Paul Huard, *The MG 42 Machine Gun was Hitler's Buzz-Saw*: https://medium.com/war-is-boring/the-mg42-machine-gun-was-hitlers-buzz-saw-aaebfde958e4
10. http://witnify.com/germans-americans-recall-hell-omaha/
11. NWWIIM: Franz Gockel, typescript.
12. http://witnify.com/germans-americans-recall-hell-omaha/
13. SWWEC: DBR0159-44C, Gockel, typescript account.
14. See ibid. and NWWIIM: Franz Gockel, typescript.
15. 'Beast of Omaha', *Scotsman*, 6 June 2004: http://www.scotsman.com/news/world/beast-of-omaha-weeps-as-he-recalls-slaughter-of-thousands-on-beach-1-1394712

16. SWWEC: DBR0159-44C, Gockel, typescript account.
17. NWWIIM: Warner Hamlett, typescript.
18. Ibid., Jack Ellery, typescript.
19. Roger Brugger, cited in Michael D. Hull, *The Battle for Omaha Beach*, Warfare History Network, http://warfarehistorynetwork.com/daily/wwii/the-d-day-invasion-the-road-to-operation-overlord/
20. NWWIIM: Warner Hamlett, typescript.
21. NWWIIM: William Otlowski, typescript account.
22. NWWIIM: Warner Hamlett, typescript.
23. NWWIIM: Harry Bare, typescript account.
24. OUCR: Barton Davis, interview.
25. NWWIIM: Jack Ellery, typescript.

Chapter 15: Gold

1. OUCR: Helmut Lang, typescript interview.
2. David Irving, *The Trail of the Fox*, p. 336.
3. OUCR: Koch, *Erwin Rommel*, typescript translation.
4. Irving, *The Trail of the Fox*, p. 336.
5. OUCR: Helmut Lang, typescript interview.
6. Carell, *Invasion*, p. 95.
7. Helmut Meyer, interview in Miller, *Nothing Less than Victory*, p. 238.
8. Irmgard Meyer, interview in ibid., pp. 238–40.
9. IWM: 19906, Walter 'Wally' Blanchard, interview.
10. OUCR: Peter Martin, interview.
11. IWM: 19906, Walter 'Wally' Blanchard, interview.
12. OUCR: Peter Martin, interview.
13. Ibid.
14. IWM: 13420, Ronald Mole, interview.
15. IWM: 20602, Robert Palmer, interview.
16. OUCR: Stanley Hollis, interview typescript.
17. Mike Morgan, *D-Day Hero*, p. xvi.
18. Ibid., p. 19.
19. OUCR: Stanley Hollis, interview typescript.
20. Ibid.: see also IWM: 1648, Stanley Hollis, interview in *D-Day: Beachhead Fighting*, oral interview
21. Ibid.

Chapter 16: Juno

1. Michael J. McKeogh, *Sgt Mickey and General Ike*, Nabu Press, 2011.
2. Butcher, *My Three Years with Eisenhower*, p. 489.
3. BBC message cited in Cornelius Ryan, *The Longest Day*.
4. SWWEC: DBR0252-41C, Georges Regnauld, *Résumé de ce que fut l'occupation allemande à Bernières-sur-mer de juin 1940 à juin 1944*.
5. Ibid.
6. MdeC: MEMO_ARCH_03625, Marie-Amélie Notteau-Wiarre, diary.
7. SWWEC: DBR0252-41C, Georges Regnauld, *Mes souvenirs de ce que fut le jour le plus long c'était à Bernières-sur-mer*.
8. Mark Gollom, 'Charles Dalton, KStJ, ED OC B Company, D-Day 1910–1998', *National Post*, 24 February 1999. The quote is from Corporal Joe Oggy.
9. Ibid. The quote is from Barney Danson, chairman of the Canadian War Museum's advisory committee and colleague of Colonel Dalton.
10. Mark Zuehlke, 'Assault on Juno': http://zuehlke.ca/excerpt-from-assault-on-juno/
11. Jean Portugal (ed.), *We Were There*, vol. 2, *The Army*, Introduction to the Dalton Brothers, p. 636.
12. Charles Dalton: https://qormuseum.org/soldiers-of-the-queens-own/dalton-charles-osborne/
13. John Fotheringham, 'See You on the Beach': https://www.junobeach.org/see-you-on-the-beach/
14. Charles Martin and Roy Whitsed, *Battle Diary*, p. 4.
15. https://qormuseum.org/2016/06/06/1998-interviews-with-three-qor-d-day-veterans/
16. Doug Hester, *War Memoir*, unpublished. See also https://qormuseum.org/soldiers-of-the-queens-own/hester-doug/
17. Jim Wilkins, 'D-Day Recollections': Jim Wilkins: http://users.erols.com/wolfy/qor/html/body_wilkins.html
18. https://qormuseum.org/2016/06/06/1998-interviews-with-three-qor-d-day-veterans/
19. John Missions, interview in Portugal (ed.), *We Were There*, vol. 2, *The Army*, p. 681f.
20. Elliot Dalton, interview in ibid., p. 637f.
21. Bob Rae, interview in ibid., p. 661f.
22. Elliot Dalton, interview in ibid., p. 637f.
23. John Fotheringham, 'See You on the Beach': https://www.junobeach.org/see-you-on-the-beach/

24. Elliot Dalton, interview in Portugal (ed.), *We Were There*, vol. 2, *The Army*, p. 637f.
25. Bob Rae, interview in ibid., p. 661f.
26. Joe Wagar, interview in ibid., p. 648f.
27. John McClean, interview in ibid., p. 606f.
28. Elliot Dalton, interview in ibid., p. 637f.
29. Mark Gollom, 'Charles Dalton, KStJ, ED OC B Company, D-Day 1910–1998', *National Post*, 24 February 1999.
30. Charles Tubb, interview in Portugal (ed.), *We Were There*, vol. 2, *The Army*, p. 904f.
31. Cited in Tim Saunders, *Juno Beach: Canadian 3rd Infantry Division – July 1944*, McGill-Queen's University Press, 2004, p.80.
32. Bailey, *Forgotten Voices*, p. 224.
33. Charles Belton, interview in Portugal (ed.), *We Were There*, vol. 6, *The Army*, p. 3038.

Chapter 17: Cliff-top Guns

1. Omar Bradley and Clay Blair, *A General's Life*, p. 249.
2. W.C. Heinz, 'I took my son to Omaha Beach', *Collier's Magazine*, 11 June 1954.
3. Ronald Lane, *Rudder's Rangers*, p. 68.
4. Christopher B. Bean, *James Earl Rudder: A Lesson in Leadership*, doctoral thesis.
5. Thomas Hatfield, *Rudder*, p. 88.
6. John Raaen, cited in ibid.
7. Omar Bradley, *A Soldier's Story*, p. 269.
8. OUCR: Herman Stein, typescript interview.
9. W.C. Heinz, 'I took my son to Omaha Beach', *Collier's Magazine*, 11 June 1954.
10. Hatfield, *Rudder*, p. 88.
11. OUCR: Herman Stein, typescript interview.
12. NWWIIM: James Eikner, typescript account.
13. OUCR: Herman Stein, typescript interview.
14. Cited in Symonds, *Neptune*, p. 293.
15. OUCR: William Petty, typescript interview.
16. NWWIIM: George Kerchner, typescript account.
17. NWWIIM: Leonard Lomell, typescript account.
18. OUCR: William Petty, typescript interview.

19. W.C. Heinz, 'I took my son to Omaha Beach', *Collier's Magazine*, 11 June 1954.

20. NWWIIM: Elmer Vermeer, typescript account.

21. Ibid.

22. OUCR: William Petty, typescript interview.

23. NWWIIM: James Eikner, typescript account.

24. Ibid.

25. OUCR: William Petty, typescript interview.

26. OUCR: Herman Stein, typescript interview.

27. NWWIIM: George Kerchner, typescript account.

28. W.C. Heinz, 'I took my son to Omaha Beach', *Collier's Magazine*, 11 June 1954.

29. NWWIIM: Leonard Lomell, typescript account.

30. Ibid.: Elmer Vermeer, typescript account.

31. http://www.historynet.com/d-day-interview-with-two-us-2nd-ranger-battalion-members-who-describe-the-attack-at-pointe-du-hoc.htm

32. NWWIIM: Leonard Lomell, typescript account.

33. OUCR: William Petty, typescript interview.

34. NWWIIM: Leonard Lomell, typescript account.

35. http://www.historynet.com/d-day-interview-with-two-us-2nd-ranger-battalion-members-who-describe-the-attack-at-pointe-du-hoc.htm

36. NWWIIM: Leonard Lomell, typescript account.

37. http://www.historynet.com/d-day-interview-with-two-us-2nd-ranger-battalion-members-who-describe-the-attack-at-pointe-du-hoc.htm

38. NWWIIM: Leonard Lomell, typescript account.

39. NWWIIM: Salva Maimone, typescript account.

40. Cited in Stephen Ambrose, *D-Day*, p. 416.

Chapter 18: The Mad Bastard

1. http://www.bbc.co.uk/history/ww2peopleswar/stories/38/a2366138.shtml

2. DDMA: 2001.687/DD 2000.5.2, Pat Blandford, interview, recorded April 1991, oral history transcript.

3. http://www.bbc.co.uk/history/ww2peopleswar/stories/38/a2366138.shtml

4. Jean Watson, interview as cited in Peter Liddle, *D-Day*, p. 240f.

5. Bill Millin obituary, http://www.independent.co.uk/news/obituaries/piper-bill-millin-the-mad-piper-who-piped-the-allied-troops-ashore-on-d-day-2059271.html

6. DDMA: DD/2008/54/2, Rupert Curtis papers.

7. Lovat, *March Past*, p. 306.

8. Ibid., p. 309.

9. Ibid., p. 308.

10. DDMA: DD/2008/54/2, Rupert Curtis papers.

11. Lovat, *March Past*, p. 301.

12. Ibid., p. 310.

13. LHCMA: Cliff Morris, *United We Conqered (sic) or The Diary of a Commando Soldier*, unpublished handwritten manuscript.

14. Lovat, *March Past*, p. 310.

15. LHCMA: Cliff Morris, *United We Conqered (sic) or The Diary of a Commando Soldier*, unpublished handwritten manuscript.

16. MdeC: MEMO_ARCH_02893, Lionel Roebuck, *The Five Yorkshire Tykes*, unpublished typescript.

17. Lovat, *March Past*, p. 311.

18. http://www.pegasusarchive.org/normandy/bill_millin.htm

19. DDMA: DD/2008/54/2, Rupert Curtis papers.

20. IWM: 11614, William 'Bill' Millin, audio interview.

21. Lovat, *March Past*, p. 311.

22. Ibid., p. 313.

23. Ibid., p. 314.

24. NWWIIM: Peter Masters, typescript account.

25. LHCMA: Cliff Morris, *United We Conqered (sic) or The Diary of a Commando Soldier*, unpublished handwritten manuscript.

26. LHCMA: Mills-Roberts, *Clash by Night* (author's hand-corrected proof).

27. Ibid.

28. OUCR: Frederick Mears, typescript interview.

29. Miller, *Nothing Less than Victory*, p. 312.

30. DDMA: PORMG 2004/3585, *D-Day Before and After: The Memoirs of George Jowett*.

31. LHCMA: Cliff Morris, *United We Conqered (sic) or The Diary of a Commando Soldier*, unpublished handwritten manuscript.

32. LHCMA: Mills-Roberts, *Clash by Night* (author's hand-corrected proof), p. 96.

33. Lovat, *March Past*, p. 319.

34. http://www.pegasusarchive.org/normandy/bill_millin.htm

35. OUCR: Josef Priller, typescript interview; but see also Trevor Constable and Raymond Toliver, *Horrido!*, p. 252ff.
36. OUCR: Josef Priller, typescript interview.
37. Lovat, *March Past*, pp. 303–4.
38. http://www.telegraph.co.uk/obituaries/2016/06/21/ren-rossey-french-commando-obituary/
39. Cited in Maurice Chauvet, *It's a Long Way to Normandy*, p. 323.
40. Decroix memoir in Jean-Pierre Guéno, *Paroles du Jour J*, p. 59.

Chapter 19: Deadlock on Omaha

1. Günsche's report cited in Meyer, *The 12th SS*, vol. 1, p. 97.
2. OUCR: Karl von Puttkamer, typescript interview.
3. OUCR: General Walter Warlimont, typescript interview.
4. Ian Kershaw, *Hitler, 1936–1945*, p. 640.
5. OUCR: Karl von Puttkamer, typescript interview.
6. David Irving, *Göring*, p. 427.
7. NWWIIM: James Van Fleet, typescript account.
8. Bradley, *A Soldier's Story*, p. 270.
9. Bradley and Blair, *A General's Life*, p. 251.
10. IWM: 19906, Walter 'Wally' Blanchard, audio interview.
11. NWWIIM: William Marshall, typescript account.
12. Bradley and Blair, *A General's Life*, p. 251.
13. NWWIIM: Felix Branham, typescript account.
14. http://articles.latimes.com/1994-05-31/news/wr-64225_1_d-day-invasion/11
15. NWWIIM: Carl Weast, typescript account.
16. Joseph Balkoski, *Omaha Beach*, p. 195.
17. Ibid.
18. Combat Studies Institute, *Studies in Battle Command*, especially chapter XVI: Major Stephen C. McGeorge, 'Seeing the Battlefield: Brigadier-General Norman D. Cota's "Bastard Brigade" at Omaha Beach', Fort Leavenworth, Kansas, n.d.
19. Ibid.
20. Balkoski, *Omaha Beach*, p. 193.
21. http://articles.latimes.com/1994-05-31/news/wr-64225_1_d-day-invasion/11
22. Cited in Balkoski, *Omaha Beach*, p. 194.
23. Ibid., p. 196.
24. NWWIIM: Jack Shea, typescript account.

25. NWWIIM: John Raaen, typescript account.
26. NWWIIM: Victor Fast, typescript account.
27. OUCR: Captain McGraw, typescript battlefield account.
28. NWWIIM: Jack Shea, typescript account.
29. NWWIIM: Harry Parley, typescript account.
30. NWWIIM: John Raaen, typescript account.
31. NWWIIM: Victor Fast, typescript account.
32. NWWIIM: Jack Shea, typescript account.
33. NWWIIM: Carl Weast, typescript account.

Chapter 20: Cracks in the Wall

1. NWWIIM: Edward Duffy, typescript account.
2. Morison, *Invasion of France and Germany*, p. 143.
3. Symonds, *Neptune*, p. 295.
4. Kenneth Janda, Jeffrey Berry, Jerry Goldmand and Deborah Schildkraut, *The Challenge of Democracy: Government in America*, Cengage, 2015, p. 249.
5. Drez, *Voices of D-Day*, p. 283f.
6. Ibid.
7. Morison, *Invasion of France and Germany*, p. 144.
8. NWWIIM: Edward Duffy, typescript account.
9. NWWIIM: Felix Podolak, typescript account.
10. Milano and Conner, *Normandiefront*, p. 98.
11. NWWIIM: William Gentry, typescript account.
12. Drez, *Voices of D-Day*, p. 285.
13. NWWIIM: Carl Weast, typescript account.
14. NWWIIM: John Shea, typescript account.
15. Hein Severloh, *WN62*, p. 65.
16. Ibid., p. 63.
17. SWWEC: DBR0159-44C, Franz Gockel, typescript account.
18. Severloh, *WN62*, p. 70ff.
19. Ruppenthal, *Omaha Beachhead*, pp. 82–3.

Chapter 21: Race to the Bridge

1. Howard and Bates, *The Pegasus Diaries*, p. 131.
2. NWWIIM: Harry Clark, typescript account.
3. Howard and Bates, *The Pegasus Diaries*, p. 131.
4. NWWIIM: Harry Clark, typescript account.

5. NWWIIM: Wally Parr, typescript account.

6. Howard and Bates, *The Pegasus Diaries*, p. 135.

7. NWWIIM: Wally Parr, typescript account.

8. Edwards, *The Devil's Own Luck*, pp. 47–8.

9. NWWIIM: Wally Parr, typescript account.

10. Howard and Bates, *The Pegasus Diaries*, p. 133.

11. NWWIIM: Wally Parr, typescript account.

12. Ambrose, *D-Day*, p. 569.

13. Howard and Bates, *The Pegasus Diaries*, p. 136.

14. Masters, *Striking Back*, p. 157. The German phrase is: *Ihr seid vollkommen umzingelt – Ihr habt keine Chance. Werft Eure Waffen fort und kommt mit den Handen hoch 'raus wenn Ihr leben wollt. Der Krieg ist aus fur Euch!*

15. Stan Scott and Neil Barber, *Fighting with the Commandos*, p. xxii.

16. Cited in ibid., p. xxiii.

17. Scott and Barber, *Fighting with the Commandos*.

18. IWM: 20940, Stanley Scott, audio interview.

19. Edwards, *The Devil's Own Luck*, p. 54.

20. http://www.pegasusarchive.org/normandy/bill_millin.htm

21. Edwards, *The Devil's Own Luck*, p. 55.

22. NWWIIM: Wally Parr, typescript account.

23. http://www.pegasusarchive.org/normandy/bill_millin.htm

24. Howard and Bates, *The Pegasus Diaries*, p. 137.

25. MdeC: MEMO_ARCH_03492, John Butler, *Diary of the Taking of Pegasus Bridge*, handwritten account.

Chapter 22: The Bombing of Caen

1. Hansard, available online at: http://hansard.millbanksystems.com/commons/1944/jun/06/ration-books-thefts

2. Harold Nicolson, *Diaries and Letters, 1939–1945*, p. 159.

3. http://hansard.millbanksystems.com/commons/1944/jun/06/liberation-of-rome-landings-in-france

4. Nicolson, *Diaries and Letters*, p. 159.

5. http://hansard.millbanksystems.com/commons/1944/jun/06/liberation-of-rome-landings-in-france

6. Nicolson, *Diaries and Letters*, p. 159.

7. Hansard, available online at: http://hansard.millbanksystems.com/commons/1944/jun/06/ liberation-of-rome-landings-in-france

8. SWWEC: LEEWW2001.987, James Kyle papers.

9. Madame Hélène Hurel, testimony in Miller, *Nothing Less than Victory*, p. 382.
10. Bernard Goupil, testimony in Michel Boivin et al., *Villes normandes sous les bombes*, p. 87ff.
11. Madame Pernelle, testimony in Miller, *Nothing Less than Victory*, p. 384.
12. Miller, *Nothing Less than Victory*, p. 384.
13. Madame Quaire, testimony in ibid., p. 385.
14. MdeC: MEMO_ARCH_03207, Denise Harel, *Mon journal*, handwritten diary.
15. MdeC: MEMO_ARCH_03276, Geneviève Vion, typescript testimony.
16. Bernard Goupil, testimony in Boivin et al., *Villes normandes sous les bombes*, p. 91.
17. Madame Quaire, testimony in Miller, *Nothing Less than Victory*, p. 385.
18. Guéno, *Paroles du Jour J*, pp. 61–2.
19. Bernard Goupil, testimony in Boivin et al., *Villes normandes sous les bombes*, p. 87ff.
20. Heinz, interview in Miller, *Nothing Less than Victory*, pp. 383–4. See also Heinz interview in *Ville de Caen: Récits de la vie caennaise 6 juin–19 juillet 1944*, Brochure réalisée par l'Atelier offset de la Mairie de Caen Dépôt légal: 2e trimestre 1984. See also 'Paroles de témoins': Propos recueillis par Nadège Orange, Michel Follorou et Willy Oriou, *Caen Magazine*, special sixtieth anniversary. And see http://paril.crdp.ac-caen.fr/_PRODUCTIONS/70e/co/heintz_hopital.html
21. Cited in Robin Neillands and Roderick de Normann, *D-Day 1944*, p. 298.
22. Cited on http://sgmcaen.free.fr/vieacaen.htm#LEBONSAUVEUR
23. Antoine Magonette, testimony in Guéno, *Paroles du Jour J*, pp. 60–1, originally in Antoine Magonette and Christian Colle, *Le Ciel est troublé*, France Europe Editions, 2002.
24. Bernard Goupil, testimony in Boivin et al., *Villes normandes sous les bombes*, p. 87ff.
25. Antoine Magonette, testimony in Guéno, *Paroles du Jour J*, pp. 60–1, originally in Magonette and Colle, *Le Ciel est troublé*.

Chapter 23: Counter-Attack

1. OUCR: Hayn, *Die Invasion*, typescript translation.
2. MdeC: MEMO_ARCH_03563, Alfred Sturm, *Normandie 6 juin 1944*, typescript.
3. Allan Michie, *Honour for All*, p. 118.

4. Cited in Atkinson, *Guns at Last Light*, p. 90.
5. http://www.bbc.co.uk/programmes/articles/ LL62CYPxJb5no XChgJ8sMT/d-day-1pm-correspondents-reports-continued
6. NWWIIM: Vandervoort report, typescript.
7. NWWIIM: Otis Sampson, typescript account.
8. NWWIIM: John Fitzgerald, typescript account.
9. NWWIIM: Vandervoort report, typescript.
10. NWWIIM: Otis Sampson, typescript account.
11. NWWIIM: John Fitzgerald, typescript account.
12. NWWIIM: Charles Sammon, typescript account.
13. NWWIIM: Vandervoort report, typescript.
14. OUCR: Anton Wuensch, typescript interview.

Chapter 24: Victory at Omaha

1. Miller, *Nothing Less than Victory*, pp. 443–5.
2. *Paris News*, Texas, 27 May 1984, p. 11.
3. Clifford Graves, *Front Line Surgeons*, Frye and Smith, 1950, p. vi.
4. Dennis L. Breo, 'June 6, 1944: Two Doctors Relive D-Day Dangers', *Journal of the American Medical Association*, 8 June 1994.
5. Graves, *Front Line Surgeons*, p. 203.
6. Treadwell Ireland, 'The Youngest Surgeon', *Action Medical Journal*, 2 June 1994 (typescript in NWWIIM).
7. OUCR: Alfred Eigenberg, interview typescript, and Eigenberg's letter to *Reader's Digest* (also in OUCR).
8. Cited in Miller, *Nothing Less than Victory*, p. 411f.
9. Balkoski, *Omaha Beach*, p. 269.
10. Miller, *Nothing Less than Victory*, p. 458.
11. NWWIIM: John Raaen, typescript account.
12. Balkoski, *Omaha Beach*, p. 274.
13. NWWIIM: Carl Weast, typescript account.
14. Balkoski, *Omaha Beach*, pp. 292–3.
15. NWWIIM: William Gentry, typescript account.
16. https://www.defensemedianetwork.com/stories/d-day-horace-flack-margaret-flack-and-the-uss-harding/3/
17. NWWIIM: *Harding Action Report*, typescript account.
18. Balkoski, *Omaha Beach*, p. 288 (from an interview with Captain Joseph Dawson).

Chapter 25: Frontier Fighting

1. Bailey, *Forgotten Voices*, pp. 319–20.
2. OUCR: Donald Gardner, typescript interview.
3. Liddle, *D-Day*, p. 148.
4. IWM: 12778, Peter Martin, audio interview.
5. IWM: 21290, Richard Gosling, audio interview.
6. IWM: 9297, Harold Siggins, audio interview.
7. Cited in Martin Bowman, *Air War D-Day: Gold, Juno, Sword*, p. 153.
8. Robert Kershaw, *D-Day*, p. 305.
9. Bob Rae, interview in Portugal (ed.), *We Were There*, vol. 2, *The Army*, p. 661f.
10. Bob Rae, interview in ibid., p. 1458f.
11. Mark Zuehlke, *Juno Beach*, p. 324ff.

Chapter 26: Panzer Attack

1. OUCR: Colonel von Oppeln-Bronikowski, typescript interview.
2. Ibid.
3. OUCR: Werner Kortenhaus, typescript interview.
4. OUCR: General Edgar Feuchtinger, typescript interview.
5. OUCR: Colonel von Oppeln-Bronikowski, typescript interview.
6. Captain Herr, interview in Miller, *Nothing Less than Victory*, pp. 395–9.
7. OUCR: Colonel von Oppeln-Bronikowski, typescript interview.
8. OUCR: Hayn, *Die Invasion*, typescript translation. .
9. OUCR: Wilhelm von Gottberg, typescript interview.
10. Captain Herr, interview in Miller, *Nothing Less than Victory*, pp. 395–9.
11. OUCR: Wilhelm von Gottberg, typescript interview.
12. OUCR: Colonel von Oppeln-Bronikowski, typescript interview.
13. Captain Herr, interview in Miller, *Nothing Less than Victory*, pp. 395–9.
14. OUCR: Walter Hermes, typescript interview.
15. OUCR: Colonel von Oppeln-Bronikowski, typescript interview.
16. IWM: 18004, George Rayson, audio interview.
17. Ibid.
18. IWM: 20009, Leslie Perry, audio interview.
19. Ibid., quoting Jim Hunter.
20. IWM: 18004, George Rayson, audio interview.
21. http://nvx.franceinfo.fr/leur6juin1944/hans/
22. IWM: 13390, John Barnes, audio interview.

23. Cited in Ken Ford and Howard Gerrard, *D-Day 1944: Sword Beach and the British Airborne Landings*, p. 69.
24. IWM: 17979, Arthur Blizzard, audio interview.

Chapter 27: Twilight

1. Lovat, *March Past*, p. 327.
2. IWM: 20940, Stanley 'Scotty' Scott, audio interview.
3. Donald Gilchrist, *Don't Cry for Me*, p. 64.
4. LHCMA: Mills-Roberts, *Clash by Night* (author's hand-corrected proof).
5. LHCMA: Cliff Morris, *United We Conqered (sic) or The Diary of a Commando Soldier*, unpublished handwritten manuscript.
6. Ibid.
7. Ibid.
8. Cited in Miller, *Nothing Less than Victory*, p. 467.
9. LHCMA: Cliff Morris, *United We Conqered (sic) or The Diary of a Commando Soldier*, unpublished handwritten manuscript
10. Miller, *Nothing Less than Victory*, p. 467.
11. LHCMA: Cliff Morris, *United We Conqered (sic) or The Diary of a Commando Soldier*, unpublished handwritten manuscript

Chapter 28: Night

1. Miller, *Nothing Less than Victory*, p. 454.
2. IWM: 14987, Irene Gray, audio interview.
3. IWM: 12590, Patrick Bayly, audio interview.
4. IWM: 29996, Mike Brown, audio interview.
5. IWM: 21877, James Cramer, audio interview.
6. NWWIIM: Sam Gibbons, typescript account.
7. NWWIIM: Otis Sampson, typescript account.
8. OUCR: Helmut Lang, typescript interview.
9. Lionel Ellis, *Victory in the West: The Battle of Normandy*, vol. 1, p. 216.
10. Miller, *Nothing Less than Victory*, p. 448.
11. OUCR: Koch, *Erwin Rommel*, typescript translation.
12. OUCR: Helmut Lang, typescript interview.
13. LHCMA: Cliff Morris, *United We Conqered (sic) or The Diary of a Commando Soldier*, unpublished handwritten manuscript.
14. Miller, *Nothing Less than Victory*, p. 468.
15. Ibid., p. 472.
16. Ibid., p. 462.

17. IWM: 18827, Harry Pinnegar, audio interview.
18. Miller, *Nothing Less than Victory*, p. 471.
19. NWWIIM: Harold Baumgarten, typescript account.
20. NWWIIM: Robert Miller, typescript account.
21. Ernie Pyle and David Nichols, *Ernie's War: The Best of Ernie Pyle's World War II Dispatches*, pp. 277–80. See also http://teachers.sduhsd.net/mgaughen/docs/OnWWII.pdf

Afterword

1. See Lieutenant Colonel F.A. Osmanski, *Logistical Planning of Operation Overlord*, Archives Section, Library Services, Fort Leavenworth, Kansas, Doc No.: 2128.67.

Bibliography

THE SOURCE MATERIAL for *D-Day: The Soldiers' Story* is drawn in large part from personal testimonies (handwritten and type-script), audio interviews and oral transcripts, as well as unpublished memoirs, diaries and letters. Detailed references can be found in the Notes and Sources. The most useful published accounts – both primary and secondary works – are listed below.

Ambrose, Stephen E., *Supreme Commander: The War Years of Dwight D. Eisenhower*, Doubleday, 1970
——, *Pegasus Bridge: June 6, 1944*, Simon and Schuster, 1985
——, *D-Day: June 6, 1944: The Climactic Battle of World War II*, Simon and Schuster, 2016
Atkinson, Rick, *The Guns at Last Light: The War in Western Europe, 1944–1945*, Little, Brown, 2013
Axelrod, Alan, *Eisenhower on Leadership: Ike's Enduring Lessons in Total Victory Management*, Jossey Bass, 2006
Bailey, Roderick, *Forgotten Voices of D-Day*, Ebury, 2010
Balkoski, Joseph, *Omaha Beach: D-Day, June 6, 1944*, Stackpole Books, 2006
——, *Utah Beach: The Amphibious Landing and Airborne Operations on D-Day, June 6, 1944*, Stackpole Books, 2006
Barber, Neil, *The Day the Devils Dropped In: The 9th Parachute Battalion in Normandy, D-Day to D+6*, Leo Cooper, 2002
——, *The Pegasus and Orne Bridges: Their Capture, Defences and Relief on D-Day*, Leo Cooper, 2003
Baumgarten, Harold, *D-Day Survivor: An Autobiography*, Pelican, 2007
Beevor, Antony, *The Battle for Normandy*, Viking, 2009
Boivin, Michel et al., *Villes normandes sous les bombes: juin 1944*, Presses Universitaires de Caen, 1994

Bowman, Martin W., *Air War D-Day: Bloody Beaches*, Pen and Sword Aviation, 2013

——, *Air War D-Day: Gold, Juno, Sword*, Pen and Sword Aviation, 2013

Bradley, Omar, *A Soldier's Story*, Henry Holt, 1951

—— and Blair, Clay, *A General's Life: An Autobiography by General of the Army Omar N. Bradley*, Simon and Schuster, 1983

Butcher, Harry Cecil, *Three Years with Eisenhower: The Personal Diary of Captain Harry C. Butcher, Naval Aide to General Eisenhower, 1942 to 1945*, Heinemann, 1946

Carell, Paul, *Invasion – They're Coming!*, Harrap, 1962

Chauvet, Maurice, *It's a Long Way to Normandy, 6 juin 1944: Le débarquement vu par un des 177 du commando Kieffer*, J. Picollec, 2004

Cheall, Bill and Cheall, Paul, *Fighting through from Dunkirk to Hamburg: A Green Howard's Wartime Memoir*, Pen and Sword Military, 2011

Constable, Trevor J. and Toliver, Raymond F., *Horrido! Fighter Aces of the Luftwaffe*, A. Barker, 1968

Coquart, Marie-France and Huet, Philippe, *Le Jour le plus fou: 6 juin 1944, Les Civils dans la tourmente*, Albin Michel, 2004

Cunningham, Chet, *The Frogmen of World War II: An Oral History of the U.S. Navy's Underwater Demolition Teams*, Pocket Star Books, 2005

Darlow, Stephen, *D-Day Bombers: The Veterans' Story: RAF Bomber Command and the US Eighth Air Force Support to the Normandy Invasion 1944*, Grub Street, 2004

Dear, Ian, *Ten Commando: 1942–1945*, Leo Cooper, 1987

Delaforce, Patrick, *Churchill's Secret Weapons: The Story of Hobart's Funnies*, Pen and Sword Military, 2007

D'Este, Carlo, *Decision in Normandy*, Barnes and Noble, 1994

——, *Eisenhower: A Soldier's Life*, Cassell Military, 2004

Drez, Ronald J. (ed.), *Voices of D-Day: The Story of the Allied Invasion Told by Those Who Were There (Eisenhower Center Studies on War and Peace)*, Louisiana State University Press, 1996

Dunning, Robert, *The Fighting Fourth: No. 4 Commando at War 1940–45*, History Press, n.d.

Edwards, Denis, *The Devil's Own Luck: From Pegasus Bridge to the Baltic 1944–45*, Pen and Sword Military, 2009

Edwards, Kenneth, *Operation Neptune*, Collins, 1946

Eisenhower, David, *Eisenhower: At War, 1943–1945*, Outlet, 1991

Eisenhower, Dwight David et al., *The Papers of Dwight David Eisenhower*, vol. 3, Johns Hopkins University Press, 1970

Ellis, Lionel Frederic et al., *Victory in the West*, 2 vols, Stationery Office Books, 1962

Ford, Ken and Gerrard, Howard, *D-Day 1944: Sword Beach and the British Airborne Landings*, Osprey, 2002

—— and Lyles, Kevin, *Gold and Juno Beaches*, Osprey, 2002

Fraser, David, *Knight's Cross: A Life of Field Marshal Erwin Rommel*, HarperCollins, 1993

Gavin, James M., *Airborne Warfare*, Battery Press, 1980

Giesbert, Franz-Olivier, *Les Héros du 6 juin: Le débarquement de 1944*, Michel Lafon, 2004

Gilchrist, Donald, *Don't Cry for Me: The Commandos, D-Day and After*, Robert Hale, 1982

Gockel, Franz, *La Porte de l'enfer: Omaha Beach, 6 juin 1944*, Éditions Ronald Hirlé, 2004

Guéno, Jean-Pierre, *Paroles du Jour J: Lettres et carnets du débarquement, été 1944*, Éditions de la Loupe, 2004

Hargreaves, Richard, *The Germans in Normandy*, Stackpole Books, 2008

Harrison, Gordon A., *The European Theater of Operations: Cross-Channel Attack*, Office of the Chief of Military History, Department. of the Army, 1951

Hastings, Max, *Overlord: D-Day and the Battle of Normandy*, Simon and Schuster, 1984

Hatfield, Thomas M., *Rudder: From Leader to Legend*, Texas A&M University Press, 2014

Hayn, Friedrich, *Die Invasion von Cotentin bis Falaise*, Vowinckel, 1954

Hennessey, Patrick, *Young Man in a Tank*, privately printed, n.d.

Herval, René, *Bataille de Normandie: Récits de témoins*, 2 vols, Éditions de Notre Temps, 1947

Hills, Stuart, *By Tank into Normandy*, Orion, 2002

Hitchcock, William I., *The Bitter Road to Freedom: A New History of the Liberation of Europe*, Free Press, 2009

Holborn, Andrew, *D-Day Landing on Gold Beach*, Bloomsbury Academic, 2017

Holbrook, David and Halson, Geoffrey, *Flesh Wounds*, Longmans, 1968

Hooton, E.R., *Eagle in Flames: The Fall of the Luftwaffe*, Brockhampton, 1999

Howard, John and Bates, Penny, *The Pegasus Diaries*, Pen and Sword Military, 2008

Howarth, David, *Dawn of D-Day*, Collins, 1959

Irving, David, *Göring: A Biography*, Avon Books, 1988

——, *The Trail of the Fox*, Avon Books, 1990

Isby, David C., *Fighting the Invasion: The German Army at D-Day*, Skyhorse Publishing, 2016

Janda, Kenneth et al., *The Challenge of Democracy: Government in America: 1999–2000 Update*, Houghton Mifflin, 2000

Jefferson, Alan, *Assault on the Guns of Merville: D-Day and After*, John Murray, 1987

Keegan, John, *Six Armies in Normandy*, Viking, 1983

——, *Churchill's Generals*, Warner Books, 1993

Kershaw, Alex, *The Bedford Boys*, Da Capo Press, 2003

Kershaw, Ian, *Hitler, 1936–1945: Nemesis*, W.W. Norton, 1999

Kershaw, Robert J., *D-Day: Piercing the Atlantic Wall*, Ian Allan, 2008

Keusgen, Helmut von, *Sainte-Mère-Église und Merderet: US-Luftlandeunternehmen*, HEK Creativ, 2010

Kiln, Robert, *D-Day to Arnhem with the Hertfordshire Gunners: Personal Account*, Castlemead Publications, 1992

King, Martin et al., *To War with the 4th: A Century of Frontline Combat with the US 4th Infantry Division, from the Argonne to the Ardennes to Afghanistan*, Casemate Publishers, 2016

Koch, Lutz, *Erwin Rommel: Die Wandlung Eines Grossen Soldaten*, W. Gebauer, 1950

Lane, Ronald L., *Rudder's Rangers*, Ranger Association, 1979

Leménicier, Christian, *Chronique d'un été brûlant*, Association Cocktail Culture de Rots, n.d.

Lemonnier-Gruhier, François, *Parachutés le 6 juin: Témoignages américains et français*, Editions Spes, 1949

Lewin, Ronald, *Rommel as Military Commander*, Ballantine Books, 1968

Liddle, Peter, *D-Day: By Those Who Were There*, Leo Cooper, 2004

Lovat, Simon Christopher Joseph Fraser, *March Past: A Memoir*, Weidenfeld and Nicolson, 1985

Luck, Hans von, *Panzer Commander: The Memoirs of Colonel Hans von Luck*, Praeger, 1989

McKee, Alexander, *Caen: Anvil of Victory*, Souvenir Press, 1964

Macksey, Kenneth, *Armoured Crusader: The Biography of Major-General Sir Percy 'Hobo' Hobart, One of the Most Influential Military Commanders of the Second World War*, Grub Street, 2004

Marshall, Charles F., *Discovering the Rommel Murder: The Life and Death of the Desert Fox*, Stackpole, 2002

Martin, Charles Cromwell and Whitsed, Roy, *Battle Diary: From D-Day and Normandy to the Zuider Zee and VE*, Dundurn Press, 2008

Masters, Peter, *Striking Back: A Jewish Commando's War against the Nazis*, Presidio, n.d.

Mayo, Jonathan, *D-Day Minute by Minute*, Short Books, 2014

Meyer, Hubert, *The 12th SS: The History of the Hitler Youth Panzer Division*, 2 vols, Stackpole Books, 2005

Michie, Allan A., *Honour for All*, Allen and Unwin, 1946

Milano, Vince and Conner, Bruce, *Normandiefront: D-Day to Saint-Lô through German Eyes*, Spellmount, 2012

Miller, Russell, *Nothing Less than Victory: The Oral History of D-Day*, Michael Joseph, 1993

Mills-Roberts, Derek, *Clash by Night: A Commando Chronicle*, W. Kimber, 1957

Milton, Giles, *Wolfram: The Boy Who Went to War*, Sceptre, 2011

Morgan, General Sir Frederick, *Peace and War*, Hodder and Stoughton, 1961

Morgan, Mike, *D-Day Hero: CSM Stanley Hollis VC*, Spellmount, 2014

Morison, Samuel Eliot, *The Invasion of France and Germany, 1944–1945 (History of United States Naval Operations in World War II)*, Little, Brown, 1957

Neillands, Robin, *The Battle of Normandy, 1944*, Cassell, 2002

—— and Normann, Roderick de, *D-Day 1944: Voices from Normandy*, Cassell Military, 2004

Nicolson, Harold, *Diaries and Letters, 1939–1945*, Weidenfeld and Nicolson, 2004

Nordyke, Phil, *Four Stars of Valor: The Combat History of the 505th Parachute Infantry Regiment in World War II*, Zenith, 2010

Payne, Roger, *Paras: Voices of the British Airborne Forces in the Second World War*, Amberley, 2016

Piekalkiewicz, Janusz, *Secret Agents, Spies and Saboteurs: Famous Undercover Missions of World War II*, David and Charles, 1969

Pitcairn-Jones, L.J., *Battle Summary No.39: Operation Neptune, Landings in Normandy, June 1944*, HMSO, 1994

Pogue, Forrest C., *Pogue's War: Diaries of a WWII Combat Historian*, University Press of Kentucky, 2001

Portugal, Jean E. (ed.), *We Were There: A Record for Canada*, 7 vols, Battered Silicon Dispatch Box, Vanderburgh, 1998

Prados, Edward, *Neptunus Rex: Naval Stories of the Normandy Invasion, June 6, 1944*, Presidio, 1998

Pyle, Ernie and Nichols, David, *Ernie's War: The Best of Ernie Pyle's World War II Dispatches*, Easton Press, 2000

Reeman, Douglas, *D-Day, 6th June 1944: D-Day Remembered*, Arrow, 1984

Renaud, Alexandre, *Sainte-Mère-Église*, Julliard, 1984

Roberts, Mary Louise, *D-Day through French Eyes: Normandy 1944*, University of Chicago Press, 2014

Ruppenthal, Roland G. et al., *European Theater of Operation: Omaha Beachhead, 6 June–13 June 1944; Utah Beach to Cherbourg, 6 June–27 June 1944; Saint-Lô, 7 July–19 July 1944; Small Unit Actions, 6 June–6 December 1944*, Historical Division, War Department, American Forces in Action, 1948

Ryan, Cornelius, *The Longest Day: June 6, 1944 D-Day*, Fawcett Publications, 1959

Saunders, Hilary St George, *The Green Beret*, Michael Joseph, 1949

Scott, Stan and Barber, Neil, *Fighting with the Commandos: The Recollections of Stan Scott No.3 Commando*, Isis, 2008

Severloh, Hein, *WN62: A German Soldier's Memories of the Defence of Omaha Beach, Normandy, June 6, 1944*, HEK Creativ Verlag, 2011

Simonnet, Stéphane, *Commandant Kieffer: Le Français du Jour J*, Tallandier, 2012

Speidel, Hans and Colvin, Ian Duncan, *We Defended Normandy*, Jenkins, 1951

Stagg, James Martin, *Forecast for Overlord, June 6, 1994*, Ian Allan, 1971

Stanké, Alain and Morgan, Jean-Louis, *Histoires vécues du débarquement*, Archipel, 2014

Strong, Michael, *Steiner's War: The Merville Battery*, CreateSpace, 2014

Studies in Battle Command, Faculty Combat Studies Institute, Kansas, n.d.

Summersby, Kay, *Eisenhower Was My Boss*, Dell Publishing, 1948

——, *Past Forgetting*, Simon and Schuster, 1976

Symonds, Craig L., *Neptune: The Allied Invasion of Europe and the D-Day Landings*, Oxford University Press, 2014

Taylor, Maxwell D., *Swords and Plowshares*, Da Capo Press, 1990

Tootal, Stuart, *The Manner of Men: 9 PARA's Heroic D-Day Mission*, John Murray, 2014

Trez, Michel de, *Colonel Ben Vandervoort, 'Vandy,' 0-22715: Commanding Officer, 2nd Battalion, 505th Parachute Infantry Regiment, 82nd Airborne Division*, D-Day Publications, 2004

Winter, Paul, *D-Day Documents*, Bloomsbury, 2014

Wood, James A. (ed.), *Army of the West: The Weekly Reports of German Army Group B from Normandy to the West Wall*, Stackpole, 2007

Young, Desmond, *Rommel: The Desert Fox*, Quill/William Morrow, 1987

Zaloga, Steve and Gerrard, Howard, *D-Day 1944, Omaha Beach*, Osprey, 2003

——, *D-Day 1944, Utah Beach and the US Airborne Landings*, Osprey, 2004

Zuehlke, Mark, *Juno Beach*, Douglas and McIntyre, 2005

Index

Bénouville
  strategic importance of
    bridge, 51, 369
  glider-borne troops capture
    bridge, 65, 73–8, 81,
    289
  parachute landings, 92
  Lovat's commandos advance
    on and relieve, 294,
    317–18, 321, 323, 325–6,
    397
  German counter-attack on,
    384
  devastation, 400
Bensman, Norman, 178
Berchtesgaden, 151, 291
Berghof, 151, 231, 291
Berlin: liberated (2 May 1945),
  419
Bernaville, Château de, 153–4
Bernières-sur-Mer, 247–8,
  250, 252–5
Biéville, 387–8
Blanchard, Wally, 232–5,
  293–4
Blandford, Pat, 273–4
Blin, Monsieur (of Vierville),
  198
Blizzard, Arthur, 394
Block, Major, 160
Bluff, Sergeant, 11–12
bocage (terrain), 363
Boland, Oliver, 74
bombardments *see* naval
  bombardments
Bone, Corporal Harry, 191–2
Bormann, Martin, 151–2
Borzikowski, Lieutenant, 87

Boston, Mission, 102
Bowen, Private Dennis, 371,
  413
Bradley, Bruce, 180
Bradley, General Omar
  and attack on Pointe du
    Hoc, 260
  and Omaha landings, 292–3,
    295, 314
  Eisenhower rebukes for lack
    of information, 346
Brandenburg, Lieutenant,
  80–1
Branham, Felix, 296
Brannen, Malcolm, 154–5, 240
Brantley, Lloyd ('Red'), 39–40
Braun, Eva, 151
Breeze, David, 96
Bretteville-l'Orgueilleuse, 380
Bréville, 400–1
Brewer, Charlie, 179
Brierre, Eugene, 185
British Broadcasting
    Corporation (BBC)
  broadcasts to French local
    inhabitants, 246
  live radio report from
    bomber, 346–7
British military formations
  Divisions
    6th Airborne, 65, 82, 317,
      407–8
    79th Armoured, 163
  Regiments
    1st Hussars, 380
    Cheshires, 374
    East Yorkshire, 136, 259,
      275–6